P9-AQS-172

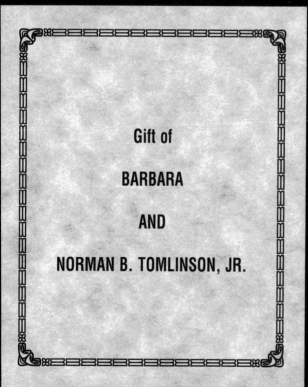

Gift of

BARBARA

AND

NORMAN B. TOMLINSON, JR.

Reimagining Canada

Reimagining Canada

Language, Culture, Community,
and the Canadian Constitution

JEREMY WEBBER

McGill-Queen's University Press
Kingston & Montreal • London • Buffalo

LIBRARY
COLBY-SAWYER COLLEGE
NEW LONDON, NH 03257

JL
27.5
.W433
1994
c.1

To my parents,
Bernard and Jean Webber

#29025/02

© McGill-Queen's University Press 1994
ISBN 0-7735-1146-6 (cloth)
ISBN 0-7735-1152-0 (paper)

Legal deposit first quarter 1994
Bibliothèque nationale du Québec

Printed in Canada on acid-free paper

This book has been published with the help of a grant from the Social
Science Federation of Canada, using funds provided by the Social
Sciences and Humanities Research Council of Canada.

"Dancing" from *The Dance Is One* by F.R. Scott, is used by permission
of the Canadian Publishers, McClelland & Stewart, Toronto.

Canadian Cataloguing in Publication Data

Webber, Jeremy H. A., 1958–
Reimagining Canada: language, culture, community, and the
Canadian constitution
Includes bibliographical references and index.
ISBN 0-7735-1146-6 (bound) -
ISBN 0-7735-1152-0 (pbk.)
1. Canada – Constitutional law. 2. Canada – Constitutional law –
Amendments. 3. Canada – Constitutional history. I. Title.
JL27.5.W42 1993   342.71'03   C93-090546-6

This book was typeset by Typo Litho composition inc.
in 10/12 Baskerville.

LIBRARY
COLBY SAWYER COLLEGE
NEW LONDON, NH 03257

Contents

2

8 Practical Implications   260

CONCLUSION

9 The Canadian Conversation   309

Notes   321

Index   365

Preface

This book is the product of two aspirations.

First, it results from engagement in a very practical controversy. In the winter of 1989–90, Wade MacLauchlan and I, increasingly disturbed by the popular debate over the Meech Lake Accord, were instrumental in launching a group called "Friends of Meech Lake." The federal government had, we believed, treated the public with disdain, failing to offer convincing justifications for the accord. As a result, the debate was polarized. On the one hand were the self-proclaimed upholders of constitutional principle, opposed to any special recognition of Quebec. On the other were the political movers and shakers, trying to sell their political compromise on the simple grounds that Quebec liked the deal and might leave if it were rejected. We vehemently opposed both those positions and sought to foster a substantial public debate, one that expressed our conviction that the accord was founded on a coherent vision of Canada, a vision consistent with constitutional principle and firmly rooted in this country's character.

It was, of course, an uphill battle, which ultimately failed. But the experience convinced us that our vision of Canada – a principled and democratic vision responsive to the richness of Canada – needed better expression, no matter what the outcome. We therefore began, even before the end of Meech, to think about the case for the longer term. This book thus began as a joint project. It eventually fell into my lap alone, in part because of Wade's appointment as dean of the University of New Brunswick's Law School. The first objective remained the same, however.

At the same time, the book has had a more general vocation. Over the course of our constitutional debates, it became apparent that the problems Canada was wrestling with (whether and how we should recognize cultural difference in the design of public institutions; how individual rights intersect with collective recognition) were of great importance throughout the world. Similar issues were raised, for example, in the protection of the Turkish minority in Bulgaria or of Hungarians in Rumania, in the devolution of power to Scotland, or in the drive for greater autonomy in Corsica. There had long been similar tensions in the ethnically and religiously diverse societies of Africa and Asia. The issue of aboriginal rights raised comparable questions in Australia and the Americas. Many of the conventional tools of political and legal philosophy were profoundly unhelpful. Often they utterly failed to address issues of cultural diversity or assumed that those issues could be handled by banishing them to the private sphere. Significant rethinking was necessary, and Canada provided a rich storehouse of experience on the accommodation of linguistic, religious, and cultural difference. This book is an attempt to examine that neglected store, drawing out some of its many lessons.

The book therefore speaks to two audiences. It is very much rooted in a Canadian experience and speaks most directly to Canadian concerns, but it also offers insights to all those interested in the accommodation of cultural difference in law and public institutions, throughout the world.

There are many people to thank for their help in the realization of this project. First, of course, is Wade, who was not only a splendid and irrepressible comrade during the Meech debate, but who also contributed the other half of the conversations out of which this book emerged (and indeed was responsible for the interesting part of this book's title; I claim responsibility for the tedious tail section). My thanks as well to the other members of Friends of Meech Lake, too numerous to mention, whose dedication in a not very popular cause was always an inspiration. I owe special thanks to Robert Stanfield, Solange Chaput-Rolland, and Stephen Lewis, whose service to Friends, especially in the initial stages, was crucial.

I would not have been able to write this book without the generous support and criticism of a number of my colleagues at McGill. I owe a great deal to Rod Macdonald and Jim Tully, who read the entire manuscript, returning chapters very quickly, always with helpful suggestions. Daniel Jutras, Colleen Sheppard, and David Hawkes provided very useful comments on a number of chapters. I have also benefited from the fine comments of the readers for the McGill-

Queen's University Press, from the Aid to Scholarly Publications program, and from the expert editing of Judith Turnbull.

I must thank a number of students in the Faculty of Law, especially René Brewer, Christine Bush, Michael Bush, Stephen Lloyd, and the participants in my seminar on Social Diversity and the Law, who read and commented on much of the argument. I am especially indebted to those students who worked as researchers: Jacques Neatby, Christoph Sicking, and Allison Bond.

Finally, my thanks to the members of my family, especially my wife, Carolyn. Carolyn, my parents, and my brothers and sisters all read parts of this argument at different times. As families do, they gave unfailing support. They also contributed mightily to keeping the style readable.

My thanks to the Faculty of Law at McGill University for its financial assistance. This book has been published with the help of a grant from the Social Sciences Federation of Canada, using funds provided by the Social Sciences and Humanities Research Council of Canada. It has also benefited from work done under a research grant from the Social Sciences and Humanities Research Council.

Introduction

1 Crisis and Community

THE CRISIS UPON US

In 1990 Canada entered the most serious crisis of its 123-year history. The crisis took most Canadians completely by surprise. Its cause seemed absurdly small. The Meech Lake Accord – a bundle of constitutional amendments that attracted little impassioned support and that even the accord's most vigorous proponents described as modest – failed to obtain the unanimous provincial approval needed for ratification. Even in Quebec, for whose benefit it had been drafted, the accord enjoyed less than overwhelming support. And its rejection was full of ambiguity. All federal political parties and all but two provincial legislatures had, in the end, supported the agreement. Although there was widespread popular opposition outside French-speaking Quebec, the reasons were diverse, many having nothing to do with the chief concerns of Quebec. Yet the failure of Meech plunged Canada into its worst constitutional crisis, one that threatened to result in the secession of its second-most-populous province.

Paradoxically, the crisis was more severe precisely because of the modesty of its cause. The suddenness and seriousness of the breakdown shocked Canadians, unprepared as they were for a collapse of their national debate. If this little bundle of amendments could provoke such a reaction, perhaps Canada was in worse shape than everyone believed. Perhaps we had all been living one long misunderstanding.

The reasons for this sense of disappointment and exasperation varied from one part of the country to another. In Quebec the accord had been seen as an act of reconciliation, designed to end the debate over Quebec's fundamental adherence to Canada. It was a way of leaving the referendum on sovereignty-association behind, of declaring that, with these few amendments, discussions could occur through ordinary federal-provincial relations, no longer dominated by the threat of secession. Indeed, most Quebecers saw the accord as a way of saying yes to Canada. It effected no revolution. It simply codified what they had long considered to be their province's place within Canada. For them, the failure of Meech represented a rejection of that place – a rejection of Quebec in Canada. That hit Quebecers hard. For many, it was bitter confirmation that English Canadians could never accept Quebec's distinctiveness within Canada. It made little difference that many Canadians opposed the Meech Lake Accord for reasons having little to do with Quebec. It was clear that many others could not accept recognition of Quebec as a distinct society, or that they would subject that recognition to so many qualifications and additions that the clause became meaningless.

For Canadians outside Quebec, on the other hand, and for most of Quebec's anglophone population, it was the manner in which Quebec first defended Meech and then reacted to its failure that grated. During the ratification period, Quebec refused to accept any changes or additions to the accord's text. This was seen by many not only as intransigent and undemocratic, but as profoundly ungenerous. Quebec seemed to be grasping for what it wanted without any consideration for the priorities of other sections of the country, especially aboriginal people, women, and those provinces favouring Senate reform. The idea that Quebec was only out for itself was reinforced by Quebec's fierce (and successful) lobbying for federal procurement contracts, particularly the maintenance contract for the CF-18 fighters; by its defence of the clause in Meech that required the unanimous approval of all existing provinces before new provinces could be created in Yukon and the Northwest Territories; and (in Newfoundland) by its continued insistence on the terms of the Churchill Falls contract (in which a previous Newfoundland government had agreed to sell hydroelectric power to Quebec at a price that was now far below the market rate). In the context of an exercise in national reconciliation, Quebec's actions seemed to be narrow, exclusive, and parochial, lacking all consideration for a larger Canadian interest. This perception was strengthened during the

Meech Lake debate by Quebec's enactment of Bill 178, which reaffirmed elements of a law banning the use of English on commercial signs, a law that had just been struck down by the Supreme Court of Canada. At a time when it was being "welcomed back into the constitutional family," Quebec seemed bent on suppressing other aspects of the Canadian identity. Many Canadians began to doubt whether Quebec had any adherence to Canada as a whole, and as long as they doubted that adherence, fears of separation were unlikely to prompt much compromise. Quebec's reaction to the failure of Meech Lake only seemed to confirm widespread doubts about that province's ultimate commitment to the country.

Thus, in Meech Lake and after, the two traditional sides to Canada's constitutional dialogue came to doubt the other's commitment to an acceptable idea of Canada. But Canada's constitutional discussions no longer involved just two sides. To begin with, in provinces outside Quebec (and among Quebec anglophones), constitutional issues were not seen in exclusively French/English or Quebec/rest-of-Canada terms. To the extent that westerners or Maritimers cared about the constitution at all, they were concerned with the country's responsiveness to perspectives outside the central Canadian axis. Sometimes these concerns were framed in terms of Senate reform, but often the very preoccupation with the constitution was seen as a central Canadian phenomenon. Issues of economic development, of interest rates, of agricultural assistance, of the fisheries were much more important to citizens of the Atlantic or western provinces.

Secondly, the Meech Lake debate made clear that many groups that represented communities that did not define themselves in geographical terms had become key constitutional players. They too had their unique claims upon the definition of a Canadian identity (or identities).

The most prominent of these were the aboriginal peoples. In the four years prior to the conclusion of the Meech Lake Accord, a series of federal-provincial conferences had been held to give some precision to the recognition of aboriginal rights in the constitution. These conferences ended in failure, increasing the frustration of peoples already fed up with the slow pace of negotiations on land claims. In aboriginal eyes, the reluctance of several provinces, particularly in the west, to agree to a status for aboriginal peoples acceptable to those peoples smacked of the same kind of easy disregard that had characterized previous treatment of Indian, Inuit, and Métis. It reinforced the alienation many aboriginal people felt, not

just from a particular province, but from Canada as a whole. Canada
seemed unwilling to ensure an honourable place for the First Nations within its contemporary constitutional structure.

The swift conclusion of the Meech Lake Accord, following close
on the heels of the failed aboriginal round, only served to fire the
accumulated sense of outrage, outrage that found its outlet in opposition to the accord itself. Meech would not directly affect the aboriginal constitutional agenda, except that it would make provincial
status more difficult to achieve in Yukon and the Northwest Territories (in which aboriginal peoples made up a very large proportion of
the population), but it served as a symbol of the ease with which the
larger society arranged its affairs without regard for the concerns of
Native people. A Cree member of the Manitoba legislature, Elijah
Harper, was responsible for Manitoba's inability to ratify the accord
before the deadline. And in the months that followed, Canadians
got a taste of aboriginal frustration in the long confrontation between Mohawk Warriors and Quebec's provincial police (later replaced by the Canadian army) at Kanesatake and Kahnawake. One
police officer was killed in that confrontation, and for seventy-eight
days, barricades established by armed Warriors blocked roads near
Oka as well as approaches to the bridge linking Montreal to its
south-shore suburb of Châteauguay, causing deep bitterness between the aboriginal communities and their neighbours. Similar
confrontations occurred across the country, although none as violent and disruptive as those near Montreal.

The Meech debate also reinforced the constitutional role of other
groups, groups variously referred to as "multicultural communities"
(communities with a cultural heritage other than British, French, or
aboriginal) and "Charter communities" (groups enjoying specific
recognition in the Canadian Charter of Rights and Freedoms:
women, racial minorities, the disabled, and, again, multicultural
communities). While often lumped together, these groups in fact
presented a variety of perspectives on the constitution. They tended
to share a strong commitment to individual rights and a suspicion
that communal claims might undermine their ability to become full
and equal participants in Canadian society. But even here there was
considerable variation. Women's groups in Quebec and the rest of
Canada took dramatically different positions, the Quebec groups accepting that formal recognition of Quebec's distinctiveness was compatible with women's equality, the groups outside Quebec fearing
the possible effect of cultural recognition on women's rights. And in
the aftermath of Meech, the representatives of women's groups
tended to share the sense of exasperation and bitterness common to

their part of the country. Quebec women generally saw the rejection of Meech as one more example of English Canadians' inability to accept Quebec's distinctiveness. Many women outside Quebec came to doubt Quebec's commitment not only to an idea of Canada as a whole, but also to basic human rights. There was a widespread feeling, for example, that many Quebec women had let their nationalism get in the way of their commitment to equality.

Members of the multicultural communities generally shared the fear that communal claims might trump individual rights (although the strength of this fear varied from one community to another), but this was usually coupled with a somewhat different concern: the strong suspicion that the Meech Lake Accord enshrined the "two nations" or "two founding peoples" conception of Canada. Many read the accord's distinct society clause as an attempt to define Canada only in terms of English and French, ignoring – perhaps even demeaning – the cultural heritage and contribution to Canada of Canadians of other backgrounds. Manitoba broadcaster Izzy Asper voiced the sentiment of many when he said: "If Quebec is a distinct society, then what are the rest of us – so much chopped liver?"[1]

The adamant desire of multicultural communities to be included continued into the post-Meech period. It generally did not result, however, in the kind of steadfast opposition to compromise expressed by some Canadians in the months following Meech's failure. This is so for a number of reasons. First, having more knowledge of other countries (and perhaps having experienced the reality of communal strife firsthand), members of the multicultural communities generally kept their faith in the value and vitality of Canada at a time when others doubted the country's prospects. After all, for many members of these communities, Canada (including Quebec) is the country they chose. Second, although many did have concerns about the persistence of racism or lack of acceptance within the broader society, these problems were not particular to Quebec, but applied to Canada generally; they were unlikely to be solved by a break with Quebec. Third, at a more practical level, some of the most influential multicultural communities (for example, the Jewish, Italian, and Greek communities) spanned the country, having a very substantial presence in Montreal. The separation of Quebec would have caused a painful disruption. Consequently, one often found among the multicultural communities a strong desire to find solutions to the impasse.

This desire was even more apparent among members of yet another group: francophones outside Quebec. Unlike the members of the multicultural communities, they saw their language as a public

language, one which, because of the vitality and weight of both English and French in the national make-up of Canada, should continue to be a means of political discussion, education, and the
provision of public services in areas where substantial numbers of
French-speaking Canadians lived. Their language served as an important link to the heritage of their ancestors, but it was also the language through which they had contributed to the public life of
Canada. Its use in this land was not merely a way of preserving ties
to a cultural home, it was part of preserving the homeland itself.
More than any other group, more even than Canadians of British
origin, French Canadians had long considered their "old country" to
be Canada, not France.

Francophones outside Quebec responded to the crisis with a mixture of desperation and resolution. At first, many had opposed
Meech Lake because of that document's emphasis on the coincidence of language with provincial boundaries, conceding the predominantly English character of Canada outside Quebec. By the
end, however, organizations representing all French-language minorities had declared their support for the accord and were working
to find some mutually acceptable compromise. Quebec's secession
would simply have been too damaging. Although some communities
were probably strong enough to survive (the New Brunswick Acadians are the best example), separation would undoubtedly have
undermined the commitment to bilingualism in what was left of
Canada, reducing services and increasing the pressure towards
assimilation. For French-speaking minorities, a united Canada was
essential.

FRAGMENTS OF A PUBLIC DEBATE

This, then, was the mood of Canada on the defeat of Meech, a mood
that ranged from bewilderment and disappointment to the severe
disaffection and alienation of many aboriginal people. There was a
feeling that Canada had lost its conception of itself, or worse, had
proven incapable of developing any coherent and convincing vision
of how it could be a country. Both Quebecers and Canadians outside
Quebec had come to question each other's basic commitment to a
land that included the other, and especially to a bilingual (or bicultural) country. The very notion of biculturalism (or, for that matter,
aboriginal self-government) now had to compete with visions in
which all individuals, all cultures, or all provinces would be treated
in precisely the same way. Aboriginal peoples, although their voice
was now much louder than it had been before, continued to be out-

siders in these debates, trapped between a desire for unique recognition and self-government on the one hand and the persistence of a debilitating form of special status and dependence on the other. Looking across Canada, it now seemed impossible to reconcile allegiance to the whole with allegiance to its constituent parts.

This loss of confidence infected the debate following Meech's failure. At first, the constitutional discussions that occurred – and there were many Canadians who wanted nothing more to do with the constitution – focused on the development of consensus at the provincial or regional level, or on opposing and uncompromising assertions of national visions. Indeed, the lines of the Meech debate were still very much in evidence, with each side making little attempt to work beyond them towards a new national consensus. The attempt to articulate a broadly acceptable conception of the country seemed to have dropped out of sight. Positions were often justified simply in terms of the interests of one part of the country, seldom addressing how they made sense in terms of the whole.

Part of the problem was the federal government's utter loss of credibility under Prime Minister Brian Mulroney. Even before the last days of Meech Lake, that government had become extremely unpopular outside Quebec. Some of this was due to policies largely unrelated to Canadian identity or the constitution – the introduction of the goods and services tax (GST), for example, or the management of the east coast fisheries. But other policies caused many Canadians to doubt the Mulroney government's commitment to, or perhaps understanding of, elements they considered essential to Canada's existence and cohesion. These policies included deep cuts to such Canadian institutions as passenger rail service, the Canadian Broadcasting Commission (CBC), and the National Film Board (NFB); the limitation of transfer payments to the provinces; a weakening of support for universal social programs; and the pursuit of a conservative economic agenda at odds with the economic nationalism of a significant number of Canadians, an agenda that involved the privatization of crown corporations, the replacement of the Foreign Investment Review Agency (FIRA) with an agency much more favourable to takeovers of Canadian-owned companies, and, finally, the conclusion of the Free Trade Agreement (FTA) with the United States. The government's handling of the CF-18 maintenance contract and the Meech Lake debate reinforced the perception that the government was incapable of achieving an adequate balance either among Canada's regional identities or between those identities and a clear federal interest. Above all, Canadians lost all faith in their ability to have any influence over federal policy, given the gov-

ernment's disdain for reasoned public debate (or even public justification of its policies), a disdain evident on a range of issues but
particularly on free trade and Meech Lake. For very many Canadians, the federal government had simply ceased to be their government.

In Quebec, the reason for the federal government's incapacity was
different. Most Quebecers agreed with such controversial measures
as free trade and Meech Lake. They did not, then, share the antip-
athy towards the substance of federal policy. But they too had been
appalled by the indignity of the final manoeuvring on Meech, and
they certainly doubted the Mulroney government's ability to speak
for the rest of Canada, given the public repudiation of the accord
outside Quebec. The federal government could take some of the
sting out of Meech's failure by giving more administrative autonomy
to Quebec in, for example, immigration, but Quebecers knew it was
not well placed to develop a convincing federal consensus.

This meant that there was, during the first months following
Meech's failure, a void at the centre. Instead of confronting the
issues head on, the federal government focused on other questions
(the Mohawk confrontation, the adoption of the GST) and engaged
in a series of diversionary tactics on the constitutional front (the
Beaudoin-Edwards Commission on constitutional amendment; the
Citizens' Forum on Canada's Future, headed by Keith Spicer), designed to restart discussion in a manner apparently divorced from
federal government direction. When, in April 1991, the government
did move to intervene directly in the debate, former minister of
external affairs Joe Clark took charge of the dossier, retaining the
appearance of distance from the prime minister.

Throughout all of this, neither of the other principal federal political parties was able to fill the vacuum. Jean Chrétien, by an unfortunate coincidence, had been elected Liberal leader on the very
weekend the Meech Lake Accord failed. He had initially opposed
the accord (but had relaxed his opposition in the last days). Within
Quebec he was seen as a man out of touch with his province, vacillat-
ing between loyalty to the centralist vision of his mentor, Pierre
Elliott Trudeau, and his growing awareness that a refusal to recognize Quebec as a distinct society would threaten Quebecers' confidence in Canada. His consequent vulnerability became evident in a
by-election in the long-time Liberal riding of Laurier-Sainte-Marie,
seven weeks after the expiry of the Meech deadline. The Liberal
candidate, a strong supporter of Chrétien, obtained 19 per cent of
the vote. The riding was won by the sovereignist Bloc Québécois,
with 67 per cent.[2] Liberals had chosen Chrétien as their leader in the
hope that he would reawaken latent support for Trudeau's vision

within Quebec. As it became clear that he carried little weight in that province, Chrétien's personal authority began to wane in the rest of Canada as well.

The New Democratic Party also had a relatively new leader, Audrey McLaughlin. It too had great difficulty developing a strong position on the constitution, although this was probably due more to the nature of the party itself than to the qualities of its leader. The NDP's position on Meech Lake had been ambiguous. Under its former leader, Ed Broadbent, the party had officially declared its support for the accord. However, many New Democrats (including McLaughlin herself) dissented for a variety of reasons – some because of their fears that the accord would weaken the central government and federal spending programs such as medicare, many because of their solidarity with aboriginal peoples, women's organizations outside Quebec, or the aspirations of the northern territories, and all because of their suspicion that the accord was one more undemocratic element in the neo-conservative agenda of its chief promoters, Brian Mulroney and Quebec premier Robert Bourassa. These concerns surfaced with a vengeance at the party's convention in early December 1989, the convention at which McLaughlin was selected leader. Although the party did not reject the accord in so many words, its demand for changes severely qualified its commitment. From then on, the NDP's claims that it still backed the accord seemed like a weak attempt to be all things to all people.

Underlying the NDP's hesitations on Meech itself, and impeding its attempt to find a new consensus after Meech, was a more fundamental difficulty. The party had, at least during the previous twenty-five years, embraced two firm commitments relevant to the national question. First, it retained its traditional support for a strong central government that acted as guarantor for a set of Canada-wide social programs. Second, it recognized Quebec's unique character and particularly that province's right to self-determination. Finding the right combination of these two commitments has been difficult. For many within the party, Quebec's demands for greater power over social programs threatened those programs' integrity. In addition, the country's preoccupation with constitutional renewal diverted attention from the more important (to New Democrats) social and economic issues. The constitution has been, then, for many New Democrats, a perennial source of frustration, frustration compounded by the party's lack of electoral success in Quebec.

There was a way of eliminating the tension, in a manner apparently consistent with the NDP's two commitments. The recognition of Quebec's uniqueness could find expression simply in support for Quebec's right to self-determination. No concessions would be made within Canada's constitutional structure. Quebec could choose either to be in or out. Prior to the Meech debate, this position had never been dominant within the party; the party's leaders had generally sought an acceptable consensus *within* Canada. But as many NDP members came to question Quebec's commitment to the country – and indeed some doubted whether an acceptable structure could ever be found – the blunter option gained support, especially at the grass roots. Even if many New Democrats remained committed to a federal alternative, the readiness of many others to put Quebec to the choice sapped the party's ability to find a solution.

The problems that each of the federal parties had developing a new Canadian consensus revealed the extent to which the popular debate was pulling apart. This tendency was dramatized by the rise of political parties expressly opposing constitutional compromise. The Bloc Québécois was founded by federal members of Parliament who had left the Conservatives and Liberals at the time of Meech's failure to work for the secession of Quebec. In January 1992 polls suggested that the Bloc was supported by 32 per cent of voters in Quebec. In the western provinces, the new Reform Party did not argue for Quebec's separation, but it did eschew any attempt at compromise. Quebec could take Canada as it was, or leave it. Indeed, Reform argued that Quebec (and French Canadians generally) had already extracted too many concessions. When, in the spring of 1991, the Reform Party decided to accept members from provinces east of Manitoba, it made clear that it would not seek members from Quebec precisely so that it could represent the interests of the rest of Canada (as it saw them) unimpeded by any need to please Quebecers. In January 1992 Reform had the support of 39 per cent of voters in the Prairie provinces, more than any other federal party.[3]

The inability (or unwillingness) of federal parties to bridge the chasm had its counterparts in the provincial sphere. This was most pronounced in Quebec, where the collapse of Meech prompted a sudden re-evaluation of the province's status. The dominant terms of the debate (although not the only terms) were now very different. Meech had been seen as a way of accommodating Quebec's unique character within a modestly changed structure. When that accommodation was rejected – when, in French-speaking Quebecers' eyes, the rest of Canada rejected any recognition of Quebec's uniqueness – many Quebecers decided that the province's only choice was to build political structures without regard to the rest of Canada. Previously, constitutional proposals had been premised on Quebecers' participation in a broader Canadian political community, but henceforth Quebec would fashion its institutions in its own interest. There might still be, at the end of the day, an entity called Canada, but Quebec's participation would be justified in terms of Quebec alone, implicitly setting aside any broader Canadian allegiance. Quebecers would be Canadians in the same way that the British are Europeans.

This sentiment clearly informed the recommendations of the two reports bearing upon Quebec policy in the aftermath of Meech Lake: the Allaire report, drafted by a committee of the Quebec Liberal Party; and the report of the Bélanger-Campeau Commission on the Political and Constitutional Future of Quebec.[4] Those documents, like many committee reports, contain a rich array of themes and variations not always consistent with each other. In some ways, the reports are best read for how they say things or for what they leave unsaid rather than for what they say. But if one looks just at the formal recommendations and their justification, it is clear that both reports took the relevant political community to be Quebec alone. Ties to the rest of Canada were not excluded. On the contrary, both reports emphasized the value of preserving, perhaps enhancing, the Canadian economic union. But these links were justified simply in terms of the interests of Quebec. There was no acknowledgment (at least no express acknowledgment) of any loyalty Quebecers might have to an idea of Canada. The reports' recommendations reflected that starting-point. The Allaire report suggested a very extensive decentralization of powers. The powers left to the federal government could be justified in terms of the various provinces' interests in building an economic union and pursuing a common defence policy, but little remained that would permit the federal government to serve as an independent object of allegiance for Canadians. For its part, the Bélanger-Campeau Commission refrained from specific proposals on the division of powers. Rather, it recommended a political process for determining Quebec's future status. Like the Allaire report, this process clearly focused on Quebec as the only relevant political community. The federal government was treated as the government of Canada outside Quebec, from which Quebec would receive offers of a new constitutional pact.

Quebec was the province most dissatisfied with its constitutional status, and it was the only province to push the constitutional agenda forward in the immediate wake of Meech. The initial response of other provinces was to let matters lie. Most Canadians simply would not support a resumption of the same old constitutional debate. This was doubly so when Quebec insisted that it would only negotiate with Ottawa, a government now perceived as having very little legitimacy outside Quebec. Discussions that did occur at the provincial level occurred between governments alone and tended to focus on regional responses to the threat of Quebec's separation. The risk of separation injected new life into the movement for regional cooperation in the Maritime provinces. The western premiers also met to reassess their position for the post-Meech period.

Governments were not the only agencies having a hard time bridging the cultural divide. Popular organizations also split along linguistic lines. This was the case in the labour movement. During the Meech debate, some unions and union leaders worked to find a common, generally acceptable position. A few unions held seminars, for example, to bring together representatives from Quebec and the rest of Canada to discuss the accord. Leaders such as Bob White, Leo Gerard, and Richard Cashin favoured Meech's adoption, even though they were no friends of the federal government, objected to the way in which Ottawa handled the constitutional debate, and represented many English-speaking members opposed to the accord. Their actions were the exception, however. Unions that crossed the linguistic divide tended to take a less stressful (if less courageous) approach: since their English-speaking members opposed the accord because it went too far and their French-speaking members opposed it because it didn't go far enough, the unions simply opposed the accord. As long as no reasons were given, this could mask the unions' internal divisions. When reasons became necessary, the mask dropped. At the national convention of the Canadian Labour Congress in May 1990, a resolution on Meech Lake was withdrawn and extensively redrafted in order to prevent Quebec delegates from walking out.[5] The labour movement's divisions have continued into the post-Meech period. The union representatives on the Bélanger-Campeau Commission were among the strongest supporters of Quebec's separation, and they have remained so since, even when support in Quebec has waned.

A similar division occurred in the women's movement. During the initial hearings at the federal level on the Meech Lake Accord, the National Action Committee on the Status of Women (NAC) took the position that the accord could be approved if section 28 of the Charter were protected from the amendments. (Section 28 provides that Charter rights are guaranteed equally to men and women, notwithstanding any other provision in the Charter, and was included in the Charter as the result of an extensive battle by women's groups during the patriation of the constitution in 1981.) In the 1987 hearings, NAC's president, Louise Dulude, testified that the committee had adopted this position despite the misgivings of some members that section 28 alone was insufficient. It did so largely because the principal women's organization in Quebec, the Fédération des femmes du Québec (at that time a NAC affiliate), argued that the distinct society clause was not a threat to women's equality.[6]

NAC's 1987 position constituted a real attempt at compromise between feminists in Quebec and those in the rest of Canada. Over the course of the next two years, however, the position of NAC hardened against Meech, approaching that of a number of other predominantly English-speaking women's groups (especially the Ad Hoc Committee of Canadian Women on the Constitution). This accentuated tension with French Canadian feminists. In 1989 the Fédération des femmes du Québec, representing (in 1992) 102 women's organizations in Quebec, left NAC because of differences on Meech Lake, the absence of simultaneous translation in NAC meetings (making English the *de facto* working language), and the fact that the Fédération's size was not reflected in its voting rights in NAC. Some prominent English-speaking feminists (and some women's groups) continued to work for common ground, despite the emerging split. They argued that when the issues were of primary concern to Quebec women, Quebec women had to be heard. But the dominant English-speaking voice increasingly opposed the accord, particularly because of the possibility that the distinct society clause might affect the Charter (especially the equality guarantees). It paid little heed to the arguments of Quebec feminists. Some opponents of Meech even suggested that Quebec groups like the Fédération could not be trusted to speak for Quebec women – that their support for the accord was influenced by their dependence on government grants or their unwillingness to stand up to an oppressive, male, nationalist consensus (arguments that would have deprived Quebec feminists of any legitimate role in the debate). Towards the end of the ratification period, many Quebec feminists gave up, withdrawing just as many of their male counterparts were doing. The fact that during the last days of Meech many English-speaking women had no idea that Quebec feminists had taken a different position on the accord showed the extent to which the debate had split apart: the voice of the most prominent English-speaking organizations had become, simply, the voice of women. The division continued into the post-Meech period. In May 1991 the Fédération des femmes du Québec adopted, for the first time, a resolution in favour of Quebec's secession.

Canada's traditional federal-provincial and French-English debates were therefore in disarray following the collapse of Meech. There seemed to be no compelling vision of the whole. Canadians appeared to be concentrating on defining their own sectional interests largely without reference to, perhaps in outright opposition to,

those of others. It was into this context of division and recrimination
that the aboriginal peoples forced their claims. The interaction between aboriginal rights and secessionist tensions has not been easy.

Aboriginal leaders did use the Meech debate very effectively to get
their concerns before the Canadian people. Throughout the debate,
the First Nations' objections were among the most influential. The
manner of the accord's demise also focused attention on aboriginal
alienation: the Manitoba legislature's inability to ratify Meech was, in
the end, due to the actions of Cree MLA Elijah Harper, actions tele-
vised across the country. But just as the aboriginal peoples had used
the Meech deadline to achieve some influence, the passing of the
deadline risked ending that influence. In the days following Meech's
failure, it seemed that aboriginal concerns might again be pushed
off the table, as the federal government withdrew offers it had made
during the Meech discussions.

The First Nations did retain their role in the constitutional debate,
in part because of continued support throughout Canada, but also
because of the events of the summer of 1990. The blockades at
Kanesatake and Kahnawake – those long confrontations between
the Canadian army and armed Mohawk Warriors – shocked Canadians, graphically demonstrating the effects of Canada's failure to deal
with aboriginal claims. But the demonstration had a cost. Relations
between Kanesatake, Kahnawake, and their neighbouring communities, which of late had been relatively free of friction, became very
tense, generating deep frustration and incidents of outright racism.
Even within Mohawk communities, the stand-off deepened existing
divisions, some members supporting the Warriors' actions, others
opposing the armed confrontational tactics (although they shared
the deep disaffection with the government's aboriginal policy).
Quebec public opinion generally became very hostile to aboriginal
claims. Given the proximity between these events and the defeat of
Meech, there was even suspicion in Quebec that aboriginal rights
were being used as a pretext for attacks on the province. This suspicion reflected a profound misunderstanding of the aboriginal position and revealed the extent to which Quebec's preoccupation with
French-English relations could distort consideration of other issues.
Regrettably, it was given a semblance of reality by the fact that some
English-speaking Canadians who had never sympathized with the
aboriginal cause nevertheless used it as a way of undermining
Quebec nationalism, seizing upon Cree and Inuit arguments for
self-determination to claim that an independent Quebec would lose
the northern lands.

The situation in Quebec has gradually improved. The notion of aboriginal rights as pretext has faded, especially as Quebecers have heard the voices of the First Nations themselves. Hostility and incomprehension were never universal, and following the blockades a number of initiatives showed a commitment on the part of Quebecers to a constructive dialogue.[7] In the debates over the Charlottetown Accord, both the provincial Liberals and the Parti Québécois supported, at least ostensibly, aboriginal self-government (although the PQ, opposing the package, did play upon popular fears about aboriginal claims). The movement towards accommodation is fragile, however. It probably could not survive another confrontation as bitter as that at Oka. In fact, one gets the impression that for Canadians generally the engagement with aboriginal issues is delicately balanced between sympathy and unease.

In recent years, the arguments of some Native leaders have been less conciliatory, claiming that the First Nations are utterly alienated from Canadian society, evoking the possibility of violent clashes of the kind seen at Kanesatake and Kahnawake, or arguing for the complete sovereignty of aboriginal peoples over their lands, sovereignty excluding both provincial and federal governments. These arguments reflect real disaffection within the First Nations. They also serve an important strategic role. When people are faced with a government that shows little commitment to their fundamental concerns – when a government disregards aboriginal peoples because of their lack of political power – extreme rhetoric itself becomes a source of power. The strategy has its dangers. It may reinforce the position of those within aboriginal communities (now the minority) who genuinely do oppose accommodation with the larger society, or if the balance is lost between expressions of alienation and willingness to talk, it may frighten away sympathetic members of the broader public. Our objective must be to move beyond the rhetorical sparring, so that we can find some reconciliation between the aspirations of aboriginal communities and Canada's other societies.

LONGING FOR COMMUNITY

In the months immediately following the collapse of Meech, it often seemed that our national debate was splintering. There was little agreement on what our country might mean, little will to search for agreement. We seemed to be drifting into rigid camps, gradually pulling apart. Meech Lake had apparently killed many Canadians' taste for compromise. Greater support for Quebec's separation, in

Quebec and elsewhere, suggested that many were giving up on Canada altogether. And yet, as time passed, it became increasingly clear that many Canadians still longed for a solution.

This was most evident outside Quebec. When English-speaking Canadians doubted whether Canada could continue – when they fell back on the exasperated "Let Quebec go" – they rarely did so out of a conviction that Quebec should secede. Theirs was a separatism of reaction: tired of the problem and despairing of a solution, they responded to Quebec's demands by embracing the only outcome that offered hope of settling the matter once and for all. Indeed, for many there was no real acceptance of separation. Letting Quebec go was just a way of calling Quebec's bluff. Many were convinced that if put to the test, Quebec would remain within Canada. For Canadians who did accept that Quebec might separate, letting Quebec go was a solution of last resort: convinced that Quebec's aspirations were incompatible with their conception of Canada, they would rather have seen Quebec go quickly than have the country gradually stripped of significance by concessions designed to keep Quebec in.

There was also considerable commitment to Canada within Quebec, despite the polls in favour of sovereignty. It is true that some Quebecers had cut their ties to Canada and were now confirmed *indépendantistes*, but they remained a decided minority even of French-speaking Quebecers. Many favoured the Parti Québécois more out of frustration or a strategic calculation that the PQ would best protect Quebec's autonomy than out of any conviction that Quebec must be politically separate. Indeed, many advocates of sovereignty, especially at the grass roots, retained significant residual loyalty to Canada. One of the chief attractions of the PQ's policy of "sovereignty-association" was that it permitted Quebecers (at least in theory) to reconcile their dual loyalties to Quebec and Canada. Those dual loyalties have been a consistent theme throughout Quebec politics – one that Quebecers themselves have begun to recognize, not least in the post-Meech discussions – and they remain present (in various degrees) across the political spectrum. They lay behind the remarkable voting patterns in Quebec in the late 1970s, when the same electorate voted for PQ governments in Quebec and for the strongly centralist Trudeau Liberals in Ottawa. The comedian Yvon Deschamps, at the time of the 1980 Referendum, caught the paradox in a marvellous and now famous joke: "What do Quebecers want? But it's quite simple: a free and independent Quebec in a strong and united Canada."[8] Allegiance to Quebec – even the belief that Quebec must be independent – did not exclude attachment to Canada.[9]

Indeed, a continuing (though bruised) commitment to Canada was often evident in the very manner in which disaffection was expressed. I cited above the Quebec Liberal Party's Allaire report as an example of the weakening of confidence in Canada. That report was prepared over the winter of 1990–91 and approved by the party in March 1991. Its link to government policy was ambiguous: it was a party document, not adopted by the government, prepared when Robert Bourassa was in a Washington-area hospital for cancer treatment. It caught, however, the mood of Quebecers profoundly disappointed by the defeat of Meech. It proposed a very extensive devolution of powers. The Canada it envisaged was patterned on the European Community, with the relationship between the provinces and Ottawa roughly equivalent to that between the states of Europe and the EC. Its proposals seemed (as some commentators noted) to be not all that far from the PQ's goal of sovereignty-association.

Some members of the Quebec Liberal Party accepted that option wholeheartedly. There was a constituency within the party – their numbers swollen by Meech's defeat – that spoke of Canada predominantly in terms of economic integration and efficiency; for them the ideal would have been a largely independent Quebec operating within a context of liberalized trade and conservative economic management. The recommendations of the Allaire committee reflected the views of that constitutency (which included the committee's chair, Jean Allaire), but they also contained a number of contrasting themes pointing in a very different direction, themes which gave a more accurate picture of the stance of the party as a whole.

One remarkable feature of the report was its preoccupation with the lost opportunity of Meech Lake. There was little passion in its discussion of the building of a new Quebec. The positive justifications for its blueprint were surprisingly thin. Passion was reserved for descriptions of how we got to where we were, and especially for the rejection of Meech. In this context, the proposals for a strongly decentralized federation came across as distinctly second-best. The report did recommend a substantial break with Canada as it is now, but it did so reluctantly, with a long backward glance at what might have been. This response was common in Quebec's post-Meech constitutional discourse, and shortly after Meech's defeat it prompted a perceptive comment by that unrepentant *indépendantiste* Pierre Bourgault on the increasing tendency of many Quebecers to identify themselves as pro-independence: "I don't believe it," he said. "They still care too much what the rest of Canada thinks. When you're a true sovereignist, you no longer care what they think."

This commitment to a more-accommodating solution was also ev-

ident in the Allaire report's treatment of future constitutional discussions. A substantial caucus within the Liberal Party, particularly
the youth wing, wanted to exclude all negotiations on the grounds
that that route had been tried, had failed, and that now was the time
to end the nonsense. According to these activists, the report should
have been presented as a take-it-or-leave-it proposition. The party
rejected this approach. It preserved room for negotiations – room
that also existed in the conclusions of the subsequent all-party
Bélanger-Campeau Commission. Both reports resisted the call for
an immediate referendum. The referendum would be held in June
or October 1992 and would deal with Quebec's sovereignty only if
no agreement had been reached with the rest of Canada in the
meantime.[10] Even if it did deal with sovereignty, Quebec would not
attain independence until one year after the vote, again permitting
negotiations (only this time probably on the kind of association
between an independent Quebec and the remains of Canada rather
than on a solution within the Canadian federation).

When read as a whole, then, the Allaire report began to look less
like a bottom line and more like a warning of what would come next
if the constitutional actors neglected negotiations. The report was
best read not as the Liberals' firm vision of a radically decentralized
Canada, but rather as an attempt to convey the level of dissatisfaction within Quebec – a plea to the rest of Canada to come to grips
with the issue before it was too late.[11]

But perhaps the best indication that there was still, throughout the
country, considerable commitment to a Canadian solution was the
fact that negotiations did begin again, eventually resulting in the
conclusion of a new package of amendments, the Charlottetown
Accord, although the subsequent collapse of that accord also showed
that fundamental problems remained.

In the wake of Meech, circumstances were far from favourable for
a resumption of talks. Most Canadians outside Quebec wanted nothing to do with the constitution. They had been appalled by the
Meech debate, they distrusted their leaders, and, while they might
have constitutional demands of their own (Senate reform, for example), they generally believed that other issues were far more important. They were especially resistant to Quebec's demands, still
considering that province to be the spoiled child of Confederation
and questioning its commitment to the country. The situation was
further aggravated by Quebec's apparent desire to force negotiations with (as one prominent Quebec commentator put it) "le cou-
teau à la gorge"; there was very strong feeling outside Quebec that
a country founded on knives at the throat was not worth having.

Quebec's insistence on bilateral negotiations with Ottawa and its refusal to attend federal-provincial conferences until all parties had agreed to the contents of Meech merely rubbed salt in the wounds.

Given the situation in Quebec, however, the constitutional debate could not be shelved – not, at least, without giving up altogether. Quebecers had channelled their hurt and disappointment into a resolve to settle matters once and for all. This could not be ignored, even by those strongly committed to federalism. The most that could be gained was time, and even this was short. Given the mood in Quebec, a referendum could not be postponed indefinitely, and October 1992 became the effective deadline. This was a very tight schedule for negotiations that, to have any legitimacy outside Quebec, would have to deal with the whole gamut of constitutional demands: Senate reform, aboriginal self-government, Ontario's proposals for a social charter, federal proposals for a stronger economic union, as well as the issues promoted by Quebec.

Slowly, in the months following Meech, Ottawa, the provinces, and a number of independent organizations (the C.D. Howe Institute, the Donner Foundation, and others) worked to foster popular acceptance of and participation in further discussions. A number of committees, forums, commissions, and conferences debated the issues. Gradually, opinion outside Quebec began to move, so that there was a measure of toleration, though hardly enthusiasm, for further talks. Formal discussions began again, haltingly and with considerable acrimony. On 28 August 1992, in Charlottetown, an agreement in principle was concluded.

As a solution to Canada's impasse, that agreement was a failure. It was put to a pan-Canadian referendum just within Quebec's deadline, on 26 October 1992, and was defeated by a majority of Canadians across the country and in all provinces except Newfoundland, New Brunswick, Prince Edward Island, and Ontario (where the result was a virtual dead heat). Clearly, even if Canadians had been willing to countenance further talks, their leaders had gone too far, making compromises that their constituents would not support. Still, the process was not a loss. Canadians had taken their involvement very seriously, participating in forums, reading the accord, and turning out to vote. Public opinion had evolved during the debate. The lines established in Meech had blurred. One had the impression that a more constructive conversation had begun, although only just. Moreover, the fallout was much less damaging than that resulting from the defeat of Meech. Ironically, the extent of Charlottetown's rejection made for a less serious crisis. Quebec was no longer isolated; it too had rejected these proposals.

But, of course, agreement in saying no was not the same as saying yes to something else. The abortive Charlottetown process may have demonstrated that there was still commitment to a Canadian solution, but what solution? Was there any conception of this country that could adequately capture the allegiances of Canadians? Charlottetown proposed trade-offs on specific reforms – a set of deals and side deals – but the problem of vision remained. In the absence of an acceptable vision of the whole, many Canadians, in all parts of the country, were unwilling to go along. Charlottetown failed, above all, because it remained a saw-off, unsupported by a persuasive sense of what this country might be.

Charlottetown and Meech before it demonstrated that goodwill alone – a general commitment to something called Canada – was not enough. Although some of us may claim to be "unconditional Canadians," the truth is that there are few (if any) francophone Quebecers who are willing to remain within Canada on any terms, just as there are few (if any) other Canadians who are ready to solve our current crisis simply by letting Quebec rewrite the constitution. On all sides, our commitments must be to a particular kind of Canada. In recent years, we have come to doubt whether essentially all Canadians share the same conception. And the more we doubt, the more we wonder whether we should compromise to preserve what seems to be an empty shell. We are torn between our genuine desire to continue with this country and our suspicions that we may no longer have compatible ideas of what the country should be.

Our problem therefore runs deeper than this or that clause in the constitution. It concerns our ability to agree on a vision of this country satisfactory to all. We have to consider our various perspectives to see whether they are reconcilable. This involves exploring whether we can accommodate our particular loyalties within Canadian political life. It also involves understanding how our differences might fit within a coherent sense of the whole. Our problem is not how to live apart, but how to live together. We have to see how individuals can find freedom and fulfilment in their own pursuits and in their sense of belonging to Canada's constituent societies; we have to see how those societies can prosper and grow, all within the broader Canadian community; and we have to grasp what it means for Canadians to belong to that broader community – how, in other words, Canada makes sense as a country.

TERMS OF DISUNION

I believe there is a vision of Canada that responds to these aspirations, a vision firmly rooted in our experience as a country and capable of supporting a profound allegiance to this land and its future. That vision has often been implicit in relations between our various communities. It is reflected (imperfectly) in our constitutional structure. It has been a consistent, though not always dominant, theme within our political practice. But we have generally lacked the vocabulary to grasp it, develop it, and understand how it could be just. We have treated our diverse and complex institutional structures as the product of nothing more than the politics of power, as compromises of our conceptions of national identity and citizenship that may have been necessary, but were hardly admirable. In our constitutional practice, we have often fashioned workable structures for accommodating difference, but in our constitutional theory we have failed to see how those structures were good or how they could work together to make a country.

That is the tragedy of our current constitutional debate. We are caught between a practice that can be responsive to the complexity of our community and a theory that makes us profoundly doubt that practice. Canadians can – and to a large extent do – share a conception of community and nationhood that underlies the best of our experience, although we have yet to find the words to express it. We need to find those words now, not only because they are essential to understanding the place of Quebec within Canada, but also because they are fundamental to building a political community acceptable to all Canadians, including the First Nations.

This book describes the contours of that vision of Canada. It reviews the constitutional debate of the last thirty years, explores the relationship between political community and culture, shows how that discussion relates to prominent themes in Canadian political life, and finally suggests specific implications for the Canadian constitution. Its premise is that we have been badly served by the terms of the present debate and that those terms need to be reconceived. Developing that reconception will take up the bulk of this volume. It may help now, however, to sketch its main lines.

The terms "nation" and "nationalist" have often framed the controversy. Is Canada one nation or two – or more? Is a particular Quebecer a nationalist or a federalist? Is he or she a Canadian nationalist or a Quebec nationalist? In this book, I avoid the language of nation, preferring to speak of political communities or societies. I do not do this because I object to considering Quebec or the aboriginal peoples as distinct societies with their own identities, or because I want to reduce their status in comparison to the Canadian state. On the contrary, I argue in this book that Quebec and the First Nations are legitimate objects of allegiance, possessing substantial social autonomy that should be reflected in institutional autonomy. My quarrel with "nation" concerns two additional connotations. First, the term often leads to an easy equation of membership in a political community with ethnic identity. Ethnicity frequently is related to the sense of belonging that exists at the base of any community, including a political community. But the relationship between ethnicity and political community is often much more complex than identity. Separating the concepts can help us think through the issues in a more careful fashion, so that we might understand especially how our communities can include as full members people of diverse ethnic backgrounds.

The second problem with "nation" is its exclusivity. The term usually carries the assumption that an individual can only have one nation. But the crucial fact about Canada is precisely that people do belong to more than one political community at the same time. Canadians are members of the broader Canadian society and they are also members of less-extensive communities. Where those communities have their own cultural or linguistic character and serve as centres of political life largely autonomous from the broader society (as is the case for aboriginal nations or Quebec), they may rival or surpass the broader society in their significance for their members. Which, then, is the nation? In many ways, the best answer is that they both are. Quebec is a nation for its people for some matters, and Canada (including Quebec) is a nation for its people (including Quebecers) for other matters. This use of the term sits uncomfortably, however. We seem to be compelled to argue over which is *the* nation to which we belong. "Political community" lays aside that baggage, permitting us to talk about multiple communities and multiple allegiances.[12]

The question of multiple allegiances will be crucial. One of the defining features of a nation (once it has been weaned from ethnic identification) is the powerful feelings of allegiance it inspires. In Canada, many of our arguments over nation seem to come down to arguments about allegiance. Many English-speaking Canadians recoil at the suggestion that Quebec might be a nation precisely because this seems to place in doubt Quebecers' loyalty to Canada. We saw that suspicion in the Meech Lake debate, when Quebecers were confronted with the challenge: "Are you Quebecers first, or Canadians first?" For those asking the question, the only acceptable answer was "Canadians first"; they believed that Quebecers should be willing to lay aside recognition of their distinctive society in favour of a broader Canadian identity. Many Quebecers balked at this, further increasing the suspicions of Canadians outside Quebec. But the problem was the question, not the answer. Its very terms assumed that Quebecers had to choose between their loyalties as Quebecers and as Canadians, that it was not possible to be both a good Quebecer and a good Canadian. But why should Quebecers have to make that choice? Isn't it enough to ask whether they have sufficient allegiance to Canada to make this country work? It doesn't matter that they have strong allegiance to Quebec, as long as their allegiance to Canada is also strong.

The challenge to Quebecers is reminiscent of an older challenge that we now recognize as extremely objectionable: "Are you a Canadian first, or a Jew first?" The point is that there are certain choices we have no business asking people to make. Requiring people to choose is just another way of saying that the characteristic – allegiance to Quebec or, in the older challenge, Jewish identity – is somehow incompatible with being a good Canadian. By putting the challenge to Quebecers in that way, we risk slipping into the trap that suggests that any desire of Quebecers to maintain their distinctive community, perhaps even their cultural identity, places that allegiance in jeopardy: to be good Canadians, they have to be willing, if it comes to that, to sacrifice their cultural identity for the whole.

That kind of requirement fundamentally misconceives the nature of Canada and distorts how Canadians in many parts of the country – not just Quebec or the First Nations – think about their relation to the whole. Many Canadians cherish not just their identity as Canadians but also their particular, more local identities. They have probably never asked themselves whether they are Canadians first or, for example, Newfoundlanders first (at least not until the Meech debate made it the fashion) precisely because there was no need to choose. If they had asked themselves, the question wouldn't have made much sense. They are both Canadians and Newfoundlanders, and they know that they can continue to be both because being Canadian doesn't require that they surrender all other allegiances: being a vigorous Newfoundlander is perfectly compatible with being a good Canadian.

Most English-speaking Canadians have had difficulty seeing that the same goes for Quebec. The extent of attachment to local communities does vary from group to group across this land, and there is no doubt that the loyalties of Quebecers are among the strongest. Moreover, the demands for constitutional change by Quebec "nationalists," coupled with the threat of separation, have made it seem to many that loyalty to Quebec is, at least in the long run, much less compatible with loyalty to Canada. Indeed, there are some Quebec nationalists – confirmed sovereignists – who believe that loyalties to Canada and Quebec are fundamentally irreconcilable, that Quebecers must choose their country, and that the only sensible choice is Quebec. But for many Quebecers, including people often called nationalists, the two can exist at once. That is the truth underlying Yvon Deschamps's joke. Quebecers do want "a free and independent Quebec" in "a strong and united Canada."

One of the ironies of the present situation is that the two groups at the extremes of the opposing camps both share the same exclusive conception of nationalism. The core of confirmed separatists insist that Quebecers can only have one country: Quebec. Some strong centralists would force the same kind of choice, but they want Quebecers to choose Canada. In each case, the protagonists are working with an exclusive notion of allegiance that conflicts with the pattern of loyalties in Canadian society, denies some of the things we most value about Canada, and has within it the seeds of intolerance. This book attempts to recapture the ground that those notions exclude, making room for the various ways in which each of us is Canadian. This does require a more complex idea of Canadian identity. Finding the appropriate role for each of our communities is not easy, especially given the differences between them. But we have traditionally accepted that challenge in Canada, believing that tolerance of our diverse attachments is one of the things that makes our society valuable.

Responding to that challenge is going to require sensitivity to differences between groups. Not all groups face the same challenges; not all have the same aspirations. If we are to develop the proper recognition for each group within the structure of the whole, we have to be ready to distinguish between different kinds of group attachment and identity.

Drawing these distinctions can be a tricky business, as we saw in the debate over Meech Lake's and then Charlottetown's distinct society clause. If one group is given special recognition, others may feel excluded or demeaned. It sometimes seems that we are caught between two poles: either all groups should get special consideration or none should. We may be tempted to follow the Reform Party's approach, avoiding the problem altogether by treating all identically. Culture would then be considered a matter of private preference, carrying no public consequences. That does not resolve the problem, however. It hides it. We cannot escape the presence of culture in our public institutions. Whether we like it or not, they are shaped by culture. If we pretend they are neutral and refuse accommodation of minority cultures, we will end up subjecting those minorities to domination by the majority. That was the tragedy of Native children caught within an ostensibly neutral but ultimately insensitive and self-defeating system of child adoptions. It was also the problem during the first half of this century when English was required to be the predominant language of instruction in heavily francophone areas of Ontario. [13] Policies take shape within communities that have a cultural character, are delivered by individuals who express cultural characteristics, and are stated in one language or another. If we want to respect cultural diversity, we have to come to grips with the recognition of distinctive groups in institutional design.

That means looking carefully at the intersection between different kinds of cultural diversity and political community. We have fallen into the habit of treating any distinction as an element in a hierarchy: the distinct society clause would, we imagined, have given Quebecers more rights than any other group; recognizing Quebec's unique identity would make Quebecers "first-class citizens and everyone else second-class." Some of the images we use reinforce that impression, especially the phrase "two founding peoples." That phrase does capture the special salience of the English and French cultures in Canada's history, but it does so in a way that excludes the contribution of aboriginal peoples and Canadians of other ethnic backgrounds. By focusing on "peoples" and justifying the preeminence of English and French in historical terms, the phrase also suggests that individuals of English and French descent will always, because of the presence of their ancestors at the origin of this country, have a privileged place. Surely all this confuses the issue. The only acceptable justification for recognition of Quebec's distinctiveness is not what happened many years ago, but the character of that community and its situation within Canada today. In part, that is the result of history, but it goes well beyond some idea of initial entitlement to include the continued strength and cohesion of Quebec's society, the size of its population, the challenges it faces within today's North American environment, and above all its use of French as its primary language of commerce and debate. The reason we might wish to recognize Quebec's uniqueness is not because francophone Quebecers should stand above all others, but because the character of Quebec society, being different, may justify different treatment.

Similar arguments might be made for aboriginal peoples, Canadians of other cultural backgrounds, French Canadians outside Quebec, and perhaps other groups as well. In each case, different kinds of accommodations are appropriate, depending on the nature and aspirations of the members of the group itself, all considered within a viable vision of Canada as a whole. In some cases, the accommodation may take the form of specific guarantees of individual rights, but in many it will have little to do with rights. Constitutions are not just about the protection of rights, but also about the institutions through which we govern ourselves – the communities within which public debate occurs and public decisions are taken.

This brings us to another failing of our present constitutional discourse. Canadians have become obsessed with the language of rights. The protection of individual rights is a crucial function of constitutions, and this book will have much to say about the relationship between the recognition of communities and individual rights. But by talking about everything in terms of either individual or group rights, we have fallen into a simplistic opposition in which one or the other must lose: either the group triumphs and individual rights suffer, or the individual triumphs and the group suffers. The language of rights virtually begs us to see group and individual as opposed.

Many of the kinds of recognition at issue, however, are not concerned with the ability of groups to restrict individuals. They relate primarily to the communities and structures within which public decisions are taken. When aboriginal peoples want control over family law, economic regulation, and the administration of justice, as they affect their members, they simply want those areas to be shaped, at least in part, by the aboriginal communities concerned. When Quebecers want Quebec to have control over immigration, social policy, or even language, or when they want the constitution interpreted in a manner sensitive to Quebec's uniqueness, they too are concerned with the context in which decisions are made, not the ability to repress individuals. All public decision making takes place within a cultural and institutional context, and constitutions play a crucial role in defining that context. The decisions taken by our institutions may adversely affect individuals, and certain institutional arrangements may pose more of a threat to individual liberties than others. Consequences for individual rights, then, must be considered. But not every constitutional recognition of a community threatens individual rights, and we should adjust our language accordingly.

Indeed, one consistent theme running through this book will be the ways in which the Canadian constitution serves as the institutional exoskeleton of our political communities, defining the channels through which we engage in public debate and decision. The constitution is important not just for its guarantees of individual rights, but also for its role as a vehicle for self-determination. It must therefore be responsive to the complexity of our communities, for those are the forums within which public discussion takes place and public initiatives find their legitimacy. Like any exoskeleton, the constitution will impose its own constraints and indeed will shape communities in its own image. We are caught in a constant dialogue, then, between institutions and society. But any decent constitutional theory has to catch both sides of that dialogue. It must be a theory grounded in conceptions of community, country, and allegiance that have resonance in the society it serves.

This book suggests how the range of our commitments to Canada and to our more particular identities can and should find expression in our constitutional structure. It shows how those commitments can work together with a vision of the country as a whole, a vision largely implicit in our practice and sufficient to support continued allegiance to the Canadian project, one we have risked losing in recent years as we have tried to squeeze this richly diverse country into rigid and anachronistic forms of nation and allegiance. Its proposals will not settle the constitution for all time. It neglects some items now on the table. This book simply suggests how, from the perspective of one standing in Canada in 1993, we should think about the broad structure of our country and our constitution. Constitutions are not meant to resolve all our conflicts. They merely suggest a framework through which we can wrestle with them through time.

WHAT WE MIGHT LOSE

The previous section placed this book's argument against the terms of the present debate, suggesting that we can and should reconceive those terms. The rest of this book will develop that reconception. One might ask, however – especially given the present state of our constitutional debate – "Why bother?" Maybe this reconception is simply one imaginative attempt to save a country not worth saving.

Clearly I don't believe that. This book is (perhaps all too obviously) the product of passionate commitment to this country and its future. Like all passions, mine is hard to justify in coldly rationalistic terms. In many ways this book simply trusts that others share its passion. Given the extent to which we have begun to doubt ourselves, however, perhaps I should say a word about what I think we will lose if we let this country slip from us.

Over the past 125 years and more, and especially in the last 30, we have struggled to express the "Canadian identity." The expressions we have used have been partial. It is as though no single image could contain the essence of this society. Some images, such as those stressing Canadians' relationship to nature or their willingness to use the state for the construction of a better society, capture central themes in Canadian life, but in the end they seem strangely bloodless, neglecting the richly diverse character of Canada's peoples. Others, like the expressions "two founding peoples" or "British Canada," evoke important aspects of our cultural heritage but leave little room for other contributions, especially those of aboriginal peoples or the multicultural communities. I will not attempt a new synthesis in this space but will address one part of the whole now in doubt: the contribution of Quebec to the country. What does it mean to a British Columbian (as I am) that Quebec was and remains part of Canada?

We may be tempted to answer, "Not much." After all, the dominant image of relations between French-speaking and English-speaking Canada is one of "two solitudes," each pursuing its own dynamic in isolation from the other, and it is true that many British Columbians have little direct understanding of French Canadian society. But our answer would be wrong, for it would have focused only on the most obvious kinds of cultural interchange, ignoring the more subtle ways in which we have shaped each other. It would have assumed that we were members of either a British Columbian or a Quebec community and would have then asked how those communities have influenced each other. But each Canadian is also, at the same time, a member of another community, one that crosses those regional divides. That membership makes one Canadian, and it is at that level that British Columbians have been most obviously shaped by the encounter with North America's French culture. To the extent that British Columbians consider themselves Canadians – and they do – they lay claim to an identity that is manifestly not formed solely within the linguistic group in which they live.

The presence of the French fact within this pan-Canadian community is clear from the traditional account of the events of Canadian history: the role of French Canadians in the fur trade; the extension of civil rights to Canadian Catholics at a time when Catholics in Britain suffered a series of disabilities; the struggle for responsible government during the 1830s; the Confederation debates; the Riel Rebellion; the gradual severing of ties with Britain; the arguments over conscription in World Wars I and II; the search for a Canadian identity in the postwar period. Canadian history is much more than a dialogue between two founding peoples. Accounts of some of these events, especially of the Riel Rebellion, have suffered from an excessive emphasis on central Canadian linguistic conflicts. But the linguistic divide was one of the elements that made those debates what they were, and it therefore shaped the political community of today.

Those debates continue to influence our institutions and political culture. The original division of powers between provincial and federal governments was itself designed in part to accommodate a Catholic, francophone Quebec. The design of many lesser institutions has drawn upon similar principles of cultural accommodation. This is most apparent in social policy, notably education. The constitutional guarantee of Catholic and Protestant schools in Ontario and Quebec was a direct result of the Catholic-Protestant encounter in central Canada, an encounter in which the Catholic side was represented by Irish and Scots, but above all by the French Canadians. Quebec has since moved away from denominational school boards towards boards based on language, but the principle of publicly funded denominational schools has been adopted by other communities, especially by recent waves of predominantly Catholic immigrants. Guarantees of separate schools were also very important at the time of Newfoundland's entry to Confederation. The original constitutional provision served as a potent support for the recent extension of full funding to Catholic schools in Ontario. Beyond denominational schools, the influence of French Canada is of course very apparent in the language of education – in the presence of French schools in provinces with anglophone majorities, English schools in Quebec, and immersion classes in all jurisdictions.

Examples could be multiplied. Most of our public debates in fields as diverse as foreign policy, the ownership of family property, regional economic development, and cultural policy have been coloured by the presence of a vibrant French-speaking society within Canada. This is not to romanticize what has often been an uneasy coexistence. The conscription crises of the world wars split the country, largely along linguistic lines. Quebec's opposition to the federal spending power (the federal government's power to provide services in areas of provincial jurisdiction) has sometimes impeded the creation of standard social programs across the country (although the design of programs has benefited from distinctive initiatives developed in Quebec – the structure of the Quebec pension plan,[14] for example, or Quebec's system of community health clinics). French Canadians have also had their share of frustrations. They, after all, were on the losing side in the conscription debates. They worked in an economy dominated by anglophone firms, in which the language of work was often English. They paid taxes to a federal government, which until the Diefenbaker years sent cheques to them only in English, and in which, in some departments, English was the exclusive language of work as late as the 1960s.

The point is not that we have lived in a cultural paradise, but simply that our diversity has shaped our sense of ourselves, certainly at the level of our politics, but also, with more subtlety, at the level of our social relations generally.

At its simplest, this has meant a greater awareness of and perhaps tolerance for cultural diversity in Canada. From its origin, our country has had to cope with the existence of deep cultural differences. We have had to find a way to accommodate those differences in public policy. We didn't always like it. Protection of the minority's view sometimes required compromises the majority would rather not have made. Separate schools are a good example. Protestant reformers in nineteenth-century Canada, as in the United States, would have preferred a unitary system, to give students a common set of values. But we were forced to make special allowances, allowances that later formed the basis for our ability to accommodate other groups: Newfoundland Catholics, Italian Canadians, or the cultural communities served by heritage language programs. The lessons learned at home may also have given us greater sensitivity to cultural distinctions on the international plane, contributing to our impressive diplomatic record. This sensitivity may also have made us less rigidly individualistic, with more respect for the meaning of community in a host of public policies.

Our identity has been marked not only by the fact of cultural diversity, but also by the nature of our cultures. Among these, two great European traditions, the British and the French, have had dominant roles within Canada's cultural life, shaping its access to the world. The influence of these traditions goes beyond linguistic ability or express borrowings from Europe, although those have been important. The two traditions have served as media through which Canadians have understood their experience in this land, developing parallel, distinctively North American visions. At that level, the French Canadian expression has been influential throughout the country – in the myths of the French Canadian trader, logger, or emigrant to the United States in search of work; in the French Canadian version of the attempt to preserve an ordered and upright community in a wild land; or in the French Canadian evocation of the contrast between a cohesive, cooperative society and a cold, forbidding landscape.

No doubt we could have made better use of our cultural heritage. Like any people, we have had our share of missed opportunities, misunderstandings, and outright chauvinism. The treatment of the First Nations is one such example, including the attempts to obliterate their religions, languages, and ways of life – certainly our failure to pay more attention to and draw more of our sense of ourselves from their traditions. Nor have we always understood how to make room for people of origins other than English or French. One thinks of the denial of the vote to Canadian citizens of Asian origin living

in British Columbia, a disenfranchisement reversed only in the
1940s. But we have also had our successes, and these together with
the lessons we take from our past can provide the basis for a vigorous and tolerant society, one that has room for our particular allegiances and particular values and also for our attachment to the
broader Canadian community. An integral part of that process is the
ability to draw upon the wealth of experience and aspiration presented by our history.

That history has made us. It furnishes the bank of experience and
myth that gives substance to community. It helps us define what it
means to be Canadian as we wrestle with questions of cultural and
intercultural solidarity, trying to build vibrant and humane societies
both in our particular communities and at the level of Canada as a
whole, all in a large and magnificent land. The French Canadian culture has been part of that story. It has served as an important component of our myths of strength, determination, and openness.
Surely we do not want it to become a myth of failure.

I have often been struck by the way Canadians, when they want a
gift that symbolizes Canada, reach for artwork or crafts reflecting
folk cultures with roots deep in this land – often folk cultures of an
origin other than their own. How can we see our nation in an Inuit
carving or Cowichan sweater when we have left so little room for aboriginal peoples in our society and when most of us have little real
engagement with Indians or Inuit? I believe it is one more indication
that our idea of Canada is more than is manifested in our present institutional arrangements or habits of interaction, or is expressed by
our theories of what it means to be a nation. The choice of symbols
also reflects an aspiration towards inclusion of and respect for
Canada's constituent communities, although we may not know how
to act on that aspiration. Lying behind the often awkward or bitter
terms of our present debate, Canadians (including Quebecers) hold
a vision of their country that embraces the whole and draws upon
our history for symbols of identity and models of justice. It is a vision
that needs expression, a Canada that needs reimagining.

LIBRARY
COLBY-SAWYER COLLEGE
NEW LONDON, NH 03257

PART ONE

National Identity and Constitutional Change, 1960 to 1992

Introduction to Part One

How did our debate evolve to the present impasse, where we now have difficulty reconciling our particular identities with commitment to the whole? At one level, the roots of the crisis predate Confederation, encompassing all the rivalries, conflicts, and collaborations throughout our long history in this land.[1] But at another, the roots are found in the last thirty years of debate over Canadian nationality and identity and in the movement for constitutional reform generated by that debate.

Thirty years ago, Canada was going through a time of renewal, a process that, while often disconcerting, seemed, by the end of the 1960s, to hold the promise of a new Canada. We were leaving behind old conceptions of the national character, conceptions which generally focused (in English-speaking Canada) on the tension between allegiance to Britain and a belated pro-Americanism and (in French-speaking Canada) on the central role of the church. We were searching for distinctively Canadian voices, in literature, the arts, broadcasting, education. We transformed our national symbols, adopting a new anthem and flag. Canadian governments began to pursue a more active role in promoting Canadian nationalism, encouraging cultural industries, limiting foreign ownership in the domestic economy, and pursuing an increasingly independent foreign policy.

In this process of revision and rethinking, the most contentious issues had to do with the relationship of Canada's cultural groups to the emerging identity. The most prominent of these concerned

French Canadians, and especially French-speaking Quebecers. Quebec was undergoing its "Quiet Revolution," a set of dramatic changes that offered both challenges and opportunities to Canada. As a result of that revolution, some Quebecers began to question the very existence of Canada. At the same time, the ending of Quebec's cultural isolation suggested that now Canada might fashion an identity appealing to both French- and English-speaking Canadians. This opened a long debate over the place of Quebec within – or outside – Canada, and led to reforms in the operation of the federal government that were designed to make Ottawa more accessible to French Canadians. This change in turn generated its own set of tensions, as some who had been comfortable with the previous English dominance or who had a cultural heritage other than English or French contested the attention to French Canadians.

The period also marked the emergence into popular consciousness of other sources of grievance. At the time these seemed unrelated to Canada's identity or constitutional structure, but they would eventually find expression on both fronts. One was the condition of aboriginal peoples. The late 1960s brought a surge of concern about that condition, differing from the paternalistic intervention (or neglect) of previous decades in the self-assertion and defiance of the aboriginal peoples themselves.[2] It was also during this time that women's equality forced its way back onto the public agenda. Again, the focus was on questions which had little to do with the constitution: women's participation in the workforce, equal pay, child care, the status of married women, and sexual stereotyping in education.[3]

Indeed, few of the issues animating anglophone Canadians in the late 1960s were conceived in constitutional terms. Even the popular debate over what it meant to be Canadian generally ignored the constitution. But there was one crucial intersection between identity and constitutional order: the demands of successive Quebec governments for greater powers and, in response, the positions adopted by the federal government.

At first, constitutional discussion was largely confined to these issues, but by the end of the period, the debate had expanded to embrace a wide range of social claims and counter-claims. A constitutional discourse initially preoccupied with the arcana of the division of powers between Ottawa and the provinces ultimately became the focus for redefining all of Canada, the prism through which all questions of identity were refracted. The constitutional conversation of the past thirty years, and the failures of that conversation in the 1990s, can only be understood in the context of the broader discussion about Canadian identity and its relationship to the demands of

Quebecers, aboriginal peoples, multicultural communities, women, and all the rest of this country's rich fabric. Through the constitutional debates of the 1960s, 1970s, and 1980s, several disparate and initially quite independent themes were brought into conjunction, creating the complex and unwieldy dilemmas of today.

2 Competing Nationalisms, Competing Identities

In the 1960s the impetus for constitutional change came from Quebec. Other provinces had their own agenda, and in later years their demands would be pressed with a vigour rivalling that of Quebec. But in the 1960s Quebec's concerns drove the process. Indeed, for many Canadians, the constitutional discussions often seemed like a battle between Quebecers, with the rest of Canada looking on as sometimes-bemused, sometimes-anxious spectators.

Those who sought greater constitutional powers for Quebec have often been called, collectively, "Quebec nationalists," a term including everyone from turn-of-the-century Liberal MP Henri Bourassa to Parti Québécois premier René Lévesque, from Liberal premier Jean Lesage to the terrorists of the FLQ. The term hides more than it reveals. It was not true in the 1960s, and is not true now, that all Quebec nationalists were opposed to the continuation of Canada, that all ultimately wanted a sovereign Quebec and disagreed only on tactics. Most were committed to Canada, although they did want constitutional reform. Nor was it true that all Quebec nationalists systematically pursued the interests of Quebec, disregarding those of Canada as a whole. Some did, but others retained an allegiance to Canada that went beyond the parochial self-interest of their province.

What passes for "nationalism" in Quebec is really a broad stream, including persons having very different objectives, very different strategies, and sometimes different conceptions of what makes

Quebec unique, what makes it worth defending.[1] It is not a cohesive movement, with members uniting around a common platform. Quebec nationalists belong to the whole range of federal and provincial parties and fight vigorously with other "nationalists" over just about everything. In fact, the term itself is elastic. For those French-speaking Quebecers who now describe themselves as nationalists, it normally indicates commitment to extensive autonomy (if not complete independence) for Quebec (this usage is itself different from that of the 1950s or the early years of this century). Those opposed to the constitutional recognition of Quebec's uniqueness apply the term to a much broader swath of the political spectrum. For them, "nationalist" seems to apply to all who believe Quebec has a special role in the expression of North America's French culture, or who are dissatisfied with the constitutional status of Quebec. This use of the term has gained most currency in English-speaking Canada. It obscures much, damning with the taint of separatism all who support change in Quebec's constitutional powers.

The constitutional upheaval of the last thirty years (even setting aside, for the moment, the demands of aboriginal peoples, the western provinces, the Atlantic provinces, and others) cannot be understood simply as a fight between two easily defined sides: nationalists and federalists, René Lévesque and Pierre Trudeau. The controversy only makes sense when the different varieties of nationalism – and federalism – are appreciated. And the first of these is the nationalism of Maurice Duplessis, premier of Quebec from 1936 to 1939, then again from 1944 to 1959.[2]

Duplessis was the heir, or, more accurately, the opportunistic, self-proclaimed guardian, of a long tradition of conservative, Catholic nationalism in Quebec. Throughout his time in office he presented himself as the defender of Catholic virtue, French Canadian culture, and the legislative jurisdiction of the province of Quebec. His regime was authoritarian and corrupt – it eventually earned the nickname, *la grande noirceur* (the great darkness) – but it rode resentment of Ottawa and defence of Quebec's identity to a series of impressive electoral victories (often tainted by fraud). It was against this brand of nationalism that the "three wise men" of federal Liberal politics, Jean Marchand, Gérard Pelletier, and Pierre Trudeau, cut their political teeth. But Duplessis was equally considered the enemy by many who in their different ways would later advocate a new constitutional status for Quebec, people like Jean Lesage, André Laurendeau, Claude Ryan, and René Lévesque. All the principal political forces of Quebec in the 1960s were formed, in part, by their opposition to Duplessis.

The essence of the traditional, Catholic nationalism of Quebec was the inseparable identification of nationality, culture, language, and faith. The French Canadian "nation" was characterized not just by its language, but also by its commitment to the one true religion. The foundation of its identity, the bulwark that had defended it against the English language and Protestant materialism for so many years, was the church. The church was the repository not just of moral virtue, but of the national culture of French Canada. The national identity of French Canadians found its expression not so much in the public sphere of governmental action as in the private sphere of family, church, and neighbourhood. The conservative nationalists were concerned with public affairs. They believed that the moral teachings of the church should shape governmental action, just as they should guide every sphere of human activity. They certainly believed that government should not pursue, and perhaps should not permit, conduct at odds with Christian precepts. But the focus of French Canadian nationality lay elsewhere; government was neither the principal agent nor the principal interpreter of French Canada's national life.

This fact was reflected in the respective functions of church and state in Quebec in the 1950s. Elementary and high school education was run by denominational school boards. There was no provincial department of education until 1964. French-speaking universities were confessional. The province largely abstained from the direct provision of social welfare in order not to interfere with the voluntaristic, charitable impulse expressed in the church's ministry to the poor. Most hospitals were run by religious institutions. The province's economic policy reflected the church's deference to private property and individual initiative, bolstered by a not particularly religious commitment to economic growth based on the private ownership of capital. Government ownership was very rare, regulation of industry lax, and non-Catholic unions – even militant Catholic unions – vigorously attacked. In short, the national role of the Quebec government was to preserve the space within which the church could fulfil its historic mission and, in those areas in which direct government action was appropriate, to ensure that public policy was consistent with Catholic morality and social doctrine.

This conception of church and state informed the Duplessis government's position on the constitution. That position was predominantly defensive, asserting that the province was uniquely responsive to the French Canadian way of life, and resisting what were said to be federal intrusions into provincial jurisdiction. This traditionally involved strong opposition to the federal power of disallowance (under which the federal cabinet could annul validly enacted provincial laws; disallowance was last used in 1943 and many constitutional lawyers now consider it obsolete) and the federal declaratory power (under which the federal Parliament could unilaterally assume jurisdiction over works normally under the control of the provinces). But most important, Quebec opposed the federal government's use of the spending power to establish programs in areas of provincial jurisdiction, especially in education, health, and welfare. These areas were within the exclusive jurisdiction of the provinces; the federal government had, by the constitution, no right to regulate them. Rather than regulate them directly, then, Ottawa tried to support such matters as technical education, universities, hospitals, and financial assistance to families either by giving money directly to the persons concerned or by offering to share the costs of specific programs (the terms of which Ottawa would have a hand in determining) with the provinces. A province might be able to opt out of these programs, but the federal government would continue to use tax dollars obtained in that province to pay for the program in the rest of the country. Not only would the province's taxpayers have to pay for services they didn't get, but there would be little space left – little "tax room" – for the province to raise money to support its own programs.

Other provinces (although not all) occasionally objected to Ottawa's use of its taxing and spending powers, but the situation was particularly galling to the Duplessis government in Quebec. Its social policy had been based largely on government abstention. This left a vacuum easily filled by federal programs, programs the traditional Quebec elites argued were insensitive to the province's Catholic and francophone character but that were very difficult, politically, to reject. Once the vacuum was filled, it would be next to impossible for the province to reoccupy the field. The Duplessis government argued strongly, but with very little success, against the use of the federal spending power and in favour of increasing the provinces' share of taxation. It backed its resistance by refusing to participate in the building of the Trans-Canada Highway in 1950 and by rejecting federal support for universities in the middle years of that decade.

Conservative nationalists of the kind championed by Duplessis were generally not separatists. They did cherish the memory of a Canada before the British Conquest, of a time when French Canadians could look forward to being masters of their own destiny. But as long as the autonomy of church and province was respected, they accepted that independence must remain an unattainable dream. The stability of Canada was preferable to the hazards of secession. Conservative nationalists simply wanted the federal government to stay within its own space, leaving Quebec to govern its own affairs. They often seemed to have little more than an instrumental commitment to Canada. They were happy with the Canadian connection insofar as it allowed French Canada to preserve its faith and its language. They looked to the Quebec government as the jurisdiction most reflective of French Canada's identity. But the feelings of allegiance, of national belonging, were focused on the religious-linguistic community. This was the "nation," a nation that excluded even those Quebecers who spoke another language or had another faith. Quebecers of other languages or religions rarely were persecuted by church or state. Conservative, Catholic nationalists generally acknowledged that others had communal rights, especially the established Protestant community. (Jews did not benefit from the same recognition. Until 1930 they were denied the right to establish their own public schools – although after they obtained that right, they chose to remain within the Protestant school boards – and they were more likely to be discriminated against by institutions and individuals.) There was far less acceptance of individual liberties, especially when the exercise of those liberties threatened (in the traditionalists' eyes) the cultural integrity of Quebec. Thus, the Duplessis government acted vigorously to suppress Communist political action and harassed Jehovah's Witnesses because of that sect's anti-Catholicism.[3]

There were many who strongly opposed Duplessis, and towards the end of the 1950s criticism of his corruption, authoritarianism, and policies that placed few constraints on business while ruthlessly repressing unions, had become intense. On 7 September 1959 Duplessis died. A brief interregnum followed, during which the remnant of his Union Nationale government tried to fashion an image of reform and liberalization, not just to answer Duplessis's critics outside church and party but also to satisfy a growing sentiment within those bastions of conservative nationalism. The attempt at renewal failed, however, and in the election on 22 June 1960 the Liberal government of Jean Lesage took power. The Quiet Revolution had begun.[4]

The Quiet Revolution represented, above all, a period of reevaluation in Quebec's social and political life, during which the nationalism of the past was discarded and the relationships between church and state and between government and economy were transformed. The movement for change was not strictly anticlerical – liberal clerics provided much of the intellectual justification upon which reformers relied – but the Quiet Revolution nevertheless brought about a dramatic secularization of Quebec society. By stages, the church's role in education and health was reduced. A comprehensive system of state-delivered social assistance was devised. The government also pursued a much more interventionist policy in the economic sphere, nationalizing the remaining private power companies to give the state-owned Hydro-Québec a monopoly, increasing regulatory controls on industry, enacting labour legislation more favourable to unions, and rationalizing the government's administrative and procurement practices. All this resulted in a huge increase in the size of government. Still more profound changes occurred in the non-governmental sphere. In the archdiocese of Montreal, the percentage of Catholics practising their religion declined from 61 to 30 during the years 1961 to 1970. The birth rate dropped from 30.2 in 1955 to 16.1 in 1970.[5]

One of the reasons for the Lesage government's strong focus on economic policy was French-speaking Quebecers' deep discontent with the fact that large sectors of the economy were owned by anglophone interests (often based outside Quebec), conducting their business predominantly in English – a situation that had apparently been abetted by Duplessis's abstentionist economic policies. There was widespread frustration that French-speaking Quebecers suffered discrimination in employment, frequently having to switch to English if they wanted to advance beyond the lowest echelons of the workforce.[6] A study for the Royal Commission on Bilingualism and Biculturalism (B&B Commission) found that in 1961 *unilingual* anglophones had the highest average incomes in Quebec ($6,049). They were followed by bilingual anglophones ($5,929), bilingual francophones ($4,523), and, at the bottom, unilingual francophones ($3,107).[7] In the popular culture these findings were supplemented by countless anecdotes about unilingual anglophone foremen forcing francophone workers to adapt to the foreman's language, about managers of companies' Quebec divisions communicating with their employees exclusively in English, and about French Canadians passed over for promotion. Discrimination in employment generated the most severe criticism, although anglophone firms were also blamed for insensitivity to the predominantly French character of Quebec, particularly when they failed to provide adequate service in French. The Lesage government's economic activism was designed in large measure, then, to overcome the material and psychological effects of the dominance of English in the economic life of the province, reasserting a French Canadian presence under the slogan "maîtres chez nous" (masters in our own house). The growth of government services, the expansion of Hydro-Québec, and the founding of new crown corporations opened up many technical and managerial roles to francophone Quebecers and projected an image of competence and dynamism in public and private administration.

The turn away from the church, the secularization of social services, and the heavy emphasis on the economic sphere radically transformed nationalism in Quebec. No longer was the church the principal custodian of French Canada's national identity. In fact, Catholic piety had largely disappeared from the popular image of what it meant to be French Canadian, at least in Quebec's cities. For most francophone Quebecers, the state was now the focus of nationalist sentiment. It was the guardian of their culture, the vehicle that would establish the conditions necessary for the flourishing of French language and culture in Quebec. And the change was even greater than the mere substitution of state for church would suggest. In many ways the whole idea, the whole significance of culture had been transformed. The economic reforms, the slogan "maîtres chez nous," the growth of government, all spoke of French-speaking Quebecers' desire to control their economic destinies. They appealed to Quebecers' frustration with economic subordination, lower wages, less education, and haphazard social services. They promised francophone Quebecers a greater say in the governing of their society in both public and private realms. The reforms were about economic and political self-determination (in the broadest sense of that term, not necessarily implying secession from Canada) rather than the mere preservation of a culture and a language. Culture remained part of the package but in a very different way than under the conservative nationalism of Duplessis. The economic reforms were not directed solely at the achievement of economic prosperity. They were designed to allow francophone Quebecers both to retain their culture and to progress economically – to have a flourishing linguistic community, but one that flourished not just on the shop floor, in the corner grocery, and on the farm, but also around the drafting table, in the accountant's office, and in the boardroom. For the new nationalists, culture was not something to be preserved intact, sealed against all change, confining its members to an economic ghetto; it was an integral part of every francophone Quebecer's identity, something he or she should be able to retain and develop in every sphere of activity. Seen this way, culture was dynamic, a dynamism reflected in the surge of francophone artistic creation in the 1960s and 1970s.

This placed a whole new cast on the constitutional positions of the Lesage government and its successors, the Union Nationale under Daniel Johnson and Jean-Jacques Bertrand (1966 to 1970) and the first two Liberal governments of Robert Bourassa (1970 to 1976), all of which, in their different ways, shared the presumptions of the

Quiet Revolution. The whole tenor of constitutional debate had changed. No longer was Quebec a sullen and reactionary naysayer, trying to block the social agenda of a pragmatic and popular federal government. No longer was it a grumpy anachronism, complaining but doing little to occupy its own jurisdiction. Quebec laid vigorous claim to that jurisdiction, filling it with new and often innovative programs. At first, federal politicians welcomed this, hoping that Quebec would now become a full partner in the construction of the postwar welfare state, an enterprise Canadians outside Quebec generally associated with Ottawa. Soon, however, the potential for conflict became evident, and because the conflicts were now between two direct competitors they could be fiery indeed, as the dispute over the creation of the Canada Pension Plan made plain.

In 1963 the federal government announced it would sponsor the establishment of a national, contributory system of pensions, the kind of social program that would normally have been within provincial jurisdiction but which Ottawa proposed to establish using the spending power. Discussions continued over the next nine months, with Ontario and Quebec both voicing objections. The dispute came to a head at a First Ministers Conference in Quebec City in the spring of 1964. To Ottawa's chagrin, Quebec proposed its own provincially administered scheme, in which the revenues would be used to fund economic activity within the province. Quebec's plan was persuasive, well documented, and presented very forcefully. It provoked a major confrontation that threatened to degenerate into a serious constitutional crisis. Eventually, however, Ottawa backed down. Quebec established its plan, and Ottawa adopted a parallel regime for the rest of the country (borrowing a number of features from the Quebec proposal). Quebec received tax room to compensate for the fact that its taxpayers would otherwise have had to pay for both programs. The federal and Quebec regimes were coordinated, so that taxpayers moving between them could retain their benefits.[8]

The pension controversy demonstrated that Ottawa could no longer count on retaining the political initiative in federal-provincial relations. It also dramatized how the central concerns of Quebec had changed. The pensions dispute was not about language and culture in the traditional sense. It was about control – about who would design and run the program. Here, culture was relevant, but in the new way described above: if the plan was controlled by Quebec, French-speaking Quebecers would determine its structure and could apply the pension funds to the more general aim of supporting Quebec-based economic activity. The plan would have an indirect effect on the preservation of Quebec's language and culture (by increasing opportunities for employment in French, it would help reduce pressure for assimilation), but its relationship to self-government would be immediate and direct. Once again, French-speaking Quebecers would be taking control of their own destiny, declining to participate in a federal plan under the wing of an anglophone majority.

But here was a problem. If Quebec's distinctive identity demanded control of pensions, why shouldn't Quebec control banking, communications, even national defence? Why shouldn't it control everything? The principal concern of the earlier, conservative nationalism – the defence of language and culture – had had its own intrinsic limits: some things were cultural, others were not. Those limits were especially clear when national identity was entrusted to the church, which had a clearly defined body of doctrine and a stable institutional structure. Once the state had replaced church, however, and the focus of nationalism had shifted from the preservation of culture to self-determination, what limits were left? Where would self-determination end?

Quebec politicians themselves were unsure. On one occasion, Prime Minister Lester Pearson asked Premier Jean Lesage where the latter thought his province was going. Lesage responded, "I don't know."[9] Successive Quebec governments argued for the expansion of provincial jurisdiction, seeking a greater role in broadcasting, immigration, international relations, and a range of economic fields. Quebec nationalists adopted different positions across the spectrum of possibilities, some arguing that Quebec should have jurisdiction over an expanded but still finite range of matters, others moving quickly towards the ultimate in self-determination, complete independence. They used a variety of terms to describe their aspirations. Lesage's "maîtres chez nous" was elastic enough to include a vast range of outcomes. Daniel Johnson's "égalité ou indépendance" implied a continued dialogue between English and French Canada, but with the possibility of moving towards separation if negotiations were unsuccessful. And René Lévesque, one of Lesage's principal ministers, pushed the logic of self-determination further than any of his colleagues, demanding increased provincial control over a whole range of matters and eventually presenting a proposal for sovereignty-association to the 1967 provincial Liberal convention. When the convention rejected the proposal, Lévesque left the party to found the Mouvement souveraineté-association and then, after joining with other pro-independence groups, the Parti Québécois.

Above all, the situation was fluid. If there were any limitations to the aspiration for self-determination – and it is a central argument of this book that there were – they were very difficult to see in the heady days of the 1960s. Most Quebec politicians agreed that Quebec should remain within Canada, but on what basis and with what powers? With the rejection of the old nationalism and the acceptance of the new, everyone was left wondering where the limits were.

Other aspects of the new nationalism also appeared unstable. For many, the new nationalism had a purely positive message: French-speaking Quebecers would now take a leading role in the economic and political life of their province. For others, it had a hard, negative edge: English dominance would be cast aside by casting aside the English, an attitude symbolized by the rough reception Queen Elizabeth experienced in Quebec City during the royal visit of 1964. Some believed that the only true Quebecers spoke French. Others insisted that all residents of Quebec were valued members of the political community. Most Quebecers probably shifted (and shift still) between the two positions. Quebec was special precisely because it was the only jurisdiction in which French Canadians could directly control their destiny. This almost automatically meant that the aspirations of Quebecers were assumed to be those of its French-speaking citizens. But if the subject was raised expressly, all Quebecers were acknowledged to be equal citizens, entitled to full political rights.

The new nationalism carried a more definite implication for linguistic minorities, however, this time for francophone minorities outside Quebec. The older, conservative nationalism had identified the nation not with Quebec as such, but with the French language and Catholic faith throughout Canada. Its people were not *Québécois* but *Canadiens français*. It recognized, then, a special solidarity among all French Canadians. That solidarity had never been complete. The Acadians of the Maritime provinces or the Franco-Manitobans of the Prairies had always had their own traditions, their own histories, and therefore their own myths, all developing in considerable autonomy from those of Quebec. This sense of separation had been reinforced by the great linguistic crises of Canadian history: the attempts by various provincial governments (often inspired by the more virulent forms of British nationalism) to suppress the French Canadian presence outside Quebec. These efforts convinced many Quebecers that French Canada's future lay predominantly within a strong and autonomous Quebec, the only jurisdiction in which French Canada's institutions were safe. The new nationalism significantly reinforced this tendency. To the extent that it substituted the government of Quebec for the religious-linguistic community, it severed the bond with francophones outside Quebec. The bond never completely disappeared (many francophone Quebecers retained an allegiance both to their province and to their linguistic community), but on many issues, especially the guarantee of minority language rights, the divergence became pronounced.

There was ambiguity generally about the extent to which the new nationalism carried forward the themes of the old, especially the relationship between individual rights and cultural protection. Quebec's traditional nationalism, at least as practised by Duplessis, had little time for individual rights, emphasizing instead the rights of collectivities. The new Quebec was much more liberal, attaching great importance to individual liberties. Polling data taken in 1981 revealed that questions of language aside, Quebecers had become among the most individualistic of Canadians.[10] In 1975 the Bourassa government adopted an extensive Charter of Human Rights and Freedoms.[11] The new nationalists acknowledged, however, that particularly in language policy individual rights had to be balanced against what they termed "collective rights." The precise balance was a matter of debate, but the acknowledgment of collective rights made the most convinced advocates of individual rights nervous, especially in the anglophone community.

Finally, there was yet another strand of nationalism on the scene, one devoted not to greater francophone participation in a reformed capitalist economy, but to the revolutionary transformation of both state and economy. Taking its cue from the national liberation movements of the Third World, it combined nationalism and Marxism in a struggle that its partisans hoped would simultaneously secure independence for Quebec and overthrow capitalism. This radical and uncompromising nationalism attracted the support of only a small proportion of the population, but its public profile was considerable. It was embraced by a small but vocal segment of Quebec's university students. Its search for a *projet de société* was joined by a number of Quebec intellectuals and trade unionists. But most dramatically, it provided the ideological justification for the FLQ's terrorist activities. The FLQ was a tiny group, but its bombing of mailboxes and other acts punctuated the political upheaval of the 1960s with sharp bursts of violence and menace, and culminated in the kidnappings and murder of the October Crisis of 1970.

THE FEDERAL RESPONSE

Ottawa's response to the Quiet Revolution was tardy, beginning only with the Liberals' electoral victory in 1963. John Diefenbaker's Conservative government was in power during the first three years of Lesage's government. Significant federal-provincial discussions did occur, especially regarding the sharing of taxation (a series of arrangements were concluded allowing the provinces more tax room) and the amending formula (it was at this time that the so-called Fulton-Favreau formula began to take shape, a formula eventually rejected by Quebec). But these either continued trends begun when Duplessis was premier of Quebec or constituted the first, faltering attempts by the Lesage government to work out the constitutional implications of its policies. The consequences of the Quiet Revolution for federal-provincial relations were not yet evident. Diefenbaker, whose understanding of Quebec was (to put it charitably) imperfect, had not grasped the need for a new response.

Liberal leader Lester Pearson, on the other hand, did realize that a new strategy was necessary. In a major speech in December 1962, he signalled that the Liberals would act vigorously to ensure that the federal government reflected the linguistic duality of the country. He also promised to appoint an inquiry to study the bilingual and bicultural character of Canada.[12] Following the Liberals' victory in the April 1963 election, he immediately moved to increase the use of French in cabinet and caucus, established a special committee under Quebec MP Maurice Lamontagne to develop objectives for bilingualism in the federal administration, and, in July 1963, appointed the Bilingualism and Biculturalism Commission to study what might be done in the public service, in the private sector, and through language education to reflect the bilingual and bicultural nature of Canada. The bilingualization of the federal government thus became a key theme of federal policy. That theme is worth exploring in some detail because of its centrality in Ottawa's response to Quebec, its highly controversial nature, and the different linguistic strategies it reveals.

Bilingualism in the public service was designed to make Ottawa the government of French- as well as English-speaking Canadians. At the beginning of the 1960s, the linguistic character of the federal government was overwhelmingly anglophone. In 1946 (the last year for which the B&B Commission could find reliable figures), 29 per cent of the country's population spoke French; less than 13 per cent of federal civil servants were francophone, and that proportion had fallen dramatically over the previous three decades. The B&B Commission reported that in the 1960s, French Canadian civil servants, underrepresented in the service as a whole, tended also to be concentrated at the lower levels of the administration. Although many governmental services were available in French (mainly in Quebec;

the situation was worse for francophones outside the province), the language of work within the administration was often English, even for francophones. This was true not only in Ottawa and regional centres outside Quebec, but also in Quebec itself, largely because of the prevalence of unilingual anglophones throughout the public service. Pearson and others realized that if Ottawa continued to act as a predominantly anglophone government, French Canadians' aspirations would inevitably focus on Quebec to the exclusion of Ottawa. His policy of bilingualism therefore had two objectives: to increase the extent to which government services were available in French and to institute measures that would permit French Canadians to work within the federal government without abandoning their language.[13]

The government initially pursued these objectives by focusing on the language use of individuals. It encouraged all civil servants to learn both languages, permitted individual civil servants to use either language in internal communications (in communications, that is, with other members of the administration), and tried to make it possible for citizens generally to deal with the government in the language of their choice. In the late 1960s, however, the government adjusted its approach in response to the findings of the B&B Commission. The commission argued that the two problems – the language of services and the language of work – called for different solutions. Services could be handled on an individual basis, but a purely individual approach to the language of work was likely to be both impractical and ineffective. Unless the vast majority of civil servants understood both languages, internal communications would inevitably have to adapt to the common denominator: if a civil servant only understood one language, anyone wishing to communicate would have to speak that language. Since most anglophone civil servants were unilingual and most francophones bilingual, this meant that in practice English would continue to be the dominant (if not the exclusive) language. The commission recommended that to avoid this the government should return to what it took to be the government's principal goal in this area: "institutional" (rather than individual) bilingualism, in which the administration as a whole provided services in both languages and individual civil servants looked to the administration as a whole (rather than to any particular section of it) for employment in their own language. This more precise objective, the commission argued, did not require that all civil servants be bilingual or that all parts of the administration work in both languages. Rather, specific units could work in English or French. Within those units, employees would only need to know that language. Individual bilingualism would be an asset, required for positions that straddled the linguistic divide or provided services to a bilingual public, but most posts could be staffed by people knowing only one language. These recommendations were adopted and became the organizing principle for bilingualism within the civil service.[14]

In many ways, these recommendations were a specific application of the more general principles enunciated in the first volume of the commission's report, although these more general recommendations, as we shall see, enjoyed less acceptance than the proposals for the civil service, even within the federal government itself. The commission had been formed to inquire into the state of bilingualism and biculturalism in the country and recommend measures to promote the equality of the English and French linguistic groups in Canada. In its various reports, it made very clear that it did not expect all Canadians to become bilingual. Its conception of a bilingual and bicultural Canada was not one in which both languages were used interchangeably or every individual was a member of both cultures. On the contrary, it concluded that an exclusive emphasis on individual bilingualism could work to the detriment of the minority-language group, especially if members of that group had to conduct most of their daily activities in their second language. In such situations, the minority language could become marginalized over time, gradually displaced by the dominant language. The commission also recognized that even for a fully bilingual person, having to function in his or her second language was frequently stressful and often unnecessary. The commission concluded, then, that the best regime would include a measure of separation between linguistic groups. French- and English-speaking Canadians should have equivalent opportunities to work, to progress, and to participate in public affairs in their own language, but these opportunities could well exist, for the most part, in parallel English and French spheres.

The strategy adopted by the commission therefore reflected the interplay between three kinds of linguistic accommodation. First, the commission recognized that it was inevitable (and even desirable) that there be areas in which each language was predominant. These were the "unilingual nuclei" which formed, in most bilingual states, the "great mass of the population" and "around which each of the major language groups tends to cluster." It would be futile and self-defeating to try to break these up in order to achieve complete integration. Instead, the positive role played by these linguistic heartlands should be recognized. They were the areas in which each of the cultures could flourish most fully, with its own extensive array of institutions. In the Canadian context, this meant that Quebec would always play a central role in promoting French language and culture in Canada. It was Quebec's four million French-speaking citizens who, the commission argued, gave reality to the idea of "equal partnership" between English and French in Canada. Indeed, the commission coined the phrase "distinct society" to refer to the autonomous character of the two dominant linguistic groups in Canada, especially Quebec's French-speaking society.[15]

The commission's second form of linguistic accommodation dealt with the rights of official-language minorities. Francophone and anglophone citizens who lived in predominantly English-speaking or French-speaking areas would not be abandoned. On the contrary, they would benefit from an array of municipal, provincial, and federal government services in the minority language, expressly recognizing, for example, Canadian parents' right to have their children educated in either official language. The extent of the services would depend on the numerical strength of the community. They would be most extensive in specially designated bilingual districts, created throughout Canada wherever official-language minorities exceeded approximately 10 per cent of the population (on this rule, bilingual districts would exist in every province except British Columbia and Newfoundland). In these districts the language regime would include the right to use both official languages in municipal government, the right to use English or French before the courts, and the provision of many governmental services in both languages. Finally, the commission recommended that Quebec, New Brunswick, Ontario, and any other province with an official-language minority constituting more than 10 per cent of its population declare themselves to be officially bilingual, and that all provinces permit English and French to be used in legislative debates.[16]

Finally, the third form of linguistic accommodation focused on establishing bridges between the cultures, making shared institutions bilingual and providing ways of increasing understanding between the linguistic groups. The commission recognized that institutions at the level of Canada as a whole had to provide equal opportunities to both linguistic groups if they were to retain the allegiance of both. It therefore strongly supported the Liberal government's commitment to making the federal administration bilingual. And although it argued that this could be achieved without requiring that all civil servants speak both languages, it also recognized that bilingual civil servants – and bilingual citizens generally – were necessary to maintain and extend the interaction between linguistic groups. The commission therefore made a number of detailed recommendations to improve second-language education throughout the country.[17]

These recommendations were never accepted in their entirety. One reason was strong public opposition to the report. Many criticisms focused on cost, especially the cost of French services at the provincial and municipal levels outside Quebec. Why, the critics argued, should scarce resources be funnelled into services in French when francophones might be no more than 20 per cent of the local population, when virtually all of them spoke English, and when there were other, equally numerous ethnic minorities (Ukrainians, Germans, Italians)? Why should French Canadians benefit from special privileges, privileges that also implied that they would have special access to government jobs? For many Canadians, the recommendations contemplated a scandalous waste of money on a manufactured problem. When they looked at their immediate community, they saw little linguistic strife. Francophones, like members of the immigrant communities, had adjusted to life in a land in which English was dominant. And even if resources were devoted to French-language services, did anyone really believe that French would become a viable language on the Prairies, in Nova Scotia, southern Ontario, or British Columbia? Especially for many westerners, bilingualism was another example of a central Canadian agenda imposed upon communities for which it made no sense.

These criticisms often mingled with a more fundamental objection – one focused on national identity. Many English-speaking Canadians resisted the very idea of defining Canada as a bilingual country. In its early years, Canada might have had a substantial French character, but many believed that was all in the past. For them, the French fact had been undermined by the British Conquest, had been eroded by immigrants who chose English as their second language, and would inevitably disappear because of the simple fact that English was, in their view, the universal language of commerce and technology. French had survived, they believed, only because of the closed nature of Quebec under Duplessis. Resurrecting the French fact would divide the country, and to what end? Simply to delay the inevitable assimilation? The country should be one, and the way to make it one was not to preserve the divisions of the past, but to get on with the business of economic development.

For some English Canadians, this attitude was the product of residual attachment to the idea of British Canada or hostility towards Catholicism. For most, however, it was simply their perception of the nature of the country. Our conceptions of national identity are frequently projections of what we see in the part of the country we know. For most Canadians outside Quebec, even for many anglophones from the western suburbs of Montreal, the French fact was virtually invisible. Most anglophones had little personal contact with

French Canadians, and when they did, the contact occurred in English. Their understanding of languages other than English was based on the immigration model. Immigrants' languages might survive, but they were used in the private sphere, within the family and in voluntary associations. English was the language of politics and economy. Why should others have to adapt to what was seen as the private language of French Canadians? This perception applied not just to the status of French outside Quebec, but to linguistic relations in Canada as a whole. Most English-speaking Canadians had little concrete understanding that, in 1961, French Canadians in Quebec formed a society of more than four million people (more than the population of Alberta, Saskatchewan, and Manitoba combined), conducting virtually all their activities in French and most of whom (like anglophone westerners) were unilingual. Their misunderstanding was reflected in the traditional complaint of anglophone visitors to Quebec: "I asked a French Canadian on the street for directions and he refused to answer. You know they can speak English, but they just won't." It was equally likely that the French Canadian couldn't speak English, or at least felt about as comfortable in English as the anglophone felt in French. But lack of contact between the societies reinforced anglophones' perceptions that there was, in reality, only one society in Canada, a society whose public language was English.

There was thus widespread resistance to bilingualism, and this resistance impeded the introduction of bilingual districts and greatly limited any move towards provincial and municipal bilingualism outside New Brunswick. The federal government had its own reservations about the B&B Commission's report, but for very different reasons, reasons particularly associated with the influence of Pierre Trudeau.[18]

Trudeau had entered federal politics along with Jean Marchand and Gérard Pelletier in 1965, becoming parliamentary secretary to the prime minister in 1966, minister of justice in 1967, and prime minister in 1968. Trudeau believed firmly that the federal government had to be, both in appearance and reality, the government of all Canadians. He strongly supported bilingualism in the public service, and in 1969 was responsible for implementing one of the B&B Commission's principal recommendations, the enactment of an Official Languages Act.[19] He agreed, then, with one of the central themes of the commission's report. He vehemently disagreed, however, with another: the report's express acknowledgment that Quebec had a special role to play in the promotion of the French culture within North America, and the implication that this might justify a unique legal regime for Quebec.

Trudeau had long been a fierce opponent of Quebec nationalism in all its forms. In his view, all nationalisms, even if expressed in purely positive terms, inevitably identified the interests of the state with the interests of one ethnic group. They always contained within themselves, then, the seeds of oppression, especially the oppression of members of other ethnic groups. They tended to make their own members parochial and backward, continually gazing inward, their development stunted by the failure to engage a wider world. These consequences had been patent under Duplessis. They would also, Trudeau was convinced, be true of the nationalism of Lesage and Lévesque, even though the latter might not realize it. To Trudeau, those tendencies were already apparent in the extremes of separatist rhetoric, in the prospect of an alliance between conservative nationalists and René Lévesque (the alliance ultimately consummated in the Parti Québécois), and in the increasing attacks on the prominence of English in Quebec. He responded by trying to turn the course of the Quiet Revolution's immense release of energy away from the provincial scene and towards the federal, where there would be no danger of confusing state power with a particular ethnic identity.

Trudeau's implacable opposition to Quebec nationalism made him suspicious of any claim to a special cultural role for Quebec. He vigorously opposed all arguments for increased powers for that province, for the recognition of two nations within Canada, or for special status for Quebec. All of these he equated with nationalism. He occasionally conceded that Quebec had a role to play in the preservation of the French culture in Canada, but the acknowledgment was grudging, often accompanied by attacks on the ignorant and backward character of what would be protected. In any case, he argued, Quebec's present constitutional powers were more than adequate to fulfil that role. Any additional tinkering would inevitably, he believed, set Quebec on the road to separation. There was no logical stopping place between the present extent of Quebec's jurisdiction and outright independence. Any increase in that jurisdiction could only be based on nationalism, and as he remarked in a 1964 article, "when a tightly knit minority within a state begins to define itself forcefully and consistently as a nation, it is triggering a mechanism which will tend to propel it towards full statehood."[20] He much preferred that that mechanism work in favour of Ottawa, that nationality become the same as citizenship.

His strategy therefore had two crucial aims: (1) making Ottawa a principal focus of allegiance for French-speaking Quebecers; and (2) undermining Quebecers' allegiance to Quebec. In the same 1964 article, Trudeau noted that one way of countering separatism was to invest "tremendous amounts of time, energy, and money in nationalism, *at the federal level.*" Although he then went on to renounce that option, arguing for a politics based on reason, not emotion, his later programs do seem to have emphasized the creation of a direct emotional bond between francophone Quebecers and the federal government. The emphasis on bilingualism in the federal administration had both a functional and a symbolic aim: it brought Quebecers into the public service but it also projected an image of the federal government as the government of all. The development of the National Capital Region, especially the extensive construction of government buildings across the river from Ottawa in Hull, had a similarly strong symbolic motivation. Ottawa's sudden expansion of diplomatic relations with francophone countries, including its commitment to the *francophonie*, was prompted not so much by the country's external interests as by the policy's domestic impact. There was nothing wrong with this. For too long, the symbolic character of the federal government had borne little evidence of a third of the country's population. But it is disingenuous to suggest that Trudeau's policies were purely functional, setting aside questions of emotion and nation. They were about shifting Quebecers' national identification from Quebec to Ottawa.[21]

This is particularly evident in Trudeau's attempts to undermine the identification of French Canadian culture with Quebec. He consistently denied all claims by the government of Quebec to speak for French Canada or even for a substantial section of French Canada. With some justification, he asserted that his voice, as that of Canada's prime minister, was as much a voice of French Canadians as the Quebec government's. Substantial federal funding for cultural activities gave concrete form to Ottawa's role as protector and promoter of all Canadian cultures. In his arguments and policies, Trudeau emphasized the existence of francophones and anglophones across the country: Quebec did not include all French Canadians, nor was it exclusively French Canadian. He resisted all attempts to link language to territory, emphasizing instead the linguistic rights of individuals, rights that would in principle be the same from one end of the country to the other. English and French Canadians should, the slogan went, feel equally at home in any part of the country. Often, this emphasis on the individual slid towards advocacy of full bilingualism for all Canadians. For Trudeau, the ideal Canada would be one in which all Canadians could talk to each other in either language.

This focus on the rights of individuals and on individual (rather than territorial) bilingualism was characteristic of Trudeau's policy. Its emphasis on individualism complemented his support for civil liberties. Indeed, he had already combined advocacy of civil rights with uncompromising anti-nationalism in his opposition to Duplessis. But Trudeau's individualism was not quite all it seemed. In his early writings, he had focused exclusively on individual choice, insisting that the only true test of a culture's quality was how it stood up in the competition with other cultures, a competition in which the state should remain rigorously neutral. He had argued that individual freedom to choose, unencumbered by government preference, was the only true standard of cultural worth. But in practice, the Trudeau government did not stand back and let unconstrained liberty take its course. It actively promoted the use of French, creating incentives for individual bilingualism in the federal civil service and crown corporations, insisting that certain positions be filled by bilingual candidates, and funding bilingual services across the country. Individualism in language policy went hand in hand, not with government abstention, but with a strong federal role. Not only would that role be the best guarantee of respect for linguistic minorities, but, in a kind of symbiosis, an emphasis on language as an individual phenomenon would keep attention focused on the federal government, not the provinces, as the chief guarantor of language and culture. If language was associated with distinct linguistic communities or territorial homelands, then Quebec's position – its claim to a special cultural vocation because of the concentration of French Canadians in Quebec – would be strengthened. A purely individual approach, on the other hand, focused attention on the centre, bypassing the provinces and all other subdivisions of the state. All citizens would owe their linguistic rights directly to Canada; the dimensions of their linguistic community would be the whole country, not a part; and all citizens, in all provinces, would be subject to precisely the same rules. Canada, not Quebec, would be the chief forum for linguistic debate. Ottawa, not the provinces, would be the repository of linguistic and cultural value.

Trudeau's government therefore laboured to shift the focus of linguistic policy (and with it, national allegiance) from Quebec to Ottawa. It refused to concede that Quebec needed more powers to fulfil a cultural role. The openness to constitutional decentralization signalled by Pearson was no longer part of Ottawa's plan.[22] This did not mean that Trudeau's policies were relentlessly centralizing. At the practical, administrative level, he was willing to countenance the kind of flexibility initiated by Pearson, although to a lesser extent. Trudeau's Ottawa did not renounce the use of the federal spending power to establish new social programs, but a 1969 discussion paper did suggest that provinces would be able to opt out of future programs without financial penalty.[23] Under Trudeau, a series of agreements with Quebec clarified federal and provincial roles in immigration (under the constitution, an area shared between Ottawa and the provinces). But at the symbolic level of national allegiance, his stance was single-minded in its centralism. As he would often tell Quebecers, they had to choose between two alternative – not complementary – objects of allegiance: Quebec or Canada. Although Trudeau's administration preached respect for provincial jurisdiction, when it came to allegiance he used the language of a unitary state.[24]

The popular reaction to Trudeau's attempt to redefine Canadian nationalism was mixed. In the aftermath of Meech, Quebecers would sometimes say that they had never cared about bilingualism, that bilingualism responded to Ottawa's priorities, not theirs. That certainly was not true. The majority of francophone Quebecers did appreciate (and still appreciate) Trudeau's efforts to make Ottawa the government of all Canadians. The overwhelmingly English character of the federal government had excluded francophones from employment, had placed francophones at a disadvantage in their dealings with federal agencies, and had given a distinctly English Canadian bias to a host of policies, from immigration to the organization of the armed forces. If Quebecers were going to be subject to the Canadian government – and the vast majority wanted to remain Canadian – they naturally desired a place in that government. They balked, however, at the second limb of Trudeau's nationalism: the denial of a distinctive cultural vocation, of a special status, for Quebec. Francophone Quebecers realized that whatever Ottawa might say or do, they would never be equally at home in Ladner, BC, Lethbridge, Alberta, or St John's, Newfoundland. Most believed that the future of French Canada had to depend, in part, on the cultural and linguistic policies of the government of Quebec, the only jurisdiction in which they formed a majority and the only province in which French could be the principal language of commerce and politics. They were very happy to become full members of the Canadian community and would vote for Trudeau for that reason, but they would not renounce their attachment to their province.

Outside Quebec, the reaction was still more complex. The vast majority of anglophone Canadians were relieved that someone was finally standing up to the nationalists in Quebec. Here was a French Canadian who fought for a united Canada, who attacked the pretensions of the Quebec government, and who even echoed English Canadians' criticisms of French Canadian culture in terms more vitriolic than their own. But there was less unanimity on the content of Trudeau's new Canadian nationalism. Some English-speaking Canadians, in all parts of the country, accepted that federal institutions had to reflect the existence of French Canada. Others, however, remained bluntly sceptical about the merits of bilingualism, especially as they saw the face of their government changing beyond their recognition. In some ways, Trudeau's strong opposition to linking language to territory fuelled this scepticism. Western Canadians might accept bilingualism in Ontario and Quebec, but why across the country? Resistance to bilingualism became part of the long-standing complaint that Ottawa should be more responsive to regional differences.

Two groups, however, overwhelmingly supported bilingualism: the anglophone minority in Quebec and the francophone minority in the other provinces. Both shared Ottawa's strong resistance to Quebec's tendency to identify itself as the exclusive spokesperson for French Canada. The linguistic minorities' very existence belied that claim. But even in their support for bilingualism, there were subtle variations between the anglophone and francophone minorities.

First, they differed in their motivation. The anglophone community in Quebec did not consider itself threatened with extinction (at least not prior to the Parti Québécois victory in November 1976). For its members, bilingualism was a way of stemming the rising tide of Quebec nationalism, a way of fighting Quebec's attempts to promote, through legislation, the use of French within the province. For francophones outside Quebec, bilingualism appeared much more fundamental to their continued existence. It was a guarantee of survival, especially in those parts of the country (like Manitoba) where the rate of assimilation was high.

Second, in part because of the different challenges they faced, the two minorities responded differently to various aspects of Ottawa's policy. Anglophone Quebecers, confident in their language's ability to survive and increasingly reconciled to the need to learn French as a second language, tended to embrace the entirety of Trudeau's individualistic form of bilingualism. They generally accepted a vision of a Canada in which all citizens would know both languages, but in which the language actually used would be left to the individual. Francophones outside Quebec, on the other hand, tended to have a more precise, less grand objective. They were concerned with the survival and prosperity of particular communities in the face of very real pressures. They pushed for services targeted directly at those communities rather than for a generalized, individual bilingualism.

To many, the latter seemed an unrealizable dream, liable only to provoke the antagonism of their English-speaking neighbours. They wished to secure their own position, not reach for an unattainable, largely symbolic goal. To the extent that this sentiment tended to emphasize a new kind of territoriality, focusing on specific communities in specific places (although communities whose linguistic character would not be defined by provincial boundaries), it diverged from the more thoroughly individualistic policy of Trudeau.

These were the positions adopted by Canadians identifying themselves with the traditional divisions within Canada's cultural-linguistic community – anglophones and francophones, inside and outside Quebec. But the increasing emphasis on bilingualism throughout the 1960s triggered another reaction, one which would also leave its mark on the constitutional debates of the 1970s and 1980s. Canadians of cultural origins other than English, French, and aboriginal insisted that their identities be woven into the national fabric. Multiculturalism had emerged to challenge biculturalism.

MULTICULTURALISM VS BICULTURALISM

In 1961 Canadians of British ancestry made up 43.8 per cent of Canada's population, those of French ancestry 30.4 per cent, aboriginal 1.2 per cent, and "other" 24.6 per cent.[25] This "other" category formed the constituency for multiculturalism. It was a diverse and rapidly growing group, united only by the fact that its members were not descended from either of the "two founding peoples" or from the First Nations. Although often referred to as immigrants, some members of the multicultural communities had come to Canada long before many members of the "founding peoples." Different multicultural groups had arrived in different waves of immigration, resulting in dramatic variations in their patterns of settlement, in the extent to which they retained their ancestral cultures, and in the cohesiveness of their communities. They were often divided among themselves. Treating them as a single "third force" frequently underestimated the rivalries between groups, the experience of greater or lesser degrees of prejudice, and the feelings of superiority and subordination between earlier and later arrivals.

The groups also differed in their cultural aspirations. Many immigrants had purposely abandoned their ancestral culture, refusing to teach their children their language, urging their children to become "Canadians" without any vestige of what had come before. Others (though very few) sought to preserve their language and culture intact, employed in precisely the same way for precisely the same purposes as in the old country. Many fell between these extremes, trying to hold on to some traditions of their former land (especially their religion), sometimes continuing to speak their language in their homes and ethnic organizations, but sending their children to school in English, finding jobs in English, and using English as the language of commerce, of political life, and generally of discussion with those outside their community.

Multicultural communities differed in their relationships to the established English and French linguistic groups. Most adopted English as their public language, although some chose French because of their geographical location or prior affinity for that language. The preference of most immigrants for English had two crucial consequences: (1) it contributed to French Canadians' sense of cultural insecurity, as Canada's linguistic balance appeared to shift against them; and (2) it impeded the development of a mutual understanding between French Canadians and members of multicultural communities. Until recently, French Canadians tended to think of their society as racially and culturally homogeneous. They therefore neglected the task of accommodating cultural diversity within a society concerned chiefly with preserving distinctively French Canadian traditions. For their part, many English-speaking members of the multicultural communities had little feeling for the sociological weight of the French language and culture within Canada. To them, English was the language of North America, and they could not understand the prominent place accorded French in Canada.

The divisions within the multicultural communities meant that they very rarely acted as a political unit. The controversy over a new identity for Canada did, however, produce a widely shared position. This emerged most clearly in reaction to the B&B Commission. The terms of reference of that commission had adopted the image of "an equal partnership between the two founding races"; they then referred, almost as an afterthought, to "the contribution made by the other ethnic groups to the cultural enrichment of Canada." This singling out of English and French "races," followed by such an offhand reference to "other ethnic groups," struck many members of the multicultural communities as the recognition of an ethnic hierarchy in which they occupied the bottom rungs. They let the commission know their displeasure in no uncertain terms. The commission found itself, in public meetings and in its reports, continually defending its terms of reference, denying that the intention had been to establish first- and second-class citizenship, a "hereditary aristocracy," or a "special birthright" of the founding peoples. It argued that bilingualism and biculturalism were not about ethnicity, but about cultures and languages, attributes that were not intrinsic to individuals but were the products of education and social interaction, products that immigrants could – and did – freely adopt. The commission faced an uphill battle, however, especially given the terms of reference themselves, which did speak in terms of ethnicity. J.B. Rudnyckyj, a commissioner of Ukrainian origin, issued a dissenting statement to volume 1 of the commission's report, in which he argued for constitutional recognition of certain "regional languages" in addition to English and French. Although the commission later consecrated a fourth volume to the multicultural communities, it was largely unable to repair the damage the initial controversy had caused.[26]

The heart of the problem was that the commission still wished to distinguish between, on the one hand, the English and French languages and cultures and (for lack of a better term) the immigrant languages and cultures. As long as the issue was phrased in terms of ethnicity, any attempt to differentiate ran up against the most fundamental aspiration of virtually all members of the multicultural communities. They wanted to be treated as full members of Canadian society, able to participate equally in all spheres of Canadian life. Building distinctions based on ethnicity into the conception of the Canadian nation would consign them and their descendants to a lower status for all time to come. The problem was less severe when phrased in terms of culture, but it still raised objections. The vast majority of members of multicultural communities were willing to adapt to the fact that they were living in Canada. They were, to some extent, willing to become "acculturated." But they also wanted to preserve their distinctive heritage. If there were two official cultures, would they be forced to reject their own to be considered part of the mainstream? If they chose to preserve their identities as Italian Canadians, Chinese Canadians, or Ukrainian Canadians, would they suffer discrimination? Would they be *allowed* to integrate into the broader society?

Faced with these objections, the Trudeau government dropped biculturalism and focused solely on bilingualism. There would be no official cultures. All would have equal status. Bilingualism would only refer to the citizen's ability to use either language in communication with the federal government, and to the requirement that both languages be used in government functions, government publications, and certain spheres of economic activity (such as product labelling). This, after all, was also consistent with the individualism of Trudeau's language policies. The recognition of two official cultures would have come altogether too close to an acknowledgment of specific, territorially based French and English Canadian communities. The emphasis on many cultures throughout Canada, none of which had a claim to precedence, undermined the claim for a distinctive, French Canadian society centred on Quebec. This separation of bilingualism from biculturalism was reinforced by the Trudeau government's formal adoption of the policy of multiculturalism in 1971, followed by the appointment of a minister responsible in 1972. Under this policy, the government provided financial support to cultural events, festivals, newspapers, voluntary organizations – indeed, a whole range of activities reflecting the cultural diversity of Canada.[27]

This reorientation away from biculturalism and towards bilingualism was much more acceptable to the members of multicultural communities, especially when supplemented by the policy of multiculturalism. Virtually all immigrants had, after all, recognized the practical necessity of adopting one of the official languages (usually English) in their relations with the broader Canadian society. Not all acquiesced in Trudeau's bilingualism, however. Some, particularly in the West, continued to balk at the increased profile given French. For many, their reasons were virtually the same as those of westerners generally. They implicitly considered English as the standard language of public communication in North America. French was conceived in the same terms as Ukrainian or German. It was, within Canada (or at least in western Canada), a language of the private realm or the ethnic community, which French Canadians were welcome to preserve but which should not be "forced" on others. A few (though in the end not many) even turned this argument on its head, arguing that if French were given increased status, so should their languages. (This was the approach taken in Rudnyckyj's report, which would have given some recognition to a handful of "regional languages," although less than that accorded English and French.) Others continued to oppose bilingualism simply because for them it still implied social inequality. By moving away from a single, standard language – by recognizing a second language as part of the very structure of Canadian society – the policy of bilingualism abolished (in their view) the common basis of Canadian citizenship. People would no longer be on the same footing. Now there would be two national languages for Canadian citizens, English and French. Bilingualism, in its alleged divisiveness and potential for inequality, was just as bad as biculturalism.

In general, however, Trudeau was successful in harnessing the multicultural communities' dissatisfaction. The abandonment of biculturalism defused much of the opposition. The policy of multiculturalism allowed the multicultural communities to become an integral part of the reconception of Canada – a reconception that many believed was a marked improvement over the idea of a British Canada, which, like biculturalism, had limited appeal for those of other cultures. Finally, members of the multicultural communities, always concerned with freedom from discrimination, liked the strong emphasis on individual rights in Trudeau's policies. This emphasis (as we will see) would occupy a prominent role in his constitutional proposals.

THE CLAIMS OF ABORIGINAL PEOPLES

There was one more kind of cultural-linguistic community whose conceptions of nation would be important to the constitutional debate: the aboriginal peoples. The unity of the aboriginal peoples, like the multicultural communities, should not be exaggerated. They are not one people. The differences between status Indians, non-status Indians, Métis, and Inuit are profound in terms of their histories, their cultural identities, and their status under Canadian law. Even within the group "Indians," there are many peoples, differing fundamentally in their languages, traditions, structures of government, economic organization, and the extent and nature of their contact with European societies. And within each aboriginal community, as in any community, there are deep disagreements between individuals. Despite these differences, however, the development of aboriginal demands has tended to follow a common trajectory. This section describes that movement.

Over the last thirty years, the principal demands of aboriginal peoples have changed in emphasis. Initially they were concerned with redressing economic and social inequality, later they focused on land claims, and most recently they have emphasized self-government. Each of these demands flowed, however, from a common source. Aboriginal peoples have sought, above all, for a way to reclaim their cultural heritage, for a way to rebuild their self-confidence as Kwakiutl, Ojibway, or Métis, and to carry that identity with them in their engagement with contemporary Canadian society. They have not tried to return to a distant past or become exhibits in a living museum. They have tried to make their way in today's world, on a basis of equality but without abandoning their identities as distinctive peoples with their own cultural value and their own social institutions. They have tried to work out, in other words, what it should mean to be (for example) Montagnais in today's Canada.

The first step in this process, a step that clearly occurred in many Native communities in the 1960s, was to reclaim their cultures and languages and to rebuild their self-respect. Here, the great variation in aboriginal communities was significant. Some still retained a vibrant and living culture, spoke the ancestral language, and possessed the resource base necessary to support a viable community. Most, however, had suffered in different degrees from prolonged contact with the settler society, the destruction of their traditional relationship to the land, disease, alcoholism, the loss of language and customs through an unsympathetic educational system and a host of other policies designed to destroy what was considered by government and church to be an anachronistic and backward way of life. For a great many years, Natives had been pushed to adopt the Christian religion and the English or French language, to leave traditional economic activities for agriculture or waged labour, with the objective eventually of assuming rights and obligations identical to those of any other citizen. Particularly in the 1960s, Native Canadians, especially the youth, rejected this model with a vengeance, insisting on rediscovering their own identities and using those as the basis for engagement with the world.

This renewed defiance was often accompanied by anger at the poverty of their communities, which had often been stripped of their traditional lands and access to fish and wildlife. A chief target for this anger was the federal Indian Act. That act did establish a form of local government for Indian reserves, but these band councils had limited powers, and even the exercise of those was frequently subject to prior approval or after-the-fact nullification by government officers. Even certain actions by individuals – the making of a will, for example – were subject to the discretion of the government's agent. Aboriginal people attacked the act for giving them little control over their own destiny, little ability to shape their societies in accordance with their customs (indeed, for areas outside the bands' jurisdiction, none at all), and for placing them at the mercy of sometimes well-meaning, sometimes neglectful, always non-aboriginal officials.

Many of these criticisms found a responsive audience. Canadians generally were appalled by conditions on reserves. The Indian Act's paternalism struck many as condescending, likely to perpetuate the ills the act sought to cure. For many non-aboriginal Canadians, the situation seemed analogous to apartheid in South Africa or the civil rights struggles in the United States. The solutions too should be the same: aboriginal people should be fully integrated into Canadian society. They should not be treated as a different class of Canadian, segregated on their reserves. They should become full and equal Canadians, holding their land in full ownership, each pursuing his or her own individual economic and cultural destiny. This philosophy became the basis for the Trudeau government's 1969 white paper on Indian policy.[28]

That paper argued that the government should attempt to phase out the special status of aboriginal peoples under legislation and the constitution, and work towards the complete integration of Native people into the society at large, on the basis of individual equality. Aboriginal rights would not be recognized (although treaty rights, because of their origin in contract, would be respected, though perhaps only temporarily). The reserves would be abolished, and aboriginal people would become Canadian citizens like all others. They would certainly be free to retain their cultures if they wished, but they would not be subject to any unique legal regime. The approach was the same as Trudeau's stance on Quebec. Governmental powers and legal rights should not be related to ethnic or cultural characteristics. The only safe, liberal form of government – the only form sufficiently respectful of equality – was one that treated everyone as identical individuals. Indeed, the language could have been lifted out of one speech and put in another: "We can go on treating the Indians as having a special status. We can go on adding bricks of discrimination around the ghetto in which they live and at the same time perhaps helping them preserve certain cultural traits and certain ancestral rights. Or we can say you're at a crossroads – the time is now to decide whether the Indians will be a race apart in Canada or whether it [sic] will be Canadians of full status." In Trudeau's view, this was a choice not just for the aboriginal peoples but for Canadians generally. Did Canadians want to have, within their country, "a group of Canadians with which we have treaties, a group of Canadians who have as the Indians, many of them claim, aboriginal rights or whether we will say well forget the past and begin today?"[29]

Aboriginal peoples vehemently rejected the proposal, with great unanimity. They did not want their aboriginal identity washed out in a sea of undifferentiated Canadian citizenship. They wanted to find a place – an equal place – in Canadian society, but not at the expense of their aboriginal identity. An approach that saw culture as a purely private matter, which individuals could pursue in their spare time but which was excluded from government or law, was insufficient. Their identity presupposed a way of life and a relationship to the land that could only be satisfied in cohesive communities, in which certain decisions were made as communities. But more fundamentally, they knew that if they accepted the government's offer and became, legally, like all other Canadians, the realm they would enter would not be neutral in its culture. It had its own, very definite culture, a culture in which aboriginal peoples would be a tiny minority, with little ability to make their distinctive presence felt. Canadians of other backgrounds might be blind to the cultural character of their political life (perhaps because it coincided so closely with their own), but aboriginals could see it well enough. They wanted to find a role within that broader society, and they were willing to make accommodations to do so, but they also had to preserve a sphere in which their distinctive identities could flourish.

This did not mean that aboriginal peoples generally rejected individual rights. Indeed, within the next few years, Indian women who had married white men would use the equality provisions of the Canadian Bill of Rights to challenge their loss of status under the Indian Act (and consequently their loss of the right to live on reserves). These claims were not, however, intended as an attack on the legal recognition of aboriginal peoples. The women's objective was to share the life of aboriginal communities, not destroy it. When they eventually won their case – not in the Supreme Court of Canada but in the United Nations Human Rights Committee – they did so on the basis of the international right of members of ethnic minorities, "in community with the other members of their group, to enjoy their own culture." Their opponents among the aboriginal peoples had attempted to invoke communal rights against them, arguing that any change would put too much strain on an already inadequate land base. The women's response stressed not only individual rights, but also a shared concern with the future of aboriginal communities. The problem was, in their view, how to accommodate individual rights within the structure of strong aboriginal communities – how to reform the legal structure governing those communities in a manner that would respect the integrity of the communities.[30]

The arguments of the aboriginal peoples won the day. The Liberal government backed down, accepting that a distinctive, Indian status would remain.

During the 1970s, Native land claims occupied a prominent place on the public agenda. Land claims were important to aboriginal peoples for both cultural and economic reasons. Aboriginal cultures generally were premised on a special relationship to a particular territory and to the creatures within that territory. Without that territory, the traditional way of life and the religious beliefs based on that life were severely impaired. The taking of the territory also undermined the economic viability of communities, especially when the settlement of the surrounding land, the advent of white hunters, trappers, and fishermen, and the regulation of hunting and fishing (often to protect non-aboriginal uses) reduced the availability of fish and game. The loss of the land was frequently a major cause of the demoralization of Native communities and their dependence on government. Re-establishing control over land was a way of re-gaining control of their lives.

There was a widespread perception among many non-aboriginals – a perception echoed in the quotation from Trudeau's speech above – that these claims were attempts to get compensation for wrongs long in the past. Sometimes it was true that the dispossession had occurred many decades before, but very frequently the loss of the land had occurred within living memory. Many claims related to lands removed from Indian reserves in this century, confiscated to make room for the expansion of towns or the construction of public works for the benefit of non-aboriginals. In other cases, the dispos-session was occurring at the present time. Fishing or hunting regulations were being enforced against traditional Native uses. Un-surrendered lands were being taken at that very time, without compensation, even though Native people had always lived on the land and harvested its resources. Historically, land had usually been surrendered and Indian reserves established only when non-aboriginal Canadians wanted the land and its resources. In many parts of the country, that process was occurring now. In some, re-serves had never existed because until recently there had been little conflict over the land.

The largest claims were based on subsisting aboriginal title, the basic right of those using and occupying land to retain their rights to that land, even after the assertion of sovereignty by a European power. Because they were based on a prior property right, the claims usually covered all lands traditionally used by the people con-cerned, even though some land might now be occupied by someone else. The claims were not necessarily designed to bring all of this area back into aboriginal hands. Frequently, aboriginal peoples were willing to accept complete control of a lesser area, with compensa-tion for the balance. Making the claim was a way of forcing negoti-ations to achieve a viable land base for the people.

Three events during the 1970s were crucial in the development of land claims. All were based on aboriginal title. In the late 1960s, the Nisga'a people of northern British Columbia took their long-standing claim to the courts. In 1973, the Supreme Court of Canada delivered its decision in the *Calder* case.[31] The judgment gave little immediate satisfaction to the Nisga'a. They lost, three judges sup-porting the claim, three holding that the BC government had extinguished Nisga'a title prior to Confederation, while the seventh and deciding judge rejected the claim on a procedural technicality. For aboriginal peoples generally, however, the judgment was a victory. Six judges had affirmed in no uncertain terms that aboriginal title had existed, even though three (not a majority) had held that in the specific case of the Nisga'a it had been extinguished. The judgment prompted the Liberal government to agree, at least in principle, to negotiate claims founded on aboriginal title.

In April 1971, while the Nisga'a case was wending its way through the courts, the Quebec government announced its intention to develop the hydroelectric power of a number of rivers flowing into James Bay. Hydroelectric power had, since the early 1960s, been an important component of the Quiet Revolution's attempt to boost French Canadian participation in the commercial and industrial life of the province. The James Bay project, the most ambitious so far, was the centrepiece of Premier Robert Bourassa's economic policy. In formulating the proposal, the government had taken little account of the Native population of the area. Indeed, from the perspective of southern Quebec, the region appeared empty. It seemed inconceivable that less than 10,000 people, spread around the fringes of an area larger than the province of Ontario, could block the aspirations of six million Quebecers. The government tried to proceed without settling aboriginal claims. In November 1973 the Cree and Inuit obtained an injunction prohibiting work until their subsisting aboriginal title was dealt with. The injunction was overturned one year later on appeal, but the proceedings had already postponed construction.[32] Rather than risk further delays while the matter went to the Supreme Court, the province, Hydro-Québec, and the federal government began negotiations with the aboriginal inhabitants of the area, the Cree, Inuit, and Naskapi.

These negotiations resulted, two years later, in the James Bay and Northern Quebec Agreement.[33] The agreement covered two-thirds of the province of Quebec. It was essentially a modern-day treaty, purporting to extinguish aboriginal title over the entire area in return for specific rights granted the aboriginal peoples. In the case of James Bay, these included a cash settlement, exclusive rights over some specifically designated lands (the rough equivalent of reserves), the exclusive right to harvest fish and wildlife in a larger area, and, throughout the entire region, the continued right to harvest fish and wildlife where possible, combined with participation in economic and environmental regulation. In addition, the agreement provided for a strong aboriginal role (if not outright control) in health and social services, education, policing, and game regulation. Many aboriginal representatives have criticized the agreement for extinguishing, rather than reaffirming, aboriginal rights in the territory. Peoples covered by the agreement have frequently complained of a lack of cooperation from Quebec in establishing and running the joint regulatory structures. Nevertheless, the agreement remains significant for its demonstration of the relevance of aboriginal title to the economic development of vast areas of the country, and for the substantial powers obtained (at least in theory, perhaps eventually in practice) by the Cree, Inuit, and Naskapi.

The last event was the Berger inquiry into the proposal for a pipeline down the Mackenzie Valley in the Northwest Territories.[34] The OPEC crisis of 1973 had prompted the Trudeau government to unveil a new energy policy, one component of which was the development of alternative sources of petroleum. One such source was the Canadian Arctic. The Mackenzie Valley pipeline was designed to transport that oil to markets in the south. In March 1974 Mr Justice Thomas Berger of the BC Supreme Court was appointed to study the social, environmental, and economic impact of the pipeline. His inquiry lasted three years, in the course of which he criss-crossed the North, holding hearings throughout the territory. His chief recommendation was a moratorium on pipeline construction in the valley for a period of ten years, during which time the claims of the aboriginal peoples could be settled. That recommendation was accepted; no pipeline was built. In fact, there has yet to be agreement on the resolution of the Dene people's claims.[35] The Berger inquiry – the manner of Berger's investigation as much as the report's findings – did, however, sensitize the Canadian public as never before to aboriginal concerns. It also made clear the link between land claims and the next major development in aboriginal demands: self-government.

The changing outward character of the aboriginal demands over time (first equality, then land claims, and ultimately self-government) tends to hide their fundamental unity. In many ways, each was a different manifestation of the aspiration of the aboriginal peoples to regain control over their own destinies. Each step was another attempt to express that aspiration in terms understandable to both the aboriginal communities and the broader Canadian society. Aboriginal peoples did not seek equality, for example, in order to be treated precisely the same as all other Canadians; they had differences they wanted to preserve, and their conception of equality involved equal respect for these differences, not their obliteration. For Natives, equality meant freedom from dependency and from presumptions of racial inferiority. Land claims were one way of reclaiming independence and self-reliance. They were a way of obtaining the necessary resources for viable and self-determining societies, drawing upon concepts of property that had a strong foothold within the broader society. But in the end, self-government was the most direct way of expressing the aspiration. Aboriginal peoples wanted to be recognized as distinct societies, with their own character, and having an inherent right – not a right conferred by others – to shape the development of that character through time. This did not mean separation from Canada. All but the naive (and these remain very few) realized that accommodation would be necessary, that they would continue to participate in (or at least work with) the broader society on many issues. But they wanted to preserve a sphere which they would control, in which discussion and decision would occur through the institutions of their own communities, not through those of a much larger society in which they formed a small minority.

This relationship between all their demands, and particularly between land claims and self-government, is apparent in the divergent interpretations of the treaty process, including the modern equivalent of treaties, agreements like that regarding James Bay. Canadian governments have often treated these as though they were contracts for the sale of land, perhaps producing obligations for the future, but to be read narrowly. Aboriginal peoples, on the other hand, have tended to interpret them as pacts between peoples, as "treaties of peace and friendship," establishing a broad framework for future cooperation. The provisions of the James Bay Agreement dealing with joint regulation of the economy and environment are the contemporary translation of the aboriginal perspective – for aboriginal peoples, concrete expressions of the heart of the deal. The failure of these provisions in practice is largely attributable to the divergent perceptions of the aboriginal peoples and Quebec regarding the nature of the agreement.

Prior to the debate over the patriation of the constitution in the early 1980s, indeed perhaps before the debate over the Meech Lake Accord in the late 1980s, aboriginal peoples focused on securing their own autonomy and self-reliance, and very little on redefining the country as a whole. Their arguments had obvious significance for the broader debate, however, as the controversy over the 1969 white paper and their increasing emphasis on self-government suggested. In many ways, the questions posed by aboriginal peoples paralleled those of Quebec's Quiet Revolutionaries. Both struggled to reconcile the recognition of distinct societies with participation in Canadian society. Both believed that some decisions should be made in forums where their culture was the majority culture. But both also acknowledged that there had to be some issues (what issues?) determined at the broader, Canadian level. Both were concerned with reconciling an emergent sense of self-determination with a seemingly inevitable commitment to the whole.

3 Constitutional Themes

These were the questions of identity and nation that would come together in the constitutional discussions of the 1960s, 1970s, and 1980s. Those discussions were not, however, the product of debates over identity alone. Constitutional discourse had its own themes and preoccupations, intersecting in fascinating and sometimes complex ways with questions of identity. To understand those issues, one has to understand something of the constitutional language.

THE DIVISION OF POWERS

One of the dominating facts of the Canadian constitution is the country's federal character: the division of the power to make laws between the federal and provincial legislatures. Under the relevant part of Canada's constitution (originally the British North America [BNA] Act, 1867, now renamed the Constitution Act, 1867),[1] Ottawa has exclusive jurisdiction to make laws on some subjects, such as defence, fisheries, international and interprovincial trade, criminal offences, and matters specifically concerned with the Indians and Inuit. The provinces have exclusive jurisdiction over, among other things, education, municipalities, trade within provinces, and most of the private law (the law of contracts, property, and compensation for wrongful injury). A few areas (such as agriculture and immigration) are concurrent; both the federal and provincial levels of government may regulate them, although in cases of conflict the federal law prevails.

This division defines the sphere of action of each government. It defines what the provinces can do and what must be left to Ottawa. The division can give rise to considerable frustration when a government wants to regulate something but finds that the question falls outside its jurisdiction. Most Canadians (except those advocating the separation of Quebec, or the small number who would like a unitary Canadian state) accept that a federal system of government – and the resulting frustration – is necessary in a country as large and diverse as Canada. They may well disagree, however, on whether a particular power should be exercised by Ottawa or the provinces.

Part of the trouble is that any specific division of powers can be justified on a wide range of grounds. Some of these are more appealing in some parts of the country than in others. Some provoke considerable passion, touching on issues of cultural survival, political self-determination, or economic equality. Others are based on arguments of economic rationality or organizational efficiency.

One criterion is simple administrative convenience: some things (such as tariffs and money) are best determined at the level of the country as a whole; others (such as municipal services) are best determined locally. Another is the ability to participate in the democratic process: it may be easier for a Nova Scotian to have her voice heard in Halifax than in Ottawa, both because she has to travel further to get to Ottawa and because, once there, she has to compete for attention with people from across the country. Ottawa may be preferred for a particular subject where there is a widespread belief that laws on that subject should, as a matter of citizenship, be identical for every Canadian (criminal law might be an example). On other matters, the provinces may be preferred because there is a general belief that, in those areas, policies should be tailored to regional differences. The provinces might, for example, be best placed to determine what should be taught in history classes so that, although all students should learn about other parts of Canada, Newfoundlanders will explore in detail the history of conflict and cooperation along their shores, Saskatchewan children will understand the settlement of the West, and students in the lower Skeena will know something about the Tsimshian people. In a province like Quebec, the concern with regional variation may be given much greater force by the concentration of one cohesive cultural group in the province. There, a federal system of government may permit that group to retain control over many aspects of its own political life, so that at least with respect to those matters it is not at the mercy of a majority belonging to another culture. Then there are reasons having nothing to do with who is best able to perform a task. Some have argued that a federal division of powers allows for political experimentation and even healthy competition between jurisdictions – a competition that produces better policies for all Canadians.[2] Some say this is what happened in the 1964 conflict over the federal pension scheme. As a result of Quebec's stand, the federal plan was better than it would otherwise have been. Others have argued that having two levels of jurisdiction builds checks and balances into our political system, so that the unwise or oppressive policies of one level can be offset by the other.

During the past thirty years, the division of powers has been a principal subject of constitutional negotiations. Some of these have addressed the integrity of the scheme. Provinces have resisted what they consider to be encroachments by the federal government into their realms. They have tried to ensure that they alone set the priorities, they alone make the rules within the areas given to them by the constitution. This is the basis, for example, of the provinces' traditional opposition to the power of disallowance (which permits Ottawa to annul laws enacted within provincial jurisdiction).[3] It is also the reason why many provinces have sought to limit the federal spending power (which Ottawa has used to establish programs within what is normally exclusive provincial jurisdiction). These concerns, especially the limitation of the federal spending power, played a large role in the Meech Lake debate.

Other discussions have dealt with *changes* to the division of powers. In fact, the series of constitutional conferences that began in the late 1960s were largely driven by Quebec's requests for greater powers to regulate (within its borders) communications, social policy, immigration, and, to a lesser extent, economic development. Quebec also wanted to develop direct relations with foreign countries on matters related to provincial jurisdiction and French culture. In the 1970s, Quebec's demands were joined by the jurisdictional demands of other provinces, especially Alberta, Saskatchewan, and British Columbia (seeking greater control over the taxation and marketing of natural resources) and Nova Scotia and Newfoundland (seeking a role in the regulation of offshore resources and fisheries). In the late 1970s and early 1980s, Ottawa retaliated by arguing for increased powers of its own so that it could eliminate barriers to the movement of goods and services between provinces.

The federal division of powers, then, has formed a crucial component of the constitutional debate. It defines the legislative authority of the two levels of government and has been the target of those favouring greater autonomy, on the one hand, and more centralized decision making, on the other. At times these demands have been portrayed as blatant attempts to grab power, and no doubt self-aggrandizement and empire-building have played their role in constitutional negotiations. But the division of powers, by determining the context within which we pursue public goals, also speaks to fundamental concerns of political community, democratic participation, economic equality, and cultural identity.

THE FINANCIAL STRUCTURE OF CONFEDERATION

The fiscal authority of Canadian governments may seem the most prosaic of subjects, but it has been at the core of much of the discussion of Canadian federalism. Throughout the 1940s, 1950s, and 1960s, most federal-provincial conferences were preoccupied with who should have the power to impose taxes and how tax revenue should be shared. Although fiscal questions were pushed from the spotlight in later conferences, they nevertheless formed the backdrop of many of the thorniest issues of the 1970s and 1980s.[4]

The issues raised by taxation are surprisingly diverse. Some concern the redistribution of income from richer to poorer parts of the country. From the time of Confederation on, a series of special grants were made from the central government to provinces having weaker tax bases. In the postwar period, these grants took the form of equalization payments, designed to permit poorer provinces to afford social services approaching those of the richer provinces. The amendments to the constitution adopted at the time of patriation in 1982 included a formal commitment to the principle of equalization.[5] Other federal programs, to the extent that they raise money predominantly in the richer regions but pay benefits in the poorer (for example, unemployment insurance or regional development funds), also redistribute income across the country. Together, these programs are the concrete expression of a solidarity that crosses Canada's regional divisions.

Occasionally, disputes over taxation serve as a surrogate for conflicts over regulatory jurisdiction between the provinces and Ottawa. During the 1970s, the battle between Ottawa, Alberta, and Saskatchewan over the pricing of natural resources was fought largely in terms of taxation. In the 1974 budget, Ottawa changed its income tax rules so that resource-extraction companies could no longer treat provincial royalty payments as a business expense, effectively increasing Ottawa's share of resource revenues. Ottawa also imposed a tax on oil exports to force the western provinces' petroleum onto the domestic market at lower prices. In the late 1970s, a Saskatchewan royalty scheme was successfully challenged in the courts on the grounds that it constituted a form of taxation denied the provinces under the constitution. This running battle led to the enactment, in the 1982 patriation package, of a new constitutional provision clarifying provincial control over natural resources and extending provincial powers of resource taxation.[6]

But the most pervasive effects of the fiscal issue stem from the fact that although the power of provinces to make laws is extensive, their taxing power is, at least in practice, sharply circumscribed. To begin with, their constitutional authority is less than that of the federal government. Ottawa can impose both direct and indirect taxes; the provinces are generally limited to direct taxation alone.[7] More importantly, however, Ottawa is dominant even within the field of direct taxation. In 1941, as part of its assertion of control over the entire wartime economy (and influenced by the report of the Rowell-Sirois Commission on Dominion-Provincial Relations),[8] Ottawa took over income tax and succession duties, to the exclusion of the provinces. The federal government then made a series of grants to the provinces to compensate for their lost revenue. This structure continued into the postwar period, the federal government controlling the chief sources of taxation, the provinces relying on grants from Ottawa.

This arrangement severely constrained the provinces. They had extensive constitutional responsibilities, requiring ever-higher funding, but were dependent on money from Ottawa to pay for them. Their power to establish programs and their ability to set priorities within their jurisdiction were limited by the revenue they received from Ottawa. They could have raised their own taxes, but once the federal government had occupied a field, this became extremely difficult. Citizens could only bear so much taxation. They already had to pay the taxes imposed by Ottawa. Unless Ottawa was willing to reduce its take – unless it would give the province more tax room – additional provincial taxes might well overburden taxpayers. Thus, throughout the postwar period provinces demanded increased revenues, ideally revenues roughly equivalent to their constitutional jurisdiction. They wanted a larger share of the taxes collected by Ottawa, and they asked for greater room to impose their own taxes.

The nature of the fiscal structure had a crucial effect on the debate over the spending power. Some provinces alleged that Ottawa was able to establish programs within provincial jurisdiction precisely because Ottawa's control of tax revenue gave it too much money, money it could then use to encroach on the provinces. The poorer provinces would often accept these programs willingly, but others were reluctant, annoyed that matters within their jurisdiction were dictated by Ottawa, disturbed that their priorities were distorted by the financial power of Ottawa, and fearful that once a program was established, Ottawa might reduce its contribution, leaving the province holding the bag.[9] The provinces could have refused some of these programs, but this was difficult, in part because the programs were popular with the electorate, but also because if the provinces refused to participate (without securing financial compensation), their citizens would continue to pay taxes to Ottawa for a program from which they gained no benefit. Thus, criticisms of the spending power were inevitably linked to demands for compensation (in the form of additional grants or tax room) to any province opting out. In the negotiation of the patriation package in 1980–81 and of the Meech Lake Accord in 1987–90, many of the discussions over the spending power (and, for similar reasons, the ability to opt out of certain future constitutional amendments) ultimately came down to this question of financial compensation.

The federal government had arguments of its own for retaining its fiscal dominance. One of these was economic. Ottawa considered itself responsible for macroeconomic policy, for the management of government spending and interest rates in order to fight inflation and maintain employment. Its control of taxation enabled it to ensure, within limits, that the provinces went along with its policies in this area. But it had other, less technocratic reasons for opposing reform. A single, country-wide system of taxation and the social programs created through the use of the spending power contributed (some governments claimed) to a sense of Canadian identity. The Trudeau Liberals, for example, resisted granting provinces a blanket right to opt out of spending programs with financial compensation for fear this would result in the dismantling of programs that had become an integral part of Canadian identity. Some analysts also opposed reform because the federal nature of taxation and programs automatically helped reduce regional disparities in income: the federal government would naturally obtain most of its revenue from the more prosperous parts of the country, but would then provide equal benefits to the less wealthy regions. The issues of federal fiscal control and equalization were not identical – it was certainly possible to provide greater latitude to the provinces while maintaining or even increasing fiscal transfers (provinces might, for example, be permitted to opt out of spending programs with financial compensation, as long as equalization payments were adjusted to allow all provinces to provide similar services) – but the questions were sufficiently close to complicate immeasurably the negotiations on the limitation of the spending power.

Thus, the issue of financial resources was integrally linked to two central issues of the Canadian constitution (indeed Canadian citizenship): (1) the integrity of the existing division of powers and (2) equalization. The question of financial compensation often became a sticking-point in the negotiations of the 1970s and 1980s.

FROM COLONY TO NATION: PATRIATION AND THE AMENDING FORMULA

This is one of the classical themes of Canadian constitutional history: Canada's evolution from British colony to independent nation. Like its patriotic counterpart – the commitment to a British Canada – the concern with imperial relations now seems obsolete, the relic of another era. But it too has left its mark on our recent constitutional debate.[10]

For many years, it was the dominant concern of Canadian constitutional change. Canada, by a series of incremental measures, gradually established its independence from Britain.[11] Many of these changes occurred through political practice, without fanfare, but the evolution was punctuated by the enactment of the Statute of Westminster in 1931 (recognizing Canada's legislative sovereignty) and the abolition of civil appeals to the British Privy Council in 1949, making the Supreme Court of Canada Canada's highest court.[12] At the beginning of the 1960s, two substantial links to Britain remained, however: (1) the British monarch was still Canada's monarch and (2) the principal document of the Canadian constitution was an ordinary statute of the British Parliament – the British North America Act, 1867 – which Britain alone could amend.

The second link was generally considered the more serious defect in Canadian nationhood. From the negotiations over the Statute of Westminster on, successive Canadian governments periodically sought to "patriate" the constitution, to remove the constitution from the control of the British Parliament so that it could be amended in Canada, by Canadians. Before it could be patriated, however, the constitution had to have an amending formula, a description of the process to be followed, the consents to obtain, in any future amendment to the constitution. Despite a series of conferences devoted to the issue, Ottawa and the provinces failed to agree on a formula. In the absence of agreement, the constitution remained in Britain.

In federal countries, amending formulas usually require the consent of the central government and of a certain number of provinces (sometimes with express provision for public input through the holding of a referendum or formal public hearings). Provincial consent is required for the same reason provinces exist. In a large and diverse country, a federal constitution guarantees that some matters will be decided close to home, in a forum in which the inhabitants of a particular area form a majority. If the constitution could be changed without provincial consent, those guarantees would be worth little, subject to change by the central government alone, without regard for minority interests. At the same time, no one wants an amending formula so strict that it is next to impossible to change the constitution. Amending formulas therefore balance the importance of the constitutional protections against the need to permit amendments. Different kinds of amendments require different degrees of consent.

Often, amending formulas assume that all provinces will have roughly similar interests in a particular kind of amendment. Thus, requiring that a certain number of provinces consent is assumed to protect the most fundamental interests of all. Other formulas assume that interests may differ depending on the region of the country. Those formulas may expressly require consent in each region or may require a total number of consents sufficient to ensure that all regions will be represented. Occasionally, one province has a special interest in preserving its autonomy, an interest not shared (at least not in the same degree) by other provinces. Quebec has long claimed that it has such an interest because it is the only province in which French Canadians form a majority. For that reason, Quebec has traditionally claimed a veto over many kinds (if not all) of constitutional change. The denial of that veto in the patriation package of 1982 was one of the main reasons for Quebec's rejection of that package.

Governments may not agree on how to balance all these interests, on the issues to which they apply, or even on whether distinctive interests exist. It can therefore be very difficult to achieve agreement on an amending formula, especially when, as in Canada prior to 1980, it was generally assumed that any formula should have the support of all, or virtually all, provinces. Many of the discussions of the 1970s and 1980s – and those today – foundered on the appropriate degree of consent required.

All governments agreed that the constitution should, if possible, be patriated, that going to London to amend our constitution was a vestige of our colonial past which should be ended. That consensus was one of the elements that kept the constitutional process moving in the years prior to 1982. It was also one of the traditional constitutional themes that appealed most to Pierre Trudeau, complementing his will to create a new Canadian nationalism independent of allegiance to Britain. This appeal was most evident in his questioning of the other remaining link with Britain, the monarchy. Reform of the monarchy was of little interest to other strong advocates of constitutional change. It was also political dynamite, arousing vigorous opposition in some quarters. But it remained a latent component of Trudeau's constitutional vision, appearing briefly in Ottawa's 1978 proposals.[13]

HUMAN RIGHTS AND CIVIL LIBERTIES

A concern with human rights has long been a real, though elusive, theme in Canadian constitutional thought. It has been elusive largely because until 1982 there was no constitutionally entrenched charter of rights binding Canadian governments. There were other ways in which rights were valued and protected – the history of human rights certainly did not begin with the Charter – but these did not have the clarity or symbolic presence of a constitutional guarantee.[14]

Before 1982 – and, one could argue, after as well – the principal means protecting individual rights were the commitment of Canadians to their freedom, their ability to engage in open debate, the presence of strong traditions of tolerance and fair play, and the responsiveness of the political system to Canadian society. These forces were far from negligible. They remain indispensable today, given the inability of the courts to remedy every injustice, the prohibitive cost of access to the courts, and the intrinsic value of broad, public decision making. But they were not perfect. Canada has provided its share of examples of governmental disregard for individual freedom, including the internment of Japanese Canadians during the war, the suppression of the potlatch among Indians on the west coast, the forced relocation of Inuit villages in the North, anti-Semitism in immigration policy, and the persecution of Jehovah's Witnesses and Communists throughout Canada, especially in Duplessis's Quebec.[15] These and other abuses led some Canadians to call for a constitutional guarantee, enforced by the courts.

Prior to the Charter, courts did play a role in defending basic human rights against state action. A host of general legal principles, especially in criminal and administrative law, were designed to protect individual liberties. Courts would interpret ambiguous or abstract statutory language in a way that would preserve, as much as possible, the freedom of the individual. Occasionally, in constitutional cases, a concern with human rights shaped decisions on division of powers: the courts, uncomfortable with the human rights implications of a law enacted by one level of government, would hold that the law encroached on the exclusive jurisdiction of the other level of government, rendering it unconstitutional. For a time, the Supreme Court of Canada toyed with the notion that Canada's original constitution contained an "implied bill of rights," lurking in the terms of the preamble or in the principle of parliamentary government.[16] Finally, Saskatchewan in 1947, the federal government in 1960, Alberta in 1972, and Quebec in 1975 all enacted their own statutes, providing for judicial review of state action on human rights grounds.[17] But these statutes were limited. They applied solely to the government that enacted them, they could be changed or set aside by subsequent legislation, and the courts interpreted the federal Bill of Rights in particular in a restrictive, even timid, fashion.

Consequently, some human rights advocates strongly supported the constitutional entrenchment of a charter of rights, often modelled on the US Bill of Rights, applicable to all levels of government, overriding incompatible legislation, and beyond the control of one government to amend. This civil libertarian theme played a strong role in the discussions leading to patriation. But the adoption of a charter of rights was not about freedom alone. Some participants saw the Charter as the focus of a new Canadian identity, a set of rights forming the common content of Canadian citizenship. It would symbolize that all Canadians, no matter who they were, no matter where they lived, would be treated identically. For these participants, that symbol itself was essential, quite apart from its consequences for human freedom. They would not, for example, have been satisfied with a set of provincial or regional charters even if those had guaranteed precisely the same rights.

INSTITUTIONAL REFORM

Constitutions do not simply divide power between two levels of government or place restrictions on the scope of governmental authority. They also define the state's basic institutional framework: how laws are made, how elections are held, how courts are established, and how governments are created and controlled. Some of these institutional issues played an important role in the recent constitutional negotiations. Virtually all of the discussion focused on central institutions, and especially on the implications of Canada's diversity and federal structure for the redesign of those institutions.[18]

One set of proposals was intended to make Ottawa more responsive to the country as a whole. These were promoted most strongly by the western and Atlantic provinces, which argued that federal institutions often reflected the interests of Ontario and Quebec and ignored those of less-populous provinces. Two solutions were particular favourites of the western and Atlantic provinces. The most important was Senate reform. In 1978 British Columbia, then in later rounds a number of other provinces (especially Alberta and Newfoundland), pushed for a complete restructuring of the Senate to give that body a greater role in the representation of interests outside central Canada. Representation in the federal House of Commons is apportioned among the provinces based roughly on each province's population. Because Ontario and Quebec contain more than half of Canada's population, most MPs come from those provinces. The advocates of Senate reform suggested that the Senate be used to offset this central Canadian dominance. Representation in the Senate would give more weight to geography, so that more senators would come from the western and Atlantic provinces than justified by their population. Indeed, since the 1980s, Alberta and Newfoundland have argued that every province should have equal representation, so that Newfoundland with 568,474 people would have the same number of senators as Ontario with 10,084,885.[19]

Those favouring Senate reform have also proposed new ways for selecting senators. Under the present constitution, senators are appointed (in practice) by the prime minister of Canada, and for a very long term (until age seventy-five).[20] Not only does this reduce democratic accountability, but it undermines the Senate's professed role as representative of the regions, since each senator owes his or her job exclusively to the central government. Proposals for reform have usually opted for one of two methods of selection, combined with a limited term: appointment by provincial governments, or direct election. The various proposals also discuss the Senate's powers. Most would preserve the House of Commons as the dominant institution so that representation by population would remain paramount. The Senate would have jurisdiction over a limited range of subjects or would have power to delay but not defeat legislation. Finally, some proposals have attempted to structure the Senate to give weight to interests other than those of the western and Atlantic provinces – French-English duality, for example, or the concerns of aboriginal peoples.

The second strategy for increasing the federal government's responsiveness is to give the provinces (or a reconstituted Senate) a role in certain key federal appointments. Saskatchewan, for example, might have a say in appointments to the Wheat Board. Provinces might also participate in the appointment of judges.

Another objective of institutional reform is to ensure that institutions fundamental to the country's federal structure complement that structure. This is the chief rationale for reform of the Supreme Court of Canada. The structure and powers of that court are determined by legislation of the federal Parliament and could therefore be changed by the will of Parliament.[21] There was virtually unanimous agreement that this was insufficient; the court should be given a constitutional basis, especially since it had to rule, in the last analysis, on the validity of federal as well as provincial legislation. There was similar (though not unanimous) criticism of the fact that Supreme Court judges were appointed by the prime minister, acting (if he or she wished) alone. Some proposals would have required consultation with – perhaps even the agreement of – representatives of the provinces. Finally, a number of proposals would have required that three of the nine Supreme Court judges come from Quebec. This has been consistent practice for a very long time and is justified on the grounds that the Supreme Court is the final court of appeal for cases arising under Quebec's civil law.[22]

Finally, some institutional reforms were supported by functional concerns largely unrelated to the federal character of Canada. In the late 1970s, for example, the New Democratic Party suggested that one hundred extra seats be added to the House of Commons, allocated regionally in proportion to each party's popular vote in the general election. This proposal would have allowed parties to attract excellent candidates for these seats, because candidates high on their party's list would be virtually assured of election. It would also have given parties representation in provinces where they had significant support but not enough to win seats. This would have prevented the dramatic imbalance in party support that occurred during the late 1970s, when there were virtually no Liberal MPs from the West and only one Conservative and no New Democrats from Quebec. Functional concerns also contributed to the impetus for Senate reform. Some wished to reform the Senate simply because it was an embarrassment. The federal NDP, for example, wanted it abolished. Finally, one strong argument for a provincial role in judicial appointments was functional in nature: such a system would reduce the number of appointments based on political patronage.

The reform of central institutions, then, was yet another strand in the complex web of constitutional debate. In some ways it formed an alternative response to regional disaffection: instead of granting more autonomy to the provinces, Ottawa would keep its existing jurisdiction, accommodating western and Atlantic interests *within* central institutions. Ottawa would continue to make laws, but those laws would (one hoped) be more responsive to other parts of the country. Sometimes these reforms were criticized for "regionalizing" the federal government, for making it too dependent on the will of the provinces, and some of the reforms may have had this effect. But western Canadian advocates resented this criticism, believing that it demonstrated the central Canadian tendency to equate the interests of Ontario and Quebec with those of Canada. They saw increased western influence not as anti-Canadian, but as an attempt to make Ottawa more representative of the whole – more Canadian, rather than merely central Canadian.

RELATIONS BETWEEN CULTURAL AND
ETHNIC COMMUNITIES

Lying behind many of these discussions was an older, often unrecognized, sometimes expressly denied theme of Canada's constitutional history: a concern with relations between diverse cultural and ethnic groups. In recent years, there has been a strong tendency to talk of ethnic or cultural diversity only in terms of individual rights – rights to equality, to education in one's language, to one's own religion. But there is an older tradition that deals with cultural diversity in terms of relations between groups, sometimes between peoples. That older tradition shaped Confederation and continues to play a role in today's debates.

It was especially prominent during the earliest period of Canada's constitutional history, evident, for example, in the place of aboriginal peoples in Canada's first constitution following the British Conquest, the Royal Proclamation of 1763. That proclamation established a new government of Quebec under British sovereignty. It also took steps to ensure that the "several Nations and Tribes of Indians ... who live under our Protection, should not be molested or disturbed in the Possession of such Parts of Our Dominions and Territories as, not having been ceded to or purchased by Us, are reserved to them." To that end, the proclamation restricted extensive areas to the exclusive use of the Indians, and established procedures for the purchase of lands outside those areas. It dealt with aboriginal "Nations and Tribes" as collectivities, recognizing their autonomy and providing for negotiations between the sovereign's representative and each tribe as a group. The relationship was one between peoples, a structure later continued in treaties for the surrender of Indian lands.[23]

A similar concern with relations between distinctive, largely autonomous cultural groups shaped the general government of the new British colony. The Royal Proclamation contemplated that

English law (or a local variant) would apply to Quebec. The Quebec Act, passed eleven years later to secure the loyalty of French Canadians during the American Revolution, reinstated the bulk of Quebec's private law (based on the French legal tradition) and eliminated discrimination against the Catholic religion. This produced consternation among the small English-speaking population, which strongly resisted the application of French law to their activities and the use of the French language in the government of the colony. Consequently, in 1791, Quebec was divided into two colonies: Upper Canada (the nucleus of Ontario), predominantly anglophone and adopting the English tradition in private law; and Lower Canada (Quebec), predominantly francophone and continuing the French legal tradition.[24]

At first sight, each of these structures seems to have been based on principles quite different from the autonomy recognized in aboriginal-white relations, principles much more consistent with our usual understanding of political competition, among individuals of diverse backgrounds, within a single political community, rather than with group autonomy as such. In the old province of Quebec, for example, there was a single structure of government applicable to all white residents. The disagreements seemed to occur within common institutions over which single system of laws, which system of government, would apply to all the residents. In fact, the situation was much more complex. The institutional structure did seem to treat the residents of the colony as the individual members of a single, unified political entity, but in practice political life tended to be preoccupied with the existence of two distinct cultural groups. Law and government were conceived in terms of the relationship between these groups, not between individuals. This was evident in the language of political debate at the time, but it also had its reflection within the formal legal structure. It was not at all clear that the same laws applied to all white residents of the colony. Under the Quebec Act, for example, the Crown had reserved the right to grant lands under English, not French, tenure, and such grants were made (especially in Quebec's Eastern Townships). For a very long time it was presumed that these lands were subject to the property law of England, not the French-derived law applicable elsewhere in the province. Old British subjects within Quebec also resisted the application of the French law to their activities, claiming that they should be governed by English law. They achieved some success in the courts and legislative council. Indeed, the very institutions of government – the courts, the executive and legislative councils – were structured and their membership determined with an eye towards the ethnic balance.[25]

In short, two principles – political unity and the recognition of distinct cultural groups – were in tension within the old province of Quebec. This tension was partially resolved in 1791 by the division of the province into Upper and Lower Canada, institutionalizing a measure of cultural autonomy by allowing each of the separate colonies to act as a political unit in its own right. But the close relations between the two colonies meant that the tension between cultural autonomy and political unity remained, a tension captured in Lord Durham's famous description of Canada in 1838–39 as "two nations warring in the bosom of a single state." Durham was appalled by the deep divisions between English and French, and recommended the reunification of Upper and Lower Canada in order to create a single, cohesive political community through the gradual elimination of the French language and culture.[26] The colonies were united in 1841. Cultural autonomy reasserted itself, however, despite attempts to suppress it. A ban on the use of French in the Union Parliament was soon dropped, and by the time of Confederation there were, in many portfolios, separate ministries for the former colonies of Upper and Lower Canada. In some legislative fields, Upper and Lower Canada continued to be governed by separate laws, and this *de facto* division in legislative authority – some things dealt with at the level of the whole, others at the level of the former colonies – later influenced the division of powers in the Canadian constitution.[27] That later constitution also expressly guaranteed certain minority rights within Quebec and Ontario: the political representation of the anglophones of Quebec's Eastern Townships was protected by section 80 of the BNA Act (limiting Quebec's ability to change certain electoral boundaries); and the existence of Catholic and Protestant separate schools was entrenched in section 93.[28] These protections did not take the form of rights granted to individuals, but rather community control over certain public institutions.

All this may seem like ancient history, but the concern with relations between groups – the attention to cultural autonomy – is a living force in today's constitutional debate, although one which often exists in uneasy relationship with the present focus on individual rights. It is no accident that the aboriginal peoples rely heavily on the Royal Proclamation of 1763 in their arguments for land and self-government. They wish to use similar forms of institutional autonomy to fashion a distinctive place for their communities in today's Canada. Similarly, most French-speaking Quebecers consider the federal division of powers to be a guarantee of their cultural existence. Like Durham, they expect that the loss of political autonomy would bring the gradual extinction of their culture. For them, Quebec continues to have special significance as the only government uniquely responsive to French Canada. That perception has informed Quebec's constitutional demands over the years, including the attempt to have Quebec recognized as a distinct society in the Meech Lake and Charlottetown accords. It is also the perception against which Pierre Trudeau fought so vigorously throughout his academic and political career. He resisted all attempts to protect minorities through distinctive legal or political institutions. In the case of aboriginal rights he eventually relented, abandoning the stance of the 1969 white paper. But he maintained his opposition to any recognition of Quebec as a French Canadian homeland, choosing instead the ideal of a federal government bilingual from coast to coast, with each language protected in all parts of the country by means of individual guarantees of education and governmental services.

In many ways, then, Canadians are still struggling with two contrasting political tendencies. One emphasizes the unity of the nation and insists that to have unity all individuals have to be in the same relationship to the Canadian state. This perspective finds it very difficult to recognize distinct societies within the country, and seeks to deal with cultural and linguistic differences by translating them into individual rights, by banishing them to the private sphere, or (in the most extreme case) by urging their elimination. The other emphasizes that distinct aboriginal or French Canadian societies can and should be accommodated *as societies* with their own autonomy within the broader state. It argues that they cannot be adequately accommodated through individual rights alone because all social action has a cultural character. If the recognition of minority cultures is confined to the level of the individual, political equality will not be furthered (aboriginal peoples, for example, will not feel more at home in political institutions). Rather, the political system will be dominated by the culture of the majority. Thus, each society should have its own measure of autonomy so that it can have a public sphere within which its culture will be dominant. This does not mean (at least not necessarily) that individual rights will suffer within these communities. Each community may protect individual rights equally, but its public institutions will tend to reflect the cultural characteristics of the principal cultural group.

The two sides of this dialogue have therefore continued to today, often arguing on the symbolic rather than the practical plane, each scrutinizing the other's language for centralizing or decentralizing tendencies – one fearing that focus on the centre will undermine its position as a minority, the other concerned that any recognition of distinct societies will set Canada on the road to incoherence and disintegration. And shaping the two sides of this dialogue, forcing it into terms in which compromise seems impossible, is our continual stumbling over the idea of "nation," our tendency to treat allegiance as all or nothing, exclusively focused on the cultural community or exclusively focused on Canada.[29]

4 Towards Patriation: Constitutional Reform, 1960–1982

The constitutional negotiations of the last thirty years were formed by these two strands of public debate: first, the political conversation about nationality and the place of Canada's cultures within the whole, and second, the drier, more specialized argument over constitutional law. The negotiations began with an attempt by Quebec to achieve specific, technically conceived reforms. They became, by the late 1960s, a struggle over different visions of the country and particularly of the place of Quebec within Canada, a struggle that assumed added urgency in the 1970s as the Parti Québécois worked actively for Quebec's secession while other provinces lobbied hard for increased powers over natural resources. By the end of the period the debate had evolved still further, reaching well beyond a preoccupation with federal-provincial relations to become the focus for virtually all attempts to achieve recognition and equality within Canadian society. Aboriginal peoples, multicultural communities, women's groups, the disabled, the gay community, low-income Canadians, unions, and others all sought express mention within the constitution, and when successful (and even when not), tried to vindicate their rights before the courts. The constitutional conversation, which in the 1940s and 1950s had addressed a set of specialized and precisely focused issues, had become the arena within which the entire country sought to define itself and all its people.

This evolution occurred in three stages. The first began with the election of the Lesage government in 1960 and lasted until the victory of the Parti Québécois in 1976. During that time, the traditional preoccupations of constitutional lawyers took on new significance as successive Quebec governments grappled with the consequences of the Quiet Revolution for the evolution of the constitution. The 1976 election of the PQ forced the debate into a second stage, throwing into question the very survival of the federation. That stage was punctuated by the victory of the "No" forces in the 1980 referendum on sovereignty-association and culminated in the patriation of the constitution, complete with a charter of rights, in 1982. Patriation changed the formal structure of the constitution and, equally importantly, created new constituencies claiming a strong interest in constitutional change, constituencies that demanded participation in future negotiations. Patriation also left certain tasks unfinished, the most prominent being the definition of aboriginal rights, the securing of Quebec's consent to the constitution, and Senate reform. These issues dominated the third stage of negotiations, from 1982 to 1992. This chapter will examine the discussions of the first two stages. Chapter 5 will examine the third.

THE QUIET REVOLUTION AND
THE CONSTITUTION, 1960–1976[1]

During the 1950s, federal-provincial conferences had generally been preoccupied with two relatively confined questions: fiscal relations between governments and the search for an amending formula. They tended to follow a standard form, dictated by Ottawa's control over sources of taxation: the provinces first demanded a greater share of revenue; Ottawa then made a set of concessions. The Quiet Revolution transformed this staid relationship. As francophone Quebecers came to consider the province (rather than the church) as the primary vehicle for promoting their language and culture, they began to probe the limits of that province's jurisdiction, questioning whether it had sufficient powers to fulfil its new role. The initiative began to shift from Ottawa to Quebec. Quebec's representatives aggressively defended provincial autonomy and began to argue for a greater role in areas of federal dominance (communications, immigration, international relations). This change (like the social changes in Quebec) did not happen all at once. But the Quiet Revolution had assumed its own trajectory, one that transformed the terms of discussion.

This became evident during Jean Lesage's term as premier. Lesage's first federal-provincial conference took place in the summer of 1960, almost immediately after the election that had brought him to power. It was, as usual, concerned with fiscal relations.

Lesage voiced Quebec's traditional grievances, demanding (with support from Ontario) that the spending power be restricted. He also proposed action on a new amending formula. This last proposal set in motion a series of smaller meetings resulting, four years later, in tentative agreement on the "Fulton-Favreau formula."

This formula was named for the federal ministers of justice who presided over its creation. In its final form, it would have required the unanimous consent of all governments for most significant amendments, including any change to the division of powers. Certain changes to central institutions (for example, the allocation of seats in the Senate) were subjected to less onerous requirements; they would have required approval by Ottawa and two-thirds of the provinces representing 50 per cent of the population. Finally, the formula would have permitted the delegation of powers between Ottawa and the provinces. Under Fulton-Favreau, the fundamental constitutional structure (especially the division of powers) would have been very difficult to change, but there would have been substantial room for the ad hoc transfer of powers between provinces and the federal government.[2]

At their meeting in October 1964, all premiers agreed to the formula and adjourned to consider final approval. All except Quebec eventually supported the proposal. The formula quickly came under attack in Quebec (especially by the leader of the opposition, Daniel Johnson) because of its rigidity, a rigidity that, it was feared, would prevent major reforms. Eventually, it became clear that Quebec would not approve the formula. This marked a turning-point in the province's strategy. Traditionally, it had sought to restrict the ability to make amendments in order to protect its jurisdiction. This made sense when Canadians outside Quebec favoured the expansion of Ottawa's role. Quebec had been on the defensive, opposing, in the name of its unique character, attempts to expand federal jurisdiction. Now, however, the shoe was on the other foot. Quebec was seeking changes. There was less danger of other provinces supporting federal expansion. Rigidity was no longer so appealing.

This, however, raised a nice problem of strategy. Quebec wanted change, but it wanted change on its terms. It wanted to force the pace but control the content of reform. The first objective favoured flexibility, but the second favoured rigidity, to prevent reforms being adopted without Quebec's consent.[3] In the end, Quebec decided on a twin-track approach. It insisted that any amending formula preserve its veto over constitutional change, claiming (with some justice) that its veto was both implicit in Canadian practice and justified by the need to safeguard its cultural autonomy. But it also insisted that significant change occur *before* the adoption of a new amending formula. Quebec knew that most provinces had little commitment to the kinds of reform it wanted. It also knew that provinces outside Quebec wanted patriation. It therefore decided to use the leverage it had. The province would trade its consent to patriation for significant reforms now.

This became Quebec's strategy in all subsequent negotiations, beginning in 1967. Its position transformed the debate from isolated discussions of precise, relatively constrained issues into wide-ranging attempts to rewrite the constitutional division of powers, almost always to give more power to the provinces or at least to Quebec. That strategy ran headlong, however, into the newly emerging federal approach formed under the influence of Pierre Trudeau.

Trudeau's constitutional policy was the projection into the institutional realm of his attitude towards Quebec nationalism generally: his refusal to treat Quebec as a focus of allegiance for francophone Quebecers, his suspicion of any claim to a distinctive role for Quebec in the flourishing of French Canadian culture, and his desire to replace any tendency towards Quebec nationalism with an exclusive Canadian nationalism, based on individual bilingualism and individual rights to language use. Under his influence, Ottawa forcefully opposed all calls for increased legislative autonomy for Quebec. In fact, for most English Canadians, he first came to prominence at the 1968 First Ministers Conference where, as Pearson's minister of justice, he argued against Quebec's demands for more powers. He also resisted any general weakening of the spending power, particularly if it should result in differences in treatment between Quebec and the rest of Canada. He was willing to give the provinces, especially Quebec, a greater administrative role in particular programs, and conceded that provinces should be able to opt out of some programs. But he resisted proposals that would have established general constraints on the exercise of the spending power or provided fiscal compensation for those opting out. Opting out should, he believed, continue to inflict a significant fiscal penalty on the province withdrawing. Otherwise the incentive to opt out would be too great, threatening the pan-Canadian character of spending-power programs.

Trudeau's stance in 1968 contrasted sharply with his position prior to entering federal politics, when he had strongly criticized the spending power's distortion of the division of powers.[4] The change resulted from two factors. First, he came to realize that spending-power programs were among the most popular federal services, very useful in the struggle for the people's loyalty. When it came to the crunch, Trudeau was more committed to maintaining Ottawa's contributions to the budgets of individual Quebecers (reinforcing those Quebecers' commitment to Ottawa) than to protecting the integrity of the division of powers. Second, if constraints on the spending power took the form of an unimpeded right to opt out (and given the popularity of the programs, this, rather than complete abolition, was the most likely form of constraint), Quebec would probably exercise that right more than any other province, resulting in a *de facto* special status for Quebec, an outcome he found anathema.

These were the defensive or reactive elements of the new federal policy on constitutional reform. But Trudeau also sought to regain the initiative by pushing a positive agenda to counter the decentralizing demands of the provinces. The centrepiece was the adoption of a charter of rights, fully entrenched in the constitution and applicable to all provinces and the federal government. One crucial feature of the charter would be language rights. This initiative tapped into the long-established civil libertarian strain in Canadian constitutional thought, which had first developed around the struggles of women and Asian Canadians for the vote, had then concentrated on the discrimination practised against socialists, Communists, and certain religious sects in the 1930s and 1940s, and most recently had been sharpened by revulsion against the persecution of Jews in World War II and the civil rights struggles in the United States. Indeed, Trudeau's focus on civil liberties was a natural extension of his own advocacy of individual rights during the Duplessis regime. But it also had a dimension less obviously tied to individual liberty, one that made it particularly effective as a counter to Quebec's demands. A charter would not only protect individual rights, it would help focus attention on each citizen's individual relationship to Canada as a whole; it would emphasize the oneness of Canada and of Canadian citizenship, implicitly undermining concepts of Canada that treated citizens not simply as members of the whole, but also as members of distinct and cohesive groups with their own publicly recognized identity.

The very nature of a charter of rights emphasized uniformity across the country. All citizens, no matter where they lived, would enjoy the same protections, in language rights as well as in other civil liberties. It therefore presented an image of Canada as fundamentally one. Federal proposals spoke of the charter as a statement of the common values of the nation, as an enunciation of the national will. The rights it protected, including the right to education in either of the official languages, would apply across the country, shifting attention away from the territorial concentration of linguistic groups and the dominant provincial role in education, and providing symbolic affirmation of the claim that Canadians of either linguistic group should feel equally at home in any part of the country. Moreover, a new charter of rights would focus attention on pan-Canadian institutions. The charter itself would be a pan-Canadian document, and its interpretation would be decided in the last analysis by a central institution, the Supreme Court of Canada. The charter became a key element in the federal position, in other words, because it served two purposes: it affirmed the pre-eminence of individual rights over state action, evoking the commitment of all Canadians to individual liberty and equality; and it affirmed the existence of a Canadian identity that transcended cultural or regional differences, adopting an individualistic approach to language rights that would have removed at least some aspects of language use from provincial control.[5]

This new federal strategy began to take shape in the months between the failure of the Fulton-Favreau formula and the constitutional conference of February 1968. A team was assembled within the federal Department of Justice to flesh out a new program. In the fall of 1967, Trudeau (as minister of justice) began to promote an entrenched charter of rights as a central component of future constitutional change. In 1968 the federal government unveiled its program as a whole. It proposed that three general topics be discussed (the order was significant): first, a charter of rights; second, the reform of central institutions; and third, change to the division of powers.[6]

At the same time, Quebec was articulating its position along very different lines. In 1966 Lesage had been defeated at the polls. By a quirk of the electoral system, Daniel Johnson had been elected premier, even though his Union Nationale had received substantially fewer votes than the Liberals. He developed the case for a comprehensive revamping of Confederation, giving Quebec considerably more autonomy.[7] He presented his position forcefully at the Confederation for Tomorrow Conference in November 1967, a conference of provincial premiers hosted by John Robarts of Ontario, with federal representatives attending as observers. Ottawa's and Quebec's positions came into direct conflict at the federal-provincial conference of February 1968. Johnson and Trudeau sharply debated the relative merits of provincial autonomy and language rights, sketching the positions that would dominate negotiations for the next three years and indeed characterize the debate between federalists in Ottawa and federalists in Quebec for the next twenty.

The February conference was the first of a series of meetings between 1968 and 1971 that sought agreement on a package of reforms.[8] During that time, Quebec's leadership changed twice: in

September 1968 Johnson died in office and was succeeded by Jean-Jacques Bertrand; then, in the Quebec election of 1970, the Liberals under Robert Bourassa came to power. The election of Bourassa – and the shock of the October Crisis soon after (when terrorists of the separatist FLQ kidnapped a British diplomat, James Cross, and murdered Quebec labour minister Pierre Laporte) – added new vigour to the negotiations. Quebec suggested it might agree to patriation if it were permitted to opt out of certain spending-power programs with compensation, and if it could legislate regarding other matters (such as unemployment insurance or old age pensions), its laws taking precedence over Ottawa's. This went too far for Ottawa, but negotiations continued. Finally, in June 1971, at a meeting in Victoria, BC, the first ministers came to a tentative agreement, enshrined in the "Victoria Charter."

That agreement would have made a very modest change to the division of powers, recognizing provincial paramountcy in the fields of old age, family, youth, and occupational allowances (but without prohibiting federal programs and without providing financial compensation to the provinces). It would also have patriated the constitution, complete with what came to be known as the Victoria amending formula. Under that formula, amendments would have required the consent of both Ontario and Quebec, two of the four western provinces (representing 50 per cent of the total population of those provinces), and two of the four Atlantic provinces. A charter of rights would have been added to the constitution, containing some basic freedoms and democratic rights. There was no provision for the right to education in either official language, but there was a patchwork of guarantees regarding bilingualism in the federal and some provincial legislatures, some courts, and some public services. The Supreme Court of Canada would have been entrenched, requiring provincial consultation prior to appointments and reserving three seats for judges trained in Quebec's civil law. Finally, the Victoria Charter contained a number of miscellaneous measures, reaffirming the principle of equalization, abolishing the now-obsolete federal power of disallowance, and requiring First Ministers Conferences each year.[9]

The agreement allowed a period of consideration prior to final approval. On 23 June Bourassa announced that Quebec rejected the package, ostensibly because of the uncertain effect of the agreement's terms regarding paramountcy in income-support programs. Those terms were indeed uncertain, but Bourassa's reason ran deeper than mere terminology: the limitation on the federal spending power was simply too modest – if Quebec were to agree to patriation, it wanted significant change.

Quebec's rejection put an end to the package, and indeed to the intensive series of negotations begun in 1968. In 1974 Ottawa proposed a resumption of talks, but the provinces' response was cool. It tried again in 1976, and this time serious discussion did begin. By now, however, the political climate was changing in a way that would further complicate negotiations. A series of conflicts between Ottawa and the western provinces over resource pricing had led those provinces to formulate significant demands of their own, especially regarding jurisdiction over natural resources and, for British Columbia, Senate reform. These demands were supported by Newfoundland, which sought greater powers over fishing and offshore oil production. In Quebec, the scandal-ridden Bourassa government was coming under increasing pressure from the *indépendantiste* Parti Québécois. On 15 November 1976 the PQ defeated the Bourassa Liberals at the polls, René Lévesque becoming premier. These two events – the development of clear, forceful constitutional demands in the West and the election of a separatist government in Quebec – were to cause another dramatic reorientation of constitutional debate in Canada.

SEPARATISM, REGIONALISM, AND
THE CONSTITUTION, 1976–1982[10]

The election of the Parti Québécois changed the debate in two fundamental ways. First, Ottawa and the other provinces were faced with a government committed to holding a referendum on Quebec's secession. No longer was the government of Quebec working for more autonomy within Canada. No longer was it forging a new bond between French Canadian culture and provincial power within the framework of an overarching Canadian community. The PQ was working for full political sovereignty. Following separation, it might conclude an economic agreement with the rest of Canada, but that agreement would be based on the *separate* needs of Quebec and the remains of Canada. In its constitutional negotiations, the PQ was unconstrained by any inherent allegiance to Canada or any need to compromise in the interests of a larger Canadian polity. Its actions were therefore bolder, less compromising, and more far-reaching than those of any previous government, and behind those actions lay the prospect of an early movement towards complete political independence.

The PQ was also much more single-minded in its conception of Quebec as the homeland of the French-speaking population of North America. Previous Quebec governments had embraced the province's role as the defender of French language and culture, but they had tempered it by expressly recognizing other linguistic communities, especially the English community, as integral to Quebec. In 1974, for example, the Bourassa government had introduced Bill 22, making French the official language of Quebec, encouraging French as the language of work, and requiring French on signs. Bill 22 did not demand the exclusive use of French, however. Other languages could appear on signs, provided French was used. Schooling would be available in either language (or an aboriginal language) at the parents' option, as long as the student already knew that language. Whatever the principal language of instruction, students would be taught the other as a second language.[11]

The PQ introduced its own language legislation shortly after the election. Commonly referred to as Bill 101, this legislation went much further than the Liberals'. It promoted French and actively discouraged the use of English in certain contexts. French was not only declared the official language of Quebec, it was made the predominant language of the legislature and courts (in provisions of doubtful constitutionality, struck down by the Supreme Court of Canada in 1979).[12] French was the only language permitted on public signs, except signs dealing with safety or health, with religious, political, or humanitarian activities, and with activities expressly concerned with the culture of a specific ethnic group. Municipalities and school boards could have bilingual signs and, in the case of school boards, conduct their operations in both languages only if the majority of their clientele was English-speaking or (for school boards) if the services were expressly charged with providing instruction in English. With respect to the language of instruction, the general rule was that every student wanting to take advantage of publicly funded education would have to go to French school, unless one of the parents had been educated in English in Quebec. Special allowance was made for the instruction of aboriginal peoples, especially for the use of aboriginal languages.[13]

For most anglophone Quebecers, Bill 101 symbolized the rejection of the English fact in Quebec. Not only was Quebec the homeland of French Canadians, its status as homeland now seemed to imply (at least for the PQ) the existence of a single national culture. Many believed that Bill 101 was the first step in an effort to suppress English entirely, making Quebec an exclusively francophone society. This was the aim of some extreme nationalists (who formed part of the PQ's broad constituency), but it was not the objective of the legislation's architects. Their position was more subtle. They certainly wanted to send a signal that French was the dominant public language of Quebec: it was the common medium of communication in commerce and government, the language that all Quebecers should know and that all organizations serving the public must know. In their view, anglophone Quebecers should not be able to ignore the French fact, speaking only English and expecting francophone Quebecers to deal with them in that language. The province would not, in other words, be bilingual if bilingualism meant that it was appropriate for anglophones to function exclusively in English. English could remain as the distinctive language of the anglophone minority of Quebec, still having a public presence in that minority's schools, universities, hospitals, and social services (although immigrants to the province would be expected to educate their children in French). Bill 101 did not attack the use of English in cultural activities and in ordinary private interaction, indeed even in communication between individuals and the provincial government. But in the public realm, and certainly in the realm of public symbolism, the two languages would not be on the same plane. French would be the *lingua franca* of Quebec, the common medium of communication for the society as a whole.

These two aspects of the PQ's policy – the rejection of any sense of allegiance to Canada and the denial of bilingualism at the provincial level – made the party's position very different from that of previous Quebec governments. It expressed a thoroughly binational vision of the country and of linguistic relations within the country – or rather "countries," for the binational vision was taken to its ultimate extension: complete sovereignty for Quebec. Its challenge was more threatening than that of any previous government because the PQ accepted, even embraced, the prospect of failure in the talks. Indeed, the Parti Québécois had already declared its commitment to push the constitutional question to the point of crisis.[14]

At the same time, other provinces – especially Alberta, Saskatchewan, British Columbia, and Newfoundland – had developed more coherent demands of their own, demands that made them more forceful actors in the discussions of the late 1970s. The concerns of these provinces were usually grouped together under the term "regionalism." Their common element was the sense that federal policy routinely ignored the interests of the eastern and western sections of the country.

The perceived bias in federal policy was often attributed to the concentration of population in the central provinces, enabling Ontario and Quebec to dominate the federal House of Commons. Together those provinces elected well over half the country's MPs. This often meant that federal governments were largely ignorant of areas with less population and few (if any) cabinet ministers. Their grasp of the problems of the Newfoundland or BC fisheries or their commitment to the marketing of grain, for example, sometimes seemed vague and irresolute, insufficiently responsive to the importance of the issues to the regions concerned. But there was also a harder, economic edge to the perception of a central Canadian bias. Westerners had long believed that many of Ottawa's policies were driven by the economies of Ontario and Quebec, not by the interests of the West. This sense of grievance had deep roots. The very settlement of the West had, on this view, been marked by a colonialist policy on the part of the central government, under which Prairie markets had been preserved for overpriced central Canadian goods and the West's resources had been shipped to Ontario and Quebec to serve as cheap raw materials. Traditionally, complaints centred on railway monopolies (especially that of the Canadian Pacific Railway); the imposition of high tariffs on imported manufactured goods, forcing westerners to buy machinery from Ontario instead of cheaper goods from the United States; and the maintenance of Ottawa's control over public lands and natural resources until 1930 (long after the creation of the provinces of Manitoba, Alberta, and Saskatchewan) even though lands and resources in other provinces fell squarely within provincial jurisdiction.

Except for the issue of Prairie lands and resources, these grievances had generally focused on the economic policies of the federal government, not on the constitution. This changed in the 1970s. The catalyst was the long confrontation between Ottawa, Alberta, and Saskatchewan over energy pricing, a development closely tied to the explosive rise in the world price for oil through the 1970s. Prior to that time, western oil and gas had benefited from a protected market to the east. Federal policy had reserved the area west of (roughly) the Ontario-Quebec border to Canadian sources of supply. This was to Alberta's and Saskatchewan's benefit, since their petroleum was generally more expensive than the world price. It ceased to be a benefit in the early 1970s when the international price of oil skyrocketed.

Alberta was especially determined to take advantage of the higher prices. Indeed, the Conservatives under Peter Lougheed had just formed the government in 1971, pledging a vigorous program of economic development based on oil revenues. Its policies on prices and royalties set in motion a series of federal and provincial manoeuvres designed, on the federal side, to secure oil for central Canadian consumers at less than the world price (as well as more federal revenue) and, on the provincial side, to increase the income and consequently the industrial base of the province. A similar conflict occurred between Saskatchewan and Ottawa over the taxation of oil revenues and the marketing of potash. British Columbia's newly elected NDP government also tangled with Ottawa over the deductibility of mineral royalties from federal taxes. Finally, Newfoundland joined BC's long-standing attempt to assert provincial jurisdiction over offshore resources, a jurisdiction Newfoundland wanted so that it too could use oil as the foundation of regional economic expansion.

In large measure these battles turned on a set of constitutional questions: the relative taxing power of the provinces and Ottawa; the balance between federal jurisdiction over interprovincial and international trade, on the one hand, and provincial authority over business within the province, on the other; the province's ownership of public land and natural resources within its boundaries; and the precise location of those boundaries. Some of these battles were fought in court in actions designed to clarify existing constitutional authority. In other skirmishes, each side used its jurisdiction to frustrate its opponent, trying to force the latter to come to terms. Thus, Alberta eventually secured an agreement over oil pricing by cutting back on production, causing Ottawa more losses in terms of foregone revenue and subsidies for expensive replacement oil than Ottawa could gain through its higher tax rate.

But the disputes also gave rise to demands for constitutional change, which then became part of the broader debate. These demands were of two kinds. First, some governments argued for greater control over the taxing and marketing of natural resources, including, in Newfoundland's case, offshore resources. This demand certainly contemplated a legislative decentralization, but of a fairly limited kind, tightly focused on a specific sector. With the exception of Alberta and perhaps British Columbia, the provinces that spoke for regionalism were not in favour of an extensive decentralization of federal power. They all, despite their quarrels, remained committed to a significant role for the federal government. Several of them, especially Saskatchewan, Newfoundland, and Manitoba, had economies fragile enough – and memories of the Great Depression vivid enough – to prevent any action that might imperil federally administered programs or equalization payments. These governments were not, then, grand decentralizers, but advocates of very specific transfers of powers.

The second kind of constitutional demand focused on the reform of federal institutions, especially the Senate, to give greater weight to the voices of the Atlantic and western provinces. The hope was that with solid representation at the centre, the interests of the western and Atlantic provinces would figure more prominently in Ottawa's decision making. A reformed Senate might also have a role in appointments to sensitive federal agencies, injecting a western or Atlantic voice into such bodies as the National Energy Board or the Wheat Board. In the mid-1970s, British Columbia was the main advocate of Senate reform, although the policy also had supporters in other provinces, particularly Alberta.

These events – the election of the Lévesque government in Quebec and the emergence of clear constitutional priorities in the western provinces and Newfoundland – injected into the negotiations both a sense of urgency and a belief that fundamental change was possible. Now provinces other than Quebec were willing to contemplate reform to the division of powers. Change seemed necessary if the separatist challenge was to be surmounted. The crisis provoked a flurry of activity. A host of studies were commissioned by governments, private think-tanks, and concerned individuals. Conferences were held, newspapers commented, and a plethora of individual initiatives tried to promote understanding between francophone and anglophone Canadians.

Discussions also continued at the governmental level. A series of interprovincial conferences resulted in a broad front in favour of greater provincial power over communications, resources, fisheries, and immigration. British Columbia continued to push for Senate reform, arguing that the Senate should consist of delegates appointed by provincial governments. The PQ participated actively in these discussions and formed part of the emerging decentralist alliance, assuring the other provinces that until the people of Quebec had endorsed secession in a referendum, it would take part in federal-provincial negotiations in good faith. In all the discussions, the PQ especially defended provincial jurisdiction over language. It claimed that it was not against increased protection for minority languages, but argued that protection should occur through bilateral agreements between provinces. For its part, the federal government began, in the late 1970s, to show more openness to change in the division of powers, though without agreeing to any specific scheme. It continued to stress the need to protect individual rights, especially language rights, through an entrenched charter. It also proposed reform of central institutions, but in ways that would provide a much more modest role for the provincial governments than that contemplated in the BC proposal. In all its statements, Ottawa strongly resisted any implication that provincial governments were the chief spokespersons for their citizens, asserting that federal members were just as representative of their regions as the premiers of Quebec or British Columbia.

But despite these intense discussions and the multitude of blue-prints proposed, the federal-provincial talks of the late 1970s produced no immediate action, for very good reasons.[15] Even though Ottawa and the provinces conceded that constitutional reform was urgent, it was inconceivable that the PQ government, committed to complete sovereignty for Quebec, would approve any form of renewed federalism prior to a referendum. Quebec knew this, and Ottawa knew it too. Their negotiations during the late 1970s were designed not to secure agreement, but to stake out positions for the upcoming referendum debate. Quebec tried to portray itself as the reasonable negotiator, unable to achieve even minimal gains within the federal system but willing to negotiate calmly and effectively for an agreement with the rest of Canada if it won the referendum. Ottawa emphasized its flexibility on all aspects of the constitution (including the division of powers), its commitment to individual rights across the country (including those of francophone minorities outside Quebec), its steadfast support for federal spending pro-grams (which, it suggested, an independent Quebec could not af-ford), and attempted to underline the prestige derived from the French Canadian presence at the federal level in Canada.

In 1978, knowing that it would never get the PQ's agreement to a constitutional package, Ottawa tried yet another strategy in order to show its willingness to make significant reforms. It proposed a two-step approach to constitutional renewal, an approach reflected in its proposal of that year, Bill C-60.[16] First, Ottawa would act alone on matters that lay (it claimed) within its exclusive jurisdiction: the cre-ation of a charter of rights, which would apply only to federal legis-lation but which provinces could choose to accept; the expansion of the Supreme Court of Canada, resulting in a larger portion of the court appointed from Quebec; reform of the Senate to improve re-gional representation, but with a complex structure so that virtually every federal and provincial party would be represented; and a set of other measures that would increase provincial input into certain federal decisions. Other matters (such as the division of powers and the amending formula) would be addressed at a second stage, once the provinces were ready to agree. Unfortunately for the federal government, the proposal was too diffuse, too complex, and pre-sented in such an ineffective manner that it never caught the popu-lar imagination. Ottawa was left on the defensive throughout the meetings of late 1978 and early 1979. In the fall of 1978, it submit-ted a reference to the Supreme Court of Canada, asking whether the federal Parliament could unilaterally reform the Senate; in Decem-ber 1979 the court held it could not.[17] In the meantime, however, the political situation had changed dramatically. In May 1979 the

federal Liberals had been defeated at the polls, and the federal torch
had passed to the Conservative minority government of Joe Clark.

The Clark government was short-lived, with very sparse representation from Quebec. It moved towards a concept of the country embracing regional diversity, but did not get far beyond a slogan:
Canada would be a "community of communities." The Conservatives
were defeated in the House of Commons on 13 December 1979 and
lost the general election of February 1980. Trudeau was once again
prime minister.

All parties were now caught up in the rush to Quebec's referendum, slated for 20 May 1980. The PQ would use the referendum to
ask Quebecers for a mandate to negotiate sovereignty-association,
an arrangement under which Quebec would have sovereignty but
would maintain an economic association with the rest of Canada.
Committees were created to argue for each side in the debate, one
for the "Yes," one for the "No," the former led by the PQ government, the latter by the Liberal opposition. The Quebec Liberals
staked out their position in a "Beige Paper."[18] It proposed a redistribution of powers, imposing some limits on the spending power and
providing for a greater (though seldom exclusive) provincial role in
a number of fields. It supported an entrenched charter of rights,
with language rights more extensive than those in today's Charter. It
recommended that aboriginal peoples have a right to schooling in
their languages, participate in constitutional talks, and have their
historic rights respected. It proposed major Senate reform and the
entrenchment of the Supreme Court of Canada. Its amending
formula was very close to the Victoria formula. But the time for detailed negotiations had passed. Now the question was much more
blunt: Would Quebecers give reform one more chance, or would
they break with the rest of Canada, attempting to negotiate an
association?

The referendum debate was intense and exhausting for all concerned. Throughout the province neighbours and families, communities and organizations, argued over whether change was possible
within Canada and what the future might hold if Quebec were outside Canada. The "No" side based its arguments on (1) the likelihood
that any move towards independence would result in a costly, complete separation, with no association to follow, and (2) a positive
commitment to "renewed federalism." The Quebec Liberal Party
used the Beige Paper to express its vision of renewed federalism.
Ottawa's meaning was much less clear. It did not adopt the Quebec
Liberals' position. In fact, relations between the two parties were
tense during the campaign, Ottawa disagreeing with the Quebec

Liberals' campaign strategy. Nevertheless, the federal Liberals did
rely on the phrase, especially in one critical intervention.

On 14 May 1980, six nights before the referendum, Prime Minister Trudeau addressed a crowd in Montreal's Paul Sauvé arena. It
was here that Trudeau made his famous commitment to renewed
federalism. His precise words, as reported by a news release from
the Prime Minister's Office, were as follows:

The Government of Canada and all the provincial governments have made
themselves perfectly clear.

If the answer to the referendum question is NO, we have all said that this
NO will be interpreted as a mandate to change the Constitution, to renew
federalism.

I am not the only person saying this. Nor is Mr. Clark. Nor is Mr. Broadbent. It is not only the nine premiers of the other provinces saying this. It
is also the seventy-five MPs elected by Quebecers to represent them in Ottawa who are saying that a NO means change.

And because I spoke to these MPs this morning, I know that I can make
a most solemn commitment that following a NO vote, we will immediately
take action to renew the Constitution and we will not stop until we have
done that.

And I make a solemn declaration to all Canadians in the other provinces,
we, the Québec MPs, are laying ourselves on the line, because we are telling
Quebecers to vote NO and telling you in the other provinces that we will not
agree to your interpreting a NO vote as an indication that everything is fine
and can remain as it was before. We want change and we are willing to lay
our seats in the House on the line to have change.

This would be our attitude in the case of a NO vote.[19]

Trudeau would later claim that this did not mean he was accepting
any of Quebec's traditional positions on the division of powers,
namely the transfer of jurisdiction from Ottawa to the provinces,
limits on Ottawa's spending power, or greater autonomy for Quebec. Clearly his words were sufficiently vague to embrace virtually
any constitutional change. But given the context of the "No" campaign, and given Trudeau's own flexibility on the division of powers
in the conferences of 1978–79, his audience understood and, it
seems clear, was meant to understand that just such a commitment
had been made. Trudeau might have had a private definition of a
renewed constitution in mind, but if so, it was not communicated.
This did not mean – could not mean – that from that moment
Canada was morally bound to change the division of powers. A
promise by one politician on the referendum stump could not

possibly bind the country. But it strongly contributed to the sense of betrayal of many Quebecers, especially Quebecers who had worked for the "No" side, when the constitution was patriated with only a gesture towards Quebec's traditional concerns.

On 20 May, Quebec's voters demonstrated their faith in Canada by voting "No" in the referendum. The question was defeated by the margin of 59.56 to 40.44 per cent. Immediately following the referendum, literally the next day, the federal government began contacting provincial governments, beginning again the quest for agreement.

The full story of that quest has been told elsewhere.[20] Events proceeded quickly, on a number of fronts. Trudeau wanted to strike while the iron was hot, taking advantage of the fatigue and demoralization in the separatist camp. Extensive meetings were held over the summer, leading to the First Ministers Conference of September 1980. In the wake of the referendum victory, the federal stance had hardened; Ottawa showed less flexibility on the division of powers than it had in 1978–79. Attempts to achieve agreement with the provinces failed. On 2 October, Ottawa announced its intention to proceed unilaterally and ask the United Kingdom Parliament to amend the Canadian constitution despite provincial opposition.

The federal proposal, initially worked out in a series of meetings within the federal cabinet, would have patriated the constitution, adopting the Victoria amending formula, but also providing for the use of referenda to bypass provincial assent. It would have entrenched a charter of rights, guaranteeing (among other things) the right to an education in either English or French, depending on one's mother tongue. An interpretive clause was added to ensure that a strongly individualistic reading of the Charter could not be used to erode the distinctive status of aboriginal peoples. There was no general affirmation or entrenchment of aboriginal rights in the initial document, however.[21]

In the days that followed, Ontario and New Brunswick expressed support for the measure. The leader of the federal NDP, Ed Broadbent, also pledged his support, after extracting a promise that the Charter would be stengthened and provincial jurisdiction over natural resources extended. In this way, natural resources became the only element of the division of powers directly affected by the patriation package, addressing some of the concerns raised by Alberta and Saskatchewan in the late 1970s.[22] The package as a whole was then referred to a special joint committee of the House of Commons and Senate for hearings over the winter of 1980–81. Those hearings resulted in many amendments that extended and strengthened the Charter. Among these was a new clause promoted by the NDP (initially with the agreement of all major aboriginal organizations) that "recognized and affirmed" aboriginal and treaty rights. The clause also made clear, for the first time, that "aboriginal peoples" included the Métis. A new interpretive clause required that the courts apply the Charter in a manner consistent with Canada's multicultural heritage. During the committee hearings, women's groups argued for a stronger guarantee of gender equality, saying that the existing provisions could justify the limitation of women's rights on a variety of grounds, including particular cultural traditions (especially given the interpretive clause concerning multiculturalism). These concerns resulted in the adoption, on the floor of the House of Commons, of a special super-guarantee of gender equality.[23]

Not all parties supported the package, however. The federal Conservatives participated actively in the committee hearings, proposing and voting on amendments, but they also vigorously opposed the federal government's willingness to act unilaterally. They argued that such far-reaching changes to the constitution should not be made without the consent of the provinces. They urged the government to go back to the bargaining table, and by stalling debate in the spring of 1981, they eventually forced the government to delay the package until the Supreme Court had ruled on its legality. The Supreme Court's decision, in September 1981, played a decisive role in forcing Ottawa back to the table, resulting in further changes to the constitutional package.

Eight of ten provinces – the "Gang of Eight" – also opposed the federal initiative. All rejected the way it was being done, through action by Ottawa alone. For most provinces, this, rather than any dispute over substance, was the chief grievance. A few, however, did have substantive concerns. Some provinces, including Alberta and Newfoundland, objected to the lack of action on the division of powers. The only provisions dealing with powers concerned natural resources, and these were of limited effect. Most of the criticism, however, focused on the amending formula and the Charter of Rights. Alberta was the strongest critic of the amending formula. It objected to the fact that under the federal proposal only Ontario and Quebec would be guaranteed a veto. It argued that the principle of equality of the provinces required that all provinces be treated in exactly the same way, and advanced an alternative plan under which no single province would have a veto. British Columbia also disagreed with the Victoria formula, but on different grounds. It accepted that formula's use of regional vetos (under which Ontario,

Quebec, two western, or two eastern provinces could block certain changes), but asserted that British Columbia should, like Ontario and Quebec, be treated as a region in its own right.

Criticism of the Charter was more widespread among the provinces than criticism of the amending formula. Some of this focused on specific guarantees (Prince Edward Island, for example, opposed the entrenchment of property rights). But the governments of two western provinces, Saskatchewan and Manitoba, were sceptical about the very idea of an entrenched charter. Saskatchewan's NDP premier, Allan Blakeney, believed that the Charter would place political choices under the control of unelected and often conservative judges, judges who might use it to strike down social legislation (as the US Supreme Court had done during one period of its history, invalidating, for example, minimum-wage legislation). He argued that the best protection for individual rights was a healthy, egalitarian political community, actively participating in the legislative process. That kind of protection was never perfect, but it was better than the abdication of public decision making in favour of an unrepresentative, fallible, and probably conservative judiciary. Manitoba's Sterling Lyon made a similar argument from a strongly conservative perspective, asserting that a written charter of rights was incompatible with British traditions of parliamentary government. But the most bitter opposition came from René Lévesque. He denounced the Charter because it would restrict provincial powers without the provinces' consent, especially in the cultural field. He was particularly incensed with the guarantees of minority-language education rights, which specifically overruled aspects of Quebec's language law, Bill 101. In his view, the proposed charter was not so much about individual rights as about the restriction of Quebec's powers; Trudeau was trying, through the Charter, to impose his vision of the country on Quebec, directly amending the existing law of the province and subjecting future laws to control by a central institution, the Supreme Court of Canada, dominated by judges chosen by Ottawa alone, most from outside Quebec.

Given this diversity of interest, the dissenting premiers were initially very loosely allied, united more by their resentment of Ottawa's methods than by agreement on the substance. Over the winter of 1980–81, however, they tried to develop a common position, eventually releasing a counter-proposal in April 1981. That package would have permitted patriation, but with a different amending formula and no charter. Under that proposal, most amendments would have been subject to the "Vancouver formula," which required the approval of two-thirds of the provinces representing 50 per cent of the Canadian population (the formula was often referred to as the "seven and fifty formula" because with ten provinces in all, the approval of seven would be necessary). This meant that although large provinces might well carry more weight in the decision, no province would have a veto. Any province would, however, be able to opt out of amendments that transferred jurisdiction from the provinces to the federal government. The eight dissenting provinces all agreed to this package – even Quebec, which for the first time (and despite strong objections from the provincial Liberals), gave up its traditional claim to a veto over constitutional change. On Lévesque's insistence, the amending formula also provided for full financial compensation to provinces opting out. The PQ government had effectively decided to trade the veto for opting out, even though there were many amendments (especially concerning the reform of central institutions) from which opting out was impossible.[24]

Finally, two of the three major aboriginal organizations – the National Indian Brotherhood (NIB, representing status Indians and the forerunner of the Assembly of First Nations) and the Native Council of Canada (NCC, representing Métis and non-status Indians)[25] – decided to oppose the package, mounting a vigorous lobbying campaign among British MPs and launching an action in the British courts. When Ottawa's original proposal had been released in October 1980, all three organizations had rejected it because of the minimal recognition given aboriginal rights. Led by the Inuit, their representatives had lobbied Canadian politicians for something better, eventually securing the clause recognizing and affirming aboriginal and treaty rights. For a time it looked as if all three organizations would support the amended package. Later, however, both the NIB and the NCC (but not the Inuit) reconsidered their position and opposed the package despite the change. In one sense, the decisions of the NIB and NCC were based on a straightforward evaluation of the force of the clause, which was admittedly vague and of uncertain effect, but they also revealed the fundamental difficulty of accommodating aboriginal concerns within the process of constitutional renewal. This problem continued to haunt the treatment of aboriginal issues in subsequent negotiations.

There were three aspects to the problem. First, the timing of the two sets of questions – federalism and human rights on the one hand, aboriginal rights on the other – did not mesh well. Federalism and human rights had long been debated; positions were clear and reasonably well understood. The issue of aboriginal rights was new to most Canadians, including politicians. Many Canadians felt an obligation towards aboriginal peoples, but there was little understanding of what concrete form this obligation should take. Indeed, the demands of the aboriginal peoples themselves had evolved rapidly over the previous decade (and would continue to evolve over the next). This already-difficult situation was further complicated by differences in the structure of decision making in aboriginal and non-aboriginal communities. The non-aboriginal process consisted of closed-door negotiations among a very small number of governments, complemented by public hearings whose pace was largely controlled by government MPs. The aboriginal process was much more decentralized and more dependent on decision by consensus. Aboriginal leaders needed time to build that consensus. They could not take binding positions in private discussion; they had to refer initiatives to their constituencies.

The second aspect of the problem concerned the scope of aboriginal demands. The kinds of changes likely to make a real impact in aboriginal communities (the recognition of aboriginal governments that would act autonomously, wield significant powers, and possess adequate resources) required very detailed and complex negotiation. What specific powers should be exercised? Would they be exercised over aboriginal peoples only or also (for some purposes) over non-aboriginals? What mechanisms would regulate the boundary between aboriginal and non-aboriginal jurisdiction? At what level would aboriginal authority be exercised – Canada as a whole, confederacies of aboriginal peoples, individual peoples, bands, communities? Who would speak for aboriginal peoples – traditional governments (if so, which ones) or elected band councils? How would those governments be funded? All of these issues should have been resolved in a manner sensitive to the traditions of particular peoples, their geographical situation (in the North, for example, provincial status was an option), and the unique challenges faced by such groups as urban non-status Indians or the western Métis. The time-frame and structure of constitutional negotiations made this kind of detailed consideration inconceivable. The most that could be achieved were general statements of principle, to be developed later through negotiations or actions in the courts. To peoples as frustrated as the First Nations, such vague generalities were inevitably insufficient. Once again, it seemed that politicians were delaying serious consideration of aboriginal concerns.

Third and finally, the demonstrated lack of commitment among nonaboriginal politicians further undermined their ability to deal with these issues. If there had been more trust, aboriginal peoples may have been willing to accept the inclusion of a statement of principle in the constitution, which could then have served as a framework for further negotiations. But government resistance to claims for land and self-government gave aboriginal peoples little hope that attention to their issues would survive patriation. Some of the western Canadian provinces were patently hostile to aboriginal claims. The Trudeau government, which had (since the late 1970s) been receptive, showed by its actions that its commitment was limited: its original proposal provided scant recognition of aboriginal rights; during the committee hearings it resisted additional protection; and in later negotiations it did little to defend the clause the aboriginal peoples had secured. Given the record, the aboriginal peoples were understandably sceptical of promises for future action.

The federal Liberals might have withstood all opposition to the package and pressed on regardless had it not been for the decision of the Supreme Court of Canada in late September 1981. The previous fall, three of the dissenting provinces had asked their courts of appeal to rule on the constitutionality of Ottawa's unilateral action. The opinions in those courts had been divided, some judges ruling it constitutional, others unconstitutional.[26] Those judgments were then appealed to the Supreme Court of Canada. Following the Conservatives' filibuster of spring 1981, the federal government agreed to wait for that court's decision before proceeding to London. The Supreme Court's ruling altered the situation dramatically. A majority of the judges held that Ottawa's action did not violate constitutional law, but a majority also held that it violated constitutional convention – a set of rules recognized as binding, but unenforceable before the courts.[27] Although Ottawa's unilateral procedure was legal in a strict sense, it was unconstitutional in a broader sense. The legitimacy of its action undermined, Ottawa convoked another constitutional conference for early November.

After long and sometimes acrimonious debate, that conference did result in agreement – an agreement uniting the federal government and all provinces except Quebec. Its substance was worked out by several provincial delegations, not including Quebec, during what PQ politicians would later call "the night of the long knives." The first of its elements was the addition of the notwithstanding clause to the Charter of Rights. That clause would permit legislatures to remove a law from the application of some (but not all) of the provisions of the Charter by enacting a declaration that the law applied "notwithstanding" the Canadian Charter of Rights and Freedoms. The exemption would lapse automatically after five years but could be renewed as many times as the legislature wished. The notwithstanding clause was not promoted by Quebec. Indeed, by the time it was accepted, Quebec had already been left behind in the negotiations. British Columbia proposed it, with support from Alberta and Ontario. The clause represented a compromise between a fully entrenched charter of rights (under which courts would always have the last word) and the principles of democratic accountability espoused by premiers Blakeney and Lyon. Supporters of the clause believed that its use would be rare; governments would run a serious political risk if they invoked it without solid justification. But where it was used, it might have a beneficial effect, promoting a kind of dialogue between courts and legislatures over the content of fundamental rights and generating vigorous public debate over the appropriate balance between rights. Among the Charter provisions exempted from its reach were (at Ottawa's insistence) minority-language education rights – guarantees that were central to Trudeau's concept of the country and that directly overruled one aspect of Quebec's Bill 101. Under the November agreement, no government (not Quebec, nor any other government) would be able to opt out of those provisions.

The second element was a revised version of the Vancouver amending formula, the formula originally proposed by the Gang of Eight. At the beginning of the November conference, the federal government had continued to press for the Victoria formula, under which Quebec (and Ontario) would obtain a veto over constitutional change. It surrendered this position during the final bargaining. Under the new agreement, most amendments would require the approval of seven provinces representing 50 per cent of the population, with no province possessing a veto. Provinces would still be able to opt out of amendments transferring jurisdiction to Ottawa, but under the agreement there was (again at Ottawa's insistence) no provision for financial compensation. Ottawa remained implacably opposed to a general right to compensation, fearful that if opting out were costless, Quebec could use that method to achieve a piecemeal special status. In retrospect, Lévesque's decision to support the Vancouver formula had been fateful: not only had Quebec lost its claim to a veto, it had now lost the condition it had demanded when agreeing to the Vancouver formula, the right to opt out with full compensation.

From the point of view of the first ministers, these were the major changes accomplished at the November meeting, the two changes that made agreement possible. The agreement also included a number of other modifications, however, which seemed of marginal importance to governments but two of which provoked enormous controversy once the revised package was released to the public. One of these was the elimination of the clause affirming aboriginal rights. Some provinces, especially British Columbia and Alberta, had never liked that clause. They wanted its exclusion. During the private discussions of November 1981, the other governments acquiesced, a turn-around they found easy to rationalize, given the continued opposition of the NIB and NCC. The ministers misjudged the public mood, however. Both aboriginal and non-aboriginal Canadians branded the governments' decision as yet another betrayal of aboriginal peoples. The avalanche of criticism forced the governments to readopt the clause, although this time it was confined to "existing" aboriginal rights.[28]

The other controversial casualty of the November meeting was the super-guarantee of equality between the sexes. Over the winter of 1980–81, forceful presentations by women's organizations had, with considerable difficulty, secured this additional clause protecting gender equality. The clause could be read as suggesting that gender equality would be exempt from the interpretive standards and potential limitations affecting other Charter rights (even such rights as racial equality). The November agreement removed this super-guarantee, although gender equality remained protected by section 15 of the Charter, the general provision forbidding discrimination on the basis of such grounds as race or ethnic origin. This deletion provoked outrage from women's organizations and the public-at-large. Soon it too was back in the Charter.[29]

Thus, the constitutional package took its final form, or almost its final form. Continued hostility from the Quebec government and the possibility of a mobilization of opinion in that province against the package continued to worry Ottawa. The federal government proposed two additional changes, readily accepted by all provinces except Quebec, to make the package more palatable. First, the minority-language education guarantees were varied so that the right to English-language education in Quebec would depend on whether at least one of the child's parents had been educated in English in Canada. This clause (usually referred to as the "Canada clause") still overruled the provisions of Bill 101, but it was less generous than the previous version, which had extended the right to all whose mother tongue was English. Many within the PQ, including Lévesque himself, had favoured extending English education to those whose parents had been educated in English in Canada, but always by ordinary legislation of the Quebec National Assembly, never within a constitutional guarantee.[30] They continued to object to the imposition of the clause in the patriation package.

The second change modified the amending formula to provide some compensation to a province opting out of a transfer of jurisdiction to Ottawa. Compensation was limited to transfers in the fields of education and culture, however. These changes were not enough for the PQ. It repeatedly stressed its rejection of the package, and on 1 December 1981 the Quebec National Assembly passed (over Liberal members' opposition) a resolution formally dissenting from the November agreement. The resolution insisted on the following conditions for Quebec's adhesion:

1 recognition that the two founding peoples of Canada are equal and that Quebec "forms, within the Canadian federation, a society distinct in its language, culture and institutions," possessing "all the attributes of a distinct national community";
2 the revision of the amending formula to provide either a veto or full compensation for opting out;
3 the redrafting of the Charter of Rights to limit its scope and especially to provide for Quebec's consent to guarantees respecting the language of education in Quebec; and
4 guarantees of equalization and increased provincial control over natural resources.[31]

Quebec also launched another lawsuit, arguing that it had, by convention, a veto over constitutional change. The judgment of the Supreme Court of Canada was rendered on 6 December 1982, after the new constitution had entered into force. It held that no such convention existed. Quebec's position had not been helped by the PQ's willingness to abandon the veto during negotiations.[32]

The two houses of the Canadian Parliament approved the package in December 1981. The following March, the United Kingdom passed it into law. On 17 April 1982 the new constitution (the Constitution Act, 1982, supplementing, but not replacing, the British North America Act, now renamed the Constitution Act, 1867) was proclaimed in force as the supreme law of Canada. On 23 June 1982 the Quebec legislature, in continued protest against the process of patriation, adopted its own law invoking the notwithstanding clause for all existing legislation.[33] From that time until the Bourassa Liberals changed the practice, each Quebec law contained a provision exercising the notwithstanding clause, no matter what the law's subject.

The patriation of the constitution with the Charter of Rights changed the structure of constitutional debate in Canada. The new Charter became, as Trudeau intended, a focus of national allegiance outside Quebec.[34] In part this was due to the powerful image of a single citizenship, a single body of rights, applicable from coast to coast, but it was also due to the process by which the Charter had taken shape. During the discussion in the joint Senate—House of Commons committee, the debate on the floor of the House of Commons, and the controversy following the November agreement, groups of Canadians had made the Charter their own, pressing their demands and vigorously defending provisions they considered the guarantee of their place within Canadian society. Nowhere was this more true than in the women's movement. The fight for section 28, the super-guarantee of gender equality, was considered a triumph for Canadian women, one that consolidated a tendency to pursue women's rights by constitutional means. The attempt to achieve gender equality through litigation became one of the principal objectives of women's organizational activity during the next few years.[35]

Aboriginal peoples accepted the new constitution with less enthusiasm, and with considerable bitterness over the cavalier fashion in which governments had dealt with their rights. As finally adopted, the package included a commitment to further discussion of native concerns. The aboriginal organizations would strongly press their demands for self-government at those conferences.

The greatest dissatisfaction existed in Quebec, however. Within the province, each side – those that rejected the package and those that supported it – claimed to speak for the majority of Quebecers. Both pointed to indicators of public opinion supporting their position, and perhaps surprisingly, both were probably right. The constitutional package, especially the Charter, carried two messages to Quebecers. The first – the protection of individual rights against state power – Quebecers generally agreed with. They were just as devoted to individual rights as were other Canadians (although they defined the content of those rights differently; many doubted, for example, whether all aspects of language and culture should be considered matters of individual right). The second message, however, was widely rejected. That was the use of the constitutional process and Charter to entrench Trudeau's concept of the country, a concept in which any claim to a distinctive role for Quebec was denied, Quebec was required to be a province just like the others, and all governments (including Quebec) would have to treat English and French in precisely the same way throughout the country, even if francophone Quebecers knew that in practice French would always face more challenges in the rest of Canada than English faced within the province. Francophone Quebecers welcomed a charter of rights, but most did not welcome the attempt to deny a distinctive cultural role for Quebec. For many, this smacked of a denial of Quebec's historic character, an attempt to put Quebec in its place.

The sense of distaste and disenchantment was reinforced by the way in which the constitution had been patriated – by agreement of all but Quebec. As a result of Ottawa's efforts, Quebec would now be bound by a constitutional order to which it had not consented, even though Quebec politicians (including Pierre Trudeau and Jean Chrétien) had consistently argued that Quebec should have a veto over constitutional change. The PQ tried to sharpen this broader grievance into an almost personal betrayal through the myth of "the night of the long knives." Quebec, they argued, had been stabbed in the back during the November conference when the other dissenting provinces had developed the final deal late at night, without inviting or informing Quebec. Like many myths, it had its kernel of truth: the provincial spokesmen had kept their former ally out of those late-night discussions, no doubt because they knew the PQ could never agree to what they were doing. But this was hardly as duplicitous as was later suggested. Many of the dissenting premiers had already made clear, in open conference, their willingness to compromise in ways Quebec would not accept. Lévesque himself had broken ranks by agreeing to fight a referendum on patriation. And the final deal was not prepared in secret; the dissenting provinces' proposal was presented in the next day's sessions in Quebec's presence, amended at the table, and agreed to there.[36] But even if the image of secret betrayal was exaggerated, there is still no doubt that the other provinces had decided they could make a constitution without Quebec's consent. In that sense, they had betrayed Quebec; they had been willing to walk away from that province, leaving it isolated.

Many have defended patriation by arguing that the Lévesque government, committed to Quebec's secession, would never have agreed to any proposal compatible with Canada's continued existence. It is probably true that agreement would have been impossible, not merely because the PQ was intent on frustrating the process (though this may have been the case), but because the PQ was, paradoxically, poorly placed to advance Quebec's traditional concerns. Lévesque was undoubtedly sincere when he said he would play the constitutional game in good faith, but successful negotiations (especially over the terms of a constitution) require more than honesty and fair dealing. They require that all parties perceive that their partners have some commitment to the relationship, a commitment that justifies the concessions and accommodations necessary to find consensus. This kind of negotiation is not just about power or some fortuitous coalescence of all parties' initial opinions. It is about working out an agreeable result through persuasion, and in order to persuade, the parties have to be able to discuss proposals in terms of some viable sense of the whole. They have to be able to justify their positions in a way that has some appeal for their partners. Otherwise, they will come across as little more than spokespersons for a narrow self-interest, an interest other parties will have little incentive to accommodate.

That was the trouble with the PQ's position. The PQ had already denied its commitment to the whole. It had made clear that it was willing to talk now, but that its ultimate goal remained the breakup of Canada. In that context, its arguments were always and inevitably weak. It could give its assent to proposals that other provinces had advanced (proposals on which other provinces had carried the burden of justification), but it had disabled itself from making convincing arguments of its own, including arguments on matters of particular concern to Quebec. All its demands (including those consistent with the positions of federalist parties in Quebec) were set against the backdrop of its commitment to step-by-step separation from Canada. Its descriptions of Quebec's requirements and of public opinion in the province were automatically suspect. The Lévesque government had chosen as its political goal a break with the rest of Canada. That choice, by denying a sense of common cause with other Canadian governments, fatally undermined the PQ's ability to argue for positions that many within Quebec, including many federalists, believed were necessary.

The great difficulty in achieving agreement did not mean, however, that patriation should have occurred without Quebec – or at least that it should have occurred in the way it did. There are some successes that are more costly than failures. Patriation in these circumstances may have been one. And even if obtaining a charter of rights was worth proceeding without Quebec's consent, Ottawa should have resisted the temptation to constitutionalize its vision of the country, to insist on sending the second message to Quebec. It should have, for example, made minority education rights subject to a right of Quebec to opt in. Perhaps most importantly, if Ottawa truly could not accept full financial compensation for provinces rejecting future amendments, it should have refused patriation without a veto for Quebec.

Constitutional politics always involves a balance between partisan political manoeuvring and the construction of a stable, long-term commitment to a new national consensus. Sometimes the building of consensus requires that partisanship be restrained so that many more citizens can see their vision reflected in the country's structure. Democratic constitutions, governing a diverse citizenry holding different conceptions of their country, should make room for a plurality of visions and should allow space for continuing debate over how those visions can be reconciled.[37] In 1982 Ottawa and the premiers got the balance wrong. Outmanoeuvring and finally marginalizing Lévesque in the final negotiations, the federal government took full advantage of its victory. At the time this seemed justified, given the extent of Lévesque's defeat and the increasing tendency to cast the question as a straight-out choice between two implacably opposed alternatives, each identified with a single individual: Trudeau's vision of Quebec within Canada, Lévesque's vision of an independent Quebec.[38] The polarization, the personalization, of the dispute obscured the fact that many Quebecers (probably the majority) sided with neither position, at least not in all its purity. They remained committed to Canada, but within a framework that could take into account Quebec's distinctive character. The entrenchment of Trudeau's vision not only excluded the separatists' vision of the country, it also undermined those federalists who retained an allegiance to Quebec as the unique homeland of French culture within Canada.

5 After Patriation:
Aboriginal Rights, Meech Lake, and Charlottetown, 1982–1992

The patriation of the constitution initiated a new phase of constitutional debate in Canada, a phase in which discussion (especially at the elite level) seemed to be expanded, not contracted. Now, however, preoccupation with the constitution took different forms.

Many Canadians, especially academics and advocacy groups, turned their attention to the practical meaning of Canada's new constitution, especially the abstract language of the rights guaranteed in the Charter. Did "freedom of association" include the right to strike, the right to bargain collectively, or perhaps the right to refuse to pay union dues? What precisely did the guarantee of "equality" mean? What could it accomplish, in practical terms, for women, visible minorities, the poor? The language of the Charter became the preferred language of social advocacy. Groups representing different segments of Canadian society explored the Charter's potential for advancing their ends, sometimes sponsoring test cases before the courts.

Other Canadians were concerned with what was omitted, rather than included, in the patriation package. The patriation process had generated extensive debate on a broad variety of questions, several of which remained on the table. A number of these became the subject of additional consideration in the years following patriation. Senate reform, for example, was studied by a joint Senate and House of Commons committee in 1983 and 1984, resulting in a recommendation for an elected Senate, weighted towards the smaller provinces (each province would not, however, have an equal number of representatives), with power to delay federal laws with which it disagreed.[1] The proposal did not lead to any immediate action, however. Many of the first ministers were unwilling to embark so soon on another major cycle of amendments, there was little consensus on the precise content of Senate reform, and in the immediate aftermath of patriation, changing the Senate was not a major priority of any government. Enthusiasm for the idea, however, gradually increased throughout the 1980s, especially in Alberta.

ABORIGINAL RIGHTS[2]

There was one issue, however, on which there was a serious attempt to find a solution: aboriginal rights. During patriation, the National Indian Brotherhood and the Native Council of Canada had objected to the clause recognizing aboriginal rights on the grounds that it was vague, qualified by the term "existing," and of uncertain legal effect. Indeed, the patriation package itself acknowledged the vagueness of the clause. Section 37 of the new constitution required that the first ministers meet within one year of the constitution's proclamation, with representatives of the aboriginal peoples participating, to define precisely what was included within aboriginal rights. This expanded definition would then be written into the constitution.[3]

That conference was held in March 1983. It sketched out the Native agenda for future discussion, including elaborating the content of aboriginal rights, entrenching self-government, securing adequate financial resources for aboriginal governments, obtaining a land base for the Métis, reforming the amending formula to permit Ottawa to act alone to create new provinces in the territories, and entrenching aboriginal participation in the process of constitutional reform. No substantive decisions were taken on most of these matters, but following the 1983 meeting a constitutional amendment was adopted to entrench present or future land-claims agreements, to guarantee gender equality in the enjoyment of aboriginal and treaty rights, and to require at least two more conferences before 1987 dealing with aboriginal rights.[4] Working groups were established to study the remaining issues in detail.

Three conferences followed over the next four years. Most of the discussions were preoccupied with aboriginal self-government, although other difficult issues were also discussed. Self-government had clearly become the first priority of the aboriginal peoples. They pressed the issue at each conference, eventually proposing a constitutional amendment backed by all the major aboriginal organizations. There was hesitant support for some form of self-government among many first ministers as well, and this support increased with each conference. In October 1983 a special committee of the House of Commons delivered a report arguing that Ottawa should adopt aboriginal self-government as its goal.[5] The following spring, immediately before the 1984 First Ministers Conference, Ottawa announced that it would pursue some form of aboriginal self-government. During the conference, it proposed an amendment addressing the issue. Manitoba, Ontario, and New Brunswick supported the federal stand. By 1987, two more provinces (Nova Scotia and Prince Edward Island) had also come on side.

These five provinces were not enough, however, and in the end the talks collapsed. One crucial reason was the consistent opposition of the Social Credit and Conservative governments of the western provinces to any expansion in aboriginal rights. Constitutional amendment required the support of seven provinces representing 50 per cent of the Canadian population. In 1987 four provinces (BC, Alberta, Saskatchewan, and Newfoundland) continued to reject Ottawa's proposal. Quebec, although it did not oppose the amendment, refused to express any opinion because of its protest against the patriation of the constitution over its objections.

Provincial resistance to aboriginal rights was only part of the reason for failure, for even though five provinces and Ottawa had agreed on an amendment, the aboriginal organizations themselves opposed the federal plan. In the absence of aboriginal consent, the first ministers would not have proceeded even if they had achieved the agreement of seven provinces. The dispute between the aboriginal organizations and the governments favouring the federal plan concerned the precise nature of the proposals, rather than the general principle of self-government. Both sides acknowledged that any practical scheme for self-government would take time to achieve. The issues were simply too complex for quick resolution, given the number of peoples involved, the uncertainty over what powers should be exercised at what levels, and the drastic variation in the traditions of and the financial resources available to the different groups. The proposals supported by the first ministers all involved, then, two steps: an immediate amendment recognizing, in principle, the right to self-government, to be followed by negotiations between Ottawa, the aboriginal group, and the relevant province to specify the content of that right – the structure of the self-governing institutions, their powers, their resources.

This was not enough for the aboriginal representatives. They wanted to achieve, as far as possible, an immediate, effective right of self-government. They knew that this could not possibly mean establishing at once a fully developed system of aboriginal governments. They, like the first ministers, were unable to propose detailed structures at this time; there simply wasn't sufficient consensus over what those structures should be. Thus, their proposals, like those of the first ministers, provided for future negotiations. They wanted, however, to make sure that any right of self-government was more than a mere declaration of principle. They wanted it to be enforceable before the courts, so that if they didn't like the way negotiations were going, they could opt out, trying to do better in the courts. They strongly resisted, then, any language suggesting that the content of self-government depended on the success of the subsequent negotiations. They argued that self-government should be considered part of the already-existing (and already-enforceable) "aboriginal rights," not a separate category, newly recognized and not yet defined. They also proposed constitutional provisions dealing with the finances of aboriginal governments, hoping that these provisions (though vague) might be used in the courts to force Ottawa to fund aboriginal organizations. They argued, too, that their right to self-government should be recognized as "inherent." This meant, at a minimum, that self-government should be seen as flowing from their very identity as peoples; it would not be something granted by superior authority, their governments merely performing a limited range of functions delegated by Ottawa or the provinces. Aboriginal governments would be political agents in their own right, having their own autonomous powers, more analogous to the provincial or federal governments than to municipalities, school boards, or the existing Indian band councils.

The first ministers balked at these demands. They were unwilling to establish another order of government without knowing what powers it would exercise or who would exercise them. The only acceptable way of establishing the new governments, they believed, was through negotiations to determine their precise scope and design. Reliance on the courts would be very uncertain and perhaps even futile, since the institutional issues would be so complex, the content of the right so vague, as to frustrate any judicial attempt to do anything more than state general principles. Indeed, recourse to the courts might delay negotiations by preserving the false hope of obtaining perfect justice by judicial decision.

The first ministers were also distrustful of the notion of an inherent right. Most accepted that the justification for aboriginal self-government lay in the cultural autonomy and historical cohesion of aboriginal societies, not on the grace of the provincial or federal governments. Most (but not all) also came to accept that the governments resulting from the negotiations should be enshrined in the constitution. The aboriginal governments should, in other words, have their own source of authority, in no way subordinate to other levels of government. In this sense, then, the first ministers could live with the language of inherent right, but they were worried that the concept might be taken further, that it might be used to justify attempts by aboriginal peoples to define the scope of self-government unilaterally, or even to deny Canadian sovereignty over aboriginal lands.

In the end, then, the conferences failed to achieve any amendment dealing with self-government. In large measure, this was due to the consistent opposition of some of the provinces to any expansion in aboriginal rights. Even if those provinces had agreed, however, there remained the fundamental difference between the proposals of the aboriginal organizations and each of the successive federal plans: the aboriginal peoples argued for a right of self-government enshrined in the constitution and enforceable now; the first ministers were willing to establish the principle of self-government and a framework for negotiation, but not more.

MEECH LAKE[6]

One of the contributing factors to the conferences' failure had been Quebec's abstention from constitutional negotiations. Any amendment would need the active support of at least seven provinces; Quebec's refusal to participate therefore had the same effect as a "no" vote. Indeed, Quebec had remained aloof from constitutional discussions ever since patriation in 1982. It claimed that patriation had been illegitimate because it had occurred over Quebec's objections – the objections, in other words, of the only province with a French-speaking majority. It refused to take part in any further discussions until its concerns were addressed, its consent to patriation secured.

This did not mean Quebecers were pushing for a quick end to the province's isolation in the months following patriation. On the contrary, most wanted to ignore the national question and concentrate on the more prosaic concerns of earning a living and building a career. They had lived through the intense, exhausting Quebec Referendum debate of 1980, a debate that had literally divided families. Most emerged with a longing for normalcy, for some measure of social cohesion. This was evident in the re-election of the Parti Québécois government in 1981, eleven months after the PQ's defeat in the referendum. It is true that one group of referendum victors (chiefly federal Liberals) were determined to exploit their victory by patriating the constitution in a way that would subject Quebec nationalism to a single-minded focus on Canada. But most Quebecers, even supporters of the "No," did not see the referendum result in those terms. They had argued for a new constitutional arrangement that would recognize their *dual* loyalties, to Quebec and to Canada. The drama of the referendum, the demoralization of the *indépendantiste* cause, and the quick conclusion of a patriation deal that had little to do with their traditional concerns left most Quebecers with no taste for further constitutional talk. They just wanted to get on with their lives, despite (or perhaps because of) their lingering disappointment with the terms of patriation. This tendency at the popular level was reinforced at the governmental level by the fact that the Parti Québécois, still the government of Quebec, was deeply wounded by the process of patriation. Before patriation they had resisted compromise with the rest of Canada. After patriation compromise was impossible.

In the mid-1980s, however, circumstances began to change, at least at the governmental level. In December 1985 the provincial Liberals returned to power under Robert Bourassa. It soon became clear that Bourassa was willing to reconcile Quebec to the new constitutional order if that order were changed to respond to some of Quebec's complaints. Moreover, the reconciliation could occur now, with a new and more receptive Conservative government in Ottawa and comparative calm in Quebec. Bourassa's justice minister, Gil Rémillard, stated Quebec's position at a conference in Mont Gabriel, Quebec, in May 1986. Five conditions would have to be met:

1 the express recognition of Quebec as a distinct society;
2 increased powers over immigration;
3 limitation of the federal spending power;
4 recognition of a veto over constitutional amendments; and
5 the participation of Quebec in the nomination of Supreme Court justices.[7]

On this basis the first ministers agreed to negotiate. On 30 April 1987, one year after the Mont Gabriel speech and one month after the failure of the last conference on aboriginal rights, the first ministers, meeting at the federal government's retreat at Meech Lake, agreed on the general terms of a settlement.[8] Over the course of the next month, civil servants drafted a set of constitutional amendments based on those terms. In June the first ministers met again in Ottawa, this time at the government's Langevin Block. There, at a meeting extending long into the night, they discussed the draft amendments, agreed on certain revisions, and put their signatures to the proposal as a whole. The text of the Meech Lake Accord was complete. To come into force, it would have to be approved by Parliament and the legislatures of all provinces.[9] Thus began the process of ratification that, three years later, would end in such disarray.

The Terms of Meech Lake[10]

The contents of the Meech Lake Accord are worth examining in some detail, not only because they are essential to understanding Meech Lake itself, but also because they served to crystallize positions in the constitutional debate, defining arguments still with us today.

DISTINCT SOCIETY. The accord's most prominent provision was the distinct society clause. That clause read:

The Constitution of Canada shall be interpreted in a manner consistent with
(a) the recognition that the existence of French-speaking Canadians, centred in Quebec but also present elsewhere in Canada, and English-speaking Canadians, concentrated outside Quebec but also present in Quebec, constitutes a fundamental characteristic of Canada; and
(b) the recognition that Quebec constitutes within Canada a distinct society.

The clause then went on to affirm the role of all federal and provincial governments in preserving French- and English-speaking linguistic groups across the country, and of Quebec in preserving and promoting its distinct society.[11]

A few things are important to an understanding of this clause. First, it was an interpretive clause. It did not directly confer any rights or powers; rather, it instructed the courts to keep in mind French and English linguistic minorities as well as the distinct character of Quebec when interpreting other provisions in the constitution. Courts always have some leeway when interpreting a legal document. Interpretive clauses tell them that they should exercise that leeway in a manner sensitive to particular concerns.

Because the influence of such an interpretive clause is subtle, colouring the very process of interpretation, it is difficult to say precisely how the distinct society clause would have applied to any specific set of facts. In the Meech Lake debate, this lack of certainty caused many to wonder whether the clause could be used to undermine anglophone rights in Quebec. Some limits were clear from the wording of the clause itself. As an interpretive provision, it could not be bluntly used to set aside constitutional rights. It sketched the backdrop against which those rights would be interpreted; the rights themselves would still have to be given effect. Moreover, the Meech Lake Accord spoke directly to the status of the English-speaking community in Quebec. Its reference to linguistic minorities as a "fundamental characteristic" of Canada imposed an obligation on Quebec (and on every other government) to preserve those minorities. A court applying the clause would have to balance Quebec's defence of its own identity against Quebec's obligation to preserve the English-speaking community. In the last analysis, the precise nature of that balance would be determined by the courts (ultimately, the Supreme Court of Canada), not by any government.

Within these constraints, however, the clause would have had an effect. It would not have been purely symbolic, as some Meech supporters claimed. An example might clarify its impact. Quebec's language law (Bill 101) requires businesses with more than fifty employees to create programs extending the use of French in their operations.[12] This was a response to the historic dominance of English in many enterprises, especially large companies. Employers often required their employees to work in English, even when the majority of the workforce was French-speaking. Bill 101's provisions regarding the language of work did not prohibit the use of other languages, and they permitted special treatment of long-service employees, of industries having cultural content linked to other linguistic groups, and of companies with operations extending outside Quebec.

Suppose these provisions were challenged on the grounds that they contravened the guarantee of equality in the Charter. If the court began with the view that equality means that the law must treat all cultures identically – or that language should be a matter of unconstrained individual choice (and this is certainly the opinion of some) – then the Quebec provisions would violate the guarantee. They would limit unilingual anglophones' opportunities for advancement without imposing the same limits on francophones. But if the court began by recognizing that Quebec has a legitimate role to play in the promotion of the French language, the mix of considerations would change. This might produce a different outcome, especially considering the phased-in nature of the programs, the protection for existing employees, the lack of exclusion of other languages, and people's ability to acquire a second language with time. Given these factors, the court might find the different treatment to be consistent with equality. On the North American continent, the economic pressure to speak English is substantial. The greater challenges faced by individuals whose language is French justify measures to redress the imbalance. The provisions on language of work do not create inequality; they represent a carefully tailored attempt to compensate for existing inequality. If the difference in treatment does amount to inequality, that inequality is justified as a reasonable limit in a free and democratic society.[13]

The distinct society clause would, then, have had an effect on the interpretation of the constitution, although that effect would have been subtle. This did not, however, account for the significance of the clause within francophone Quebec. For most Quebecers, the clause was important not so much for its practical effect as for its symbolic value, the formal recognition that Quebec had, within Canada, its own distinct identity and that the government of Quebec had a special responsibility for allowing that identity to flourish. It confirmed, within the constitution itself, Quebec's role as the principal homeland of the French Canadian language and culture.[14] It rejected the second message of the 1982 patriation; Quebec would not be denied a cultural vocation and its own sense of allegiance. Quebecers would not be forced to choose between their identities as Quebecers and their identities as Canadians. They could be both. For many Quebecers, then, the distinct society clause would have removed the lingering distaste left by patriation. They would have been able to accept Canada, as the phrase went, with honour and enthusiasm.

The importance of its symbolism did not mean that the practical effects of the clause were irrelevant, that the clause would have had the same impact in Quebec if (as some suggested) it had been reduced to a "mere symbol." Quebecers did not want simply to be told they were distinct; they wanted their unique character to be treated as an essential element of the constitution. The interpretive nature of the distinct society clause accomplished this admirably, by expressly recognizing that Quebec's identity was relevant to Canada's constitutional order generally. The kind of recognition most Quebecers wanted, the kind of symbol that would have undone the disappointment of 1982, required that the clause have effect, however subtle.[15]

DIVISION OF POWERS.   From the mid-1960s on, successive governments in Quebec had argued for a decentralization of powers from Ottawa to the provinces. They had argued, for example, for greater authority over communications, family law, and international relations, and especially for the restriction of the federal spending power. The amendments of 1982 had contained only one provision directly addressing these questions, and this was an amendment dealing with the regulation and taxation of natural resources, requested chiefly by the western provinces. Meech Lake contained three provisions that could potentially affect the division of powers.

The first was the distinct society clause itself. It applied to the entire constitution, not just the Charter of Rights. It might have been used, then, to interpret the division of powers. Almost certainly, however, its impact would have been very limited in this respect. It remained an interpretive clause, and the well-elaborated nature of the object of interpretation – the attribution of powers to the federal and provincial levels of government – left little room for major shifts in emphasis. Moreover, the distinct society clause expressly preserved the existing scope of federal authority. Thus, even if the clause would have increased Quebec's authority, it would not have reduced federal power. And if there had been a conflict between federal and provincial legislation, the general rule of federal paramountcy would have applied: the federal law would have prevailed.

The second provision dealt with immigration. Under Canada's present constitution, immigration is a concurrent field; both Ottawa and the provinces can make laws in the area.[16] Not all provinces exercise these powers, but for those that do, federal-provincial agreements tend to coordinate the exercise of the joint authority. Quebec has been the most active in the field, establishing programs for the reception and adaptation of immigrants and participating in immigrant selection. It has had a special interest in the area because of its wish to encourage French-speaking immigrants and to ensure that non-francophone immigrants are given the services necessary to learn French. Since 1971, it has entered into a series of agreements with Ottawa. The Meech Lake Accord would have given these agreements (and similar accords with other provinces) constitutional status, so that in general they could only have been changed with the approval of Ottawa and the province concerned. Ottawa would, however, have retained the authority to establish "national standards and objectives" for immigration, without the consent of the provinces.[17]

The third and most important provision affecting the division of powers was a section limiting the use of the federal spending power. Over the years, Ottawa had simply spent money to establish programs in areas that normally would have been within exclusive provincial jurisdiction. These included the Canadian Mortgage and Housing Corporation's housing subsidies and federal support for hospitals, universities, social welfare payments, and medicare.

Quebec had traditionally objected to the strong federal role in these fields, arguing that these federal programs gave Ottawa a substantial say in areas that the constitution had reserved to the provinces. Quebec had often argued that Ottawa should withdraw, transferring the resources to the provinces so that they could run the programs. In fact, it had long been argued that this exercise of the spending power was unconstitutional because of its effect on the division of powers. There had never been a clear decision on the spending power's validity, however.[18]

The Meech Lake Accord would have given the provinces a right to opt out of future spending-power programs. Any province that exercised this option would have received compensation. The province would not have had to bear, then, the double burden of paying the same level of taxes to Ottawa while paying for its own program at home. In order to receive this compensation, the province would have had to establish its own program, compatible with the national objectives.[19]

It is important to note the limited scope of this provision. It only applied to programs within exclusive provincial jurisdiction. Ottawa could still do whatever it wanted in areas of federal or concurrent jurisdiction. The provision only governed one aspect of the spending power: shared-cost programs, in which both Ottawa and the provinces contributed funds. Other spending-power programs (family allowances, for example, in which Ottawa paid money directly to individuals) would not have been affected. Moreover, it would have been limited to *future* programs; it would not have affected such existing programs as medicare or federal contributions to welfare.[20]

Nevertheless, within its scope the provision was a significant measure. It would have applied, for example, to the proposal for a national program of subsidized day-care then under active discussion. Meech Lake would not have prohibited that scheme. Ottawa could have proceeded with its plans, just as it could have done prior to Meech Lake, but any province that wanted to run its own program would have been able to opt out of the federal plan, receiving compensation from Ottawa if the provincial plan met the national program's objectives. At the least, the right to opt out would have resulted in extensive negotiations between the provinces and Ottawa over the shape of any proposed program. It might have resulted in the adoption of separate but coordinated programs, on the model of the present Canada and Quebec pension plans. Some opponents of Meech argued that it might even have prevented the creation of some programs if the richer provinces decided to opt out, depriving the national program of those provinces' financial resources.

AMENDING FORMULA.   Meech Lake also addressed Quebec's concerns with the amending formula. It did so in two ways.

First, Meech would have given Quebec a veto over certain constitutional amendments. It did this by giving *all* provinces a veto over these items. Changes to these matters would have required the unanimous consent of Ottawa and the provinces. This was the most widely misunderstood provision of the Meech Lake Accord. Many Canadians believed Meech would have required unanimity for all future amendments. This was patently not the case. The new formula only applied to a limited and precisely defined set of amendments. The 1982 constitution already required unanimity for amendments to certain key institutions: the Queen and her representatives; the minimum number of members of the House of Commons from each province; certain language rights; the composition of the Supreme Court of Canada; and the amending formula.[21] Meech would have added six more items to that list. Three were uncontroversial: amendments to the Supreme Court of Canada (some of which were already subject to unanimity in the 1982 constitution); changes to the proportion of members of the House of Commons elected from each province; and the extension of existing provinces into the Northwest and Yukon territories. Three, however, were very controversial. Two of these concerned changes to the Senate. After Meech, any significant change to the Senate would have required unanimity. Finally, unanimity would have been required for the creation of new provinces. The formula for all other amendments (those recognizing a right to aboriginal self-government, changing the division of powers, or amending the Charter of Rights, for example) remained the same, still subject to the requirements of 1982.[22]

The second change concerned compensation for amendments transferring powers from the provinces to Ottawa. As we saw above, in the negotiations preceding patriation the Lévesque government had abandoned its claim to a full veto, accepting instead a right to opt out of amendments that transferred powers to Ottawa, with full compensation. At the November 1981 First Ministers Conference, by agreement of all the premiers except Lévesque, the right to compensation was deleted. It was partially restored in the final package, but only for amendments concerning culture or education. This meant that Quebec was left without a veto and without compensation. Meech Lake would have redressed this grievance, restoring the formula agreed to by Quebec: any province that opted out of a centralizing amendment – of whatever kind – would have received compensation.[23]

CENTRAL INSTITUTIONS. Finally, Meech Lake contained a number of provisions dealing with central institutions. It would have inserted into the constitution five brief sections specifying the existence and structure of the Supreme Court of Canada. At present, the Supreme Court of Canada is governed by an ordinary law of Parliament. This is clearly inadequate, given the court's role in policing the entire constitution, including the division of powers. There is broad agreement that the court should be constitutionalized. Meech would have done this, confirming the court's present structure with one significant change. Judges had been (and still are) appointed, in practice, by the federal prime minister acting alone. Meech would have provided for a provincial role in this process: the provincial premiers would submit lists of candidates to the prime minister, who would then appoint one of the persons on those lists.[24]

The debate over the accord focused attention on another aspect of the Supreme Court. The Meech amendments would have required that three of the court's nine judges come from Quebec.[25] This had been the practice since 1949, when the court had been increased from seven to nine judges. Indeed, there had been the same proportion of Quebec judges at the time of the court's foundation in 1875; then, two of the court's six judges were appointed from Quebec. During the Meech debate, some people criticized this practice because it now gives Quebec more judges than justified by its population. The practice has, however, long been accepted as necessary, given the distinctive character of the private law of Quebec. If there were fewer than three from Quebec, cases arising under Quebec's private law would have to be decided by a panel of judges the majority of whom would be untrained in the principles of Quebec civil law.

Meech Lake also spoke to another central institution: First Ministers Conferences. It contained two provisions on this subject. First, it would have required a First Ministers Conference on the economy each year. Second, it would have required annual conferences on the constitution. The constitutional conferences were intended to address, in part, issues not covered in Meech, with two singled out for immediate attention: Senate reform and jurisdiction over fisheries. In order to show a real commitment to Senate reform, Meech specified that until a new Senate was achieved, senators would be appointed from lists of candidates proposed by the provinces, not by the federal prime minister alone (as is now the case). There was one notable omission from the list of matters to be discussed at future conferences: aboriginal rights. Meech did, however, provide for the discussion of "other matters."[26]

That was the content of Meech Lake. At first, it seemed to have broad public support. Polls revealed that shortly after the accord was concluded, 56 per cent of Canadians approved of it, and of course, the prime minister and premiers of every Canadian province had signed it. Over the next three years, however, public opinion (outside Quebec) turned decisively against the accord. By May 1990, one month before the final date for ratification by provincial legislatures, only 25 per cent of Canadians (19 per cent outside Quebec) still supported the package.[27] Some provinces were willing to ratify the accord despite public opposition: by 23 June, eight had ratified, Manitoba had declared its intention to approve, and Newfoundland had agreed to vote on the question (although it had previously rescinded its initial approval of the accord). But it was clear that at least some still opposed the package on its merits. When Manitoba failed to ratify by the deadline (because of procedural obstruction by an aboriginal member of the legislature), Newfoundland refused to hold its vote and the Meech Lake Accord collapsed.

The Reasons for Meech Lake's Failure

What was the reason for the failure? In the aftermath of Meech, many commentators put forward what they took to be "the real reason," but this invariably differed from commentator to commentator. In truth, there were a host of reasons, not always consistent with each other, some held by members of one party, some by another, some carrying weight in one section of the country, others in another. I will not attempt to recount all the events leading to Meech's downfall or to trace the complex evolution of the parties' positions through time.[28] Instead, I will concentrate on describing the range of reasons for opposing Meech, suggesting how these related to ideas of nation, Canada, and freedom, for it was in the objections to Meech that the constitutional themes of the past thirty years intersected most dramatically with conceptions of nation and identity. My focus is on arguments important in the popular debate, not on the highly specialized comments of constitutional lawyers.

THE DISTINCT SOCIETY CLAUSE AND INDIVIDUAL RIGHTS. Many of the criticisms focused on the distinct society clause. One of the most insistent of these – and one of the first to emerge in the wake of the Meech Lake agreement – concerned the effect of the clause on the Charter of Rights. The gist of this argument was that with the clause Quebec would be able to restrict individual rights in the interest of a culturally defined collectivity. The distinct society clause would, some said, create a "hierarchy of rights" in which the cultural rights of Quebec would take precedence over all others. Some critics also attacked the drafting of the clause, in particular the lack of a precise definition for "distinct society." Quebec would be able to take the clause and run, they said, giving it any meaning it wished (as indeed PQ leader Jacques Parizeau threatened to do, measuring his comments to maximize anglophone anxiety). But comments on drafting were subsidiary to the main point: taking culture into account when interpreting the Charter would, many believed, inevitably imperil individual rights.

There were a number of variants of this argument, each with its own character. Some were based on a defence of the text of the Charter against any encroachment by other interests. Alan Cairns has noted that following the Charter's adoption, some advocacy groups – often as a result of the patriation process itself – took an almost proprietary interest in rights of concern to them.[29] The rights assumed an enormous significance. They were taken as the recognition that the group's members were full participants in Canadian society. They guaranteed members' equality. Those groups resisted any attempt (as they saw it) to whittle away that recognition or undermine that equality, no matter how remote the possibility of prejudice might be. So, for example, some groups for the disabled opposed Meech Lake on the grounds that it would, in their view, create a hierarchy of rights, in which their equality would rank lower than the collective rights of Quebec – difficult though it might be to imagine any case in which Quebec's distinctiveness would justify constraints on persons with disabilities.

The strongest advocates of this kind of Charter defence were the representatives of the women's movement, or, more precisely, of the women's movement in English-speaking Canada, for feminists in Quebec did not oppose the distinct society clause. The protection of gender equality in the 1982 constitution had special significance for many Canadian feminists. The fight to achieve section 28 – the super-guarantee of gender equality – had galvanized them. Canadian women had won what their American counterparts had failed to achieve – an "Equal Rights Amendment" for women. And they had done so over the indifference or outright hostility of male politicians.

Now, however, because of Meech Lake, this achievement was in danger, many anglophone feminists believed. One of the reasons for insisting on section 28, back in 1981, had been the worry that cultural differences might be used to undermine women's equality. Concern had focused on two possibilities. First, at that time, the determination of status under the Indian Act still depended in part on a person's gender. Proposals for eliminating this inequality had been blocked by some Indian bands on the grounds that they would have undermined the viability of aboriginal communities. Canadian feminists wanted to make sure that these kinds of arguments could not be used to defeat gender equality under the Charter. Second, the 1982 constitution contained a clause directing the courts to interpret the Charter "in a manner consistent with the preservation and enhancement of the multicultural heritage of Canadians." Feminists were concerned that this might be used to shield cultural practices oppressive to women. Thus, the super-guarantee in section 28 made clear that gender equality prevailed over all other considerations.[30]

In the eyes of many feminists outside Quebec, Meech Lake would have reintroduced the kind of cultural variables that section 28 had sought to exclude. English-speaking women's groups argued that the possibility of oppression was real, especially given Quebec's family policy, which offered incentives (additional family allowances; special payments upon the birth of children; preferential mortgage subsidies) to boost the Quebec birth rate. Some even argued that Quebec might ban abortions. These fears were dismissed out of hand by feminists in Quebec. They objected to the assumption that Quebec's distinctive character was distinctively hostile to women, and wondered whether the critics were aware of the changes in Quebec since the Quiet Revolution. They especially resented the suggestions that women might be compelled to have children or that abortions might be banned, especially since Quebec had been the first jurisdiction in which free-standing abortion clinics had been securely established, and Quebec was one of the chief innovators in family law, to the benefit of married women. Above all, Quebec women cherished their identities both as women and as Quebecers, and they were not happy being told that recognition of the latter was somehow incompatible with the former.

Many anglophone feminists were disturbed by the reaction in Quebec. Some thought they should defer to the women directly affected by the distinct society clause. Others remained opposed to any effect of the clause on the Charter of Rights, anywhere in Canada. Between these two poles, there was a range of opinion. Early in the Meech debate, the principal women's organizations had argued for the insulation of section 28 from the effects of the distinct society clause. By the end, positions had hardened: it was not at all clear that this would have been enough to satisfy the chief women's organizations.

The group most directly affected by the distinct society clause was, of course, anglophone Quebecers. The majority of anglo-Quebecers had generally resisted all attempts to promote the use of French in the province, worried that their institutions and social position would be threatened, their chances of employment and promotion reduced – worried too that an express identification of Quebec with the French language and culture would make them second-class citizens. Most had, in other words, rejected the Quiet Revolution's focus on the province as guarantor of French Canada's cultural heritage. Instead, they had firmly embraced Trudeau's vision of a country in which both languages would be (theoretically) on an equal footing coast to coast, in which everyone would be able, but no one would be required, to speak a language other than their own. They looked to the federal government to defend strict neutrality in the use of English and French and had recently begun to use the Charter with gusto to attack provincial legislation in the linguistic field.[31]

The distinct society clause seemed to imperil this conception of linguistic relations, since it expressly recognized a cultural role for Quebec and, worse still, invited a reinterpretation of the Charter. Meech Lake reopened the possibility of a territorial interpretation of language rights, in which French might be predominant within Quebec and English outside Quebec. It was true that this was counterbalanced (in part) by an express commitment to bilingualism in the "fundamental characteristic" portion of the clause, but this seemed like poor compensation to anglo-Quebecers, especially given that the original Charter had been so faithful to Trudeau's linguistic vision. The Meech formula itself seemed to suggest that the promotion of French would take precedence in Quebec: Quebec had an obligation to "preserve and *promote*" its distinct society but only to "preserve" its linguistic minority.

To some extent, other official-language minorities also opposed the distinct society clause. Francophones outside Quebec were committed to the vision of a bilingual country coast to coast and initially balked at the gesture towards territoriality in Meech Lake, particularly in the specific phrasing of the "fundamental characteristic" clause. Francophones outside Quebec differed from anglo-Quebecers, however, in that they were not directly affected by the distinct society clause itself. Indeed, some were sympathetic to that clause, acknowledging that their prosperity depended on a secure linguistic base in Quebec. Thus, when Meech began to unravel, and especially when the Acadians, Franco-Manitobans, Franco-Ontarians, and others began to realize that the end of Meech might provoke a constitutional crisis, francophone organizations outside Quebec quickly moved to support the accord, becoming, in the last months, some of its strongest advocates.

One event, in the midst of the Meech campaign, seemed to give substance to the fears of anglo-Quebecers: Quebec's adoption of "Bill 178"[32] in December 1988, using the Charter's "notwithstanding clause" to re-enact legal restrictions on the language of signs following a Supreme Court decision that had struck down Quebec's previous restrictions. Bill 178 had nothing directly to do with Meech Lake. It was enacted under the existing constitutional order. Yet the passage of Bill 178 became a critical event in the Meech discussions, not only for Quebec's anglophones but also for English-speaking Canadians outside the province. It was, in large measure, the key reason English-speaking Canadians came to doubt Quebec's commitment to Canada. It contributed both to the failure of Meech Lake and to the crisis of confidence following that failure. The controversy is therefore worth examining in some depth.

The origin of Bill 178 lay in the provisions governing commercial signs in the Parti Québécois's language law of 1977, Bill 101.[33] Bill 101 had stipulated that, with certain exceptions, commercial signs were to be in French only. At that time, this requirement had enormous symbolic significance for Quebecers. It demonstrated concretely that French was now the common, public language of Quebec, which all Quebecers should be able to use, even if they were free to speak English in their daily lives, their cultural activities, hospitals, schools, social services, and other institutions. It expressed the *visage français* of Quebec. In the late 1970s, it undoubtedly played a major role in changing perceptions in the anglophone community, prompting that community to think of itself as a minority in a predominantly French-speaking society. By the mid-1980s, that process of adaptation was well advanced. In the eyes of many, including most francophones, the full rigour of Bill 101 was no longer necessary.[34] In the 1985 election campaign, the Bourassa Liberals promised (in the rather oblique way that only Bourassa can promise) the repeal of the sign-law provisions. The majority of the anglophone community accepted the offer and voted for the Liberals.

Following the election, however, Bourassa did not immediately change the law. Instead, he temporized. He let the blanket invocation of the notwithstanding clause lapse (the statute adopted by the PQ-dominated legislature following patriation, which had invoked the clause with respect to all Quebec legislation), opening the door for a Charter challenge to Bill 101. In fact, a challenge had already been initiated, and that case was now wending its way through the courts. Bourassa refused to amend Bill 101 on the grounds that the courts should first rule on its constitutionality. On 15 December 1988, the Supreme Court of Canada delivered its reasons. It held that the sign law was contrary to the guarantee of freedom of expression in Quebec's own Charter of Human Rights and Freedoms and that a related provision was contrary to freedom of expression in both the Quebec and Canadian charters. It decided that the expression of Quebec's *visage français* would justify the *predominance* of French on all signs but would not justify a complete ban of other languages.[35] One week later, the Bourassa government enacted Bill 178. It relaxed the requirements of Bill 101, especially for signs inside a store, but kept the ban on exterior English signs. Bourassa justified the measure on the basis that restrictions on signs were necessary to preserve "social peace," and argued that Bill 178 was a good compromise – it lessened restrictions on English without entirely reversing the previous policy. The government invoked the notwithstanding clause to prevent Charter review of the new law.

Bill 178 provoked a very strong reaction among English-speaking Canadians. The Supreme Court's decision certainly contributed to the strength of the outcry. The court had declared that the sign law was contrary to fundamental rights. Now, by enacting a very similar law, the Quebec government was, virtually by definition, legislating against those rights. Bill 178 provoked far more outrage than had, in recent years, the more stringent provisions of Bill 101.[36] And in Quebec the sense of injustice was compounded by the failure of the government to honour its election promise.

Bourassa probably did not anticipate the depth of this reaction. His policy revealed the one sizeable defect in his political skills. Bourassa is a master of delay, of consensus building, of the artful compromise, all justified on the grounds of what is "rational," what is expedient at the time. For many issues, this works well. There are, however, some issues on which the public wants more than expedient compromise. It wants a policy presented with a coherent justification. The policy might attempt to reconcile divergent points of view, but that result has to be justified in terms of its own merits, as something which is right in the circumstances.[37] In Quebec, language is such an issue. Both anglophone and francophone Quebecers want it treated as a matter of leadership, of decision, not as a trade-off. Bourassa finds it very difficult to recognize these issues and deal with them appropriately. His two most serious political misjudgments have involved attempts to compromise the language issue, compromises that ended up pleasing no one. The first was the manner in which he presented and defended Bill 22 in 1974, his attempt to pre-empt the PQ's language legislation.[38] The second was Bill 178.

Not only does this lack of leadership impoverish the process of resolving these issues (though this is its most serious effect), but on an issue like Bill 178, it also undermines Bourassa's own political objectives. Suppose that, immediately following the election of 1985, Bourassa had said something like this: "The sign law was necessary in the late 1970s to send a message to anglophone Quebecers that Quebec is predominantly French-speaking. That message has been sent, and the sign law now seems unnecessary. In the election I promised it would be repealed, and I intend to honour that promise. If it becomes necessary to re-enact the law, I will be ready to do so, using the notwithstanding clause if necessary." If he had then proceeded to repeal the law, there would have been a flurry of protest from a segment of nationalists in Quebec, but, in the mood of that time probably little more. Waiting for the decision of the Supreme Court, however, was fatal. By that time, any acquiescence in the court's decision would have been unacceptable to a great many francophone Quebecers. It would have amounted to an abandonment of legislative responsibility on an issue central to Quebec's unique character (and indeed its deepest historical anxieties) to an institution (the court) whose members were appointed by the federal prime minister, the majority from outside Quebec. In those circumstances, Bourassa had little choice but to invoke the notwithstanding clause.

In fact, the divergent reactions of anglophone and francophone Quebecers to Bill 178 nicely reveal their differing conceptions of the place of language rights within Canadian political life. For anglophones, language was a matter of fundamental individual right, which should be beyond the reach of political control. For francophones, language rights were equally important, but they involved the adjustment of language use to differing contexts, differing pressures. This meant that language rights had to be subject to legislative control. This explains the apparently inconsistent opinions of francophone Quebecers at the time of Bill 178's adoption. Polls showed a majority of francophones supporting relaxation of the sign law while at the same time supporting the use of the notwithstanding clause.[39] Francophone Quebecers might well be ready to accept a weakening of Bill 101's provisions, but they wanted to agree to that weakening. They wanted to ensure that language policy would remain within the control of Quebec's legislators, not be removed to the courts through constitutionalization.

Part of the concern with Bill 178 (certainly the chief concern of anglo-Quebecers) was that it might be a harbinger of how language would be treated under the distinct society clause. That suspicion was reinforced when, in the Meech debate, Bourassa mused that with the distinct society clause the government would not have had to invoke the notwithstanding clause when enacting Bill 178. But it would be a mistake to assume that the perceived oppression of anglo-Quebecers was the only motive for the vigorous reaction to Bill 178, especially outside Quebec. For many Canadians, the issue was not so much the restrictions themselves as Quebec's breach of faith with what had come to be seen as basic premises of Canadian nationhood. Anglophone Canada had, many believed, gone a long way towards recognizing the French fact as integral to Canadian identity. It had transformed the administration of the federal government, made Ottawa's image rigorously bilingual, sent its children to French immersion schools, put French on the Corn Flakes boxes, and now, with Meech Lake, was (so they were told) "welcoming Quebec into the constitutional family." And yet Quebec, in Bill 178, seemed to be throwing all this back in their faces, freezing the English community out of Quebec, denying its legitimacy. It seemed like a blunt rejection of the spirit of tolerance and accommodation that many anglophones believed they had shown Quebec.

Their reaction was, in other words, more the product of a crisis of confidence in Quebec's commitment to a new, bilingual Canada (a Canada they thought they had embarked upon precisely to please Quebec) than the product of a concern for linguistic rights as such. This is part of the explanation why some Canadians responded not by defending minority-language rights, but by attacking bilingualism outside Quebec, even though francophones in those provinces had nothing to do with Bill 178's adoption. It also explains why arguments about the actual condition of the English community in Quebec were, in large measure, beside the point. The distinct society clause was opposed as much for reasons of nationalism as for reasons of freedom. This brings us to the second set of criticisms of the distinct society clause.

THE DISTINCT SOCIETY CLAUSE AND CANADIAN CITIZENSHIP.   During the Meech debate, one often heard arguments that took this form: one cannot have the Charter of Rights interpreted differently in one part of the country from another; all Canadians should have the same fundamental rights. For some commentators, this was an argument about liberty. We should strive, they argued, for the best understanding of freedom regardless of culture, a freedom which should be available to all. But for most, it was an argument, not about freedom, but about what it takes to have a country, about nationalism. To have a real country, the argument ran, the same rules have to apply to everyone; everyone must be treated identically.

This objection was reflected in a number of expressions common in the popular criticism of Meech Lake. The distinct society clause would, some argued, create two classes of citizen: Quebecers would be first-class and all the rest second-class. The clause would, according to Newfoundland premier Clyde Wells, give Quebecers more rights than citizens in any other province. Interestingly, this last formulation was exactly the reverse of the argument that the distinct society clause might undermine individual rights: the problem now was not that Quebecers would have fewer rights, but that they would have *more*.

Sometimes the criticism focused on governmental powers. The distinct society clause would, it was claimed, give Quebec more powers, destroying the equality of the provinces. This suspicion was apparently confirmed by Quebec's insistence that the distinct society clause would indeed increase its powers. In the popular debate, this was outrageous. The constitutional grievances of the western and Atlantic provinces were precisely that Quebec (and central Canada generally) had too much power. Wasn't Quebec already the tail wagging the federal dog in, for example, the granting of the maintenance contract for the new CF-18 plane, the running of important federal ministries, or even the exclusive focus on Quebec in the Meech Lake process itself? And now the accord would give Quebec *more*! That was intolerable.

There was a fundamental problem with this argument, one that did not, however, dim its rhetorical force. The argument drew much of its appeal from a confusion between two senses of the word "power". In constitutional discussions, having more power could mean having more power in Ottawa – being able, in other words, to exercise greater influence over federal policy. This was the kind of power Quebec used in the CF-18 negotiations, the power vaunted during the Trudeau years of "French power." It was also the kind of power that western and Atlantic provinces most wanted to achieve through Senate reform. But the word could also be used in another sense. Getting more powers could mean getting greater autonomy within the federation; it could mean exercising powers on the provincial level that previously had been exercised in Ottawa. This latter meaning did not imply that a province would have greater control in Ottawa or greater influence over what happened in other provinces. On the contrary, when Quebec got this kind of power, it would generally have less impact federally than before, for the powers would be exercised at the level of the province, applicable only to the province. It was this second kind of power – power in the sense of autonomy – that the distinct society clause would have conferred (to the extent that it conferred powers at all). One might still object to this autonomy on the grounds that the power was one which should naturally be exercised in Ottawa, or that there should be no variation in the extent of autonomy for each province, but the arguments would be very different from those used to criticize the expansion of Quebec's power in Ottawa. One of the most potent of these would be the general objection to recognizing Quebec as a distinct society: treating provinces differently was incompatible with Canadian nationhood.

Indeed, underlying many of these arguments was the assumption that all Canadian citizens, all Canadian provinces, had to be treated the same. To insist that Quebec was different from others was to insist that being Canadian was not good enough for Quebec – or perhaps that Quebec's uniqueness alone was worth recognizing and that of all the rest only worth ignoring. The argument had two possible conclusions, both hostile to a "privileged" status for Quebec: the first, that Quebec should be satisfied with being a province like the others, and the second, that every province should be recognized as a distinct society. The latter, of course, was merely a long route to the former: recognizing the distinctiveness of all implicitly suggests there is nothing particularly different about one.

In some ways, these arguments represented the triumph of a unitary conception of Canadian citizenship, the triumph of what used to be called "unhyphenated Canadianism." Canadians were Canadians. They should not be treated as French-Canadians or English-Canadians, or even (although this consequence was left implicit in the Meech debate) aboriginal or non-aboriginal Canadians.[40] Canadians should not be divided against themselves, having two allegiances, one to their country, one to their more local identity. They must be Canadians first, each treated, under the constitution, simply as Canadian. The touchstone for this was the Charter of Rights. At the popular level in English-speaking Canada, Trudeau's attempt to make the Charter the acid test of Canadian nationality had succeeded. Any attempt to vary the application of those rights, taking into account Quebec's uniqueness, was to fiddle with the very basis of Canadian citizenship. It was tantamount to taking Quebec out of Canada (at least in part). If Quebec wanted to do this, some concluded, it might as well go the whole way.

This was the final indication of the extent to which arguments of nationalism had come to masquerade as arguments of rights: some opponents of the distinct society clause would rather have a separate Quebec than modify the Charter's application. This conclusion would have been strange if their concern were really the liberty of Quebecers; surely if liberty were threatened by the distinct society clause, it would be threatened all the more by outright separation. But if the concern was not liberty at all but the maintenance of the unity of Canadian citizenship, then the position made perfect sense.

MEECH LAKE AND DECENTRALIZATION.   Many Canadians opposed Meech Lake because of its apparently decentralizing orientation. This was a different objection from the desire to preserve the unity of citizenship (although they could be combined). It concentrated on the division of powers between Ottawa and the provinces and expressed the worry that the devolution of tasks to the provinces might eventually undermine the viability of Canada as a whole.

Many Canadians, especially in Ontario and the poorer provinces, remained committed to a strong central government. This was true even in those provinces critical of federal neglect. Politicians there wanted greater power, but they generally meant power at the centre, not autonomy. Apart from Quebec, Alberta had historically been the most committed to autonomy, but in the mid-1980s, even it turned towards reform of the Senate, towards reform, in other words, of the central institutions of government, not devolution of power to the provinces. In fact, in the mid-1980s the existence of conservative governments in Newfoundland and the West probably gave an exaggerated impression of support for decentralization. NDP and Liberal constituencies tended to be much more supportive of a robust federal presence. And in the less wealthy provinces of Saskatchewan and Manitoba, support for a strong role for Ottawa cut across party lines.

This defence of central government played an important role in the opposition to Meech Lake. It tended to focus on two aspects of the accord: (1) the ability of provinces to opt out of future social programs and (2) the requirement of unanimous provincial consent for certain kinds of amendments.

The first was a genuinely decentralizing amendment in the sense that it would have transferred some decision-making power to the provinces.[41] Some commentators argued that it would have made the creation of new spending programs almost impossible, although this was by no means clear, given the constraints on opting out and the substantial political costs involved in rejection of national programs. Nevertheless, for many the risk was more than they wanted to bear. For them, Meech endangered programs that had come to epitomize the Canadian welfare state, perhaps even the Canadian identity, defined in contrast to the free-marketeering presence south of the border. In the particular context of the Meech debate, this fear was given immediacy by the suspicion that the Conservative government was less than committed to Canadian social programs and indeed might use the Meech requirements as an excuse to shelve its promise of a nationally funded system of day-care. Moreover, for residents of the poorer provinces, the concern had a hard-nosed fiscal tinge. National programs tended to work to the financial benefit of poorer provinces: federal taxes came disproportionately from the rich, but benefits were paid equally if not disproportionately in the poorer provinces. If federal programs were eroded, this benefit would be lost unless equalization payments were adjusted to compensate. That said, however, Meech Lake was not uniformly negative for defenders of the spending power: its terms impliedly affirmed the constitutionality of the spending power (which had previously been doubted); it constrained future but not existing programs, and then only within areas of exclusive provincial jurisdiction; and even then it permitted Ottawa to initiate new programs, requiring the provinces to create compatible plans if they wanted to opt out and receive compensation.

The second target (the imposition of unanimity in a greater number of constitutional amendments) was much less clearly decentralist. It tended to freeze the constitution, making any change to the status quo, centralizing or decentralizing, more difficult. Perhaps here the public concern was not so much that Meech Lake transferred legislative power to the provinces, but that it gave them a more forceful role in the now-prominent politics of constitutional change.

Many critics of Meech Lake's decentralizing orientation were concerned purely and simply with the greater provincial role, but there were two important variations on the argument, both concerned in different ways with the distinct society clause. One was expressly sympathetic to Quebec's aspirations, and it therefore agreed with the general objective of recognizing Quebec's distinctiveness. Its quarrel was not with the treatment of Quebec but rather with the treatment of all the other provinces. For partisans of this approach, Meech contained too little of the distinct society, not too much.

This view was especially prevalent among some members of the NDP. They were sympathetic both to Quebec's demand for recognition and to the need for a strong central government. They objected to Meech not because it increased the powers of Quebec, but because it increased those of other provinces. It was this extension to *all* provinces that threatened excessive decentralization. Quebec got a veto over certain kinds of constitutional change, but so did every other province. Quebec would receive compensation when opting out of amendments, but so would everyone else. Every province could be compensated when opting out of shared-cost programs. Immigration agreements would be constitutionalized for every province, not just Quebec. In each case, partisans of this variation accepted that Quebec should have those powers, but they opposed their extension to others. They wanted an asymmetrical federation, one in which Quebec would have more autonomy but existing federal powers would be preserved for the rest of the country. Meech was objectionable not because it tried to accommodate Quebec, but because it amounted to an unacceptable power grab by the rest of the provinces.

The second variation was exactly the opposite of the first. It also held that Meech Lake was too decentralizing, but for it the most dangerously decentralizing provision of all was the distinct society clause. This was the descendant of Trudeau's argument that any concession to Quebec's "nationalism" would invariably move that province down the road to independence. The only viable federalist strategy was to put Quebecers to the test: Did they want to be Canadians, or did they want to be Quebecers? This was very close to the citizenship argument, but it stressed the empirical likelihood of secession rather than a principled assertion of what it took to have a country. Indeed, the two arguments usually merged together.

THEMES OF EXCLUSION AND ALIENATION.   All of the criticisms discussed so far went to the substance of the accord. But much of the Meech debate was driven, not by disagreement with the accord's text as such, but by a profound sense of alienation from the whole process of constitutional renewal. Indeed, one suspects that many criticisms of the text were fuelled as much by feelings of exclusion and alienation as by disagreement with the terms themselves. And many criticisms focused on what the accord did not contain, rather than on what it did.

The "Quebec Round" and its exclusions.   For the first ministers, Meech Lake was not intended to be a comprehensive constitutional revision. It was the "Quebec Round," designed to deal specifically with Quebec's concerns and not with the whole gamut of constitutional issues. Much of the opposition to Meech, however, went precisely to the accord's restricted scope.

This was particularly true of aboriginal peoples. In other circumstances, the First Nations might have been Quebec's allies. They too were fighting for recognition as distinct communities within the larger Canadian state. They too worked against the presumption that equality of treatment required sameness of treatment, or that recognizing cultural differences was tantamount to recognizing superiority and privilege. But the circumstances made aboriginal support for Meech inconceivable. The speed with which Meech had been drafted – so soon after the deep disappointment of the aboriginal conferences – only seemed to demonstrate to aboriginal peoples how low they ranked in the order of priorities of Canadian governments: their talks had collapsed in failure after four years of fitful discussions; Meech Lake was concluded after one year of talks. And there now seemed little prospect for improvement. Aboriginal rights were not even mentioned among the list of topics for future conferences, and until the last months of the ratification process, few provinces, Quebec included, showed any interest in reopening the aboriginal question.

The First Nations therefore opposed the accord. The primary reason was the simple fact of exclusion. How could Canada make further refinements to its constitutional order when the fundamental rights of the first inhabitants were still ignored? This motive was directly reflected in the aboriginal criticism of the distinct society clause: if Quebec was a distinct society, surely the aboriginal peoples were as well, and they too deserved recognition. Only two of the accord's provisions would have made aboriginal objectives more difficult to achieve, and even there the effect was relatively modest. The first was the requirement of unanimity for Senate reform. Some proposals for aboriginal self-government involved reserving seats in the Senate for representatives of the First Nations. The core of the demand for self-government was not seats in the Senate, however, but the exercise of governmental functions at the level of the nation or band, and that would still be governed by the 1982 amending formula. Much more important was the requirement of unanimity for the creation of new provinces (instead of the assent of seven provinces, as currently required). These provinces would be created in the North, where the population is largely aboriginal and strongly committed to the eventual achievement of provincial status. But this objection too, though real, was of less significance than might appear. The vast bulk of provincial powers could already be conferred by Ottawa acting unilaterally, simply delegating powers to local assemblies. And one wonders whether for an issue like northern provinces, the requirement of unanimity would be substantially more difficult to achieve than the assent of seven out of ten provinces.

Back in the early 1960s, during a regional meeting of the Royal Commission on Bilingualism and Biculturalism, an aboriginal chief from Vancouver Island was asked whether French Canadian demands should be met. He answered, "Certainly. If another group can succeed in doing something when we have been condemned to death, we will be glad for them." He went on to add that "my grandchildren no longer know the language of my people, but can speak French."[42] The representatives of the First Nations in the late 1980s had none of the resignation (false in any case) apparent in that quotation. But those words do evoke the acute frustration of peoples asked to support the aspirations of others, yet denied their own.

Especially by the end of the ratification period, attention focused on yet another absence from Meech Lake: Senate reform. This was not, strictly speaking, an omission. Three of Meech's provisions spoke directly to Senate reform. First, the changes to the amending formula would have required unanimity for amendments affecting the Senate; under the present formula, the approval of seven out of ten provinces was necessary. The change would have made it more difficult (at least in theory) to achieve reform, but paradoxically, Senate reform's chief advocate, Alberta, supported the change, for reasons very similar to those that led Quebec to favour unanimity in the early 1960s. Reform might be harder to achieve, but Alberta's veto would have given it more control over the precise nature of reform. It could, for example, have ensured that a reformed Senate would adhere much more closely to the "Triple-E" model (in which each province would have the same number of senators, senators would be elected, and the Senate would have real power). Moreover, the rigidity of the amending formula was partially offset by Meech's two other provisions on Senate reform. First, the Senate was placed on the agenda of future conferences. The first ministers were therefore committed to discussing, if not resolving, the issue. Second, until reform did occur, the federal prime minister would appoint senators not unilaterally as at present, but only from lists supplied by the province.[43] Thus, even if the talks failed and no final reform occurred, the Senate's ability to represent regional interests would have been enhanced.

The accord did not, however, address the substance of Senate reform. By the end of the Meech process, many advocates of reform utterly rejected the idea that reform of the Senate could wait until later. For one thing, a variety of events (including the enactment of Bill 178) had drastically eroded English Canadian sympathy for Quebec. There was little support for a Quebec Round, for dealing with Quebec's concerns first and only later addressing those of others. Furthermore, the value of the promise of later conferences was wholly dependent on the willingness of others to compromise. The perception that Quebec was acting selfishly throughout, that it had little commitment to the good of the country as a whole, under-mined the trust that further talk would resolve anything. This lack of trust was compounded by the lack of progress during the three years of waiting to see whether Meech Lake would be ratified.

At the same time the motive for Senate reform – the feeling that Ottawa ignored the concerns of the western and Atlantic provinces – continued to intensify during the late 1980s. Ottawa's decision to award the maintenance contract for CF-18 fighters to a Montreal firm, despite a superior bid from a Winnipeg consortium, had a pro-found effect on opinion in the West. The Bank of Canada's contin-ued emphasis on high interest rates to cool the economy of southern Ontario was fiercely criticized by extensive sections of the country still feeling the effects of economic recession. And the collapse of the federally managed fish stocks had devastating effects on the Atlantic region, especially Newfoundland. Perhaps in a reformed Senate, westerners and easterners could finally get Ottawa's attention. In Newfoundland the preferred objection to Meech Lake changed over time, but in the last days Senate reform was by far the most promi-nent, presented (with considerable hyperbole) as a panacea for that province's ills. Without reform of the federal second house, the premier argued, Newfoundland would continue to be a have-not province.

The frustration and disenchantment of advocates of aboriginal rights and Senate reform emphasized the extent to which constitu-tional negotiations had become all-encompassing. There is a solid practical reason for this. Constitutional amendment takes so much energy, requires such a high degree of intergovernmental consen-sus, and therefore has such a significant risk of spectacular (and very visible) failure that it is undertaken only rarely and with some trep-idation. When it does occur, all parties want to seize the opportunity to advance their cause. After all, dealing with every issue at once means, for example, that Alberta is able to trade its consent to the distinct society clause for Quebec's consent to a Triple-E Senate. Strong tactical pressures continually expand the agenda.

Moreover, at a less cynical level, constitutional reform puts in issue – by definition – the fundamental political structure of the country. Every province wants to see its interests reflected in that structure, and so does every citizen. Thus, there is a continual push to move issues up the constitutional ladder. The constitution protects rights to a fair trial. Why not language rights? The constitution protects language rights. Why not property? The constitution protects prop-erty. Why not a decent living? The constitution protects a decent liv-ing. Why not a clean environment? The constitution protects a clean environment. Why not leisure activities, so one can enjoy that environment? All these matters are very important. Many of them – like aboriginal rights and Senate reform – are without a doubt appropriate subjects for constitutional amendment. But once the dynamic of constitutional reform begins, it becomes very difficult to constrain the list of topics discussed. There is an inevitable temptation to say every issue of significance should be addressed in the constitution, that rights left within the legislative arena, rights developed through the political process, are somehow inferior. This is not the case, and we cannot fall into the trap of believing it if we are to preserve (and indeed improve) the vitality of our political institutions.

An exclusive and limiting definition of Canada.   There was another sense in which many Canadians felt excluded by the accord. The distinct society clause was widely seen as an attempt to define Canada in a limited way, adopting a formula that focused exclusively on the dichotomies of French and English, Quebec and non-Quebec. Wasn't this just another way of restating the old myth of two (and only two) founding peoples? Hadn't Canadian politicians learned anything from the demands for recognition of aboriginal peoples and Canadians of other cultural backgrounds? In the view of some, Meech was a throwback to an earlier and discredited vision of Canada.

The distinct society clause was significant precisely because it was founded upon a conception of Canada that had wide currency within Quebec. At various times, people tried to capture that conception in phrases like "the two founding peoples" or "two nations," and in the Meech debate, those phrases were used by some defenders of the accord without much sensitivity towards people who defined themselves as neither French nor English. There seemed, therefore, to be some support for the view that the distinct society clause marked a return to an exclusive and alienating definition of Canada (especially since, within the distinct society clause itself, other cultures were not expressly mentioned).

But did it? Was it a definition at all? This was one situation in which the rhetoric of the debate left the substance far behind. The distinct society clause did not provide a self-standing definition of Canada. It was intended to work as an interpretive clause, within the structure of the existing constitution. And when read as a whole, that constitution would not have defined Canada in exclusively French-English terms.

Two interpretive clauses already existed within the constitution, both addressing the cultural composition of Canada. Section 27 of the 1982 act stated that the Charter of Rights should be interpreted "in a manner consistent with the preservation and enhancement of the multicultural heritage of Canadians." Section 25 stated that the Charter should not be interpreted "so as to abrogate or derogate from any aboriginal, treaty or other rights or freedoms that pertain to the aboriginal peoples of Canada." In addition, section 35 recognized existing aboriginal rights, and section 91(24) of the 1867 act established Ottawa's special jurisdiction with respect to aboriginal peoples. Meech Lake would have left all those provisions intact. In fact, it expressly stated that those provisions were not to be affected by the distinct society clause. Meech Lake would simply have added another interpretive consideration, this time recognizing the distinctive character of Quebec.

The distinct society clause did have different terms from the previous interpretive clauses. The phrase "distinct society" was applied to Quebec alone and "fundamental characteristic" to official-language minorities alone. The clause was to be inserted in a more prominent place. It would have applied to the whole of the constitution, not just to the Charter (perhaps because the rest of the constitution was more applicable to Quebec since it dealt specifically with the powers of provinces). It did, in short, treat Quebec differently. But this was nevertheless in addition to the existing recognition of multicultural communities and aboriginal peoples. To see it as an exclusion of other cultures – as a redefinition of Canada in terms of French and English alone – is to misunderstand the role of the clause in the constitution as a whole.

There was another way (some critics believed) in which the clause reverted to a discredited vision of Canada. The very emphasis on federal-provincial relations (and cultural difference) was seen by some as an example of the old-style politics of power, rather than the "new" politics of individual sovereignty and rights supposedly ushered in by the Charter. We should stop talking about governments, so this argument went, and focus on Canadians as individuals.

This was a potent sentiment in English-speaking Canada during the Meech debate. It has remained influential in the post-Meech period. It was yet another example of the success of the Charter in reorienting English-speaking Canadians' sense of citizenship. That reorientation was much less pronounced among French-speaking and aboriginal Canadians. They cared about individual rights, but they also realized that a very important right was participation in public decision making. If Canada was to be treated as a single unit, with all Canadians treated simply as individual members of one political entity coast to coast, they knew that their ability to engage effectively in public decision making would be reduced, not expanded. They would be a continual minority, faced with, for French Canadians, English as the always-dominant language, and for aboriginal peoples, a permanent non-aboriginal majority. Most were willing to pay that price on many issues in order to permit participation in the greater Canadian whole. But they could not simply surrender their concern with provincial institutions or aboriginal self-government. The autonomy of those local forums remained crucial, for it was only there that their particular character had direct expression. A federal structure of government was not simply a power play, then, but a question of the appropriate framework for the exercise of individual rights.

Alienation from the process of Meech Lake.   Throughout the Meech debate, much of the criticism focused on the process of constitutional reform. It focused on the fact that the terms of the accord had been concluded in two long meetings, closed to the public; that the first ministers had then resisted all changes to the accord; that public hearings had (with some notable exceptions) been limited or non-existent; and that when the accord was in trouble, Ottawa began a series of cynical and manipulative manoeuvres designed to secure the agreement of the dissenting provinces. In the oft-repeated image, Meech Lake had been made by "eleven white men in a room." It had been fixed in secret, by the tactics of labour-management negotiation. Once completed, it was immune from public input. And in the end, the Canadian prime minister had (in his own words) "rolled the dice" to determine when and where further accommodation would be made.

Perceptions of the process differed markedly in Quebec and the rest of Canada, however. For Quebecers, Meech Lake was not the work of eleven lonely men, staying up late in the Langevin Block. It was the culmination of twenty-seven years of vigorous and very public debate. Its detailed provisions had a long pedigree and were not merely the product of Mulroney's or Bourassa's advisers. Quebec had been described as a "distinct society" at least as early as the B&B Commission's preliminary report in 1965.[44] Over the years there had been a number of proposals for the express recognition of Quebec's distinctive character. When, in 1981, the Quebec legislature passed a resolution protesting patriation, it expressly declared there should be a distinct society clause. This was one of Quebec minister of justice Gil Rémillard's five points at the 1986 conference in Mont Gabriel. The changes to the amending formula were also part of a long history. Their very terms represented a return to the original proposal of the group of eight dissenting provinces during the patriation negotiations. The changes to the division of powers, including the spending power, were conservative compared to what had been on the table in previous negotiations. No specific heads of power were transferred. The provision in Meech Lake dealing with the spending power largely translated into constitutional form what had been federal policy since the late 1960s.[45] Provincial participation in appointments to the Senate and the Supreme Court of Canada, and the institutionalization of First Ministers Conferences, had all been discussed many times before.

Much of this seemed new to English-speaking Canadians not because it was new, but because they had paid little attention to constitutional discussions, having (with some notable exceptions) little desire for constitutional change. The media in Quebec, on the other hand, had given constitutional matters intensive coverage. This divergence continued throughout the Meech Lake debate, reinforcing the differing perceptions.

Even the extent of direct public consultation was not that different from what had gone before. Prior to patriation, potential amendments had been approved by resolution of the Canadian House of Commons and Senate, and had then been submitted to the United Kingdom Parliament for formal adoption. The extent of public participation varied greatly. There had been federal-provincial conferences and even royal commissions on constitutional reform. Specific amendments had been agreed in conference or in informal discussion between government leaders. The resolutions had been debated by parliamentarians during passage in the Senate and House of Commons. Generally, however, amendments had been concluded by negotiation among governments, without formal public consultation and without, at the provincial level, any need for legislative ratification.[46]

In 1980–81, the patriation process was considerably more open. It had been preceded by years of public discussion, parliamentary committees, royal commissions, and extensive popular debate, but of course Meech too had been preceded by a similar period of discussion. As in Meech, during patriation much of the decision making occurred in closed meetings of first ministers or their advisers. But even so, the public debate in 1980–81 did become very substantial indeed, partly because of Ottawa's need to muster support against the dissenting premiers and mostly because particular groups seized the opportunity to make the Charter their own. Moreover, the debate had a real effect on the terms of the 1982 constitution, especially the changes introduced in parliamentary committee and the reintroduction of aboriginal rights and the super-guarantee of women's equality during the period following the November first ministers' meeting. The one exception to this openness was, of course, the treatment of Quebec.

Meech Lake, on the other hand, had more formal opportunities for consultation. It required ratification by both federal Houses of Parliament and by each provincial legislature. The federal government and a number of provinces (including Quebec) held public hearings. All legislatures debated the accord's substance. On the surface, then, the public involvement was considerable, but it remained on the surface. Meech Lake had the form of public consultation, without its substance.

In the aftermath of the Meech debacle, there was widespread agreement that the process was flawed. Most of the suggested remedies involved some institutionalized form of direct public involvement: consultative committees that would tour the country; or a referendum on the final proposals. Ottawa's initiatives following the collapse of Meech involved a multitude of hearings and other opportunities for expressing the popular mood.

These prescriptions missed the point. They were, in large measure, suggestions of last resort, born of the view that government did not care about engaging public opinion on the constitution and was incapable of doing what was necessary to develop a more substantive public role. The problem with Meech was not primarily a lack of formal consultation. It was the spirit of consultation. In the debate on Meech Lake (as in the discussion of the 1987 Canada-us Free Trade Agreement), the federal Conservatives took the position that the issues were too complex for ordinary Canadians. Rather than attempt to justify Meech on its merits, they searched for a slogan to sell it to the public. They settled on the phrase that Meech should be adopted because it would "bring Quebec into the constitutional family," and throughout the first two and a half years of the ratification process this was virtually the only justification used by Ottawa. Meech might be an imperfect deal, the government seemed to be saying, it might even be a bad deal, but it was a deal; it would suit Quebec, so it should be accepted.

By adopting this approach, the government abdicated its responsibility to provide substantive leadership and undermined the popular debate. Political deliberation was reduced to salesmanship. The public was left either to accept the slogan and trust the government's good faith or to fashion their conclusions in ignorance of the actual motives behind the government's policy. Comment and criticism were hamstrung by the lack of substantial justification. And on a question as important as the constitution, this was intensely frustrating.

Moreover, even from the government's own partisan perspective, it was very unwise. It meant, for example, that popular support for the accord was fragile. As long as all first ministers supported the accord – as long as all dissenting voices could be marginalized – the support held, but as soon as criticism of the accord began to mount, the government had nothing to fall back on, no reasoned justification of the accord on its merits, widely accessible to the public. Reasoned justifications were advanced, but late, often by academics, opposition politicians, and persons who had once been active in public life but were now retired, acting largely in default of any appropriate action by Ottawa. And when the challenges began, the content of Ottawa's slogan actually made matters worse. The slogan essentially came down to: "This is a deal that Quebec will agree to, so we should adopt it." Despite all the goodwill in the world, Canadians were unlikely to accept a major constitutional reform merely because Quebec wanted it. And when, in the aftermath of the CF-18 and Bill 178, anglophone public opinion turned strongly against Meech Lake, this impoverished justification reinforced the opinion that Meech was a cynical power grab by Quebec.

The Meech process was also criticized for the complete refusal of the principal actors to consider any modification to the accord. Towards the end of the ratification period, there may have been good reasons for refusing changes to the text itself. Some of the criticisms, especially those of Newfoundland's Clyde Wells, attacked the very premises of the agreement. To begin negotiations on that basis would be tantamount to ripping up the accord and beginning anew. Rather than do that, it was perhaps best to see whether the existing accord could achieve the support necessary for ratification.

The same arguments, however, cannot explain the lack of discussion of matters lying outside the scope of the agreement, especially aboriginal rights and Senate reform. These were ignored for a combination of reasons. First, Ottawa had other things on its agenda, particularly the implementation of Canada-us free trade and the goods and services tax (GST). Second, some of the first ministers (especially from the West) did not want progress on aboriginal rights. They had resisted a right of self-government during the previous conferences and there was no indication that they had changed their minds. Third, the fact that Meech had not been ratified provided Quebec with a convenient excuse to refuse to take part in discussions that in the end were unlikely to be of much advantage to it. Quebec's motives, like those of other provinces, blended principle and self-interest. Given that some of the most potent criticisms of Meech concerned what it excluded, however, the failure to address other issues was very unfortunate. In the end, the governments did discuss them, but with a haste and cynicism that belied any impression of sincerity.

Finally, even if there were reasons at the end of the process for refusing to reopen Meech, those reasons were much less convincing at the beginning. If there had been more openness initially, minor changes may have resulted in Meech's acceptance among English-speaking Canadians. Perhaps changes would not have been necessary; the opportunity for real discussion may have been enough. At that time, after all, there was substantial goodwill towards Quebec. And even if a willingness to change the accord had caused it to unravel in the first months, an early failure might well have been less damaging than ratification in the climate of bitterness and recrimination that prevailed at the end of the period. It would certainly have been less damaging than what actually occurred, a collapse at the end of the process.

The Meech Lake process was abominable, although it was doubtful even afterwards that the Mulroney government realized why. The problem was not that Canadians wanted yet another forum in which to speak their minds; rather, the Mulroney government, in its failure to address the merits of the accord and its refusal to consider any modifications to the accord's text, had treated the Canadian people with disdain, and they knew it.

Quebec's (and Ottawa's) commitment to Canada.   In all of this, Quebec seemed a willing collaborator – or perhaps more than a collaborator, since it was usually Quebec that was saying no. One of the chief obstacles to resolving the impasse, and one of the principal reasons for opposition to the accord in the first place, was a growing doubt among many Canadians that Quebec truly was committed to Canada. This was the view expressed, especially towards the end of the popular debate, in such comments as "I would just like to hear one of them say that they love Canada," "We are not going to give in to the blackmail of Quebec," or (especially among anglo-Quebecers) "Bourassa is just a disguised separatist."

This was the principal significance of Bill 178 for most English-speaking Canadians. More than anything else, it suggested that Quebec had no interest in any broader idea of Canada. At the very moment that anglophone Canada was extending its hand to Quebec through Meech Lake, it was rebuffed. Part of this was simply offence at seeing Quebec take a swipe at one's language, but for Canadians who had accepted the bilingual vision of the country, the disenchantment was acute. These Canadians had thought that bilingualism was the reform that would make room for Quebec within Confederation, and yet now they were being told, sometimes in no uncertain terms, that bilingualism was nothing – sometimes even that *Canada* had wanted it, not *Quebec*. This, of course, was not the case. Quebecers had long argued for bilingualism in federal institutions.[47] In the tensions aroused by Bill 178 and the distinct society clause, however, the debate soon degenerated into a stark contrast between bilingualism and provincial linguistic sovereignty. Meech Lake came to be seen as the rejection of bilingualism rather than what it was: an attempt to reconcile (on the one hand) federal and a substantial measure of provincial bilingualism with (on the other) an acknowledgment that language use was inevitably concentrated in different parts of the country and that French would always face greater challenges than English.

Quebec seemed to be out of step with more recent versions of English Canadian nationalism as well. Quebecers did not accept the Charter as the definition of Canadian nationhood. Furthermore, their two major provincial political parties had embraced the market in a manner incompatible with the economic nationalism of many English-speaking Canadians. This was apparent in Quebecers' high level of support for the Mulroney government's economic policies, especially free trade. It is true that they were joined in this market-oriented liberalism by residents of many other provinces. After all, the principal initiators of free trade had been anglophones, there was a long free trade tradition in the western and Maritime provinces, and support for a largely unregulated and untaxed economy (and for limitations on welfare spending) was strong in some parts of the country, especially Alberta. But in the minds of some English Canadian economic nationalists, the debate was now essentially between two individuals, Quebec and the rest, with all subtleties obscured. And in this world, Meech Lake, with its restrictions on the spending power, its provisions for opting out of centralizing amendments, and its hints of decentralization in the distinct society clause and the treatment of immigration, suggested an extension of the laissez-faire agenda into the constitutional arena.

Not only was Quebec at odds with common forms of Canadian nationalism, it seemed to be acting purely in its own self-interest, with little regard for the other partners in Confederation. This was the meaning some gave to Quebec's insistence that Meech be ratified before negotiations began on other matters. It was also a common reaction to the exclusiveness of the distinct society clause (among those who thought, mistakenly, that it was intended to be a definition of Canada). In two provinces – the two that failed to ratify the accord – the perception of a selfish and grasping Quebec took very concrete form. In Manitoba, public opinion was hostile to Quebec as a result of Ottawa's 1986 decision to award the CF-18 maintenance contract to a Montreal consortium instead of to a Winnipeg group that had made a superior bid. Many westerners believed that this was simply the most blatant example of Quebec wielding disproportionate influence in Ottawa. For their part, Newfoundlanders had never forgiven Quebec for refusing to revise the terms of the Churchill Falls hydroelectric contract. Under that deal, signed when Joey Smallwood was premier of Newfoundland, power from Churchill Falls was sold to Hydro-Québec for a fraction of its current value. Churchill Falls was the reason Newfoundlanders had fire in their bellies when they supported their premier's position on Meech Lake. They might not care for constitutional theory, but they knew which side they were on when Clyde Wells spoke of equality, especially when Quebec was on the other side of the table. As the provincial finance minister, Hubert Kitchen, said in the House of Assembly, "They got us by the short hair on the Upper Churchill. But now I can tell you something else, we got them in the same place on Meech Lake."[48]

Many of the criticisms of Quebec were equally applicable to Ottawa. Ottawa, too, was criticized for having no feeling for the country, and it was more involved than the Quebec government in such decisions as the CF-18. Most importantly, its neo-conservative agenda had alienated many key constituencies, constituencies that doubted the Conservatives' commitment to national social programs and opposed their policies on the railways, the post office, the funding of the Canadian Broadcasting Corporation, free trade, and a host of other issues. To them, the Mulroney Conservatives had no idea of what Canada was all about and were in the process of dismantling institutions fundamental to the Canadian identity. They did not trust Mulroney's judgment on the good of the country. They were not about to trust him on Meech Lake either.

Perhaps the most damaging element, however – one that finally produced a kind of stalemate – was the argument that Quebec might secede if Meech were rejected. This may well have been an accurate indication of the seriousness of failure, but as an argument for the adoption of the accord it had three defects. First, it sounded too much like a threat and thus provoked a strong reaction outside Quebec. Canadians should not, so the reaction went, accede to blackmail. Second, in the absence of solid arguments on the accord's merits (arguments Ottawa seemed loath to provide), it gave the impression that the *only* reason for adopting Meech was to stop Quebec leaving. Few Canadians wanted a constitution hanging on such a slender justification. Third, it led some to doubt whether Quebec's commitment to Canada was sufficient in any case: if Quebec would secede over Meech Lake, then the federation must be fragile indeed.

In all of this, there was little understanding of Quebec's point of view. During the last months of the Meech debate, one often heard two opposing predictions about the prospect of separation, sometimes from the same people, and both used to justify inaction on Meech: (1) "Quebec will never separate," and (2) "Quebec will separate anyway." This tension was the result of anglophone Canadians' inability to grasp, simultaneously, that Quebecers might be strongly committed to Canada and yet feel that, without changes, they might have to leave. When anglophone Canadians saw Quebecers' commitment to Canada, they accepted the first prediction. When they saw that Quebec might leave, they chose the second. They found it much harder to perceive that Quebecers were committed both to Canada and to change, and without that perception, they were very reluctant to compromise.

Francophone Quebecers could not understand anglophone demands for demonstrations of commitment. They felt they had shown their allegiance to Canada on many occasions, most clearly in the defeat of the referendum on sovereignty-association, but also in their continued commitment to negotiations and their agreement to the Meech Lake Accord itself. They were accused of dominating Canada, yet the constitution had been patriated without their province's consent. Amendments had addressed western concerns over resource taxation, had protected the education rights of official-language minorities, had guaranteed (in general terms) aboriginal rights, and had recognized Canada's multicultural heritage, but in all the years of discussion not one amendment had been adopted at the request of the Quebec government, not one amendment had addressed the traditional concerns of Quebec with the spending power, the division of powers, disallowance, or the recognition of Quebec's distinctiveness. Quebecers were told that they were turning their backs on Canada when they took action against English on commercial signs, but they also saw the bitter opposition to bilingualism in Manitoba in the mid-1980s and Ontario's continued rejection of bilingualism on the Quebec model. Although Quebec was the only province to restrict by law the use of another language, services to anglo-Quebecers remained superior, often vastly so, to those available to francophones outside Quebec.[49] Quebecers were told they were insufficiently grateful for a bilingual federal government, but it seemed like the most elementary justice that a government should be able to communicate with a third of its citizenry, and a scandal that this had only begun to be the case very recently.

Part of the problem was that for many English-speaking Canadians Trudeau had symbolized French Canada. Both his anglophone supporters and opponents had believed that Trudeau's position was the position of all Quebecers who were not separatists. They could not understand that many French-speaking Quebecers – probably most – strongly favoured a French Canadian presence on the federal scene but at the same time wanted their province to maintain its role in the promotion of the French Canadian culture. This had several consequences. Anglophones generally considered the changes of the late 1960s, especially bilingualism, to be *the* response to Quebec. They considered the Charter's guarantees of language rights to be the fulfilment of French Canadian aspirations. In their view, Quebec had, throughout this period, determined the agenda on linguistic and constitutional matters, and they could not understand Quebec's new emphasis on its uniqueness. Was Quebec moving the goalposts? Anglophone Canadians had trouble seeing that these developments marked the resurgence of a current that had always been there, a current that Trudeau had tried to stifle and that, through his efforts, anglophone Canadians had come to identify with Quebec nationalism (read separatism). They had trouble seeing that there could be federalists in Quebec who disagreed with Trudeau, that bilingualism on the federal level could be compatible with a vigorous role for Quebec in cultural matters, and that Quebecers could remain dissatisfied with the constitution after three decades of effort.

The lack of comprehension, the oversimplification of the other's position, was not confined to anglophones. French-speaking Quebecers were just as blinkered, although in a different way. They had long been preoccupied with the preservation of their distinctiveness and had tended to think of the constitution exclusively in those terms. Like most minorities, they tended to interpret all the discussions in terms of their conflicts: they spoke of "French" and "English Canada" as though the latter were English in the same way that Quebec was French; they treated multiculturalism as nothing more than an attempt to undermine biculturalism, realizing imperfectly that the idea had force precisely because it spoke to a real sense of exclusion; and they saw the aboriginal peoples' demands as little more than an anglophone bargaining ploy, certainly having trouble granting them the same level of significance as their own. Seeing their identity under threat, they had emphasized their difference, refraining from effusive expressions of allegiance to Canada. Committed to the economic development of their have-not province, they lobbied vigorously for favourable policies in Ottawa and had the numbers to win many battles.

All this contributed to the anglophone perception that French-speaking Quebec was closed in upon itself. Indeed, to some extent, it was. The tragedy was that it was also committed to Canada, willing and able to engage in these broader debates if the constitutional hurdle could be cleared. The dynamic of the debate made it very hard for francophone Quebecers to express this, and very hard for the rest of Canada to perceive it. All sides were trapped in the dynamic, repeating the language of old controversies, unable to find the common ground to move forward.

The Failure of the Accord

In the last days of the ratification period, frantic and not terribly honourable attempts were made to save the accord. In the end, nine provinces agreed to ratify, on the understanding that all supported a "parallel accord" addressing a number of the criticisms of Meech. The Newfoundland government refused to support ratification but agreed to hold a free vote on the issue. By that time, however, Manitoba required the unanimous consent of its MLAs in order to ratify before the deadline. All political parties supported ratification, but one Cree member of the assembly, Elijah Harper, refused consent. Manitoba therefore missed the deadline. Newfoundland declined to hold its vote. With two provinces yet to ratify, and one (Newfoundland) still advocating substantial changes, Ottawa declared the accord dead.[50]

The extent of support among provincial governments grossly exaggerated the support within the country. By the end, public opinion outside Quebec ran strongly against the accord.[51] Even within Quebec support was lukewarm at best. The all-important symbolic message of the accord – the welcoming of Quebec "into the constitutional family with honour and enthusiasm," the recognition that Quebec could be a full member of Confederation, without surrendering its distinctiveness – had been obliterated by popular opposition to the distinct society clause. Misunderstanding and re-crimination were rife.

The popular rejection of Meech was the product of all the considerations discussed above, but if there was one element unifying the opposition, it was the failure of the government's vision. Meech Lake was initially justified as a deal, as something Quebec would agree to. There was no coherent description of the whole, no explanation why Meech Lake made sense in terms of Canada. In the absence of that explanation, Meech was inevitably seen as a crass trade-off, extracted by threats from Quebec, contrary to constitutional principle. The assertion that Meech was necessary to preserve Canadian unity was a poor substitute for a principled defence. For one thing, English-speaking Canadians rejected a constitutional order based (so they thought) on blackmail, and Quebecers found it hard to be enthusiastic about a symbolic recognition extracted only by fear of something worse. Above all, the weakness of the government's defence prevented Canadians from coming to terms with the complexity of their identities and allegiances, from working towards a conception of their country that could accommodate, perhaps even build upon, the richness of their societies.

CHARLOTTETOWN

With the failure of Meech, Canada landed in the predicament described in this book's first chapter. Our constitutional debate, our very confidence in each other's commitment to the country, seemed to be breaking down. Most Canadians outside Quebec simply wanted the constitution to go away. Quebecers, however, stung by the rejection of Meech, demanded a firm resolution once and for all. They committed themselves to another referendum on a new package of amendments, or failing that on sovereignty, no later than 26 October 1992. This forced the parties back to the table before many of them, or their constituents, were ready. Nevertheless, on 28 August 1992 the prime minister, the premiers, the territorial leaders, and the representatives of four national aboriginal organizations all agreed on a new set of amendments, dubbed the "Charlottetown Accord."

In keeping with the focus of this book, I will not describe in detail the road that led to that agreement or to its subsequent failure. Indeed, for my purposes, Charlottetown is less significant than Meech. Many of the opposing positions, many of the issues still before Canada today, were clarified in Meech. Charlottetown tried to overcome those divisions and did succeed in blurring the lines, but the most fundamental challenges remained. Charlottetown is significant, however, for its attempt to address several of the issues ignored in Meech and for the consequences of its failure for the prospects of constitutional amendment in Canada. This section will briefly review the accord, examining its implications for the evolution of Canada's national debates.

The Terms of the Charlottetown Accord[52]

The Charlottetown Accord tried to reconcile a set of very severe, largely intractable tensions evident following Meech's collapse. Quebec demanded action on the constitutional front. Most other Canadians remained very reluctant. Quebec insisted that it would not return to the table until its basic concerns were satisfied – and even then it wanted recognition as spokesperson for one of Canada's two founding linguistic communities, negotiating (so the phrase went) as one of two, not one of ten. The other provinces would only negotiate if both the range of participants and the agenda were greatly expanded, rather than contracted. Quebec insisted that Meech was the minimum, indeed it demanded "Meech plus." Given the bitterness of Meech's defeat, there was little "honour and enthusiasm" left; any settlement would therefore have to go beyond largely symbolic recognition to embrace real changes in the division of powers. Many other Canadians still believed that Meech had gone too far; they wanted changes to the Meech package.

These tensions dominated the negotiating process and the eventual accord. The talks were expanded, with full participation from territorial and aboriginal leaders. A series of conferences and hearings were held to provide popular input. Meanwhile, the government of Quebec remained aloof, conveying its views through individual contacts and the comments of high civil servants until very late in the process.

The agenda too was greatly expanded. Senate reform and aboriginal self-government were now central to the talks. So was the proposal of Ontario's newly elected NDP government for a charter of social rights. In deference to Quebec's demands for Meech plus, the division of powers was discussed. Ottawa argued for greater protection for the Canadian economic union. And through all this, the negotiators sought a magic compromise, trading concessions on Senate reform for consent to changes to the amending formula, tinkering with the distinct society clause while attempting to preserve its appeal for Quebec. This resulted in a package that was much more ambitious than Meech, but that ultimately failed to satisfy many of its key constituencies.

CHARLOTTETOWN'S RELATIONSHIP TO THE MEECH LAKE ACCORD.   Most of the elements of Meech Lake were present in

substantially the same form in Charlottetown. The immigration and
spending-power provisions were virtually identical. The Supreme
Court provisions were the same, except for two measures designed
to avoid deadlock in appointments. The essence of the Meech Lake
amending formula was also retained in Charlottetown, with one
change regarding amendments to the Supreme Court, another
providing for aboriginal participation, and a new formula for the
creation of provinces out of the territories. One of the main
grievances in Meech had been that accord's requirement of unanimity for the creation of new provinces. This was resolved by permitting their creation by Ottawa and the territory alone, while
nevertheless requiring unanimity before new provinces obtained
an equal say in constitutional amendments or the Senate.[53] Even
though they stayed close to Meech, these provisions were controversial in Quebec. Some commentators noted that much of the
benefit of Quebec's veto would have been lost, since in order to get
the veto Quebec had to agree to reforms it might otherwise have
rejected. To these Quebecers, Charlottetown looked like shutting
the barn door after the cattle had fled.

The most significant changes, however, concerned the distinct society clause. That clause had been at the heart of Meech. It was the
section with the most resonance in Quebec. It had borne the brunt
of much of the popular criticism. The framers of the Charlottetown
Accord attempted to deal with that conflict by redrafting the clause
to meet some (but not all) of the criticisms while preserving its attrac-
tion in Quebec.

In the new draft, the framers sought to steer a middle course
between two of the principal grounds for opposition to the Meech
Lake Accord. First, during the Meech debate, many Canadians had
rejected the distinct society clause because of its exclusive emphasis
on French and English. Many who took this position did not oppose
recognition of Quebec's uniqueness; they simply wanted other features of Canada's cultural make-up acknowledged as well. There
was, however, a second, closely related, but more far-reaching objection. Those who adopted the second view opposed the very principle
of the clause. They wanted Quebec to be treated identically to other
provinces. One way of doing this would be to surround the distinct
society clause with a number of other recognitions so that Quebec
would fade into the background. This was the strategy adopted by
Newfoundland during the last months of Meech Lake, when it proposed that the clause be moved out of the body of the constitution
and into the preamble, placed last in a list of fundamental characteristics of Canada.[54]

The framers of Charlottetown tried to satisfy the first objection without giving way to the second. The mention of Quebec's distinct society would appear twice. First, it would be one of the elements of a "Canada clause," third in a list of "fundamental Canadian values."[55] This clause would offer the expanded definition Meech opponents had demanded. Here, recognition of the distinct society would be coupled with recognition of other cultural groups (aboriginal peoples; "citizens from many lands") as well as with an invocation of fundamental principles (democracy, federalism, the rule of law, individual and collective rights, racial, ethnic and gender equality, and equality of the provinces). In addition, Quebec's distinctiveness would be addressed in another, quite separate clause, this one affirming "the role of the legislature and Government of Quebec to preserve and promote the distinct society."[56] Where the first clause took the form of a general evocation of the characteristics of Canada, the second was much more active, affirming a specific governmental role. The framers hoped, then, that this combination would both satisfy the advocates of a more inclusive definition of Canada and preserve the kind of recognition Quebecers had found appealing. It did not work, however. Social symbolism had little time for such fine distinctions in wording. For most Quebecers, the recognition of Quebec's distinct society had now become part of a lengthy, vague definition of Canada, with none of the directness of Meech.

Charlottetown also changed the distinct society clause in one other respect. During the Meech debate, some opponents had complained that the phrase "distinct society" was too vague and could be used to achieve a far-reaching special status. Although this was often expressed as a criticism of the drafting of the clause, it was in fact another way of chipping away at the idea of Quebec's distinctiveness, an attempt to force a measure of precision that that kind of constitutional provision simply could not achieve. Nevertheless, Charlottetown tried to meet this objection by adding a definition of the phrase, apparently aiming to be as innocuous as possible. Quebec's society "includes," Charlottetown declared, "a French-speaking majority, a unique culture and a civil law tradition."[57] Almost certainly, this would have had no practical impact on the application of the clause. The definition did not purport to be exhaustive, and in any case the starting-point of any sensible conception of Quebec's character would have been its linguistic, cultural, and legal heritage. The chief effect of this change was once again at the symbolic level. The more distinct society was hedged about with qualifications and hesitations, the less it conveyed the sense of acceptance and reconciliation that was originally at the heart of Meech Lake.

These were the most significant changes to the clause. Others were discussed but were rejected or were, in the end, of little consequence. During the lead-up to Charlottetown, some proposals contemplated that the application of the clause should be largely restricted to the Charter.[58] This was not adopted and the Charlottetown version applied, as had Meech, to the entire constitution. There were arguments over the balance between recognition of Quebec and protection of official-language minorities. This led to some tinkering with the language, but these changes merely emphasized how reluctant anglophone Canadians were to adopt the clause, and triggered quarrels about whether linguistic communities were now in a favoured position compared to, say, women.

In the end, the changes to the distinct society clause satisfied few of those who had objected to Meech because of its potential impact on individual rights and national identity. These critics still rejected any suggestion that Quebec's distinctiveness should affect the interpretation of the Charter; they continued to argue that the clause created a "hierarchy of rights." In fact, some of these commentators believed that Charlottetown was worse than Meech because it would, for the first time, have expressly recognized "collective rights" in the constitution.

The changes to the clause also failed to satisfy many francophone Quebecers. The juridical effect of the revised clause – its effect on Canada's constitutional law – would probably have been much the same as Meech. In terms of social symbolism, however, its impact was greatly impaired. This put added weight on the proposals regarding powers as a means of compensating for the perceived weakening of the clause.

DIVISION OF POWERS.   Charlottetown did contain some provisions specifically affecting the division of powers. These included the measures inherited from Meech on immigration and shared-cost programs, and new measures abolishing the federal power of disallowance and restricting the declaratory power.[59] The principal discussions, however, concerned further limitations on the spending power and the transfer of areas of federal jurisdiction, and these foundered on another set of conflicts left over from Meech. To begin with, support for provincial autonomy differed greatly from one part of the country to another. Quebec, and to a lesser extent Alberta and British Columbia, wanted more autonomy; others, especially the poorer provinces, wanted to retain the existing federal role. An asymmetrical solution, where some provinces exercised more powers than others, might have satisfied both, but this ran headlong into another objection: many English-speaking Canadians rejected, on symbolic grounds, any arrangement under which one province would be treated differently from others. As a result, the parties could not agree on either a general decentralization or on a transfer of powers to certain provinces. Instead, they fell back on a compromise that seemed to treat all provinces the same but that would allow, in certain areas, a reapportionment of jurisdiction through intergovernmental agreement. The compromise took four different forms.

First, Charlottetown recognized a number of fields as provincial and directed Ottawa to negotiate agreements restricting its presence in those fields (if a province so requested). The areas affected were urban and municipal affairs, tourism, recreation, housing, mining, and forestry, all fields in which the federal presence was based wholly or predominantly on the spending power.[60]

Second, in the domains of culture and labour market development and training, Charlottetown recognized the primacy of the provinces but affirmed a federal role over certain aspects. In the case of culture, the federal role involved responsibility for "national cultural matters," especially "national cultural institutions." In labour market training, it included the ability to run unemployment insurance and job-creation programs, and to participate in the establishment of national objectives for labour market development. Once again, the precise division of responsibility would be determined through intergovernmental agreements.[61]

Third, in two additional fields (telecommunications and regional development), Charlottetown directed Ottawa to negotiate (at a province's request) agreements coordinating federal and provincial action. Here, there was no declaration of provincial jurisdiction. The existing division of powers remained unchanged.[62]

Finally, Charlottetown provided for further discussions on the use of the spending power, which would presumably lead eventually to the adoption of a general framework to govern the exercise of that power.[63]

These proposals had the merit of flexibility. The balance between federal and provincial roles could be carefully defined by means of the agreements. This would also allow the creation of asymmetry – the tailoring of powers to the demands of different provinces – without having to write those arrangements into the constitution. As a response to the sentiment in Quebec, however, the proposals were a failure. They promised much, but for the moment they delivered nothing. In the end, the Quebec government could only point to a commitment to negotiate.

SENATE REFORM.   If Meech Lake and the division of powers were Quebec's issues, Senate reform was Alberta's and Newfoundland's (with some backing from other western provinces). The motive for reform was to increase the voice of eastern and western Canadians in central decision making. Currently, the House of Commons is by far the dominant chamber in the federal Parliament. In the Commons, representation is based roughly on population, and because Ontario and Quebec have over half of Canada's population, members from those two provinces make up more than half the Commons. Senate reform would have increased the representation of the less populous eastern and western provinces, thereby providing a counterweight to the strength of central Canada in the Commons. Over the course of the 1970s and 1980s, a wide variety of schemes had been proposed, combining different forms of representation, different powers, and different allocations of seats among provinces. The debates leading up to Charlottetown were driven, however, by Alberta's proposal for a Triple-E Senate. Under that proposal, each province would have an *equal* number of senators, senators would be *elected* rather than appointed, and the Senate would possess *effective* power.

Virtually everyone agreed that the present Senate was an embarrassment. The arguments over Senate reform therefore went to the nature rather than the fact of reform. Often, these arguments could become quite arcane, dealing with minutiae that lie well beyond the scope of this account. The most fundamental conflict, however, concerned the apportionment of seats. Two problems made this issue extremely difficult. First, in Canada, the population difference between provinces is dramatic. An "equal" Senate would constitute a very substantial departure from representation by population. Moreover, because there are only ten provinces, the extra weight given one province would not be moderated (as it is in the American case) by the number of provinces. Second, the interests of two different minorities were in conflict. Senate reform was motivated by the desire to tip the balance towards eastern and western provinces and away from the majority of the population concentrated in the central provinces. At the same time, however, one component of that majority, Quebec, saw itself as the chief protector of another beleaguered minority. Strengthening one seemed to involve, almost inevitably, the weakening of the other.[64] For a long time, it looked as though these tensions would prevent agreement. Ultimately, however, the parties did compromise. The agreement provided for equal provincial representation in the Senate, but did so in a way that would preserve the dominance of the Commons.[65]

Most proposals for Senate reform acknowledged that the Commons, as the chamber most directly representative of individuals, should be the principal house. Governments would be responsible to the Commons, not the Senate, and money bills (dealing with the raising and spending of government revenue) would be within Commons control. Charlottetown added another element, a mechanism for resolving disagreements between the two houses that clearly favoured the Commons. Under the compromise, disputes over most legislation could be submitted to a joint session of the two houses. This joint session would then vote on the measure. Because the Commons was much larger than the proposed Senate, the Commons members would, in the end, have the predominant say. Some sensitive matters were excluded from this process. If the Senate defeated legislation dealing with natural resources taxation (one of the principal concerns of the western provinces) or the French language, that would be the end of the matter. But the new procedure would apply to most legislation.

This was the crucial compromise, but there were also three additional measures designed to make the Senate more acceptable in Quebec. Legislation materially affecting the French language would be subjected to a double majority in the Senate: it would require the approval of a majority of all senators and a majority of francophone senators. Second, although Quebecers' influence in the Senate would be greatly reduced, their weight in the Commons would be protected: they would be guaranteed 25 per cent of Commons seats (approximately their current proportion), even if their share of the population declined.[66] Finally, provinces would be able to choose between electing their representatives directly and having the provincial legislature elect them. Quebec would almost certainly choose the second option, ensuring that its senators expressed a unified position.

Charlottetown, therefore, attempted to carve out a compromise acceptable to all, but its success was very limited. The proposal was so complicated, the compromises so numerous and apparently ad hoc, that it left many people dissatisfied. Was the Senate truly effective or would it be so small and divided as to lack all clout? Would it have any legitimacy if some members were elected while others were, in effect, appointed by governments? The guarantee of 25 per cent of the Commons to Quebec was especially galling in the West, where the population was expanding. It seemed to contradict what many took to be the fundamental principle of Senate reform: equality of the provinces. For most Quebecers, that very principle remained anathema. French-speaking Quebecers considered themselves one of two partners of Confederation. Ideally, they wanted to be so recognized, but short of that, they certainly wanted to have weight commensurate with their share of the population. In the present Senate, they had approximately one-quarter of the seats (roughly equivalent to their population). After the reform, they would have less than a tenth, to be reduced further when aboriginal members were added. Quebec's position might in practice be adequately protected by other aspects of the accord, but the symbolism was intolerable.

ABORIGINAL SELF-GOVERNMENT. The Charlottetown Accord contained extensive provisions dealing with aboriginal peoples. It clarified federal jurisdiction over the Métis, improved the protection of Métis land in Alberta, established guidelines for the interpretation of treaties, and provided for aboriginal participation in the constitutional amendment process,[67] but its most important measures recognized the right of self-government and provided a procedure for its implementation.

Charlottetown overcame the hesitations that had, in the mid-1980s, resulted in the failure of the aboriginal conferences. Two steps were crucial. First, the provinces that had previously resisted any expansion of aboriginal rights now acquiesced in the proposal. In fact two, British Columbia and Saskatchewan, were now led by NDP governments which, along with the NDP government in Ontario, were strong supporters of self-government. Charlottetown adopted the description of the right aboriginal representatives had wanted. The right was said to be "inherent," rooted in the character of the aboriginal peoples themselves. The clause recognized self-government but did not purport to create it, leaving open the possibility that self-government might also be included within the "existing aboriginal and treaty rights" already protected in the constitution. Finally, aboriginal governments would be "one of three orders of government in Canada," equivalent in status to the federal and provincial governments, not subordinate to them.[68]

The second step involved agreement on the means for implementing the right. Aboriginal and non-aboriginal participants generally agreed that the best way to make the right effective was through negotiations. Negotiations could work out, for each aboriginal people, the appropriate form of government, the precise extent of that government's powers, and effective means of financing. Aboriginal peoples had also argued, however, that the right should be enforceable in the courts in order to prevent Ottawa and the provinces from stonewalling. This was resisted by non-aboriginal governments, who were reluctant to create an enforceable right without more clarity on its content.

The compromise that was reached did allow for eventual recourse to the courts but strongly emphasized negotiations as the preferred means of dealing with the issues. It did this by first suspending recourse to the courts until five years had passed. This would allow considerable time for negotiations – in practice much more than five years, given the expense and delay of litigation. In the meantime, the parties were subject to an obligation to negotiate, and this more limited obligation was enforceable before the courts. Even after the five years, the courts would not necessarily begin to define self-government in detail. Instead of addressing the substance of the right, they could review the history of negotiations and make orders to induce the parties to bargain more effectively.[69]

Finally, Charlottetown addressed a number of specific concerns. It made clear that the recognition of self-government would not extend (or diminish) aboriginal rights to land.[70] It stipulated that actions taken by aboriginal governments must be consistent with "federal or provincial laws that are essential to the preservation of peace, order and good government in Canada."[71] This phrase, though vague, was clearly designed to prevent gross abuses of authority. Finally, aboriginal governments were subject to the Charter, although this protection was qualified by

- the ability of aboriginal governments to use the notwithstanding clause to exempt their laws from certain Charter provisions;
- the redrafting of the Charter provision dealing with voting rights in order to allow traditional, non-elected forms of government and to permit the restriction of the franchise in aboriginal elections to members of aboriginal communities; and
- special interpretive provisions to permit affirmative action programs and to protect measures designed to safeguard aboriginal languages, cultures, and traditions.[72]

Clearly, Charlottetown contained very substantial measures on self-government. They were also controversial. Although non-aboriginal governments had come to accept aboriginal self-government and were satisfied with the conditions imposed, many of their constituents remained unconvinced. Some simply believed that all aboriginal claims were exaggerated; they had opposed land claims and now they opposed self-government. Others rejected self-government in principle, believing that it was a form of racially based government akin to apartheid. Still others questioned its practicality, being concerned with its cost, its impact on land claims, or its sheer complexity. There was dissension even within aboriginal communities. Some of this reflected the structural problems inherent in attempts to deal, at the pan-Canadian level, with aboriginal issues. Aboriginal communities were so diverse, their organization so decentralized, their needs and expectations so different, that it was difficult to develop solutions satisfactory to all. Moreover, it became clear that a constituency existed whose views were not well represented within the principal aboriginal organizations. Some aboriginal people, especially those supporting the Native Women's Association of Canada, wondered whether their communities were ready for self-government and doubted the adequacy of the safeguards proposed in Charlottetown. In the end, for all these reasons, reserve Indians voted down the package.

SOCIAL RIGHTS AND THE ECONOMIC UNION.   The Charlottetown Accord included measures dealing with social rights and with the strengthening of Canada's economic union. Neither of these spoke directly to the conflicts in Meech, and neither elicited the impassioned support typical of, for example, Senate reform or the distinct society clause. The Ontario NDP championed a new "Social Charter" in order to broaden protection beyond the traditional catalogue of individual rights, perhaps even to counter the erosion of social programs that had occurred in recent years. Ottawa pushed for a reduction of internal trade barriers as part of its commitment to economic liberalization, a commitment expressed in, for example, the Canada-US free trade agreement. Each proposal fit well with the ideological leanings of the sponsoring government. Equally importantly, however, the two issues served strategic ends in the debate. The economic union proposals allowed Ottawa to emphasize the pan-Canadian market – perhaps even argue for expanded federal powers – as a means of resisting arguments for decentralization. This was especially useful when all parties in Quebec, including the Parti Québécois, at least nominally embraced the concept of economic union. For its part, Ontario's Social Charter gave Ontarians something of their own in the negotiations, at a time when most issues required concessions from that province. It also tapped into a rich vein of pro-Charter sentiment and helped deflect arguments that social programs would be undermined by the Meech provisions on the spending power.

Each of these issues played an important role in discussions, but ultimately resulted in only modest proposals for change. While there was considerable support for reducing internal trade barriers and maintaining social programs, most governments balked at writing binding standards into the constitution. They supported the objectives in principle, but they also recognized competing priorities. They might favour a strong internal market, but they also valued supply-management schemes for farmers, government monopolies of automobile insurance, and provincially managed resource development. Would economic union threaten these? How would the commitment to social programs in a Social Charter be balanced against reducing taxes or controlling the deficit? In the end, governments wanted to be responsible for deciding those priorities. They did not want to abandon that role to judges. Moreover, in Quebec, the proposal for a Social Charter ran directly contrary to the province's traditional defence of provincial jurisdiction in the field of social programs.

This governmental reluctance had a crucial effect on the accord. Charlottetown did include a short, general statement of "policy objectives" regarding both social rights and the economic union, but these would not be enforceable before the courts. A mechanism for monitoring progress would be established at a future First Ministers Conference.[73]

NEW BRUNSWICK LANGUAGE RIGHTS. Finally, Charlottetown included one provision designed to entrench the equality of the French and English linguistic groups in New Brunswick, including the right to such distinct educational and cultural institutions "as are necessary for the preservation and promotion of those communities." This would constitutionalize benefits already extended under legislation in the province.[74] Unlike the rest of the package, it merely required the consent of New Brunswick and the federal Parliament. Following the failure of Charlottetown, it was adopted by these legislatures and is the only part of Charlottetown now in force.

The Failure of the Charlottetown Accord

The very fact that the Charlottetown Accord had been concluded was remarkable. It had been negotiated quickly, under the pressure of Quebec's referendum deadline and without, at least initially, much public support for talks. For most of the discussions, Quebec had been absent from the table. The ultimate agreement was sweeping in its scope and had won the support of the federal government, all the provincial and territorial governments, the four principal aboriginal organizations, and all major federal parties.

Ultimately, however, the accord failed. In the period following Meech Lake, a number of provinces, responding to the criticism of the Meech process, had adopted legislation requiring referenda before the ratification of a constitutional amendment. Faced with the prospect of a patchwork of votes, the federal government decided to hold a national referendum (given the symbolic significance of referenda in Quebec, that province's vote would be held under its own legislation, although at the same time as the national vote). The referendum was held on 26 October 1992. The accord still would have to be ratified by each provincial legislature (that was the procedure required by the amending formula), and so, to succeed, the referendum needed majority approval in virtually every province. It was defeated by a majority of all Canadians, by majorities in British Columbia, Alberta, Saskatchewan, Manitoba, Quebec, Nova Scotia, and the Yukon, and by a majority of aboriginal people on reserves. In Ontario the result was essentially a tie.

As in the defeat of the Meech Lake Accord, the reasons were legion.[75] Some concerned the conduct of the referendum campaign. The time between agreement and referendum – less than two months – was so short that there was little time for preparation. Some provinces had apparently given virtually no thought to their campaign strategy. The premier of Alberta announced his retirement in mid-campaign. In Quebec the "Yes" committee lurched from crisis to crisis as leaks emerged regarding high public servants' criticism of the accord. Moreover, the August agreement was merely an agreement in principle. It was not reduced to legal language until the second week of October. This delay kept many of the chief actors busy in the drafting process. The absence of a final text fed the suspicions of some Canadians – still profoundly distrustful of their politicians – that the governments were trying to hide something. Much of the early criticism of the accord, especially in Quebec, exploited the ambiguity of the August agreement's language. The lack of time for considering the implications was a major factor in reserve Indians' rejection of the accord.

The defeat of Charlottetown, however, was not simply a matter of haste or the accidents of a poor campaign. The fundamental attempt to unite Canadians around a single package of reforms had failed for several reasons of substance. First, in order to achieve broad agreement, the negotiators had allowed the proposals to be so whittled down that they ended up satisfying neither their supporters nor their opponents. This was true (as we have seen) of Senate reform and the distinct society clause. Second, many of the new provisions generated their own reasons for opposition. This was the case with aboriginal self-government (distrusted particularly in the West and Quebec), the 25 per cent guarantee of House of Commons seats for Quebec, and the equal Senate. And underlying all of these reasons for opposition was a continued inability to resolve the basic tensions left over from Meech. How could Canadians reconcile their respect for the individual with their acknowledgment of cultural difference? How could they combine provincial loyalties with allegiance to the whole, or a concern with Canadians' equality with recognition of Quebec's uniqueness? In the end, Charlottetown remained a set of largely ad hoc trade-offs, unsupported by a clear vision of the country as a whole.

Conclusion to Part One

Looking back over the last thirty years, it sometimes seems that in the very act of reaching for a new Canadian identity, we watched it slip away. In the late 1960s, we thought we were developing a coherent conception of ourselves as a nation, one building upon our English and French heritage but also adopting a distinctively Canadian view of the world, not simply an amalgam of English, American, and French Catholic visions. And in retrospect, during that period Canadians did find a distinctive voice (or voices). Canadian literature explored themes that had roots in a uniquely Canadian reality, and many of the old insecurities (the uneasy attempt to straddle the English and American cultures or, in French Canada, the attempt to preserve a culture entirely under the wing of the church) gave way to new, though tentative, self-confidence.

It was a good start, but we also stumbled upon serious challenges. The attempts to redefine Canada as a bicultural nation caused Canadians of other origins to wonder whether they had any place in this plan. Would they be relegated to the status of second-class citizens, people whose ancestors had helped build Canada but would be denied any place within the country's national myths? And what about the aboriginal peoples? If English and French were singled out because of their presence at the origin, what about the First Nations? At the very least, aboriginal peoples' long-standing claims for fair treatment demanded resolution.

There was even substantial disagreement over how to accommodate, in a practical way, the English and French linguistic communities, once we had decided that Canada should have a bilingual identity. Often the debate was framed in terms of personal-versus-territorial approaches to language. To what extent should linguistic regulation take the form of guarantees of individual rights? To what extent should it recognize and build upon the territorial concentration of language groups? Most Quebecers favoured some combination of the two: federal and many provincial services provided in both languages, but with special recognition of Quebec's role in preserving the French Canadian culture. There were some, however, who chose just one approach, rejecting the other as an offence against nature or principle. The most-committed *indépendantistes* chose an out-and-out territorial option, although within that framework they were willing to grant some privileges to Quebec's anglophones. And on the other side, Pierre Trudeau, the person who personified federalist French Canada for many anglophones, chose a rigorously individualist approach.

These disagreements reflected larger tensions within Canadian society over how to deal with social diversity, not only cultural diversity but also gender, racial, or other forms of difference. Some groups argued for some degree of governmental autonomy. This was obviously the case with the First Nations or Quebec, but there also remained considerable support for autonomy (although on somewhat different grounds) in all provinces. At the same time, there was an increasing emphasis on individual rights in the popular debate, sometimes in ways that ran counter to the governmental autonomy of groups. Some of these arguments concerned individual freedom as such, but often they were shaped by a unified conception of nation or citizenship that was fundamentally hostile to the recognition of distinct communities within the society as a whole.

During the three decades from 1960 to 1992, these conflicts of identity, equality, and nation were focused through the prism of constitutional reform. The impetus initially came from Quebec. Indeed, at first, the constitution seemed to be Quebec's own issue. The catalyst for this new phase of constitutional debate was the shift in Quebec from the church to the province as guarantor of the French Canadian cultural community, combined with a new, stronger emphasis on government-led participation in the economy as an expression of French culture in North America. This prompted successive Quebec governments to demand recognition of their distinctive role. Their demands usually focused, in the 1960s and 1970s, on restrictions on federal incursions into existing provincial powers and on arguments for the transfer of powers from Ottawa to Quebec (though with little precision as to what powers were necessary). In these arguments, Quebec politicians drew upon a long history that saw the federal-provincial division of powers as the bulwark of regional distinctiveness, particularly the uniqueness of Quebec.

In this, however, they were opposed by another forceful politician from Quebec, Pierre Trudeau, who resisted any attempt to identify French Canadian cultural aspirations with the Quebec government, fearing that any acknowledgment of such a cultural role would lead to intolerance within Quebec and perhaps the breakup of the country. He argued for a Canada in which popular allegiance would be focused on the centre, not Quebec – for a nationalism focused beyond French Canadian society. In place of the demands of Quebec, he argued for a federation in which each province would have an identical degree of autonomy, and language would be treated as a matter of abstract, individual right, identical (as far as possible) from coast to coast, and placed beyond the reach of any government in a constitutional charter of rights.

This sharp division of opinion led to stalemate in the discussions of the late 1960s and early 1970s. Then, in the late 1970s, the Parti Québécois came to power in Quebec. This altered the way in which Quebec's demands were perceived. Now arguments for Quebec's autonomy patently seemed like way stations on the road to separation. Federalist arguments for autonomy within Canada, made from the opposition benches, claimed little attention outside Quebec. Anglophone public opinion focused on the stark contrast between Ottawa and Quebec, between Trudeau's brand of federalism and the anti-federalism and anti-bilingualism of Lévesque.

Simultaneously other provinces (notably in the West) began to press for constitutional change. Their participation broadened the debate. Now, the conferences were no longer merely about "what Quebec wants." In fact, the PQ government, by taking Quebec out of the federalist camp, had given it *less* voice in a new constitutional order in Canada. Why should one reform the constitution to please a government committed to leaving, if pleasing that government were possible? The debate began to shift to a terrain in which Quebec's traditional concerns were marginalized. Trudeau's position increasingly seemed the federalist position from Quebec. Its chief interlocutors, in the attempt to achieve reform *within* the federal structure, were the governments of the English-speaking provinces.

The defeat of the referendum on sovereignty-association and the consequent demoralization of the separatist cause opened the way for Ottawa to profit from the marginalization of Quebec's traditional concerns. In the aftermath of the referendum, Ottawa forged ahead with its proposals for patriation with a charter of rights. It succeeded. The constitution was patriated, with a charter. The emphasis on individual rights – the focus on a single, undifferentiated Canadian citizenship – had caught fire among anglophone Canadians (including members of the multicultural communities) and francophones outside Quebec. As a result, the constitution took on a popular significance it had never had before. There were concessions in the Charter to the distinctiveness of aboriginal peoples, and in the years immediately following patriation there were efforts, blocked by the western provinces, to elaborate a right to aboriginal self-government. Quebec's claims to distinctiveness, however, were ignored. The whole process left many Quebecers uneasy, feeling roughly used. They generally favoured the protection of individual rights, but they saw little joy in the isolation of their government, the loss of Quebec's veto, and the rejection of the idea that Quebec should serve as guarantor of French Canadian culture. Trudeau's vision may have triumphed on the constitutional page and in English-speaking Canada, but many Quebecers still rejected its rigour and especially the constitutionalization of that rigour.

There remained in Quebec, then, deep disenchantment with the outcome of the long series of negotiations through the 1960s and 1970s. At first, because of exhaustion from the referendum campaign and the drive for patriation, Quebecers turned away from the constitution, pursuing other aspects of their lives. There was no doubt, however, that eventually the grievance would re-emerge. It therefore made sense (and was not at all the work of some "sorcerer's apprentice")[1] to attempt to find a reconciliation early, when passions were quiet, before a crisis re-emerged. Thus, the Meech process began.

The Meech Lake Accord was an attempt to recapture the other half of a long debate in Canadian constitutionalism: to build back into the constitution, alongside individual rights and a continued commitment to bilingualism (although not precisely the bilingualism Trudeau would have wished), the recognition of Quebec's special role in the promotion of French Canadian culture in Canada. It failed for a variety of reasons, but the most important was a failure of vision, an inability to show how this could make sense in terms of the country as a whole, how it could fit with the broadly accepted framework of individual rights.

The result was a loss of faith in our ability to live together as a country. Quebecers saw the rejection of Meech Lake as a rejection of what they believed Canada should be: a Canada in which it was possible to be both a good Quebecer and a good Canadian, in which one could continue to develop and thrive as a member of a distinctive linguistic community, a community whose particular character would shape the exercise of governmental power in Quebec. Canadians outside Quebec, watching that province's insistence on an accord that had no apparent justification in constitutional principle, wondered whether Quebecers had any concern for Canada as a whole. The Meech Lake debate seemed to reveal fundamental differences in what it meant to be Canadian.

We tried to overcome those differences – or at least to compromise them – in the Charlottetown Accord, concluded in the aftermath of Meech against the prospect of a new referendum in Quebec. The problem of justification remained, however, and that accord too was rejected. Paradoxically, the extent of the rejection meant that we were not thrown into full constitutional crisis, but the agreement on a "No" vote could not hide the fact that Canadians remained profoundly divided in their conception of the country. One wonders whether with each disappointment, with each abortive attempt to justify our country to ourselves, the commitment to the country becomes that much harder to sustain, the chances of failure more real.

In our recent debates, there were indeed differences in the terms we used to talk about citizenship, our allegiance to Canada and to our more local identities. But how fundamental were those differences? How reconcilable? To what extent do the concepts we use reflect the nature of a country like ours, the value of its communities and institutions, and the practical demands of liberty? How should we, as Canadians, think about the relationship between language, culture, political community, and allegiance?

It is to these questions that I turn.

PART TWO

Political Allegiance, Political Community, and the Canadian Constitution

6 Language, Culture, and Political Community

In the wake of the Meech Lake debacle, a number of Canadians responded to the widespread sense of bitterness and frustration by suggesting that we should return to fundamentals. We should decide what it means to be Canadian. We should determine what values Canadians hold in common. Then, when we are clear on our principles, when we know precisely what kind of country we want, it will be easy to redraft the constitution. And if at the end of the day we cannot come to any agreement ... well, we never had a real country anyhow, so we might as well learn that now.

This approach sought to base constitutional reform on a common sense of the national character and national objectives. The constitutional agreement would be more than just a compromise to keep the country from falling apart; it would express, as far as possible, the Canadian identity in constitutional form. It would be a kind of Canadian creed. The constitution would then be similar to such inspiring national documents as the foundational declarations of France or the United States, proclaiming a strong set of values to which all Canadians would subscribe.

This conception was very similar to Ottawa's position during its campaign for a charter of rights in the late 1960s and 1970s. That campaign had emphasized the constitution's role in defining national identity. It had tried to use constitutional change to create a robust, unified national citizenship. In 1969 a federal position paper put it this way: "The Constitution must express the purpose of Canadians in having become and resolving to remain associated together in a single country, and it must express as far as this is possible in a constitution what kind of country Canadians want, what values they cherish, and what objectives they seek."[1] Following Meech, some Canadians retained the same yearning for unity. They argued that the post-Meech period should be used not simply to find an accommodation with Quebec, but to reaffirm the content of a common Canadian citizenship.

The language of shared values was seductive.[2] Why shouldn't Canadians think about what makes them special in the world? Why shouldn't they define what is unique about their country? But the heavy emphasis on an agreed set of political objectives – on a single, constitutionalized statement of the role of language and culture in Canadian society, for example – troubled many. For those who were troubled, especially for members of such cohesive cultural minorities as francophone Quebecers and aboriginal peoples, the problem in the past had been too much emphasis on a single definition of what it meant to be Canadian, not too little. Most of them wanted to remain Canadians, but they wanted a Canada that recognized more than one society, more than one way of being Canadian. They wanted Canadian citizenship to embrace the variety of Canadian identities. The longer the list of common values written into the constitution, the less room there seemed to be for their particular form of belonging. And even when the set of values left some space for their cultures (through, for example, the toleration of aboriginal customs or official bilingualism), the structure was all wrong. If the country was defined exclusively by what people had in common, characteristics that set minority communities apart would be pushed to the margins, becoming at best protected aspects of one's personal life, at worst latent obstacles to national unity. They would not be an integral part of what it meant to be Canadian.

For some advocates of the shared-values approach, this reluctance to speak in terms of common citizenship was precisely what made Canada such a frustrating place. Canada seemed to insist on remaining an imperfect, poorly integrated country, with a large proportion of its citizenry concerned more with setting themselves apart than with building a nation together. That was the weakness that had, they believed, undermined Canada's constitutional (indeed national) development, sapped its allegiance, and prevented it from finding a coherent sense of itself. As long as that division remained, Canada seemed condemned to drift from one quarrel to another, without any national vision.

But is that the way we should think about our country? Are those the kinds of demands we should make of Canadians' sense of allegiance? There is another way of looking at questions of identity and citizenship, one that rethinks what a country is all about. It rejects the notion that countries are typified by long lists of agreed principles, and suggests that a strong focus on shared values or a canonical set of national beliefs betrays a misunderstanding of the substance of political community. Allegiance is important, but it does not require a wide measure of agreement on substantive ends. Belonging is important, but it does not require that one's values be shared by others. A small core of shared values is vital to the health of a democratic order, but the list of those truly essential values will be relatively short, including basic respect for democratic procedures and political accountability, but not everything that makes a country what it is. Indeed, the common core of democratic values may well be the same across a broad variety of democratic states. The essential problem with the language of shared values is that it is forced to carry too much weight. It leads one to over-determine what is important to a country and to citizenship, to constitutionalize visions of a country that do violence to its richness and diversity, impliedly excluding those who do not share those visions. It is often, in the end, anti-democratic, imposing exaggerated and unnecessary tests of belief on its citizens as proof of their allegiance.

This chapter develops an alternative conception of political community. It shows how a more subtle conception of national identity can make sense of Canadians' patterns of participation and allegiance, their complex ideas of themselves and their country. This conception in turn lays the foundation for a more nuanced understanding of the role of language and culture in the definition of Canada's political communities, especially the relationship between different kinds of cultural diversity and the structure of Canadian federalism.

IDENTITY AND ALLEGIANCE IN
DEMOCRACIES

Are democratic nations really defined by what their citizens agree upon? Is national identity, even in those countries with the strongest sense of themselves, typified by adherence to a single set of values?

The answer must be no. Trying to define what makes a German a German, an American an American, or a Canadian a Canadian by listing the values that citizens of those countries hold in common can only produce a caricature of a country. National identities are much more complex. Countries always contain considerable diversity. Even the most stable and apparently unified generate vigorous debates about their very essence. In fact, societies that seem to have the clearest "national character" are often defined more by their disagreements than by their agreements. It isn't so much what citizens agree upon as the way in which they disagree that is important. It is the distinctive structure of their fundamental debates – the issues that preoccupy their public life, the ways in which those issues are posed, the kinds of solutions discussed – that give a society its distinctive cast.

An example might help. The United States is one country that seems to be defined by its devotion to a single set of values enshrined in its constitution. It prides itself on its unity and presents an image of consensus and commitment to the world. Although it fought a bloody civil war, there is no present risk of secession. What then are the values it stands for? Everyone would agree they include equality among persons, democratic government, and individual freedom, especially the freedom of the market. But if we push a little harder, we find, first, that to the extent the values are shared by a consensus of Americans, they are also shared by the citizens of many other Western democracies, and second, if we attempt to make the description of values more specific in order to capture their distinctively American features, it becomes much more difficult to claim that consensus exists.

Take equality. That concept is subject to many different meanings, meanings that imply very different conceptions of society. Americans have often argued bitterly over which conception their country should embrace. The Civil War was caused in part by an inability to agree on whether Black Americans should be included at all within the sphere of equality, and there have since been many struggles over the extent of equality they should enjoy. The very content of equality has also been hotly contested. Does it include freedom from hunger, concrete provision for members of disadvantaged groups, and minimum wages and safe working conditions for employees, or is it nothing more than freedom from discriminatory legislation? Should day-care centres and maternity leaves be supported in order to permit women to participate in the workforce, or should policies founded on "traditional family values" prevail?

These debates have been far from marginal within American society. The importance of the Civil War to the American self-image can hardly be overstated, and regional divisions descended from the war continue to this day. Arguments over the relationship between property and equality were at the foundation of the severe labour disputes of the late nineteenth and early twentieth centuries. They also formed the backdrop for this century's dramatic conflict over the

United States Supreme Court's interpretation of the constitution, when that court first ruled much social legislation unconstitutional (including minimum-wage laws and the first New Deal legislation) before reversing its course in the face of popular and presidential pressure. The same kinds of divisions are evident in the judicial decisions and politics of today, most obviously in the differences between a Massachusetts liberal like Edward Kennedy and a southern conservative like Jesse Helms.

In drawing attention to these debates, I do not want to deny their specifically American character. On the contrary, the terms of the discussion, the kinds of arguments used, the balance between the contending positions, and the tentative solutions adopted all bear a distinctively American stamp. They embody an American vernacular. But it is the character of the conversation as a whole, rather than one of the sides to that debate, that makes the public life of America what it is. One of the parties may try to wrap itself in the flag and present itself as the only true American – as Joseph McCarthy did during the 1950s – but surely that does violence to the true character of the society. The McCarthy period, with its House Un-American Activities Committee, is an aberration, part of the pathology of American nationalism. The national character of the United States, like that of all other societies, is characterized by a debate through time, not by a static, single set of values.[3]

We find the same situation if we turn to the structure of Canada's identities. It has become common on the left, for example, to attempt to identify Canadianness with a strong commitment to social programs such as medicare. Without doubt, Canadians have been more committed to that kind of program than Americans, a commitment well worth cherishing. But can we really claim that that commitment is what makes a Canadian? There were many who opposed medicare on its introduction. Significant numbers are now willing to weaken it. The political party most identified with the social philosophy underlying medicare (the New Democratic Party) has always been in the minority in Canada as a whole. Are those who refuse to support the NDP un-Canadian?

What makes us Canadian is not simply a shared commitment to social programs (a commitment that is, after all, significantly greater in some European countries). Our Canadianness lies in the particular character of our public life, which has indeed produced extensive social programs but which is much richer than the bare commitment to those programs would suggest.

If we leave aside the question of Canadianness itself for a moment and look at the identity of the provincial society from which medicare emerged – Saskatchewan – we find that even its character can hardly be reduced to a willingness to pioneer socialized medicine. In the politics of Saskatchewan farm country, for example, the willingness to use the state to achieve social ends, based in part on the experience of the cooperative movement, has always had to contend with a more conservative populism, one that could produce the government of a Ross Thatcher or Grant Devine. And that is only within rural Saskatchewan. This perspective does not begin to consider the distinctive contributions to Saskatchewan's political culture of aboriginal peoples, city dwellers, or those involved in the potash, coal, uranium, or forest industries.

If one looks at any of the well-defined provincial identities in Canada, there are elements of disagreement and movement, themes and counter-themes. Newfoundland has its ancient conflicts over religion and its more recent struggles over how to reconcile a commitment to autonomy with dependence on Canada as a whole. Although outsiders may see French-speaking Quebec as a homogeneous, strongly collectivist society, once devoted to preserving a unity of faith and now using the state to impose a single culture and language, there has always been a strongly liberal strain in Quebec politics, even within the ranks of the "nationalists." British Columbia seems to be one society where even the popular stereotypes of the province's identity embrace confrontation and conflict.

In fact, whenever one moves beyond the most simplistic of generalizations, the distinctive character of societies seems to reside more in the pattern of their public life – the terms of public discussion in those societies – than in any strong set of common values. It is more about the way issues are put, how citizens define themselves in relation to the issues, how they go about resolving them, than about an absence of disagreement and discussion.

Now, this may seem like an odd basis on which to build nationality. What is left, once these elements of disagreement and contestation are acknowledged? What kind of allegiance is possible? Two very important kinds of commonality persist, more powerful than might at first appear.

First, if national identities are essentially about the character of the public discussion through time, the very willingness to engage in that discussion – to see the discussion as one's own or, in the case of those currently excluded, to desire to be included – implies a common commitment. The commitment is to the discussion itself. Each individual is willing to pursue her agenda in that forum. She cares about other members of the forum accepting the rightness of her position. She sees the community within which the debate takes place as, in some sense, her own. It may not be the only community she cares about. She may well be committed both to a national community and to one closer to home. But the very fact that she is willing to bother with discussion implies a sense of belonging.[4]

There are different degrees of commitment. Commitment may be the product of necessity or economic self-interest: one simply cannot get out of the community, or getting out would be too costly. That may seem like an impoverished basis for any lasting political community, but even this grudging allegiance may ripen into a more robust commitment as members of the community come to conceive of their public life in terms inseparable from the particular debates of that community.

That seems to be what has happened to Quebec since the British Conquest. The French colonists initially became British by compulsion, not by choice. Yet over the years, French Canadians have pursued their public goals, first within a British colonial framework, then within the Canadian state. Their political identity has been shaped by that experience, and indeed, their participation has in turn contributed to the political life of Canada as a whole. Out of that long history a substantial commitment to the whole has emerged. Quebecers may not always acknowledge that commitment. Their desire to maintain their own culture, their periodic experience of hostility or indifference in the rest of Canada, and the ever-present sense of vulnerability all discourage fulsome expressions of allegiance to Canada. They may state their commitment in terms of simple practicality – Robert Bourassa's *fédéralisme rentable* (profitable federalism), for example. But the devotion of Quebecers to a Canadian solution, the desire (even of *indépendantistes*) to maintain relations with the rest of Canada, and Quebecers' continued attachment to Canadian symbols (citizenship, the Canadian identity abroad, bilingualism, rivalries in Canadian sport) suggest a more fundamental, less instrumental allegiance. Here, as in many areas, the expression may lag behind experience.[5]

There are, of course, more enthusiastic levels of commitment, expressed with more sound and fury, and again these forms of allegiance are usually quite apart from agreement or disagreement with a country's policies. The United States is a good example. Edward Kennedy and Jesse Helms are both Americans. Although each of them would like nothing better than to have his policies prevail, it is inconceivable that they would sever the American union to get their way. Their membership in the American community is paramount, in a way that goes beyond a simple calculation of interest. It is extremely difficult to put one's finger on the focus of allegiance in each case. It certainly involves identification with the symbols and history (real or imagined) of the country, as well as some attachment to the country's geographical dimensions – a sense, perhaps, that these have been instrumental in forming one's individual identity. For some citizens, this focus may include appreciation for the very diversity that makes up their country: the qualities that specific immigrant groups have brought to the whole, for example, or the distinctive traditions of New England or North Carolina. This allegiance may not include love for all aspects of a nation's traditions. Some may be vigorously rejected (slavery and segregation in the American south, for example), but even then, a citizen might still feel his character has been marked by those struggles. Those struggles may be part of what it means to be American. One's conception of nation may draw on the very specific experiences of particular regions, cherishing their strengths while rejecting their objectionable features.

This sense of nationality can, in other words, accept the image of Canadian cultural relations coined by author Hugh MacLennan, that of two solitudes. Canadians tend to think of this phrase as capturing a regrettable, perhaps insurmountable sense of isolation between French-speaking and English-speaking Canadians. Canada consists of "two solitudes" in the same way that a century earlier Lord Durham believed it was made up of "two nations warring in the bosom of a single state." The solitudes are something to bemoan, not celebrate. We forget, however, that the phrase, which is drawn from a letter by the German poet Rilke, is a metaphor not of hopeless isolation but of love. Rilke's full sentence is as follows: "Love consists in this, that two solitudes protect, and touch, and greet each other." It captures the tension between our individuality on the one hand and our ability to communicate and share on the other. The letter emphasizes the need for those who love to continue to develop individually, a process involving some independence and even loneliness. The letter also emphasizes that men should not expect the women they love to remain within conventional female roles; women must have room to develop their full, distinctively female humanity. It tries, in other words, to capture the understanding that people can live together, can share, without surrendering their own sense of uniqueness and their own need to grow in that uniqueness.[6]

Placing the metaphor back in its context sheds a very different light on the possibility of our cultural interaction. It suggests that we can cherish the conversation between different cultures – we can see that conversation as constituting our community – without requiring the submission of one to the other. A viable allegiance can be com-

patible with the express recognition of difference as long as we remain willing to continue the national conversation across cultures.
That willingness is the very substance of our allegiance. The conversation itself is our national life. Frank Scott's poem, "Dancing," captures the extension of Rilke's metaphor in the manner suggested
above:[7]

DANCING

Long ago
when I first danced
I danced
holding her
back and arm
making her move
as I moved

she was best
when she was
least herself
lost herself

Now I dance
seeing her
dance away from
me   she
looks at me
dancing   we
are closer
held in the movement of the dance
I no longer dance
with myself
we are two
not one
the dance
is one

A second form of commonality will almost certainly be present as
well. The simple fact of conversing will very likely lead, over time, to
some sharing of perspective, of concern, perhaps even of answers to
public questions. So why aren't these answers the common principles
or common values we should write into the constitution? First, in a
country as diverse as Canada, they are likely to be difficult to identify

and heavily nuanced when we do identify them. They may well relate to how we make decisions rather than to grand constitutional principle. They may be provisional: accepted now, but subject to evolution as the relations between our communities evolve.[8] We may find, in other words, that what we most value is the health, vitality, and flexibility of our national conversation. If we insist on consensus on the details now, we may suddenly exclude our ability to continue to talk together.

Our constitutionalism, then, is likely to have a particular flavour, establishing the structures through which political discussion is focused, enshrining some general, stable, relatively uncontroversial principles (freedom of religion; the rights of a person accused of a crime), invoking the complexity of Canadian society and inviting the courts to take that into account in the interpretation of the constitution, but without trying to write the whole of Canada into the document. Rather than attempt to freeze the conversation at a moment in time, we are likely to aim for structures compatible with the shape the conversation should take.

The kind of nationalism on which this constitution would be based would be a soft nationalism – patriotism might be a better word – tolerant of diversity. That doesn't mean it would lack all character. Canadian patriotism would be unlike all others in its commitment to the distinctively Canadian conversation and that conversation's distinctive vernaculars – in its cherishing, that is, of continued community on the northern half of North America and (one hopes) of the particular contributions over time of English and French women and men, aboriginal peoples, Canadians of neither English, French, nor aboriginal background, and our great variety of regional and local communities.

Lying behind this conception of patriotism is an understanding of why nations are important to their citizens. They are important not because they pursue a long list of constitutionalized goals with which all citizens agree, but because they serve as forums for discussion and decision making. They serve as the framework, in other words, for democratic self-government. They provide the structures through which we come together, deliberate about the objectives we should pursue, and take steps as a society to achieve them. We value our country because we value the particular character of its public debate. That specific debate is ours, one we know and care about. This is rarely a matter of conscious decision. Few of us chose to be Canadians, and if we did, we rarely knew precisely what we were choosing. Rather, we found ourselves in this country by birth or by the accidents of immigration. Once here, we defined our political opinions in terms of Canada's concerns, questions, and struggles. And over time, the unique character of its public debate marked us. We may well wish to change parts of that debate. In extreme cases, we may seek to escape it altogether. But generally we will be drawn to work for change from within the debate for the simple reason that it is ours. It concerns our community, and speaks in terms we understand.[9]

REGIONAL IDENTITIES IN CANADIAN FEDERALISM

We can, then, conceive of a strong sense of allegiance both to Canada and to communities closer to home without subordinating our concern with one to the other. But why, we might ask, should this lead to the recognition of separate political units within the country? Why can't our diverse communities find expression through the institutions of a single national state? We all have different attachments, define our communities in different ways, and belong to a host of overlapping and intersecting groups. Why should some have governmental authority, others none? What kinds of differences justify governmental autonomy, and over what matters? On what normative principles should we base the sharing of governmental authority in the Canadian federation?

Once again, the close relationship between the sense of political community and the specific character of public debate provides a clue. The previous section suggested that national identity is defined, not by shared values, but by the distinctive character of a particular public debate through time. The fact that one sees the debate as one's own, that one is committed to maintaining the conversation, is the basis of allegiance. In countries where that commitment is strong, a vigorous political debate exists, embracing the entire country within its scope and addressing issues important to the country as a whole. But that nationwide forum need not be the only place of public discussion. There may be more restricted forums (or indeed broader ones – at the international level, for example) in which debates follow their own dynamic, autonomous in large degree from that of the national community. Those other forums, grouping together different sets of participants and often addressing different issues, may attract their own sense of allegiance, which may, depending on the intensity of the debate and its importance to its participants, be similar to that given the national community. Citizens may cherish both the particular character of their national conversation and that of their local political community. They may wish to see decision making structured so that some decisions are made within the wider, national political community, others closer to home.

This attempt to create appropriate local and national structures will always be approximate. Our debates are sufficiently fluid, our commitments sufficiently various, that it is impossible to achieve a perfect fit between patterns of public discussion and institutions of government. An approximate fit is better than none, however. Because of the complexity of interests involved and the impossibility of perfection, the precise scope of the institutions will inevitably be the result of negotiation, experiment, and adjustment, but there are some factors that are particularly important in defining the shape of the cohesive, highly autonomous communities of debate that demand some form of political autonomy. These factors are often a complex blend of the influence of existing political institutions on the one hand and the presence of linguistic or cultural divisions on the other. The different combinations of these factors result in different tendencies towards political autonomy. This section examines the range of considerations important in arguments over federalism and autonomy in the Canadian context, sketching their implications for the structure of Canadian government.

The Legacy of Established Institutions

Sometimes it seems that the structure of governmental institutions is the most important factor in the creation of political communities, rather than the other way around. The institutions come first, and public discussion moulds itself to them.

Thus, when colonies were established in what would later become Canada, their boundaries largely determined the dimensions of political debate in the territory. To some extent, these boundaries were based on patterns of settlement or geographical separation, and therefore reflected physical differences directly relevant to the ability to sustain community. They corresponded, in other words, to what might serve as a natural basis for political community. The correspondence was rough, however. Although there might have been a closely related core of settlements in each colony, that core was usually joined to a vast hinterland, where the existing settlements might have very little to do with the core. The colonies were sufficiently large, sparsely populated, and diverse that there was often little real cohesion prior to the establishment of the colonial government. Political activity began to conform to their boundaries only after the colonies were created, simply because those boundaries controlled where decisions would be made. If one's settlement fell within New Brunswick, the government of that colony gradually became the focus of political concern (for decisions made at the colonial level). And over time, each colony developed its own political flavour, its own coalitions, its own set of central issues. Each developed a distinctive public debate, a debate that served as a focus for its citizens' loyalty and sense of identification.

Citizens' identification with these colonial political cultures was the direct antecedent of provincial loyalties, once the colonies entered Confederation. Seven of the ten provinces – all except Saskatchewan, Alberta, and that very special case, Manitoba – were separate colonies with their own histories and traditions prior to joining Confederation. Although the governments' role changed as they moved from colonial to provincial status (and the boundaries of some provinces were extended into territories previously beyond the control of any colonial legislature), essentially the same political units persisted, only this time addressing a more restricted set of issues. It is no surprise, then, that the established loyalties remained strong. Indeed, in many areas it took some time for allegiance to the new country to rival provincial loyalties.

Thus, in Canada, the existence of strong provincial political traditions predated the development of attachments to the whole. When those attachments did develop, they supplemented rather than excluded the established provincial loyalties. I am not suggesting that because these units were once independent, they have a moral claim to retain autonomy. My argument is not based on a compact theory of Confederation, on the idea that Canada was made by agreement of the provinces, and that therefore the provincial units are primary, the federal secondary. This book deliberately renounces historical arguments of that kind.[10] The fact that colonial loyalties existed prior to Confederation is important, not because it supports a historically based right, but because it forms one foundation for the strong provincial loyalties that existed after Confederation and still exist (in substantially modified form) today. It forms a large part of the explanation for why provincial political communities have their present dimensions, why there remain strong, distinctive, provincial political cultures. Indeed, I believe this is why the compact theory has had appeal over the years: it tries (imperfectly) to capture the fact that provincial loyalties are not secondary or subordinate to Canadian loyalty. Those loyalties did not grow up under the wing of a broader Canadian nationality. On the contrary, they predate Canada.

The provincial loyalties have, of course, changed over time. The provinces are now only one of the forums for public debate, and that evolution has had a profound effect on their significance for their citizens (an effect discussed below). However, the existence of provincial governments, exercising very substantial powers over a defined territory, continues to support autonomous communities of debate that remain relevant today. That institutional structure lies behind, for example, Canadians' recognition of a distinctive Albertan or Nova Scotian or Prince Edward Island political culture.

Provincial loyalties are often criticized as artificial, especially by those who would like to see a more centralized Canada. To these critics, it is regrettable that allegiance to the whole should be sapped by the parochial interests of the provinces, interests that, from the above discussion, seem to be based on little more than historical accident. In their view, provincial positions are all too often the product of inertia, institutional self-interest, or the tendency of governmental elites to self-aggrandizement. Surely, they argue, we should be sceptical about these claims to distinctively provincial interests.[11]

Indeed we should. Institutional inertia and empire-building do play a role in the statements of provincial politicians, just as they do in all areas of human activity (including, incidentally, the positions of the federal government). But there is good reason to resist slipping from scepticism into utter disregard, good reason to recognize that even though there is an element of historical accident in the structure of provincial communities and puffery in the arguments of provincial politicians, there is a solid basis for at least some of the claims to a distinctive provincial perspective.

First, provincial communities do express real differences on the ground. The differences between the political cultures of New Brunswick and Saskatchewan cannot be reduced to institutional self-interest. They reflect the differing character of those provinces' histories, economies, and population. The precise packaging of those interests – the fact that most Acadians find themselves in New Brunswick, that the Saskatchewan-Alberta boundary follows the fourth meridian – may be a result of "accident," but the interests within those boundaries are real enough. In fact, those variations give substance to the idea that there are distinctive regional perspectives on Confederation – a western or a Maritime perspective, for example.

The existence of separate governments gives greater voice to the varying regional interests, voice that might otherwise be drowned out if the interests all had to compete on the national stage. We see this most clearly in matters falling within provincial jurisdiction: the study of the contribution of Ukrainian Canadians to the settlement of the Prairies, for example, claims a larger place within Saskatchewan schools than it would if curriculum were set by Ottawa. It is also true for matters wholly within Ottawa's jurisdiction: Newfoundland fishermen have a higher profile in national politics because of their influence in a province, higher than they would have if they had to rely exclusively on members of the House of Commons to put their case; and in the early years of this century, Prairie farmers used their provincial governments to establish at least some counterweight to the power of the Canadian Pacific Railway. In fact, although we often speak of regionalism and regional interests, those apparently transprovincial interests generally find expression through provincial governments. And the existence of provincial rather than regional governments reveals the marked contrasts that exist among provincial societies even within regions (between, for example, Alberta and Saskatchewan).

Second, the fact that a community is defined by events lacking strong justification – by the drawing of boundaries in London or by self-interested bargaining between elites, for example – does not necessarily impair that community's integrity or its significance to its members. All communities have elements of accident about them. We can point to events crucial to the definition of any society that could have occurred otherwise. Indeed, from the point of view of the individual, we virtually always join a community by accident, usually by birth. A sense of place, a sense of belonging, is more dependent on what happens after people have been thrown together than on the way they came together in the first place. After all, Canada was separated from the United States by the same kind of arbitrary process that separated the provinces from each other. The boundary between British Columbia and Washington was, at the origin, just as artificial as that between Alberta and Saskatchewan. Yet few Canadians would suggest that BC's present allegiance to Canada is artificial, or that the differences that have grown up between the United States and Canada are of no account.

The point is this: even if democratic communities are defined by institutional arrangements beyond their control – even if they are affected by the self-interested manoeuvring of elites – they can well acquire immense significance for their members, so that their continued existence is not the concern of elites alone. Although their character may, in the first instance, be determined by structures imposed by arbitrary authority, once established they take on lives of their own – lives which elites may invoke for their purposes, but which nevertheless have a real foundation in society.

Functional Justifications for Provincial Autonomy

Prior to Confederation, most colonial assemblies exercised broad legislative authority. After Confederation, provincial powers were

restricted to those specified in the new constitution, with the balance
exercised by Ottawa. Thus, although the provinces' territorial jurisdiction was essentially the same as it had been before Confederation,
their subject-matter jurisdiction was changed. Each citizen became a
member of at least two levels of political community: the province
for provincial subjects and the wider Canadian community for federal subjects.[12] The territorial boundaries might be the product of
past institutional arrangements, but the communities defined by the
federal-provincial division of powers were the result of deliberation
and choice.

When the fathers of Confederation turned their minds expressly
to the construction of political community, what principles did they
apply? English Canadian constitutional scholarship tends to assume
that they based the division of powers on the idea that political communities should be large or small depending on the nature of the
power exercised. Decisions that interest only a restricted number of
individuals should, this approach suggests, be handled by small political units. Those affecting an entire country should be handled at
the national level. Placing power in the hands of the appropriate
level leads to the most efficiency because the people with the greatest
interest make the decisions. The classic example is the authority conferred on municipalities. Garbage collection, street repair, local li-
braries, and neighbourhood parks are of little concern to the entire
country but of great concern to those who actually use a particular
service. Hence, they are governed by the most local level. Similar
analysis is used to delineate the appropriate jurisdiction of all
governments.

As an explanation for the present form of the Canadian division
of powers, this is patently incomplete. Some of the powers clearly
were allocated on grounds having little to do with functionalism;
where they do represent a functional approach, the kinds of considerations sketched above are often inseparable from attention to the
specific cultural landscape of Canada. The fact that Quebec's tradition of private law differs from that of other provinces, for example,
was undoubtedly one of the major reasons the provinces retained
control over "Property and Civil Rights," one of the most important
of the provincial powers, covering virtually all of the private law.[13]
There was no functional presumption that private law was best handled at a local level. In fact, section 94 of the 1867 constitution contemplated the unification of private law under Ottawa's jurisdiction,
although only for provinces other than Quebec. Federal jurisdiction
over marriage and divorce was another exception to the functionalist model.[14] Divorce was severed from the rest of the private law, not
because of the kind of calculation described above, but simply to en-

sure that the divorces of Quebec Protestants would be free from regulation by the laws of a Catholic legislature.

Some aspects of the division of powers were indeed based on the functionalist concerns described above, however. For example, although municipalities have no independent constitutional status of their own, they are placed under the most local level of government recognized in the constitution – the provinces.[15] The provincial jurisdiction over hospitals, asylums, charities, and such businesses as auctioneering or taverns also suggests a functionalist approach.[16] The residual power of the provinces over "Generally all Matters of a merely local or private Nature in the Province" reflects the same spirit.[17] A functionalist approach is still more evident at the federal level. The framers of the 1867 constitution made a concerted attempt to give Ottawa powers to promote the development of an integrated national economy. Ottawa obtained jurisdiction over interprovincial and international trade and commerce,[18] the infrastructure of interprovincial and international transportation and communication (railways, shipping, telegraphs, and the post office), the principal instruments of capital formation (banking, interest, and money), and a set of powers important to the settlement of the West (concurrent authority with the provinces over agriculture and immigration; control over public lands on the Prairies, eventually transferred to the provinces in 1930).[19] But even at the federal level, the functionalist approach was by no means absolute. Ottawa's power over criminal law seems to have been based, not on functional considerations (in the United States and Australia, criminal law is a state rather than a federal responsibility), but instead on the fact that at Confederation the criminal law (then uncodified) was presumed to be virtually identical in each of the colonies.

In fact, although functionalist considerations had a significant role to play in the design of the division of powers, later commentators have tended to be much more single-minded than the framers in the pursuit of a functionalist analysis. They have used functionalism as a critical tool, suggesting how the constitution should be interpreted (or amended) to better reflect functionalist concerns.[20] Usually, these criticisms have tended towards a more centralized vision of Canada, reflecting a presumption that when it comes to the economy, the larger the better. The left-leaning critics of the 1930s and 1940s argued that the economic powers exercised by the provinces were incompatible with proper economic and social planning.[21] In the recent round of constitutional negotiations, the federal government's proposal that it receive increased powers to promote a single market reflects a conservative variant of the same idea.[22] These arguments have provincialist counterparts. In recent years, for exam-

200 Allegiance, Community, and the Constitution

ple, especially given the current dominance of economics in the province's political discourse, Quebec has phrased its arguments for decentralization in functionalist terms, claiming that overlapping jurisdictions are inefficient and that Ottawa seems incapable of managing the economy effectively.[23] Nevertheless, by and large, functionalist arguments follow a centralizing trend, especially in constitutional scholarship in English.

There is no doubt, then, that functionalist arguments have influenced and will continue to influence the express definition of political communities in the Canadian constitution. But they are far from the only factors. They are best suited to the analysis of economic powers, although even there they are unable to explain the current division of legislative authority, especially the large body of provincial regulation founded on "Property and Civil Rights." Moreover, functionalist arguments have difficulty explaining why provincial autonomy should be constitutionalized in the first place. If the division of powers is simply a matter of functional devolution, why not let it occur within the framework of a unitary state? Surely a unitary government would want to use governmental power effectively by delegating when necessary. That is what happens in a state like Britain. Why require constitutional safeguards?

The fact is that the political communities shaped by the division of powers are not a matter of mere functional efficiency. They result from the complex balancing of a host of factors, including functional considerations but also including the persistence of local loyalties, established institutional interest, the historical conflicts of the Union period, and such cultural concerns as the unique character of Quebec.[24] It is to these cultural concerns that I now turn.

Language and Political Community

The previous sections explored two ways in which institutional structures shape political community. The first suggested that structures for public decision making shape public discussion and that, over time, these forums for discussion become the foundation for a strong sense of belonging, of allegiance. The second discussed the deliberate attempt to construct political communities by designing institutions on functionalist grounds. This third section deals with quite a different phenomenon: how a particular social characteristic – language – tends by its very nature to define the boundaries of political community. Language has this effect because, in addition to being a subject of public debate, it is the medium through which public debate occurs.

LINGUISTIC DIVISION AND DISCURSIVE AUTONOMY. I begin
with one of the most insightful, yet most troubling, examinations
of the relationship between language and politics in Canada: the
report of the great English liberal Lord Durham on the constitutional structure of the Canadas in the period immediately
following the rebellions of 1837–38.

Durham's report was strongly marked by the liberal nationalism
of his age, especially its tendency to consider linguistic differences as
inherently confining, inherently illiberal, limiting the sphere of mobility and choice that liberalism sought to expand. It was also
marked by an Englishman's prejudice against French Canadian culture, a prejudice evident throughout the report but especially in
Durham's infamous descriptions of French Canadians as an "unin-
structed, inactive, unprogressive people," "a people with no history,
and no literature."[25] I clearly reject both those aspects of Durham's
argument. Indeed, the whole purpose of this book is to show how
language and culture shape political community and to argue for
more effective means of accommodating the differences they create.
One of its major premises is precisely the value of preserving
Quebec's distinctive character. I also reject the central conclusion of
Durham's report: that French and English cannot coexist within a
stable country and that French Canadians must therefore abandon
their language and join the English majority. But although Durham
and I soon part company, his report remains a trenchant commentary on the influence of language on the dynamic of political interaction, a provocative introduction to dilemmas that continue to
bedevil relations between English- and French-speaking Canadians.

Lord Durham began his discussion of the situation in Lower
Canada (now Quebec) by expressing his deep chagrin that the conflict was not a straightforward fight for responsible government, but
principally a struggle over language: "I expected to find a contest
between a government and a people: I found two nations warring in
the bosom of a single state: I found a struggle, not of principles, but
of races; and I perceived that it would be idle to attempt any amelio-
ration of laws or institutions, until we could first succeed in terminat-
ing the deadly animosity that now separates the inhabitants of Lower
Canada into the hostile divisions of French and English."[26]

Durham went on to describe how language could cause such
serious divisions. In part, according to Durham, the tensions of
1837–38 resulted from the English disdain for the customs of the
French inhabitants, on the one hand, and French Canadian jealousy
of "English enterprize," on the other. But he also noted that, quite
apart from prejudice, religious and linguistic differences meant that

there was very little mixing between the populations. There was, for example, no common system of education "to remove and soften the differences of origin and language": "The associations of youth, the sports of childhood, and the studies by which the character of manhood is modified, are distinct and totally different. In Montreal and Quebec there are English schools, and French schools; the children in these are accustomed to fight nation against nation."

Newspapers were similarly divided on linguistic grounds, so that national animosities were aggravated "by representing all the events of the day in utterly different lights":

The political misrepresentation of facts is one of the incidents of a free press in every free country; but in nations in which all speak the same language, those who receive a misrepresentation from one side, have generally some means of learning the truth from the other. In Lower Canada, however, where the French and English papers represent adverse opinions, and where no large portion of the community can read both languages with ease, those who receive the misrepresentation are rarely able to avail themselves of the means of correction.

Business and leisure also tended to divide on linguistic grounds. "The two parties combine for no public object," he concluded, "they cannot harmonize even in associations of charity."[27]

Durham identified two kinds of consequences flowing from the linguistic division. First, the separation in education (and more generally in literature) resulted in different modes of argument so that "the arguments which convince the one, are calculated to appear utterly unintelligible to the other."

The literature with which each is the most conversant, is that of the peculiar language of each; and all the ideas which men derive from books, come to each of them from perfectly different sources ... Those who have reflected on the powerful influence of language on thought, will perceive in how different a manner people who speak in different languages are apt to think; and those who are familiar with the literature of France, know that the same opinion will be expressed by an English and French writer of the present day, not merely in different words, but in a style so different as to mark utterly different habits of thought.

Second, the overwhelming prominence of linguistic differences meant that language served as a focus for jealousy and resentment, embittering relations between the communities.[28]

Durham traced the origin of the problem to the simple fact that two languages existed within a single, North American society. The problem could only be solved, he believed, through the gradual assimilation of the French-speaking population. He recommended that this be done by imposing a single political structure on the Canadas, with French Canadians in the minority. This would deprive the French-speaking community of control over public institutions and create strong incentives for individuals to function in English, without abandoning the principles of democratic government. Louisiana was a good example of "the influence of perfectly equal and popular institutions in effacing distinctions of race without disorder or oppression, and with little more than the ordinary animosities of party in a free country."[29]

In the end, Lord Durham did not get his way. Although an amended version of his proposal was adopted (Lower and Upper Canada were united under a single legislature, in a way that ensured an English-speaking majority), the French Canadians proved more tenacious than expected. Many institutional differences of the previous regime were replicated within the new structure. By Confederation, twenty-eight years later, there were parallel ministries for several government portfolios, one for Lower, one for Upper Canada. Laws were often limited to one of the former colonies, and when enacted, were frequently submitted to a double majority (a majority of all members of the legislature and of all members from constituencies in the unit affected).[30]

Most importantly, Canada remained a country with two principal public languages, and this meant that its political debate also remained divided. Much of what Durham had to say about the effect of language on political discourse has a very contemporary ring to Canadians. Generally, students are still educated in one language or the other. Social interaction occurs predominantly within rather than across linguistic lines. The media of mass communication are divided, with political discussion in the French media having a dynamic quite different from that in English. The separation is certainly not total. There are bilingual Canadians, there are institutions that bring members of the two linguistic groups together in relative equality, and at least at the federal level, the raw materials of political reporting (parliamentary debates; press releases; policy documents) are generally available in both official languages. The interchange that this bilingualism makes possible is crucial to the maintenance of a Canadian political community and has expanded greatly in the last thirty years (although it is still generally restricted to the elite level).

But bilingualism has not removed – and cannot remove – the barriers completely. Most Canadians are not bilingual, and it seems unlikely that a majority will become bilingual in the future, given the geographical concentration of language groups. Proficiency in a language demands practice and a strong incentive to learn, both of which are affected by the absence of English or French in an area. Moreover, even when people are bilingual, they tend to prefer using one language. Individuals rarely feel at home in both. When they have a choice, they are likely to use the language in which they feel most comfortable. This is particularly important in defining the shape of political discussion, since public discussion tends to follow linguistic preference rather than ability. Montreal, for example, has a large proportion of bilingual residents. When it comes to choosing a television channel, a radio station, or a newspaper, however, Montrealers overwhelmingly choose one in their first language.[31] Although personal interaction is less compartmentalized, it too tends to follow linguistic lines. Despite a large measure of bilingualism, then, the major instruments of political discussion are still largely separate. Francophones write for French newspapers, anglophones write for English papers. Francophones read French newspapers, anglophones read English papers. Although some citizens may cross the lines – the English media seems to be making a concerted effort to use French-speaking commentators, and the proportion of francophone readers of English media has always been higher than the reverse – the web of political discussion remains much denser within linguistic boundaries than across them.

Over time, this results in political discussions that follow autonomous paths, where issues are treated very differently in the different linguistic communities and where the movement towards consensus or confrontation can take divergent forms. We saw this in the Meech Lake debate. The discussion of constitutional issues in the French press was much more extensive than in the English press. What seemed to English readers like the work of eleven white men in a room seemed to francophone Quebecers like the product of a series of negotiations conducted over years. Quebecers knew that women's groups in Quebec supported the distinct society clause; Canadians outside Quebec thought that all women opposed it. Canadians outside Quebec even had trouble perceiving the seriousness of the issue in Quebec. Their chief source of information was the pronouncements of federal politicians, whom they no longer trusted.

There is thus an inevitable tendency towards autonomy in our linguistically defined political debates, and as we have seen before, the unique character of those debates attracts a substantial measure of allegiance. When Canadians follow a political debate, they are usually following the version that occurs in their public language. When they care about the outcome of that debate, they do so in terms relating to the discussion they know. When they want to see the government act in a manner responsive to the public, they think of concerns expressed in their language. As Durham saw in the 1830s, public debate is marked by a different culture, a different way of conceiving of the issues, a different history of discussion, depending on the language in which the debate occurs.

This sheds more light, I believe, on the role of culture in the Quebec government's arguments for political autonomy during the 1960s. We saw above[32] that those arguments were concerned not just with securing jurisdiction over language and culture as subjects of governmental action, with protecting and promoting that limited class of things that we normally think of as "culture"; they were also concerned with culture in action, with enabling French Canadians to engage the world in their own language and from their own culture, and thus they could produce demands for an array of powers extending well beyond the "cultural." The arguments were not just about culture as a subject of law, but about culture as the context within which a whole political debate came to be framed.

This, of course, leads us straight back to Jean Lesage's dilemma: If the effect of language is so pervasive, are there any limits to the demand for autonomy? How can one preserve a pan-Canadian community, given the impact of linguistic difference? Language is an important and, at least in the Canadian context, an unavoidable determinant of political community, but we should not fall into the trap of thinking it is the only one. Over the past two hundred years, Canadians have engaged in a political debate that crosses the linguistic boundary. They have wrestled together over great national issues. They have disagreed, sometimes vehemently, but they share a political history, common points of reference in their public life, and, to a degree, an understanding of a common set of issues. Canadians of both languages have come together in political institutions to address the issues of the day. And less-formal channels of communication do persist, although they are not as broad or efficient as those within a linguistic group.

Moreover, there is still considerable willingness to treat at least some issues as extending across the linguistic boundary. There is a willingness, in other words, to participate in decision making in forums that include both groups, even if it means getting along with someone you don't quite understand, at least not all the time. This was, after all, the basis for Quebec politicians' initial consent to Confederation, and it still persists, though in a bruised form. The full extent of Durham's fears – two utterly divided societies – has not been realized. There is a genuine Canadian political community, although it is certainly not Canadians' only community.

We can see, then, the possible outline of a dual allegiance. We can perceive that there are at least two important political communities for Canadians, intersecting with the provincial communities discussed above: one based on language and the other uniting all Canadians. But how do we fix their content? How do we respond, in more concrete terms, to Lesage's dilemma? I will return to that issue below, but first we should examine the interplay between our two official-language communities and the institutional structure of Canada, especially the existence of provinces.

LANGUAGE AND POLITICAL ASYMMETRY IN CANADA. Lord Durham believed that the imposition of a single set of political institutions would lead to the assimilation of the French-speaking population. During the Union period, French Canadians successfully resisted that danger, but most recognized that Durham had a point: a single governmental structure, with anglophones in the majority, would create enormous pressure for assimilation. They therefore placed great importance on the institutional autonomy of Quebec as the guarantee of their distinctive sense of political community. Throughout our history, the province of Quebec has remained central to the political identity of francophone Quebecers, and this despite the gradual tendency of other Canadians to shift allegiance from the provinces to Ottawa.

There has never been complete identification between Canada's linguistic groups and its governmental institutions. "English Canada" stretches across all provinces, including Quebec. There are large numbers of French Canadians in New Brunswick and northern Ontario, lesser but still substantial numbers in Manitoba, and pockets in other provinces. But despite this lack of precise fit, parts of the institutional structure have been identified, in political shorthand, with specific linguistic communities, often with special constitutional provisions designed to protect the position of linguistic minorities. This is especially true of Quebec, which was from the beginning treated as the secure base of the French-speaking community, its customs, and its religion. There is no comparable province for anglophone Canadians. None was needed, given the majority status of the English-speaking population. Provinces outside Quebec, responding to the will of their anglophone majorities, generally acted as though they were exclusively English-speaking, and for much of Canada's history English was markedly predominant at the federal level. Our governmental structures have coincided with our linguistic communities, but only in an approximate and imperfect way, making for complex interactions as governmental structures reshape linguistic communities and vice versa. Our political communities are not just the reflection of our languages, then, but result from the refraction of linguistic difference through the specific structure of our governmental institutions.

This is especially clear in the tension between francophones inside and francophones outside Quebec. Quebecers have generally considered Quebec and its autonomy as essential to the preservation of a French-speaking culture in Canada. Yet paradoxically, this has resulted in a split in the francophone political community, most obviously at the level of strategy but more fundamentally at the level of allegiance. Quebec has frequently expressed support for the cause of francophones in the rest of the country and has sometimes acted to advance the interests of minorities outside Quebec, but it has resolutely refused to support any measure that might have the effect of reducing provincial autonomy. Quebec's autonomy is seen by francophone Quebecers as the fundamental, residual guarantee of the French Canadian culture, a guarantee that must never be weakened.[33] This contrasts starkly with the instincts of francophones outside Quebec, living in provinces often hostile to their concerns. They look to Ottawa for support – they must look to Ottawa as their chief defender – taking advantage of a forum in which their numbers can be bolstered by those of Quebec.

This attitude of francophones outside Quebec is not as simple as it may appear. It does not come down to a complete lack of sympathy for Quebec's demands for autonomy. Francophones outside Quebec recognize that there is, in practice, an asymmetry in provincial roles. They acknowledge that Quebec does have a special place within French Canada, that the health of the French culture outside Quebec may well depend on strong French-speaking institutions inside Quebec. This acknowledgment can influence their political strategy. It helps explain, for example, why their organizations eventually accepted the distinct society clause in Meech Lake, although they would have preferred better protection for linguistic minorities. Because of their own particular situation, however, they cannot support linguistic autonomy for provinces generally. Quebec is not their province. It cannot directly protect them, and francophones outside Quebec have little weight within Quebec's political life. If forced to choose between Ottawa on the one hand and their own province on the other, they have to choose Ottawa.

The structure of governmental institutions has therefore had a crucial impact on the allegiance of French Canadians. Francophones *inside* Quebec have a very strong commitment to provincial autonomy – that is, to the ability of Quebecers to decide issues themselves in a way that reflects their distinctive political debate. Francophones *out*side Quebec, on the other hand, may have sympathy for Quebec's autonomy, but they cannot wish for the same autonomy for their own provinces. They often have a real commitment to those provinces. After all, they remain Manitobans or Franco-Ontarians, sharing a common history and many common concerns with their anglophone counterparts. But especially when it comes to cultural matters, they have to look federally, to a community in which French is a language of public life and there is consistent support for French Canadian institutions.

Francophone Quebecers may have retained a strong attachment to their province's autonomy, but the same is not true, at least not to the same extent, for the English-speaking population of Canada. With some variation, the balance of anglophone loyalties has gradually shifted towards Ottawa.

In 1867 Nova Scotians and Prince Edward Islanders were as strongly committed to their provinces' autonomy as Quebecers were to theirs. Accounts of the Confederation debates make clear that the division of power between Ottawa and the provinces was necessary, not merely to appease Quebec, but to satisfy the Maritimes. Even then, Prince Edward Island delayed entering Confederation until 1873, and Nova Scotia tried to secede in the years following 1867.[34] Over time, however, English-speaking Canadians have developed a much stronger allegiance to Canada. This evolution was gradual at first, nudged forward by Ottawa's developmental strategies (the National Policy, railway construction, the settlement of the West) and the consequent movement of population, knitting Canada together with bonds of political alliance and familial connection. Immigrants especially adopted a strongly Canadian allegiance: their new country was Canada, and they did not inherit (at least not with the same intensity) the previous colonial loyalties. The shift in allegiance in English-speaking Canada crystallized during the two world wars. The wars have often been credited (in anglophone historiography) with forging a Canadian nation. They certainly seized the attention of English-speaking Canadians and focused it on issues that had to be decided within the pan-Canadian political community. They generated debates in which all Canadians (or at least all anglophone Canadians) participated as members of a single community, not just for the narrow purpose of raising troops and dispatching them overseas but also for the whole range of exceptional economic powers deployed by Ottawa. In wartime, for English-speaking Canadians, the politics that mattered were national politics; the issues that mattered were determined in a national forum.

Especially as a result of the wars, anglophone Canadians came to identify with that forum, to see their chief political debates as Canadian in scope, crossing provincial boundaries. Once forged, that sense of national community remained central. English-speaking Canadians continued to look to Ottawa for action on a range of social issues. Ottawa's regulatory role had expanded dramatically during the wars; it declined slowly following them. War provided the original rationale for Ottawa's intrusion into areas of provincial jurisdiction; in peacetime, English-speaking Canadians continued to look to Ottawa for leadership in those areas, a leadership Ottawa provided through the expansion of the spending power. For many issues (including many formally within provincial jurisdiction), the political debate among anglophone Canadians was now pan-Canadian in scope.

This focus on the federal level has been especially pronounced among Quebec anglophones, for many of the reasons motivating anglophones outside Quebec but also for some specific to their situation. English-speaking Quebecers have contributed substantially to the political life of their province, although the nature of that contribution has changed, particularly since the mid-1970s, when French became by far the dominant language in provincial politics. Traditionally, English-speaking Quebecers have also benefited from extensive public institutions at the provincial level (schools, universities, hospitals, social services). Nevertheless, anglophone Quebecers have a different relationship to their province than francophone Quebecers for one crucial reason. They have little direct participation, little direct stake in the central aspiration on which francophone Quebecers have based their demand for autonomy: the desire to keep Quebec as a secure home for the expression of French culture in North America. Many anglophone Quebecers (though not all) are sympathetic to that wish, but it is the sympathy of the outsider, an attachment at a lesser level of intensity. English-speaking Quebecers may feel at home in Quebec. They may participate in public life at the provincial or municipal levels. But the existence of the federal sphere, in which English remains a central public language, is essential to their sense of belonging.

All this has meant that for English-speaking Canadians across Canada (and for francophones outside Quebec), the burden of allegiance has shifted markedly towards the pan-Canadian community. When allegiance to Canada is weighed against allegiance to a province, the former carries significantly more weight for anglophone Canadians than it does for francophone Quebecers. There is, in other words, an asymmetry in allegiance to Canada and its provinces, with French-speaking Quebecers putting much more emphasis on the provincial side of the scale.

There is also a very important difference in the reasons for allegiance. The allegiance of francophone Quebecers to their province is founded on the coincidence (admittedly rough) between linguistic community and provincial institutions; it is because Quebec is the only jurisdiction with a francophone majority that it attracts such a high degree of loyalty. English-speaking Canadians do not have the same reason for preferring the federal side, or at least they do not express it the same way. They do not think of Ottawa as the vehicle for a distinctively *English*-Canadian culture. Their allegiance is (they would say) to Canada as a whole, not to a specific linguistic community.

To a certain extent, this may be misleading, hiding the true importance of language to their allegiance. After all, English Canadian political debate expanded beyond provincial boundaries precisely because citizens in many provinces spoke the same language, and when those debates did expand, the English-language discussion remained (indeed remains today) largely autonomous from the French, especially at the popular level. Thus, during the wars, although the English Canadian debate crossed provincial boundaries, there was still an enormous gulf between discussion in English and discussion in French. Indeed, one wonders whether English-speaking Canadians' wartime sense of their national community included, in any meaningful sense, French Canadians. Our intuitive sense of nation is often a projection of communities much closer to home, the communities we know. One suspects that English-speaking Canadians have frequently identified, as distinctively Canadian, phenomena that are really confined to their linguistic group.[35]

In any case, English-speaking Canadians have not had the same need to distinguish between allegiance to a linguistic community and allegiance to the truly pan-Canadian community. They could afford to run the two together because, as they were the majority, the distinctive character of their linguistic community was never threatened. They may believe that in federal politics they have to accommodate French Canadian expressions of the national interest, and they have generally accepted a conception of Canada in which the English-speaking community should not simply have its way; but the accommodation is always from a position of strength.[36] The anglophone community outside Quebec always retains the option of majority rule. Because of their numerical superiority, English-speaking Canadians can afford to focus on a pan-Canadian community, forsaking any direct institutional expression of their linguistic community.

The balance of allegiance is therefore highly asymmetrical in Canada, generating tension between (on the one hand) the pan-Canadian aspirations of both English-speaking Canadians and francophones outside Quebec and (on the other) the greater loyalty of francophone Quebecers to their province. Because of its foundation in the structure of political debate, this asymmetry seems intractable. Having developed a strong allegiance to Canada, English-speaking Canadians are not about to turn back towards their provinces. Nor can the tension be resolved by recreating a Canada of two linguistically based nations. English-speaking Canadians do not conceive of their allegiance in linguistic terms. To build Canada on a foundation of two nations would construct the country around a characteristic that is fundamental to francophone Quebecers but nowhere near as salient to anglophones. Although it may seem paradoxical, most English-speaking Canadians have more sympathy for the recognition of Quebec's unique character than they have for an emphasis on their own language as a defining characteristic of political identity. For most English-speaking Canadians (the most prominent exception being, for obvious reasons, anglophones in Quebec), English fades into the background as a basis for constitutional reform.

At the same time, the Trudeau government's attempt to displace French-speaking Quebecers' loyalties to the federal level failed, and for very good reason. Trudeau tried to accomplish the shift by treating language as an individual phenomenon: both languages would have equal status; citizens would have access to government in either official language; the symbols of Canada would emphasize both. Those measures have been immensely important in increasing the accessibility of the federal government, buttressing the conversation across cultures, and therefore building a Canada in which members of both official-language groups speak to each other at the federal level. The reforms were crucial to the maintenance and development of a pan-Canadian political community, an important step in weaning Ottawa away from *de facto* identification with English-speaking Canada. But the reforms could not be expected to displace French-speaking Quebecers' attachment to their province, or reduce it to the level of other Canadians' attachment to theirs. Apart from the guarantees written into the constitution[37] (and these are necessarily of limited scope), the use of French at the federal level remains subject to the will of the English-speaking majority. More importantly, despite the best efforts at the federal level, Quebec will always be the only jurisdiction in which the French-speaking community is the majority, and therefore the only jurisdiction in which political debate in French is the principal debate. It will remain the only jurisdiction in which there is a reasonably direct correspondence between political discussion in French and public decision making. As Lord Durham recognized, the prosperity of a linguistic community often depends upon it having its own institutions, in which participation in the language can result in public action.

Asymmetry of allegiance is therefore fundamental to the structure of Canada's political communities and results from the autonomy of Canada's francophone and anglophone forums for debate, filtered through Canada's institutions. One should not confuse asymmetry with inadequate allegiance. The fact that francophone Quebecers have a different commitment to the pan-Canadian community – the fact that they have a more substantial allegiance to their province – does not mean that commitment to Canada is unimportant or transitory. It does mean that in designing our constitution, we should take account of the fact that French-speaking Quebecers are much more attached to provincial autonomy than are other Canadians. An asymmetrical constitution may be the institutional form most compatible with our asymmetrical political communities.

GIVING CONTENT TO QUEBEC'S DEMAND FOR AUTONOMY. The intersection of language and governmental structure explains the force behind the demand for autonomy in Quebec, but only in the broadest of terms. It says little about the content of that demand, about whether Quebec should control health, regional development, or job training, for example. It fails, in other words, to answer Lesage's dilemma about how much autonomy is enough.

Many arguments are used to define the desirable balance between autonomy and central control. Often, these are functionalist in character: provinces should exercise a specific power because their governments are "closer to the people they serve"; Ottawa should have power to create a single internal market; areas of overlap should be eliminated to prevent waste. Functional arguments are important in the give-and-take of constitutional discussion, but they do not say much about the essential content of Quebec's commitment to autonomy. They are used to lobby for changes at the margins, and certainly need to be taken seriously as proposals for reform, but they do not capture the deep sense of grievance in Quebec – the sense that Quebec has insufficient powers to express its identity, that it is, under present arrangements, denied an acceptable level of self-government.

Arguments for Quebec's autonomy also draw upon the province's unique role in protecting the French Canadian culture, although these "cultural" arguments only work for a limited range of powers having a distinctively cultural character (such as education or broadcasting). These arguments come closer to the core of Quebec's interests. Many French-speaking Quebecers suspect that the Charter might be used to reduce Quebec's power to encourage French Canadian culture (this concern is, however, significantly reduced by the provinces' ability to use the notwithstanding clause to protect legislation from many Charter provisions). As to the need for new legislative authority over cultural matters, Quebec's powers are already extensive (with the notable exceptions of broadcasting and some aspects of international relations). The restricted demand for additional, distinctively cultural powers does not adequately account for the depth of Quebecers' concerns with the division of powers. In any case, Quebec's concerns clearly go beyond the strictly cultural.

But if this is so, are there any limits? Has the autonomy of Canada's linguistic communities set in motion a process which, if indulged, will inevitably lead to Quebec's separation? I think not. Except among the small minority of committed *indépendantistes*, the demands of francophone Quebecers are not all-encompassing. They draw their essential content – and their implicit limitation – from a concern which at first sight seems to have little to do with the substance of Quebec's identity: the perception that Quebec's traditional areas of jurisdiction have been eroded in the years following Confederation. The principal content of the demand for autonomy is supplied, in other words, by the original division of powers. Although the desire for autonomy is founded on the wish to give effect to the character of francophone public debate in Canada, its content is provided by history.

If one looks at Quebec's chief constitutional demands of the last thirty years, one can see the remarkable extent to which they concern the spending power – Ottawa's power, of doubtful constitutionality, to spend money in areas allocated to the provinces under the 1867 constitution. The most important provision of the Meech Lake Accord dealing with the division of powers would have constrained the future exercise of that power. Following the failure of the accord, the jurisdictional demands pressed most strongly by Quebec also concerned areas in which the federal presence was based on the spending power (manpower training, regional development, social assistance, financial support for cultural activities, post-secondary education, health) or on constitutional amendments of the 1940s permitting Ottawa to create programs closely akin to those under the spending power (unemployment insurance, old age pensions).[38] It may seem ironic that Quebec's demands for autonomy are in large measure informed by Canada's original division of powers. It seems improbable that Quebec's demands for decentralization should amount to little more than a defence of the British North America Act. (Indeed, during the Charlottetown debate, some Quebec opponents of the accord argued, in a striking triumph of form over substance, that Quebec gained nothing from limits on the spending power because Quebec already possessed those powers!) Nevertheless, given the extent of the spending power, its restriction would result in substantially more provincial autonomy. The spending power supports the federal role in many areas of the welfare state, areas that have grown dramatically in the last fifty years. Estimates suggest that 35 per cent of federal spending now occurs in areas of provincial jurisdiction.[39] This expanded federal role has support among English-speaking Canadians; Ottawa's involvement in social policy is the concrete product of anglophone Canadians' shift in allegiance from their provinces to Canada. But that shift did not take place in Quebec, at least not to the same extent. Quebec has remained hostile to the use of the spending power.

The demand for Quebec's autonomy is, then, given content by the structure of responsibilities in the original division of powers. The fact that Quebecers' demands should, in the end, draw so heavily on Canada's institutional history is not surprising. In my discussion of provincial loyalties, I suggested that institutional structures could define political communities, which over time attract a strong sense of allegiance from their participants. The desire to retain autonomy, the cherishing of the distinctive character of the community, is real enough, although its precise content results from the accidents of institutional design. The same can happen with provincial societies defined not territorially but by the nature of the powers they exercise. Allegiance to the province is founded on the distinctive character of the provincial political debate. The precise scope of that debate (in terms of the subjects it deals with) is in part the result of institutional history. Citizens become committed to the debate surrounding those subjects. The powers come to be seen as appropriately exercised at the provincial level. Over time they become a defining characteristic of the provincial political community.[40] There is a good example of this phenomenon at the federal level. Most Canadians would consider criminal law to be distinctively federal. A single, unified criminal law has become virtually an attribute of Canadian citizenship. Yet there seems to be no compelling reason why this should be. In the United States and Australia, two federations closely akin to

Canada, criminal law is a state responsibility. The criminal law did not become part of pan-Canadian political identity because it had to, but simply because Canadians have lived with a unified criminal law, have debated their criminal law in pan-Canadian terms, and now see it as a natural element of their political structure.[41]

The contribution of these kinds of institutional considerations to the definition of our political communities is no more artificial than the territorial limits discussed earlier. Quebecers' desire for autonomy is real enough, based on the distinctive character of their political debates. So is their sense of community with other Canadians and their consequent desire to remain part of a pan-Canadian society. Those two commitments have a significant, substantive foundation. But they need to be given some concrete content, and that content is supplied by Quebecers' sense of the traditional relationship between the two spheres, which in turn is founded on the institutional definition of 1867.

Thus, the majority of French-speaking Quebecers who are still attached to Canada are not caught irretrievably in Lesage's dilemma precisely because they are not driven to push the logic of linguistic self-determination to its ultimate conclusion. They are committed, above all, to regaining what they take to be Quebec's traditional powers, and they are especially concerned with retaining those powers having a specifically cultural character. They may propose other changes, but not with the same vigour or sense of entitlement – certainly not by putting the future of the country in question. Their commitment to linguistic self-determination is limited by their still considerable attachment to Canada, and the content of their demands is determined principally by their desire to regain the sphere of autonomy they had at the origin.

Multiculturalism and Political Community

So far, this argument has focused on two of Canada's linguistic groups, the French and the English. But doesn't this reproduce the tired old dichotomy of two founding peoples? What about the other groups that make up Canadian society? Have they disappeared from view?

Languages other than English and French, and especially the cultural groups identified with those languages, certainly are important to this country. This is true both of the multicultural communities, which form the subject of this section, and the aboriginal peoples, which I will address in the next. In drawing attention to the role of the official languages, I do not mean to demean other groups or to belittle their substantial contributions to Canada. But I do want to resist the assumption that all languages serve the same role or that all have (or should have) the same significance for the structure of Canada's political communities. English and French tend to shape political life in Canada because they are major languages of public debate. They are the languages citizens use to resolve the most important public issues. Other languages (except, within very specific contexts, the aboriginal languages) do not serve that role, at least not to the same extent. Languages other than English or French are important to the members of the specific cultural groups, they are well worth preserving for their contribution to the richness of Canadian cultural life, but they are not and will probably never be media of general discussion comparable to English or French.

This does not mean that multicultural languages are inferior or that Canadians who speak them are somehow second-class citizens. Although there certainly have been examples of racism or cultural denigration in Canadian history, it would be a gross distortion to conclude that the different social function of English or French is simply the result of a dominant group imposing its culture on others (at least in the case of the multicultural communities; I discuss aboriginal peoples below). The different functions of language have been implicit in the practice, perhaps even in the aspirations, of immigrant communities themselves, for very good reasons. New Canadians did not expect to remain unilingually Ukrainian, Italian, or Cantonese when they came to this country. They did not expect to be able to use their original language for every aspect of social interaction. They fully expected that they or their children would acquire the language of the new land. They went to great pains to ensure that their children would be fluent in that language. In some cases they went so far as to renounce their own language, refusing to pass it on to their children so that the children would become Canadians more quickly (so they believed). That happened, for example, in one branch of my family, where the first generation refused to teach their children Gaelic. Fortunately, we no longer believe we have to reject our roots in order to be good Canadians. The languages and cultures of our ancestors are valued, and efforts are made to retain them. But it is a mistake to assume that this renewed emphasis on preserving our cultural heritage has displaced English or French. Differences in the role of language remain. Immigrants and the descendants of immigrants do not expect languages other than English or French to be languages of debate in the federal or provincial legislatures, languages of commerce between members of different ethnic communities, or the principal vehicle of education in the schools. They admit the need for common languages of communication and usually assume that English fills that role. The roles are accepted without question. It is only when we talk about languages in the abstract that we lose sight of what we actually do in practice.

It is precisely because the languages serve different roles that their consequences for the structure of political community are different. The immigrant languages other than English or French are not used as a means of communication with the broader Canadian society. They are not a principal medium for the discussion and resolution of public issues. They are used, sometimes extensively, for interaction within the group. They may be used in the delivery of such public services as health care or social counselling. They may be employed to mobilize members of the group in municipal, provincial, or federal politics. But they do not dominate political life; they do not establish the boundaries of political engagement in the way that English and French do. In the multicultural communities, language serves a more personal role, one of great importance in preserving a link to one's heritage, fulfilling a role similar to other cultural legacies – religion, festivals, traditions, artistic forms. They are substantial contributions to the richness of Canada. They are important to the members' sense of identity and belonging. But they are not meant to delimit the sphere of political decision making. Multicultural groups do not want a linguistically based political autonomy. Their ethic is one of participation in the broader society, of involvement, of contribution.

This is seen in their political aims, which contrast sharply with the commitment to political autonomy of aboriginal peoples or francophone Quebecers. In the multicultural communities, the emphasis is on greater involvement in the wider community, on access to its institutions and full participation in its benefits. The most important objective is freedom from discrimination – an opening up of opportunity in employment, in the government, in public life. Generally, multicultural organizations also want some recognition of their heritage in official ceremonies, public symbols, and school curriculum (heritage language programs, for example). Insofar as their aims take the form of constitutional change, they have largely been satisfied by provisions of the present Charter of Rights, especially the guarantee of equality in section 15 and the interpretive principle in section 27, which says that the Charter should be interpreted "in a manner consistent with the preservation and enhancement of the multicultural heritage of Canadians." These all emphasize participation *within* Canadian society. Francophone Quebecers also seek equality within Canada as a whole – they, after all, remain members of that society – but they differ from multicultural communities in their desire to preserve a political forum in which debate in French has its own direct expression. They wish to be involved in Canada without seeing their public discourse swamped by the English-speaking majority. The multicultural communities face different challenges. They accept that their political participation will occur primarily through English (or French), and seek a greater presence within that framework.

Many members of the multicultural communities outside Quebec, like many of their ethnically British compatriots, have little use for Quebecers' desire for autonomy. "Why should French Canadians be treated any differently from other Canadians?" they ask. Why is their language better than Italian or Ukrainian? Isn't this a case of discrimination among languages? The suggested conclusion is rarely that Italian and Ukrainian should become principal languages of education or debate in the legislatures. There is virtually no demand, in other words, for parity beween these languages and English. Rather, the arguments are used solely to prove the negative: French should not enjoy the role it now does.

The problem with this kind of assertion lies in the standard of comparison. For many living outside Quebec, French looks like a language of privilege, a language of a cultural community like theirs, but given exaggerated status merely because of its political weight (or worse, some ancient claim to historical priority). Those with this view, however, misunderstand the role of French in Canadian life. The use of French is not analogous to that of Gaelic or German, for reasons that are not reducible merely to political clout or ancient right. In its social role, French is not just a language of the personal sphere, used for relations within a specific cultural community; it is a genuinely public language – a dominant language of commerce and political life in substantial sections of the country, with a role directly analogous to that which English possesses in the rest of the country.

The sociological weight of French-speaking society is sometimes missed by those accustomed to treating English as the basic language of social interaction throughout North America. Visitors to Quebec are often surprised by the inability of many Quebecers to speak English. Forty-one per cent of Montreal's population – over a million people – is unilingually francophone. Another 48 per cent are bilingual.[42] It is as possible to live in Montreal without speaking English as it is to live in Ottawa without speaking French. Quebec's French-speaking population numbers six million, more than two and a half times the population of the four Atlantic provinces put together.[43] An additional 800,000 people in New Brunswick and northern Ontario declare French as their mother tongue.[44] There are four major francophone universities in Quebec, one with campuses around the province. There is a vibrant cultural and artistic life, and a rich intellectual tradition reaching beyond the British Conquest. Indeed, listing the characteristics of Quebec's society seems a little silly, like listing the attainments of Canada's four western provinces. Quebec is fully as sophisticated and diverse as any English-speaking society in Canada. Needless to say, given the size of Quebec's population, its educational system, and its cultural vigour, the French spoken is, contrary to one of the more grotesque myths among some outside Quebec, "real" French – not some imperfect mixture with English.

The point is that French is and always has been, as a matter of social reality, a general language of debate in Canada, serving the same role in Quebec that English serves in Ontario or Nova Scotia or Manitoba. It is the dominant language of a large segment of Canada's population. That, and not some sense of historical priority, is what justifies Quebec's concern with preserving its francophone political character. Seen in that light, Quebec's aspirations are not incompatible with multiculturalism. Multiculturalism, as it exists in Canada, has always acknowledged the need for a common language of political interaction. That language has generally been assumed to be English, but there is no reason why there cannot be a multiculturalism for which French is the general language.[45]

That, I believe, is what Quebec has been reaching towards in the last twenty years. The interaction between political citizenship and ethnic identity is always slippery, the two frequently confused, especially when political institutions have an acknowledged cultural role (as they do in Quebec). But in recent years, there has been a concerted attempt to include within the "Québécois" political identity people who do not trace their ancestry to the British Conquest. Considerable attention has been paid to individual equality, protection against discrimination, and the full participation of racial minorities in Quebec's society. In return, many of Quebec's "cultural communities" participate more actively in francophone public life. The situation is certainly not perfect. Montreal, like Toronto or Halifax, has its racial tensions. There are still jarring times when public figures run citizenship and ethnic identity together. But this seems increasingly to be the exception, often denounced when it occurs. There is no necessary incompatibility between Quebec's aspirations and those of the multicultural communities.

Aboriginal Peoples and Political Community

There is, however, another kind of cultural group whose commitment to autonomy rivals – indeed probably surpasses – that of francophone Quebecers. The aboriginal peoples are not, of course, a single group. They are a number of peoples, each with its own language, traditions, history, and political structure. They differ greatly in their present circumstances, their experience of colonization, their resources, and their social cohesion. They share, however, the distinction of being the first inhabitants of North America, holding fast to their cultural identities and striving to fashion a place for those identities within the framework of an industrialized, predominantly non-aboriginal North America. Their principal ethic is not, like that of the multicultural groups, one of individual mobility and participation in the larger North American society. They generally do wish to have the rights of Canadian citizens and to deal with others on a basis of equality, but like Quebecers, they also want to preserve a sphere in which their concerns, their way of ordering their communities, can continue to shape public life. They do not want their identities to be washed out in a single, North American society, in which the aboriginal influence can be modest at best, given their small proportion of the electorate. Like francophone Quebecers, aboriginal peoples seek a measure of self-government within the framework of the broader Canadian state.

Some discussions of self-government assume that the demand for autonomy is based on the perception that aboriginal societies form uncomplicated, thoroughly united collectivities, possessing single, identifiable sets of values. Aboriginal communities are treated as though they spoke with a single voice, with little or no internal variation. The purpose of political autonomy, then, would be to preserve the set of distinctively Cree or Inuit attitudes, the presumed cultural unity, against external challenge. This overemphasis on unity in the understanding of aboriginal societies, like the stress on "shared values" in the definition of Canadian identity, distorts the situation. It is understandable, given the tendency to stress differences in any argument over autonomy, but it clouds our understanding of aboriginal self-government, generating (among other things) an excessively stark dichotomy between the rights of the individual and the recognition of cultural differences, undermining our ability to see how individual rights can work together with cultural autonomy. Aboriginal societies are not uniform, and the demand for self-government is not about imposing uniformity. Within each people, there are profound differences of opinion. There is debate about the demands of Kwakiutl or Blackfoot or Innu culture, and especially about how to reconcile that culture with non-traditional ways. There is potential for disagreement and change. Autonomy is not about the enforcement of a set of traditional values, but much more about the framework within which debates occur, about the responsiveness of public decisions to the character of an aboriginal people.

My discussions of the Canadian political community, of provincial societies, and of linguistic communities have all emphasized the importance of debate through time to members' perceptions of community and allegiance. Members come to see public issues through the framework of those debates. In their interaction within the community, they come to share common landmarks, points of reference, terms of argument, even though they may disagree vehemently on specific outcomes. That common political language means something; its vernacular becomes the vehicle for their public engagement, for public expression. Losing it can undermine members' sense of place, their sense that they belong, that their identity falls within the scope of the community's concern.

Aboriginal peoples have their own distinctive sets of references, traditions, and histories, substantially separate from those of non-aboriginal Canadians (and indeed those of other aboriginal peoples). This separateness is partly tied to linguistic differences, in the same way that English and French political discourses are autonomous simply because discussion occurs in different languages. Aboriginal languages, even though they have a smaller base than English or French, remain vital to aboriginal traditions. They retain a continuing influence over communities' oral deliberations and public symbolism, to an extent often underestimated by non-aboriginal commentators who assume too readily that English and French have displaced aboriginal languages.[46] But beyond this strictly linguistic autonomy, the traditions of aboriginal communities remain sufficiently distinct and possess sufficient salience within their communities to support a commitment to autonomy even when English has displaced aboriginal languages as the principal medium of discussion. Aboriginal cultures have, for example, developed dramatically different conceptions of property – indeed, different visions of humanity's relationship with the world generally. Aboriginal peoples have fashioned their own conceptions of individuals' roles and responsibilities within family and society. They have developed their own ways of dealing with disputes, of structuring and resolving conflict. Often, these institutions fit poorly with the legal constructs or methods of social control used by non-aboriginal society, and the only way they can be preserved is by carving out some measure of autonomy. The commitment to autonomy is not absolute. Few aboriginal peoples crave complete isolation. But they do not want their way of dealing with the world obliterated without having the opportunity to reach for some synthesis of the traditional and non-traditional. Self-government is designed to create the space for that synthesis.

This understanding of self-government also helps us see that aboriginal autonomy does not have an exclusively ethnic or racial basis. Its justification is not founded upon biological ancestry. Its concern is cultural: the accommodation of communities whose public debate has been shaped by a different set of conceptual tools, communities with their own distinct histories. This recognition is important for two reasons. First, it frees us from a static vision of aboriginal societies based on biological determinism. Aboriginal autonomy is not predicated on racial purity; the unique character of aboriginal societies is not some stable reflection of biological identity. Like other cultural phenomena, aboriginal cultures are continually evolving in response both to the dynamic of their own debates and to outside influences. Second, the status of a participant in an aboriginal culture – his or her membership in an aboriginal society – is not dependent, in any straightforward way, on ethnicity. The important criterion is not blood, but the sharing of the cultural framework. Aboriginal peoples have always had practices for accepting non-members into the aboriginal community.[47] These individuals, though not sharing in the ethnic identity, can nevertheless be full members of the society, thoroughly involved in the social interaction that justifies political autonomy. Of course, given our histories, ethnicity and membership will often coincide. We should certainly avoid the trap of confusing full participation with the sampling of the dilettante. For this reason (among others), recognition within the community will be a key criterion of membership. But the fact remains that aboriginal autonomy has a cultural, not an ethnic foundation.

CONCLUSION

This book began with a criticism of the concepts of "nation" and "nationalism." Those concepts tend to presuppose that citizens have an exclusive commitment to a single polity. We have trouble accepting that a citizen can have more than one nation, more than one national allegiance. We fall into the language of choice and preference, insisting on an answer to questions like "What is your country? Quebec or Canada?" When we work with the concepts of nation and nationalism, we slip into the language of singleness of purpose, implicitly assuming that a nation should be based on some kind of uniformity. We ask ourselves what are the national values, the national traits, the national language – perhaps even the ethnic characteristics of the national community.

All this does violence to the complicated commitments of Canadians. Canadians have been shaped by the diversity of their country. "Canadian" means what it does today precisely because of the particular character of the aboriginal peoples inhabiting this land, because of their uneasy and often unsatisfactory relationship with the colonizing population, because English- and French-speaking Canadians have argued, sometimes vehemently, over the destiny of this land, because of the richness of the contributions of Canadians of all origins and cultures, and because somehow with all this we have made a decent society, a society with a will to continue. To reduce all this to a canon of "Canadian values," to force choices between our more local commitments and our pan-Canadian allegiances, is to lose the dynamism of Canadian identity, to freeze out the arguments that lie at the heart of our community, and to stunt our potential for growth.

The core of any democratic community is not ethnicity or language or some catalogue of shared values. It is the commitment to a particular public debate through time. The specific character of that debate is of real importance to individuals. Members come to care about public issues through the terms of that debate. It sets the framework for the positions they take on questions affecting the community as a whole. Using those terms they define their place within society. Their arguments are not, in any simple sense, dictated by the community. But the framing of the issues, much of the range of argument, and the background of experience against which arguments are judged are inherited. They are, in substantial measure, the product of a history which the member neither creates nor chooses. The vernacular of the debate is crucial in the formation and expression of political opinions. The reflection of that vernacular in political decision making is central to the member's feeling of engagement and participation.

This conception of political community avoids many of the pitfalls of nation and nationalism, expressing more accurately why we cherish the specific character of our societies. It explains the sense of commonality that exists within communities – it explains, in other words, the very specific sense members have of belonging – without slipping into a presumption of uniformity. It captures both the cohesion and conflict of a society as diverse as Canada. It tolerates the fact that members frequently belong to several communities at once, communities that may deal with different issues or with the same issues at different levels of abstraction.

The existence of these communities is a matter not of philosophical principle, but of the accidents of sociological interaction. Their dimensions and content are the product of a range of factors: institutional structure, language use, geographical isolation, and others. We respect their autonomy not because they are founded on any one of these, but rather because each community, formed by whatever process, has developed its own character and this character has become fundamental to its members' sense of engagement and participation. It is the significance of a community to its members, not the accidents of its origin, that demands respect. Indeed, one of the problems with nationalism is that it misses this focus, erecting a factor which, like language, is merely one element conditioning the structure of political community, into the sole premise of nationhood. In practice our allegiances are much more complex.

This complexity does not mean that the variety of our communities can be comfortably ignored, that they dissolve in a confusion of "cross-cutting cleavages," as one branch of democratic theory tells us.[48] The communities discussed here are not sealed off from one another; there is often considerable interchange of members and ideas. But at the same time their structure is not so diffuse as to defy all accommodation. They continue to possess a stable, *relative* autonomy that means something to their members, an autonomy that makes it sensible to talk in terms of the communities having distinctive public debates, with their own internal dynamic. Although frequently less pronounced, this autonomy is not materially different from that existing between states in the international realm, an autonomy which is itself relative, not absolute.

It is because the value of a community does not depend on any one of the factors involved in its creation that there are limits on our need to justify the existence of a particular political community. Its significance to its members today is largely independent of its origins, and respect for its autonomy (in the first instance) depends on that significance. I say "in the first instance" because the respect may well be conditional, especially on the community's protection of certain basic human rights. I have said little so far about criticisms of the character of particular political communities, but it is clear that in some circumstances the definition of community deserves to be called into question even if its members do cherish its specific character. Good examples are the whites-only regimes of Rhodesia and South Africa. In those cases, the use of autonomy as a means of oppression undermines the claim to respect. I want to be very clear that the argument for political autonomy presented here is not some variant of a pure cultural relativism. It is founded on generalized assumptions about the integrity of the individual and the value of political participation. The justification for autonomy can be destroyed if those assumptions are denied. Not every case of autonomy, however, threatens individual rights. Autonomy is not tantamount to group interests taking priority over the individual. Indeed, the compatibility of cultural autonomy and individual rights is a subject of the next chapter.

Because the factors affecting the shape of political communities are so diverse, we have to be sparing in our generalizations. In any state, the structure of political community will depend on the precise constellation of commitments in that society. Generalizations may be possible regarding some elements (the existence of several languages of debate may cause similar divisions in different societies, for example), but other elements (such as the accidents of past institutional structure) may be utterly unique. Any sensible understanding has to be based, then, on the context. This chapter therefore explored the specific contours of Canadians' allegiance.

Canada can only be understood if we think of political communities as concentric or overlapping. Individuals simultaneously belong to their local or regional communities and to the pan-Canadian community. They participate in debates at each of these levels, sometimes dealing with different issues in different forums, sometimes dealing with the same issues in different ways. They generally value their engagement in each of these forums and have come to express their positions in terms appropriate to those forums, sometimes to the point of having difficulty imagining a different framework of discussion. Virtually all Canadians, for example, including the great majority of Quebecers, think about national defence in pan-Canadian terms, and indeed many apparently *indépendantiste* Quebecers think defence would continue to be pan-Canadian even after separation. On the other hand, the large majority of Canadians tend to think of labour regulation in terms of their provincial debates. Canadians' history of engagement in these forums is the real substance of politics, the basis for a genuine sense of allegiance to our provinces and to Canada as a whole.

We have seen, in the specifically Canadian context, some of the factors that shaped those communities, and how those communities evolved over time. The accidents of institutional structure – decisions about colonial boundaries or indeed the boundary separating Canada from the United States, decisions sometimes made in London without much regard for the opinions of Canadians – played a role. Differences of language influenced our perceptions of community and have had a decisive impact on the evolution of Canadians' allegiances since Confederation. The special position of aboriginal peoples continues to support their demands for autonomy. And yet alongside the factors setting us apart have been others pushing us together. Sometimes we have worked together out of necessity. We have lived too close to one another for isolation. We have had to depend on each other for survival. Our economic prosperity has required some measure of cooperation. Our political institutions have thrown us together. All these may seem like ignoble reasons for cooperation, a weak foundation for any strong sense of community. But think about the caring, collectively self-reliant farming communities of the Prairies. Their rich sense of solidarity, which often crosses linguistic or cultural divides, was not simply the result of a pre-existing disposition to generosity. In large measure, their members found the value of mutual assistance through necessity. That origin does not diminish their virtue. Once again, it is more the experience of communities once they come together, rather than the bare circumstances of their origin, that matters.

But if we can build satisfying communities that cross our linguistic and cultural divides, why should we insist on preserving separate institutions? Why shouldn't we reach for the largest, most expansive community, the one with the widest sphere of opportunity? Why can't we all be unhyphenated Canadians, at least in our governmental structures, leaving individuals to pursue other identities on their own time? The point is that the other identities mean a great deal to us. A person cares that he or she is, at one and the same time, a member of the Dogrib people, part of the broader family of the Dene, and also a Canadian, perhaps one who shares some of the perspective of other residents of the Northwest Territories. We want to retain some space for the development of those communities, and that may mean permitting autonomy in some areas of public decision making. Our cultures not only affect our private lives; those very lives exist within a framework of public institutions, themselves possessing a cultural character, determining such things as the definition of property rights, the content of familial obligations, or methods for handling controversies between neighbours. If we want to allow the traditions of local communities to survive, if we want those local attachments to retain some of their own distinctive dynamic, we may need to allow space for decisions not only at the individual level, but also in the public institutions that define the extent and structure of individual choice. How can an individual member of the Dogrib people act upon her sense of responsibility to the land if all the decisions about land use and resource management are made in a forum where the voices of her community are too few to be heard?

All this argues for some form of institutional accommodation for our diverse political communities. The precise nature of that accommodation depends on the specific character of the community, the reasons for its significance to its members, the extent of its significance, and the need for a workable balance between communities. Not every difference, not every identification, demands the same kind of accommodation. As we saw in the case of multiculturalism, we should avoid facile comparisons. We should resist squeezing everything into boxes labelled, too simply, "language" or "culture." It is because different communities have different aspirations, aspirations that do not require the utter subordination of the individual to the group, that we can conceive of the compatibility of multiple allegiances and multiple communities. Allegiance is not a one-dimensional, all-absorbing trait, either present or absent, one allegiance necessarily excluding another. In fact, to the extent that a larger community builds its identity on the character of its parts, the allegiances may be mutually reinforcing. A Mohawk need not choose between being a Mohawk and being an Iroquois. A Quebecer need not choose between being a Quebecer and being a Canadian. Before we assume that our allegiances conflict – or use a language of nationalism that forces conflict – we should first consider the substance of the relationship to see whether reconciliation is possible.

The particular kind of reconciliation may be different for different groups of citizens. The whole direction of this argument points towards different forms of accommodation. Most members of the aboriginal peoples clearly want to handle within their own communities some of the things that non-Natives prefer to leave in the hands of provincial or federal governments. Francophone Quebecers want a different balance between federal and provincial decision making than do other Canadians. Can we accommodate these various aspirations, having aboriginal peoples decide at the level of their communities matters which, for the rest of the population, are dealt with in Ottawa? Can Quebecers decide in Quebec City what other Canadians decide in Ottawa? This would mean, of course, an asymmetrical constitution, one in which powers would be apportioned differently between different provinces and the federal government, or between aboriginal peoples and the two existing levels of government.

Asymmetry has often been resisted in Canadian constitutional reform. In the late 1960s and 1970s, the Trudeau Liberals rejected Quebec's claim to a unique role within Confederation, and indeed initially argued that aboriginal rights too should be eliminated. In the late 1980s, many opposed Meech Lake's distinct society clause on the grounds that it might have resulted in Quebec having different powers from other provinces. During the debate on the Charlotte-town Accord, many opposed the package because of aboriginal self-government. Frequently, critics reject asymmetry because it clashes with their idea of nation. They see greater autonomy as divisive and perhaps even disloyal. I hope this chapter has gone some distance towards answering that objection. Others oppose asymmetry be-cause in their view it threatens individual rights and the future sta-bility of Canada: on the one hand, it seems to represent the triumph of the interests of the group over the individual; on the other, it seems to reinforce the autonomy of local communities, possibly moving us further down the road to separation. The next chapter responds to these prominent but mistaken arguments against asym-metry.

7 An Asymmetrical Constitution

What exactly is meant by "constitutional asymmetry"? In recent years, the term has been applied to proposals that provided that one province should be treated differently from others. In practice, the debate has focused on the treatment of Quebec. A constitutional provision might be adopted expressly recognizing Quebec's distinctiveness and providing that the constitution should be interpreted in a manner compatible with that recognition. The distinct society clause is an example of this approach. Alternatively, the allocation of specific legislative powers might be changed so that Quebec would make laws (with respect to Quebecers) on matters now controlled by Ottawa.

It is often said that these arrangements would give Quebec more power. This is true in one sense, because under certain kinds of asymmetry the Quebec legislature would be able to make laws that other provinces could not make. But we should be careful not to confuse this with the idea that Quebecers would get more clout at the federal level or more clout over the affairs of the other provinces. Constitutional asymmetry is not so much about citizens getting *more* power as about where they exercise power. Individual Quebecers, just like Canadians in other provinces, would still have a say over the same kinds of political decisions. It is just that they would exercise that say in a provincial rather than a federal forum.

An example might help. Quebec has long sought exclusive control over manpower training. Under our present constitution, education is already a provincial jurisdiction, but Ottawa maintains a presence in the field through the use of its spending power and its jurisdiction over unemployment insurance. What would happen if exclusive control were granted to Quebec, without any corresponding transfer to other provinces? This would create a classic case of constitutional asymmetry: although Quebec would henceforth have exclusive control over manpower training within its boundaries, other provinces would, with respect to their citizens, continue to share the field with Ottawa. Quebec would thus, in a sense, have more power than other provinces because it, unlike the other provinces, would be exclusively responsible for job training within its boundaries. But this would not mean that Quebec would have more control over the formation of policy in Ottawa or over job training in (for example) Alberta. Quebec would gain no new powers over citizens of other provinces. The change would simply mean that the exercise of authority *with respect to Quebecers* would be divided differently. Instead of being shared between federal and provincial levels of government, powers over that particular matter would be exercised by Quebec alone.

From the point of view of the individual citizens, then, the only difference would be the forum in which decisions were made. Before the change, throughout Canada, some decisions over manpower training would have been made at the provincial level, by citizens' provincial representatives, while others would have been made at the federal level, by their federal representatives. After the change, this would still be the case outside Quebec, but within Quebec, decisions on manpower training would be made at the provincial level alone. In each province, all the decisions would still be made by popularly elected bodies in which the citizens concerned had a say. It is just that within Quebec, the decision-making authority would be divided differently so that only the provincial government would look after issues of training.

Asymmetry, in other words, is more about *where* decisions are made than about *what* decisions are made. It is about which level of political community – the provincial or the pan-Canadian – makes which decisions. Asymmetry exists when, for a given subject, the answer is different in different parts of the country, when things determined at the pan-Canadian level for Nova Scotia, Ontario, or Saskatchewan are determined at the provincial level for Quebec or Alberta, or New Brunswick. Constitutional asymmetry is therefore one way of responding to the varying perceptions of political community in Canada. Quebecers' greater commitment to their provincial community might, for example, be accommodated through an asymmetrical structure: some things decided at the federal level for other Canadians might be decided at the provincial level for Quebecers. The same approach is implicit in proposals for aboriginal self-government. There too the structure of governmental authority would be asymmetrical: matters decided for most Canadians at the federal (or provincial) level would for aboriginal peoples be decided within aboriginal institutions.

To a significant extent, asymmetry already exists in the Canadian constitution. Aboriginal peoples now have a unique constitutional status. Ottawa exercises powers with respect to "Indians, and Lands reserved for the Indians"[1] that the provinces exercise with respect to other Canadians (regulating the use of aboriginal lands or establishing local government on Indian reserves, for example). Because of its historic relationship with aboriginal peoples, Ottawa also owes special "fiduciary" obligations to them, obligations not owed to other Canadians.[2] The continued existence of aboriginal rights – and, since 1982, their constitutional entrenchment – also gives aboriginal peoples a unique status within the Canadian constitution.

There are also differences in the treatment of provinces under the present constitution. The use of English and French is guaranteed in the provincial legislatures of Quebec, Manitoba, and New Brunswick but not in the legislatures of other provinces. Denominational schools enjoy constitutional protection only in some parts of the country, and where protection does exist, it varies in extent. At the time of Confederation, in order to safeguard predominantly anglophone electoral districts, special limits were imposed on Quebec's ability to redefine electoral boundaries. Indeed, special arrangements have often been concluded when each province entered Confederation. Newfoundland's entry prompted a change in the system of subsidies to less-wealthy provinces. British Columbia obtained a constitutional right to passenger rail service, Prince Edward Island a right to ferries. More important for our purposes, in recent times a variety of administrative arrangements have meant that especially in shared-cost programs (programs in which the cost is divided between Ottawa and the provinces) the balance of federal and provincial involvement can differ from province to province. We have already seen that the controversy over a national pension plan in 1964 resulted in the establishment of separate (though coordinated) plans in Quebec and the rest of Canada. Other programs have accommodated varying degrees of opting out. And in the field of immigration, Quebec has in practice been much more active than other provinces, although its constitutional authority (full concurrency with the federal Parliament) is nominally the same.[3]

This chapter will not discuss specific ways in which asymmetry should form part of Canada's constitutional structure. That is the task of the next chapter. Nor will it examine one prominent objection to asymmetry: the problems it allegedly poses to political representation at the federal level. That too is best discussed in the next chapter, after specific forms of asymmetry have been described. This one looks instead at the fit between asymmetry in general and conventional notions of equality and citizenship. Even though constitutional asymmetry seems well-suited to the shape of political commitment in Canada – and even though Canadians have often arranged their political structures in ways that recognize, implicitly, the value of asymmetry – there remains widespread suspicion of it. There is often a feeling that asymmetry is inherently unequal, that it prefers the interests of groups over the rights of individuals, or that it constitutes an unacceptable reservation on the unity of rights and responsibilities fundamental to citizenship. Does it?

ASYMMETRY AND THE "EQUALITY OF PROVINCES"

Often, the argument against asymmetry is based on the simple fact that provinces are treated differently. If Quebec has more powers than other provinces (so the argument goes), its citizens must be better off. And even when it is unclear that Quebec would actually get more of anything, it is often assumed that the very fact of differentiation must create inequality: if provinces are treated differently, almost by definition one must be treated better and the others worse.[4]

In large measure, this objection is answered by the explanation of asymmetry given above. The fact that Quebec has more legislative power does not mean that its individual citizens have more rights – or indeed, more of anything at all. Nor does it mean that citizens in other provinces have less; their powers remain unchanged. It simply means that Quebecers do at the provincial level what their neighbours continue to do at the federal level. For individuals, the number of rights remains roughly constant; just the forum has changed. It is true that under an asymmetrical system, the powers of the Quebec *government* would be different from those of other provincial governments. But before we jump to the conclusion that all provincial governments should be treated in precisely the same way, we should consider what interests we want to serve. Is there any independent value in having identical treatment of governments, or is "equality between the provinces" important only to the extent that it speaks to individual equality? If the latter (and surely that must be the focus of our concern), there may be forms of institutional asymmetry that are perfectly acceptable.[5]

Now, this may seem disingenuous. Surely the exercise of more power at the level of the province or of a particular aboriginal people must be more valuable to individuals; otherwise, why would Quebecers and aboriginal peoples fight so hard to get it? The answer is, of course, that shifting the balance between central and local institutions is valuable (or at least, is perceived to be valuable) *to francophone Quebecers and aboriginal peoples.* That does not mean, however, that other Canadians similarly see decentralization as valuable. The preference of francophone Quebecers and aboriginal peoples for a decentralized constitution is a product of the substantial autonomy of their political communities, their commitment to the terms of debate in those communities, and their minority status within Canada as a whole. They prefer a measure of decentralization precisely because they believe that in the pan-Canadian community the distinctive character of their debates tends to be drowned out, that they end up having to compete as one interest group among many in a much different society. They do realize the necessity of continuing to do this for many issues – few favour complete separation – but they tend to draw the balance between federal and local authority quite differently from other Canadians, favouring a larger local sphere in which their debates are dominant. Other Canadians too have a commitment to their local communities (Newfoundlanders or British Columbians would, for example, strongly resist any significant erosion of provincial authority), but they have developed a much stronger commitment to the pan-Canadian community, and therefore tend to support, for example, a more vigorous federal role in social policy.[6]

The difference in treatment that asymmetry would create might well conform to these different preferences of Canadians. Asymmetry may not, then, amount to inequality. It may result in a more equitable solution, since the structure of governmental authority would accord more closely with all Canadians' preferences, not simply with those of non-aboriginal, non-francophone Canadians.

An analogy can be drawn with one of the central doctrines of Canadian human rights law. That law has come to recognize that identical treatment does not necessarily produce equality. Differences between individuals may be such that the same rule may have a much more severe impact on one person than another, therefore creating, not eliminating, inequality. A good example would be a rule for assigning shift work that allows employees to refuse work on Sundays but not on Saturdays. On its face, that rule treats all employees equally – all would have to work Saturdays, all can refuse to work Sundays – but it would nevertheless impose a much greater hardship on employees who celebrate their sabbath on Saturday. In order to treat the two groups equitably, one might well have to allow a special exception for Saturday-observers. Canadian human rights law, in the interest of equality, frequently imposes a duty to accommodate just those kinds of difference.[7] The duty is not unlimited. It is constrained by the nature of the hardship and by the practical demands of the job. Practical considerations undoubtedly limit our constitutional flexibility as well (these are discussed further below). The fact remains, however, that where individuals are in fundamentally different situations – where, as in our case, francophone Quebecers and aboriginal peoples have cultural concerns that differ from those of other Canadians – different treatment may be perfectly compatible with equality. In fact, unless there is a risk of real prejudice, refusing to accommodate difference may create its own injustice. It can impose a substantial hardship on the minority without any benefit to the majority.[8]

ASYMMETRY AND INDIVIDUAL RIGHTS

Many criticisms of asymmetry go beyond this simple identification of equality of governments with equality of individuals, however, arguing instead that asymmetry poses a direct threat to individual rights. These arguments have been aimed especially at the distinct society clause, and during the Meech Lake debate they formed the main complaint of, for example, women's groups outside Quebec and anglo-Quebecers.

Inequality Resulting from the Existence of Different Laws in Different Parts of the Country

The simplest form of this argument – and one with considerable punch in the popular debate during Meech Lake – takes exception to the very fact that under asymmetrical federalism different laws would exist in different parts of the country. According to this view, equality demands that every citizen must live by the same rules, that the law should treat every citizen in the same way. The very existence of different laws in Quebec would, then, constitute inequality.

This argument is largely absent from the specialist debate among political scientists and constitutional lawyers, and in interventions by groups like the National Action Committee on the Status of Women, for the simple reason that it is, in the end, hostile to any form of federalism. Federalism necessarily assumes that there are good reasons for laws to differ from one province to another. Indeed, provincial governments exist in order to permit that kind of variation. Federalism, therefore, recognizes, at least implicitly, that equality can be reconciled with the existence of different laws applicable to different people. Equality does impose some rough standard of comparison, but in order to see if that standard has been met, we have to push beyond mere difference in law to determine precisely what kinds of differences matter. If we accept that a federal structure of government makes sense, we cannot require that everyone be subject to exactly the same laws.[9]

This conclusion may seem straightforward. Most Canadians would acknowledge that provincial differences in traffic rules or rental legislation or labour law are legitimate. We have little trouble, in other words, accepting differences that are a direct result of the existence of different provinces, each with its own legislative authority. We have much more trouble, however, accepting differences that do not directly reflect such established federal institutions: regional variations in the application of federal law (such as the Criminal Code)[10] or the differential application of constitutional standards in different parts of the country (as a result of the distinct society clause, for example). When discussing these forms of differentiation, we often slip back into the old shorthand that all citizens must be subject to the same rules. This reasoning cannot be sufficient, given our tolerance for diversity between provinces. These measures may be objectionable, but once again, we have to probe further to see whether the particular *kind* of differentiation is inappropriate.

Inequality Resulting from Different Laws Based on Differences of Culture

Many of the criticisms of asymmetry, and especially of the distinct society clause, do focus on a particular kind of differentiation: the use of culture to shape the application of law. Canadians tend to have no difficulty accepting that economic conditions may vary from place to place, resulting in justifiable differences in economic regulation. We generally acknowledge too that provincial boundaries may produce distinctive political communities, which may legitimately pursue different legislative priorities. But within Canada's anglophone political community (but not its francophone or aboriginal communities), there is much more scepticism when it comes to governmental action premised on cultural concerns.[11] For some people, this scepticism extends to any attempt to promote a particular culture through the use of law (for example, the demand of aboriginal communities to control standards of adoption for aboriginal children, or any claim by the government of Quebec that it possesses a distinctive cultural vocation). For others, opposition is more tightly focused on legislation potentially affecting what they see as important individual rights. They tend to reject, then, any suggestion that cultural difference should be taken into account in the interpretation of the Charter. In practice, the two positions often shade into one other, for legislation that serves cultural ends often seems (to many rights advocates) to veer too close to the central concerns of human rights: discrimination, racism, and religious preference. This kind of legislation apparently endorses different treatment based on personal characteristics over which individuals have no control or, worse, amounts to the enforcement of a group identity, subjecting individuals to the supposed interests of a group. Culture seems all too dangerous a category, often closely linked with ethnicity and frequently including matters (like religion) that should be left to individual choice. Suspicion is heightened by the memory of outrages committed by nationalistic regimes against their own citizens and others, not least in this century. For some, the only safe ground seems to be the utter neutrality of government and law in matters of culture.[12]

These fears are extremely important and are not to be taken lightly. The creation of a wide space for individual expression, individual religious and conscientious belief, and equality has been an achievement of real value, which we must certainly preserve. Any decent understanding of the cultural role of government must take those concerns seriously, as indeed this argument does.

But does this mean that the state should strive for complete neutrality on matters of culture? That position is, I believe, untenable for two reasons. First, it assumes that neutrality is possible – that the state can abstract from cultural difference sufficiently to treat all individuals the same. Neutrality is not possible. The actions of legislatures and governments are inevitably marked by culture, in ways I describe below. Ignoring that fact will not rid our institutions of cultural bias. A government's claim to neutrality – a claim to have transcended its particular culture – will often amount to little more than blindness to the actual role of culture in governmental action. This blindness can lead to impositions on members of minority cultures that are both unnecessary and unfortunate, in which policies drawn from one cultural context are imposed on another despite their lack of fit. This disjuncture may exist not merely because other cultures are more prejudiced or less liberal than our own. Culture affects law in ways that are often peripheral to the central concerns of individual rights, as the examples below indicate. It may even be necessary, in the interests of individual rights, to build legislation upon an express recognition of cultural difference. This is the second reason that cultural neutrality is untenable. Often individual choice – individual freedom – is dependent on its social context. Thus, judicious governmental action may further, not hinder, individual rights. An adequate understanding of the relationship of culture to law must therefore be founded upon a recognition of the inescapable presence of culture in law. Such an understanding offers a more nuanced analysis of the kinds of measures that are appropriate, instead of insisting on the mirage of cultural neutrality.

THE NATURE OF LAW AS A CULTURAL CREATION.   Culture is bound up with law in at least three ways. First, the framework of individual rights established by law embodies, in its detailed structure, features specific to a particular society.[13] My point is not that the very idea of an autonomous individual is a cultural creation. That may be, but if so, it is an idea that I firmly believe we should continue to uphold in Canadian constitutional law. I am not arguing, then, that we should dismiss the concept of the individual itself as culture-bound, inappropriate for cultures (like those of aboriginal communities) that seem to place more emphasis on the collectivity. Rather, I am arguing that even given a commitment to individual rights, the specific expression of those rights in a concrete legal order is always marked by cultural features having little or nothing to do with respect for the individual. Statements of law that work perfectly well in one culture may have to be adjusted for another, not because that other culture is any less committed to the individual, but simply because the presumptions underlying the expression of law are wrong.

Here and throughout this section, I will speak of "culture" because that is the term commonly used in the discussion of these issues. But note that in this context the range of things marked by culture may be very broad indeed, much broader than the narrow definition of specifically linguistic or folkloric characteristics. Furthermore, this idea of culture is not static, not frozen in the past. Culture as it is used here is essentially the same as the distinctive characteristics of a particular community's public debate through time, identified in the last chapter. It can be conceived of as the set of references, the ways of framing questions and making arguments, that distinguish one language of public debate from another and that are always subject to growth and evolution.

Examples of this kind of cultural difference within the law are most obvious in the aboriginal context. One thinks, for example, of the different perspectives on the scope of individual rights in land. Both the civil law of Quebec and the common law of other provinces have, in their different ways, come to regard land as subject to private ownership, with the individual obtaining an extensive, exclusive right to exploit a block of land, subject to limitations imposed by law and to rights retained by the state (especially mineral rights). The implicit model within these systems of law, then, is of a general individual right, subsequently limited by regulation in the public interest.[14] This contrasts sharply, in its conceptual foundation, with the notion of land use in at least some aboriginal societies. For the Montagnais of the north shore of the Saint Lawrence, for example, the land – like the air or the ocean in Quebec's civil law – can never be owned; rather, each part of the land is under the stewardship of a particular individual or group of individuals, who have a right to use and administer that territory, but always with an obligation to preserve its character for other users and for future generations. This obligation is founded on the premise that the resources of the land are essential to human life, not just for the present generation, but through time. The land itself cannot be subject to the unencumbered will of an individual; rights in land must be limited in their very nature, conditioned by responsibilities built into their rationale.[15]

The Montagnais and the civil- and common-law conceptions are therefore very different, at least in their initial presumptions (although one might hope for a partial rapprochement between them, especially given the growing recognition of the need for environmental protection), but that difference is not reducible to the conclusion that one is concerned with the individual, the other with the collectivity. The two conceptions do not fit onto a neat individual rights/collective rights spectrum. Each includes some measure of individual autonomy, combined with some measure of responsibility to the claims of society. The essential difference lies, not in their respect for the individual, but in the different ways they understand the context within which individuals act, specifically the nature of land and its relationship to human life. In every society, including non-aboriginal societies, this kind of understanding shapes the structure of law, establishing the detailed framework within which individuals exercise their autonomy. Permitting aboriginal societies to govern themselves in a manner responsive to their own culture – or (in the terms of our previous discussion of political community) in a manner responsive to their public debate through time – need not mean that the rights of the individual are being sacrificed to some collective interest. It may simply allow individuals to live within a structure of laws more compatible with their own understanding of the world.

Examples might be multiplied of situations where the structure of the law is shaped by its particular social or cultural context, so that law in other societies or other cultures might justifiably take a different form. The protections afforded the accused in criminal proceedings are based on the assumption that certain kinds of behaviour will be prosecuted by the state, with the accused facing the risk of severe punishment. If, in another society, the same behaviour is dealt with by different means – by, for example, a process of mediation and attempted reconciliation – those guarantees might be unnecessary, perhaps even inappropriate. What role would the privilege against self-incrimination play in such a system? Similarly, adoption laws that specify that the child must be committed to the care of named individuals may be unnecessarily restrictive in a society in which the community as a whole is able to take responsibility for the child.[16]

In these examples, my point is not to suggest that each method of handling the situation is equally effective or that the choice of method should necessarily be included within the scope of aboriginal self-government. There might be good reasons for rejecting one of the methods or for making the choice at the level of Canada as a whole. My point is simply that the existence of governmental autonomy premised on cultural differences need not be incompatible with the demands of individual freedom. All legal structures are shaped by culture, in ways that often have little to do with concerns of individual autonomy. The existence of a plurality of systems of legal regulation, each expressing a different tradition of public discussion and decision making, may therefore be compatible with individual freedom.

GOVERNMENT ACTION TO SHAPE THE CONTEXT WITHIN WHICH CULTURAL AND LINGUISTIC RIGHTS ARE EXERCISED.   A second way in which the law might justifiably intervene in matters of culture stems from the fact that certain rights – especially rights integral to the expression of cultural identity – are dependent on a particular context for their exercise. In this kind of situation, individual rights might not be served by complete state neutrality. On the contrary, government involvement may be needed to create the conditions necessary for the enjoyment of the rights. This is particularly the case with rights that cannot be exercised in any meaningful way by an individual alone: for example, the right to speak the language of one's choice. This is still very much an individual right in the sense that it is vested in individuals and protects interests of profound value to individuals: the ability to express oneself freely, to maintain the tools necessary for the preservation of one's cultural heritage. But it also has a profoundly social dimension, in the sense that its enjoyment is highly dependent on the existence of a community of people using the language. One cannot speak a language alone, or at least if one does, one gains little value from it. Because of that social dimension, the right may well require positive governmental assistance for its enjoyment.

Indeed, the existing language rights providing for bilingualism in the public service and minority language education in the schools are based on that kind of recognition. They are expressed as individual rights and one of their purposes is to allow individuals to use whatever official language they want in communication with the government, but that objective is not and cannot be achieved by the government refusing to legislate on matters of language – by the government simply keeping its hands off. On the contrary, its activities are deliberately structured to ensure that, within limits, it can respond to citizens using English or French. The government may have achieved a measure of neutrality between those languages (although even that varies from one part of the country to another), but it is an active neutrality, born of positive government policy. Even then, the neutrality does not and cannot extend to all languages; English and French are clearly the primary languages, although some more limited services are quite properly provided in other commonly spoken tongues.[17] Such deliberate action – such deliberate governmental choice – is necessary because there is, of course, no neutral ground. Services have to be provided in some language, and the choice of language will necessarily affect its use within the community. If English is the exclusive language of education, French-speaking citizens will find it more difficult to preserve their language.

This may seem like common sense and perfectly appropriate in a country in which there are two principal languages. Language legislation becomes much more controversial, however, when it favours one of the two official languages. Yet even then, given the social dimension of language use, such legislation may be appropriate.

One of the principal grievances in Quebec during the Quiet Revolution was the predominance of English as the language of work, especially in the upper echelons of companies. Even though the great majority in an area might speak French, employees frequently had to learn English in order to get a job or to advance beyond the lowest levels. This situation was reinforced by the fact that large enterprises in Quebec, like those in the rest of Canada, were frequently owned by foreign interests or, when domestically owned, by English-speaking Canadians. Both groups tended to assume that English was the natural language of economic life throughout North America. Economic privilege and language use tended to go hand in hand, creating strong resentment within francophone Quebec.[18]

In an essay written in 1965, before his entry into politics, Pierre Elliott Trudeau fiercely criticized this linguistic discrimination, arguing for a solution which he couched in terms of individual rights. After noting that French-speaking Canadians were underrepresented at all levels of the managerial hierarchy, from the very top down to the foreman, and that the extent of underrepresentation could not be explained by the inadequacies in Quebec's education system, he concluded: "It even happens that a Quebec worker being hired for industry is required to speak English as well as French – a form of discrimination that should be rigorously forbidden by Quebec law."[19] On its face, this seems fully compatible with an individualistic approach to language rights, one that sees the law as concerned, above all, with protecting individuals against specific discriminatory behaviour, not with controlling the whole structure of language use within a given social context. But in this example, one can see clearly that individual language use and social context are inseparable. Trudeau's suggestion has far-reaching implications, not just for the treatment of specific individuals, but for the entire workplace. If firms are compelled to hire unilingual francophone workers, then the predominant language will be French; at the very least, anyone communicating with those workers will have to speak French. Protecting the rights of individuals necessarily requires a fundamental change in the whole pattern of language use within the workplace.

If one takes individual rights to language seriously, then, one may well have to pay attention not just to the individual, but also to the larger context within which the individual acts. But if that is the case, is there any good reason to limit the law's role to measures phrased, like Trudeau's, in terms of individual rights? If it makes sense to prohibit discrimination against unilingual francophones in Quebec (in some circumstances), is there any principled objection to other measures designed to increase the use of French in industry in the province, measures that regulate language use directly and might well be structured in a manner more sensitive to the legitimate needs of particular firms? This, in fact, is what the Quebec legislature has done in the language of work provisions in Bill 101. Those provisions prohibit discrimination in the manner suggested by Trudeau (there is an exception for situations in which the work itself requires the use of another language), but they also require the creation of "francisation programs" in firms over a certain size. Under those programs, the use of French in the firm is increased gradually over time, there is no prohibition on the use of English (or other languages), and exemptions exist for firms having most of their business out of province or servicing a particular linguistic community.[20]

All of these measures – Trudeau's prohibition of discrimination and the francisation provisions in Bill 101 – favour the use of French. They are not even-handed. This too is often a necessary concession to the social dynamic of language use. Only in very specific situations is it possible to maintain both languages on an equal footing. In most, one language will tend to dominate, or even exclude, the other. This is obvious when individuals are not bilingual. If, as frequently occurred in Quebec, most employees of a company are bilingual but interspersed among them are a handful of unilingual anglophones, there will be an in-built bias in favour of English. It, after all, is the only common language.[21] Even where individuals are comfortable in both languages – which is still very much the exception – one language is frequently used more than another. Conversations generally occur, and documents are drafted, in one language at a time. Patterns of interaction therefore develop in which one language tends to be used more than another. It usually takes considerable effort and very extensive personal bilingualism to maintain even rough parity in language use. I work in an institution, McGill University's Faculty of Law, in which one-quarter of the professors and one-third of the students are francophone, virtually all professors are functionally bilingual and most are comfortable in either language. Almost all students are at least passively bilingual. Many courses are taught in French, course materials come from every Canadian jurisdiction, some in French, some in English, students use the language of their choice in essays and exams, and faculty members speak either language in faculty meetings. The faculty is therefore well placed to operate in a bilingual manner, and to its credit, it does to a large extent. But there is no doubt that even with these advantages, English remains the language of most interaction within the faculty.

Given the difficulty of maintaining linguistic equality in every context and the likelihood that complete personal bilingualism will remain unattainable in Canada, it makes sense to structure language policy to take into account the dynamic sketched above. Rather than aiming for identical treatment in every context, the law should aim for fairness across the broad range of activities. It makes no sense, for example, to create a blanket individual right to work in the language of one's choice. That right is unlikely to be of much value to a French-speaking Canadian in Lethbridge or an English-speaking Canadian in Chicoutimi. But the law can promote decent opportunities for employment in French in francophone areas of the country, roughly equivalent to those existing in English. This kind of approach would not mean the abandonment of bilingualism. In some contexts and for some services, the use of both languages is feasible and desirable – indeed necessary to the healthy development of a pan-Canadian political community. Governments should continue to support the achievement of personal bilingualism so that some institutions can function bilingually, binding the country together and improving discussion across the linguistic divide. But this should be a bilingualism tempered by an understanding of the dynamics of language use in Canada, not one that imposes an abstract and ultimately futile identity of treatment across the country, or one that insists on complete neutrality on questions of language. In fact, the federal policies on bilingualism recognize the existence of different patterns of language use. Although there is an effort to have many services available in both languages across the country, the basic language of work does vary from region to region. In 1991 only 29.4 per cent of federal civil service positions were classified as bilingual, in Alberta only 3.1 per cent.[22]

In the 1960s, during the hearings of the Royal Commission on Bilingualism and Biculturalism, Acadians, traditionally the strongest supporters of bilingualism, opposed fully bilingual schools. Their environment was, they argued, already saturated with English. They feared that if the Acadian schools emphasized English as much as French, the balance would be tipped decisively towards English. To create a truly bilingual society, one in which both languages were equally vigorous, there had to be some institutions in which French was dominant so that French had some room to develop.[23] Parity in treatment, in other words, required some measure of autonomy for both cultures, with the form of autonomy tailored to the actual pressures facing the community.

In linguistic matters generally, there is a legitimate role for government, a role that need not treat all languages, all cultures, identically. Government may – indeed, often must – address the concrete contexts within which individuals try to retain their languages and preserve their cultures, and may adjust its policies to meet the challenges of these contexts, just as (for example) the Canadian Radio-television and Telecommunications Commission (CRTC) regulates the extent of Canadian content in broadcasting in order to ensure an adequate place for the expression of Canadian culture.

THE ROLE OF CULTURE IN THE INTERPRETATION OF LAW. The third way in which the law may legitimately address questions of culture is a consequence of the role of culture in the interpretation of law. Legal texts are never self-executing. They never specify, with complete clarity, all the situations in which they apply. Instead, they are phrased in general terms, describing the general type of situation they govern, with what typical effect. This is especially true of constitutional norms, which are usually highly abstract, affirming broad principles applicable to a wide variety of circumstances. Determining the effect of these principles in specific cases involves a very complex set of judgments: What is the core value (or values) enshrined in the constitutional text? What kinds of conduct is it meant to control? Does this situation raise those kinds of issues? Are there competing considerations, perhaps competing constitutional norms, that need to be weighed? If the conduct is unconstitutional, what is the most appropriate remedy? This process necessarily involves difficult judgments of value and context, judgments shaped by judges' general understanding of the structure of Canadian society and the nature of its social life – judgments which should, in Canada, ideally take account of the complexity of our political communities and the varying challenges faced by our cultural groups.[24]

The complexity of constitutional interpretation – its sensitivity to different perceptions of society and of the values implicit in constitutional texts – is apparent in a norm like freedom of expression. There is undoubtedly a broad measure of agreement that "free expression" is, in its abstract formulation, an essential value within Canadian society. But determining what that means in concrete cases is not so clear. Is all expression protected by the constitution, or only certain kinds? In large measure, the answer depends on one's understanding of the purpose of the guarantee. Is expression valued simply because of its role within democratic politics, or is it valued for its own sake, as an inherently valuable aspect of individuality? If the former, it may be limited to political speech; if the latter, it may extend to other forms of expression. Even if a broad interpretation is adopted, questions remain. Does commercial advertising have anything to do with the essence of individuality?[25] Do pornographic films – films that only show sexual acts taking place, without any further communication – have anything to do with it?[26] Are negotiations with a prostitute constitutionally protected?[27] Is the content of the freedom conditioned by some principle inherent in the very notion of a right (for example, respect for individuality), so that some forms of expression (expression that is violent or incites to violence, or that is degrading and dehumanizing) are necessarily excluded?[28] In recent decisions, the Supreme Court of Canada has opted for a very broad definition of expression, including all communications except those that are, in themselves, acts of violence.[29] That does not end the matter, however, for all Charter rights are subject to "such reasonable limits prescribed by law as can be demonstrably justified in a free and democratic society."[30] The courts must therefore weigh the value of the particular expression that the legislature has sought to prohibit against competing social concerns (the value of tobacco advertising versus the protection of health, the value of pornography versus the likelihood of harm to women). In that process, the courts may consider the extent to which the limit goes to the heart of the guarantee (it may be more acceptable, for example, to limit commercial advertising than to limit political discussion), balancing this against the reasons advanced for restricting expression.

The application of the Charter therefore requires a careful appreciation of its underlying values, including their importance relative to other concerns, all within a very specific context. In some circumstances, those judgments may need to take into account the structure of language use and cultural interaction in Canada. If in British Columbia, for example, the use of English as the main language of public education were challenged on the grounds that it discriminated against those whose first language was German or Cantonese, the courts could legitimately consider (indeed, would have to consider) the cost of offering the full range of courses in additional languages, the desirability of promoting a common medium of communication, and the prevalence of English within British Columbia. In 1990, in fact, in a case involving the constitutional guarantee of minority-language education, the Supreme Court of Canada relied on similar considerations to hold that given the need to speak English in Alberta, the Alberta government was justified in requiring that all students, even those in French schools, receive a minimum level of English instruction.[31]

Because patterns of language use vary across the country, the precise effect of these cultural considerations may also vary. In the examples just given, the issues turned on the role of English within specific contexts, in the one case, British Columbia, in the other, Alberta. One can imagine situations in which the distinctive character of Quebec's society would be relevant. In the Supreme Court's 1988 decision striking down the sign law provisions in Bill 101, for example, the court acknowledged that it was legitimate for Quebec to seek to maintain a French "visage linguistique." In the pursuit of that goal, the province could require the presence of French on commercial signs – might even require the "marked predominance" of French. The court held, however, that that objective did not justify the full extent of Bill 101's interference with freedom of expression: the complete prohibition of English on commercial signs.[32]

The specific objective at issue in that case – the preservation of French as the dominant language of public expression – was clearly unique to Quebec. It gained whatever force it had from the fact that francophone Quebecers constitute a minority in a predominantly English-speaking continent and from the consequent need to maintain an environment conducive to the use of French as a public language. The same considerations could not be used to justify legislation favouring English in other provinces, for the simple reason that the pressures on English there are not equivalent to those on French in Quebec (it may be possible, however, to rely on other justifications). In a sense, then, the Charter guarantee of freedom of expression does have a different effect in different parts of the country. This strikes some as incompatible with the very nature of constitutional rights, but it is a necessary consequence of the fact that Charter guarantees do not prescribe that all signs shall be in English and French or, for that matter, that specific sexual acts should never be mentioned. They establish much broader principles, whose application depends upon the circumstances of a particular case. The fact that the Charter permits Quebec to require the marked predominance of French on signs but might not permit Alberta to do the same does not mean that freedom of expression is different in each province. The situations are different. The regulation of language in Quebec raises considerations that are manifestly not the same as those in Alberta.

To some people, this is heresy. Individual rights should, they argue, be universal, applying in the same manner regardless of cultural context. The rights of the individual should not be affected by cultural differences. But if that is so, why did we bother creating a Canadian Charter of Rights and Freedoms in 1982? Why didn't we simply adopt the US Bill of Rights, together with the interpretations of the US Supreme Court, as our own? The answer, of course, is that our society is not the United States. We want a constitution that is sensitive to the specific character of this land. If we take differences of culture into account between the United States and Canada, why can't we consider differences within Canada? This, indeed, is what our courts have done in the cases mentioned above. It is also what the distinct society clause would have us do.

RESTRICTIONS ON GOVERNMENT ACTION IN MATTERS OF CULTURE.   This discussion has explored three ways in which the law may be premised on the existence of cultural difference. Each is relevant to strategies of institutional accommodation at issue in Canada's constitutional discussions. The first – creating a measure of institutional autonomy so that in some areas the law can better reflect the traditions of a minority community – forms the main justification for aboriginal self-government (and indeed one of the principal reasons for federalism). The second – the enactment of legislation to create an environment conducive to individuals' exercise of cultural and linguistic rights – lies behind a variety of measures designed to support the vitality of minority communities. The third – the relevance of cultural differences in the interpretation of constitutional norms – is integral to the justification of the distinct society clause. In each case, the law need not remain neutral, but may be shaped in the service of cultural ends. Indeed, law is inevitably the product of cultural choices. Frequently, there is no neutral ground.

This does not mean that governments should do absolutely anything in the name of culture. While we value our cultures – while the influence of culture is inescapable in public life – we also value individual autonomy, the ability to take a path different from our ancestors or our neighbours, to reflect critically on our societies, to struggle to transform them, perhaps even to reject them outright. We know all too well the pathologies of dictatorial nationalism, in which individuals are forced to conform to a rigid mould or, if they are unable to conform, are eliminated. We have seen many less extreme situations in which restrictions on individual freedom, in the

interests of cultural ends, are excessive. I am not at all suggesting
that we should ignore these concerns and embrace a culturalist nir-
vana. We must retain our capacity for critical reflection so that we
can judge which measures are appropriate, which are reprehensible
– so that we can preserve the possibility of changing our societies in
the interests of individual freedom. My point is simply that one easy
answer – the claim that the law and government should remain utterly neutral on questions of culture, that we should somehow rip
our public life out of the particular character of our societies to
achieve some form of abstract impartiality – is no answer at all.

We are forced to search for more subtle solutions that take into account the inevitable presence of culture in all social life (the satisfaction we draw from the sense of belonging, of familiarity, of full
participation, that comes with a vibrant culture). This is not the place
to suggest how, in every case, cultural concerns and individual autonomy should be reconciled. Nor can the text of the constitution be
expected to settle everything once and for all. The situations are so
various, the cultures so unique, the challenges so diverse, that it is often best to recognize general considerations that should be taken
into account, leaving their precise consequences to be explored in
the circumstances of particular cases (as indeed we did with the
rights included in the Charter in 1982). This section can, however,
suggest general structures through which cultural policy might be
reconciled with individual rights.

The first and purest form of the strategy of declaring general
principles while leaving their implications to be elaborated in subsequent cases is adopted in the distinct society clause. That clause does
not directly speak to the content of rights. It does not limit or exclude their application. It simply states that in the complex process
of applying abstract rights to concrete situations, the courts should
keep in mind that Quebec possesses a distinctive character, one that
gives its government a unique cultural role. We have already seen
how Quebec's linguistic character might be relevant in cases involving language use.[33] The distinct society clause signals that possibility
without prejudging the result in any particular case. Courts are still
charged with enforcing the rights, although in a manner responsive
to Quebec's uniqueness. The courts may decide, then, that challenged legislation goes too far, as they did in the decision on the
language of signs in Quebec, or they may decide that certain requirements are permissible (for example, legislation making French
predominant, but not exclusive, on signs). Through the process of
incremental decision making, the courts would, one hopes, develop
principles to govern the relationship between culture and rights.

The clause alerts the courts to consider how cultural ends might be balanced against individual rights, without specifying what that balance should be.

Beyond providing an opportunity for reconciliation, the distinct society clause might also be understood as suggesting a particular way in which culture and individual rights are compatible; it may be an expression of the general principle that the same abstract right may legitimately, when instantiated within different legal traditions, take different forms, just as, for example, substantially the same commitment to private property is, in the common- and civil-law traditions, translated into quite different legal concepts. A constitutional right, in other words, affirms an abstract value, the precise expression of which may be shaped by the context of a specific society. In some circumstances, then, individual rights might be reconciled with cultural diversity by retaining abstract rights applicable to all, but by building into the constitution mechanisms that alert the courts to the fact that those rights may be tailored to their context. Aboriginal peoples may benefit from solutions structured in this manner. The Charter (or parts of it) may remain applicable to aboriginal peoples, but with aboriginal self-government (and interpretive clauses analogous to the distinct society clause) permitting variation in the ways in which these principles take concrete form. Indeed, this seems to be the approach in section 35 of the Constitution Act, 1982, which guarantees aboriginal and treaty rights but stipulates that these shall be enjoyed equally by men and women.

One can imagine a similar way of reconciling aboriginal concerns for autonomy in a domain like adoption and child care with a continuing sense that the provincial or federal governments should ensure that minimum standards are met. Those standards might be expressed in general terms, applicable across the entire society, but with the aboriginal community determining how precisely those standards should be attained in its community, as part of its structure of social services. Under this kind of arrangement, some of the standards may not directly reflect the will of the aboriginal community, but that kind of compromise would be inevitable, given that aboriginal people would remain members both of their community and of the broader Canadian society. In the imposition of both constitutional norms and minimum legislative standards, however, one should ensure that the standards are sufficiently abstract that they avoid inadvertent and unnecessary constraints, confining themselves to ends triggering the responsibility of the larger society and recognizing that essentially the same ends can be attained by very different means.

Finally, cultural ends may be reconciled with individual rights not by focusing on enabling individuals to do whatever they want in every context, but by ensuring that contexts exist in which those individuals can pursue their cultural aspirations. This, for example, is the approach taken in the provision of minority-language education. Those rights do not entitle students to be taught in English or French in any classroom in the land. Instead, they recognize that education has to occur predominantly in one language or the other. Alternative structures, therefore, are provided, so that education occurs in different classrooms, preferably in different schools, and sometimes under the separate administration of the linguistic group concerned (depending on the number of students involved). Other, more controversial measures may constitute similarly structured compromises between individual aspirations and the manifestly social character of linguistic or cultural rights. This is one justification for language-of-work legislation, as we have already seen.[34] Similarly, the reservation of lands for aboriginal communities – either under the current system of Indian reserves or under more flexible regimes – is best understood as an attempt to preserve forms of landholding consistent with aboriginal conceptions of humanity's relationship to the land. Only if we assume that individual, fully alienable ownership is the only acceptable structure of landholding – an assumption that would entirely displace, for example, the Montagnais conception of a limited right coupled with obligations to posterity – do reserves appear to be unjustifiable infringements of the freedom of movement of non-aboriginal people.

Throughout all of this, we should certainly be concerned with the quality of options available to individuals within society as a whole, and with individuals' freedom within the specific context in which they find themselves. But weighing liberty and equality becomes a much more complex process than the simple theory of state neutrality suggests. Marginal limitations within a specific context (encouraging the use of French within certain firms in Quebec or restricting non-aboriginal use of lands reserved for aboriginal communities) may be fully justified by the fact that they enable members of minority communities to prosper without abandoning their culture or to preserve institutions in accordance with their traditions. As the example of reserved land suggests, that may be done without substantial restriction on the liberty of non-aboriginal people (or, at least, with restrictions no more substantial than those resulting from the denial of public access to privately owned land) and without substantial restriction on aboriginal individuals, who remain free to choose to live off reserve. The point is simply that when the social character of cultural or linguistic rights is taken seriously, one cannot evaluate the extent of liberty or equality by concentrating solely on the presence or absence of state constraint. Recognition of cultural differences within the structure of the law may be compatible with the rights of individuals; indeed, for members of minority groups, it may be the foundation for their enjoyment of cultural or linguistic rights.

ASYMMETRY AND CONSTITUTIONAL STABILITY

The previous sections have discussed whether constitutional asymmetry threatens, by its very nature, the liberty and equality of individuals. For many, however, that discussion would have missed the point. They find asymmetry objectionable, not because it is contrary to some abstract idea of freedom, but because it is contrary to their idea of *Canada*. For them, it is inconsistent with *citizenship* to have cultural differences taken into account in the interpretation of rights. All Canadians should be treated in precisely the same way simply because they are Canadians. From this perspective, one of the arguments given above – that we can differentiate within Canada because we differentiate between Canada and the United States[35] – would have been profoundly unconvincing. Individuals are treated differently in the United States because it is a different country.

Often, in other words, arguments of rights are really arguments of nation in disguise. The concern is not with individual liberty as such, but with requiring uniform treatment across the country as part of the very idea of having a country. We have already seen that in Canada's constitutional discussions over the last thirty years the adoption of a charter of rights served two purposes, one libertarian, the other nation-building. The nationalistic role for charters of rights has a long pedigree, present at the origin of the French Declaration of the Rights of Man and the Citizen and influential throughout the development of the US constitution. This book has argued strenuously against that conception of nation, most directly in the previous chapter. The existence of a country implies a common public debate through time, and that debate does result in a cherished set of understandings, especially regarding the terms of debate, but the existence of a country does not require a uniform set of values or laws. In fact, an insistence on uniformity can be profoundly threatening to minorities within the country (in part for the reasons given above regarding the relevance of culture to law).

I do not intend to repeat those arguments here. My concern is with another reason for opposing asymmetry on national grounds – the concern that an asymmetrical structure, especially any form of special status for Quebec, will be unstable, inevitably leading to the breakup of the country.[36] Although this purports to be a purely instrumental argument, concerned with the practical viability of an asymmetrical constitution, it is often a disguised form of the substantive nationalist argument. For most of its supporters, the concern is not that the country might one day slip towards dissolution, but that asymmetry *is* a partial dissolution – a surrender of their idea of the Canadian nation. Nevertheless, this section explores the instrumental argument to see what independent value it has.

The instrumental argument is essentially founded on an empirical claim – that asymmetry would create increasing particularization, increased tension, eventually causing the country to crumble. Like most predictive claims, it is very difficult to meet head on. How does one prove conclusively that in our specific situation an asymmetrical structure is likely – or unlikely – to succeed? Some have suggested answers based on comparative studies of federations or of countries with large cultural or linguistic minorities. I propose to take a more modest tack, looking critically at the arguments of the advocates of the slippery slope, noting especially how their implicit conception of structures of allegiance in federal states relates to the arguments presented here.

The different forms of the instrumental argument are often vague on the precise mechanism generating instability. When they do specify a mechanism, most focus on the influence of political elites at the provincial level. These elites are, they suggest, predominantly interested in expanding their own role within public (or in the case of the nationalist segment of the Quebec business class, commercial) affairs. Those elites promote the level of government with which they most closely identify: the province. Because their desire for greater influence is insatiable, they tend to press for increased provincial control over virtually everything, without regard for the attitudes of the bulk of the population. They have no personal interest in achieving an appropriate balance between the federal and provincial levels. Their demands are systematically biased against the federal level. Any attempt to cater to them will merely strengthen their position, leading to an escalating series of demands that eventually undermine any viable federal authority. It is much better to refuse to make any concessions at all, in order to avoid setting foot on the slippery slope to secession.

The remarkable thing about this argument is its complete deference to *realpolitik*. It allows no room whatever for adjustments to the federal system (at least in favour of the provinces), treating all these as beginnings of the end. It tends to exclude consideration of the merits of provincial arguments, interpreting every suggestion as nothing more than self-interested grasping. Such complete deference to *realpolitik* is unusual. We are rarely so rigorous in our rejection of normative arguments. Even though we acknowledge that – human beings being what they are – all public life is affected by self-aggrandizement and empire-building, we still recognize that alongside *realpolitik* there are more substantial reasons for acting. Except in very unusual situations, we are willing to discuss them. Why the unwillingness here?

The lack of even-handedness may provide a clue. While a commitment to decentralization is portrayed as the product of pure institutional self-interest, arguments for the maintenance of a strong federal role – made by people just as fallible (or just as noble) as their provincialist counterparts – are accorded much more respect.[37] One suspects, then, that the attack on the advocates of decentralization may be more a matter of tactics than of reason. The enemies of decentralization disagree vehemently with the conclusion, so they impugn their opponents' motives.

At a more fundamental level, there seems to be another reason for the exclusive concentration on *realpolitik*: a feeling that any system of federalism is inherently unstable, and that therefore any departure from what exists is inherently dangerous. There may be a measure of stability in existing federal arrangements. A benign inertia may have developed. But once that inertia is broken, there may be no way of re-establishing an equilibrium.[38] This argument takes Lesage's dilemma seriously: the feeling that there is no defensible stopping place on the slide between a federation and a cluster of independent states. Because of this, arguments of principle are in vain, even treacherous if they lead one to tinker with the existing division of powers. In these circumstances, only arguments of *realpolitik* can prevail. And if one wants to preserve a tenuous resting-place between a single Canada and no Canada, one should leave arguments of substance well enough alone.

This is a much more serious objection than the last. It is true that agreement on a specific division of powers may be difficult to achieve, although not (I believe) because principled arguments are absent. Rather, the considerations that bear upon a particular outcome are so diverse, the number of interests so various, that it may

be difficult to build consensus around any one solution (as indeed we
have seen in our recent constitutional negotiations). Everyone wants
some agreement, and everyone may prefer a range of outcomes to
failure, but within that range it is very hard to agree on one result.

This may be good reason for constitutional conservatism – for retaining existing structures unless they are patently inadequate, and
in any case for limiting the scope of discussion. But the situation
is different once the constitutional box is opened on a specific issue
(or once there are good reasons to open that box). Then, it is no
longer sufficient to avoid reasoned argument, especially when there
are dependable criteria for preferring particular constitutional
outcomes.

What, then, about the more basic argument that there is no stable,
principled argument for any particular division of powers, and thus
that any further decentralization, or any form of constitutional
asymmetry, threatens to undermine the whole? The principal purpose of this book has been to argue that there is such a justification.
It has argued that a federal structure – and an asymmetrical structure at that – is most consistent with the actual shape of political
community and political allegiance in Canada. Canadians in all parts
of the country value both their local political communities and their
membership in the broader Canadian community. They draw the
balance between those communities in different ways (francophone
Quebecers, for reasons discussed above, tend to emphasize their
provincial society more than do other Canadians), but they retain an
allegiance to Canada nevertheless. For the majority of Quebecers,
demands for autonomy are not limitless but are balanced by a genuine commitment to retain the pan-Canadian community, a commitment whose content is, in its core, shaped by the division of powers
in the constitution of 1867.

There are, then, forces that run counter to those emphasized by
the Cassandras of the slippery slope. In fact, one wonders whether
their blindness to these other forces results from our old friend, the
tendency towards exclusivity in the language of nation and nationalism, the tendency that has bedevilled our constitutional debate generally. Those who resist all accommodation assume that political
allegiance naturally tends to be single. They therefore refuse concessions to local allegiances and emphasize a single, central allegiance in
order to maintain commitment to the whole. In doing so, however,
they suggest, usually implicitly but sometimes explicitly, that minority communities have to be ready to weaken their commitment to
their local communities in the interest of that whole – that Quebecers must be Canadians first, that they should choose between

Quebec and Canada. During the Meech Lake debate, Tom Axworthy, former principal secretary to Prime Minister Trudeau, was asked whether Quebec could still be accommodated within Canada. He answered, "Well certainly Quebecers can be accommodated within Canada, and I draw that distinction between Quebecers and Quebec – that is the government of Quebec."[39]

In a 1964 paper, Pierre Trudeau argued the need to accommodate regional differences within a federal structure. He discussed the constitutional decisions of the Judicial Committee of the Privy Council (often criticized by anglo-Canadian academics for their allegedly decentralizing trend), arguing that those judgments introduced important adjustments into Canadian law. In a now famous passage, he continued: "It has long been a custom in English Canada to denounce the Privy Council for its provincial bias; but it should perhaps be considered that if the law lords had not leaned in that direction, Quebec separatism might not be a threat today; it might be an accomplished fact."[40]

The fundamental lesson of this trenchant comment is that in a complex society like ours, a centralized political structure may not be stable. On the contrary, it may be profoundly alienating for members of the minority community, provoking disaffection and perhaps even outright rejection. A political structure is most stable, in other words, when it bears some tolerable resemblance to the character of its society. As an academic, Trudeau accepted adjustments to the federal balance that were "guided by rational deliberation," such as "most of our constitutional amendments" and the Privy Council decisions.[41] As a politician, he resisted further change, perhaps in reaction to the increasing appeal within Quebec of forms of nationalism that tended towards complete independence, forms that he identified with passion, not reason. Over time, his counter-strategy of building Quebecers' allegiance to Ottawa seemed to displace any respect for allegiance to Quebec, until eventually his position was virtually the same as that of Axworthy above. That landed him in the same trap as the anglo-Canadian critics of the Privy Council, leaving so little room for a recognition of Quebec's specificity that the dual loyalties of most Quebecers could no longer be accommodated within his Canada. Perhaps Canadians should return to Trudeau's insight of 1964, which takes seriously the existence of a federalism of allegiance to complement our federal constitution.

By vehemently rejecting the slippery slope argument in the forms given above, I do not mean to suggest that a lack of cohesion is never a problem, that any level of decentralization can be accommodated within a federal constitution. A country like Canada is premised on the coexistence of at least two levels of political community, each capable of supporting allegiance. If decentralization continues indefinitely, there would come a time when insufficient powers were left at the federal level to support a pan-Canadian government. Moreover, what constitutes sufficient powers is not (as some Quebec sovereignists assume) a matter of cold calculation. Canada is built upon allegiances that go well beyond analyses of material costs and benefits. It is founded upon commitment to a distinctively Canadian political community, a community often maintained in defiance of purely economic interest, the pull of which has tended to be north-south rather than east-west (especially for provinces like Alberta or British Columbia). If Ottawa is weakened to the point that there is too little left at the federal level to serve as an object of allegiance, many Canadians may well ask, "Why bother?" The periodic threats of the Mulroney government to institutions such as trans-Canadian passenger rail service, the Canadian Broadcasting Corporation, Canada Post, and the National Film Board have been troubling to many Canadians precisely because they do undermine channels of communication that have been fundamental to the infrastructure, both functional and symbolic, of the pan-Canadian community. If we are serious in maintaining a federal state, we have to remain alert to the viability of the whole.

Here, once again, we bump into a difficult empirical claim. How much weight at the centre is necessary to maintain allegiance? I believe that a constitutional settlement is possible that does not cross the critical line, primarily because the allegiance of francophone Quebecers to their province is not all-encompassing. The next chapter suggests how that settlement translates into constitutional form. Readers will be able to decide for themselves whether it goes too far.

ASYMMETRY AND THE LANGUAGE OF
POLITICAL DEBATE

This book has offered a vision of our country's political life that I hope is appealing, but one objection might remain. Does the vision bear any relationship to how Canadians, including Quebecers, actually think about their country? This book began with a portrait of Canadians' divergent perceptions. It has emphasized that Canada's political debates often use concepts of nation and nationalism incompatible with those preferred here. How can we recast this set of attitudes? It is all very well to show the defects of nationalism, but what if people are, simply, nationalists? The disjuncture is especially important in arguments for constitutional asymmetry. My criticisms of the slippery slope focus exclusively on objections to decentralization (and indeed, that is the focus of most who make the argument), but doesn't the added fact that the proposed decentralization is asymmetrical introduce another complication? After all, notwithstanding the clever arguments of this book, most Canadians see asymmetry as inherently unfair, as fundamentally incompatible with citizenship. In the end, is this book simply an exercise in wishful thinking, a proposal for a new way a hypothetical group of citizens living in Canada might think about their country, but one that bears no relationship to how real Canadians do think about it?

Before we jump to the conclusion that the language of exclusive allegiance and symmetrical constitutions is an inevitable part of our political culture, we should first build some subtlety into our understanding of the role of concepts like nation or nationalism in the popular debate. There is a tendency among political analysts to pick a label to describe a particular position, to flesh out the content of that position with what seem to be its essential features, and then to draw conclusions on the basis of that highly simplified, almost stylized description. Very often the descriptions are misleading, imposing a rigour and singleness of purpose on attitudes that are much more open, more diverse, than the label suggests. A good example is the treatment of Quebec nationalism in much English Canadian political commentary. A vast array of attitudes are grouped under that label, attitudes ranging from the simple assertion of a cultural role for Quebec to an uncompromising commitment to Quebec's secession. Yet frequently, all are portrayed as though they were animated by a single spirit, always focused on the cultural community, inward-looking, insufficiently respectful of the individual, and insufficiently welcoming to people of other backgrounds. Those attributes are characteristic of a particular brand of nationalism, and they have at times been influential. But to treat them as dominant features of all Quebec "nationalists" is as misleading as to treat contemporary English Canadian nationalism as though it were, in all its variations, thoroughly committed to bilingualism coast-to-coast. Even individuals who adopt a particular label rarely adopt all the implications others ascribe to it. Labels are useful shorthand, adopted with a specific end in mind, but they rarely capture the richness of a person or of a political movement.

The point is that those labels are always approximations, simplifying descriptions that may be necessary but certainly do not exhaust the currents of our political lives. Because they are approximations, they can be challenged by a richer understanding of the raw

material or by new ways of summarizing the phenomena. This book
has taken both tacks. Part 1 was concerned with developing a more
nuanced understanding of the intersection between culture, language, and the constitutional debate. Part 2 proposes a way of understanding political community and allegiance, one that avoids the
rigidity and exclusivity of the language of nationalism.

I have tried to show that this conception is more consistent with
the structure of allegiance in Canada, including Quebec, than the
language of nationalism. That conception provides a better approx-
imation of what we actually do, how we actually feel. We do not
always realize it, even (especially?) when we ourselves are directly
concerned. But once the point is raised clearly enough, it can burst
upon the popular debate with surprising force. That happened in
Quebec as a result of the famous poll by the Centre de recherches
sur l'opinion publique, published in *L'actualité* magazine in July
1992. The answers to a series of questions – most concerned with
Quebecers' attachment to Canadian symbols – demonstrated Quebecers' simultaneous attachment to Quebec and Canada, prompting
the magazine to name its issue, "Le Canada dans le peau" ("Canada
in one's skin").[42] And more important than the actual data was the
shock of recognition that ran through Quebec. Following months of
exasperation with the aftermath of Meech, Quebecers began to acknowledge that Canada had defined their identities, had been part
of their history.

I believe that kind of recognition can work for many of the elements of the analysis presented here.[43] Our history has combined a
respect (sometimes grudging) for the concerns of cultural minorities
with a commitment to build a pan-Canadian community. We have
had substantial tolerance for different ways of being Canadian and
for institutional structures reflecting those different ways.[44] We
have, in short, lived under an asymmetrical constitution. What we
need is a way of speaking about it, one that captures our practice,
what we value, more accurately.

That reconception will not settle things once and for all. For one
thing, political attitudes often persist long after the conditions that
created them have disappeared. It is striking, for example, that even
though direct economic discrimination against francophones in
Quebec is largely a thing of the past, one still hears a few (though increasingly uncommon) echoes of the old positions – French Canadians complaining about the mythical Eaton's salesperson, capable of
speaking only English; anglophones arguing that Quebecers should
adapt to the natural language of commerce (if not of the modern
world). One hopes that with time, and perhaps with the crisis we

have been through, some of those remaining attitudes will be jolted out of their ruts and onto more effective paths. And of course, in a society of different people, opinions will continue to differ. There are undoubtedly some who will always embrace an *indépendantiste* option in Quebec, although a solid constitutional settlement would shift the balance decisively against them.

At a conference on the future of Quebec and Canada in November 1990, many of the participants were discussing how, given the Meech debacle, consensus might be possible again. Barry Stuart, chief land-claims negotiator for the Yukon government, cited Yukon's experience with negotiating aboriginal land claims, a task raising issues very similar to those involved in the constitutional debate. He said that at the beginning of the process, non-aboriginal people had been hostile to the whole idea of land claims; they had argued that their settlement would give unfair preference to aboriginal people, creating two classes of citizenship and threatening the economy of the territory. The negotiators did not seal themselves off from this public reaction. Instead, they conducted the talks openly, holding sessions in local communities and actively soliciting public discussion and exchange. As the negotiations progressed – and as the aboriginal peoples explained the character of their communities, their use of the land, and the nature of their claims – public opinion began to shift. By the end, there was substantial support among non-aboriginal residents (including the representatives of mining and hunting and fishing interests) for the settlement of claims.

There are many reasons for the greater sympathy for aboriginal concerns in recent years, but at least one is the realization that special institutional arrangements are consistent with our history, and that they are frequently desirable in order to accommodate cultural difference. I have tried in this book to show why that is so.

8 Practical Implications

Thus far, this argument has remained at an abstract level, suggesting how we should think about language, culture, and political community in Canada and defending the principle of constitutional asymmetry. This chapter brings that argument down to earth by exploring some of its specific consequences for constitutional law and practice.

This book's argument is potentially applicable to many facets of Canadian statecraft. Apart from its obvious application to constitutional amendment, it might be used to shape the courts' interpretation of the present constitution. Its analysis of the relationship between language, culture, individual rights, and citizenship can help us understand, for example, how the federal aspects of our constitution relate to individual rights, or linguistic rights to guarantees of equality. In addition, the analysis is relevant to what governments do at the subconstitutional level, within the present framework. Many of its conclusions bear upon how Ottawa should exercise its spending power, or how it should approach its relationship with aboriginal peoples.

This chapter cannot possibly explore all those implications. Instead, it will focus on three of the most important issues in the recent rounds of constitutional debate: aboriginal self-government, Quebec's demands, and Senate reform. This choice flows naturally from this book's review of constitutional negotiations of the last thirty years. Despite the collapse of our constitutional process, those issues remain among the most acute grievances in Canadian political life.

Although this chapter deals with formal constitutional change, it will also discuss how those issues can be addressed without amendments. Given the collapse of the Meech and Charlottetown rounds, we have probably seen the last of full-scale constitutional reform for the foreseeable future. If we achieve reconciliation, it will probably be through adjustments within the existing framework (at least in the short term). That framework allows substantial, though not unlimited, scope for change. Moreover, adjustments can be made more easily by subconstitutional means than by formal amendment. Informal adjustments do not require the same degree of consensus; at times, they simply require that a government exercise its powers differently. They do not have the same prominence, the same symbolic charge, or the same high stakes as formal amendment.[1]

But is it legitimate to pursue the objectives discussed here by informal means, given the popular rejection of Meech and Charlottetown? The answer, I believe, is a cautious yes.

Informal means raise very different considerations from formal amendment. First, amendment creates standards that cannot be changed except by using, again, the difficult process of constitutional amendment. Subconstitutional reform, on the other hand, allows much more scope for tinkering with, extending, or reversing the changes made. There may be substantial political pressures preventing that tinkering – the net effect may be little different from a constitutionally entrenched guarantee – but in principle the changes remain subject to reconsideration. This may make subconstitutional measures much more acceptable than constitutional ones, even though their content is the same. In our recent debates, for example, many Canadians (including some governments) were reluctant to adopt the general guarantee of aboriginal self-government in Charlottetown. They would have been much happier implementing the principle in concrete terms in specific communities, where they could judge the consequences and revise the regime if necessary. Of course, the very openness of such reforms to change does make them less desirable to their beneficiaries, especially if the latter have reason to distrust the majority.

Second, formal guarantees have very different symbolic implications. In the recent constitutional debates, there was often a disjuncture between "expert" and popular discourses. Although the experts tended to speak of the practical effect of different provisions, the popular debate focused on symbolism – on whether, for example, in the Canada clause, Charter rights were on the same level as the recognition of specific communities, whether the amendments created a hierarchy of cultural groups, or whether the rights of the handicapped were assigned a lower ranking than those of Quebec. Formal

262 Allegiance, Community, and the Constitution

change raises those symbolic issues with a vengeance; subconstitutional change much less so.[2] Many Canadians, for example, care deeply whether the constitution formally grants the provinces a right to opt out of new national social programs, and they do so largely because of what such a provision would say, in abstract terms, about the commitment to national cohesion. They are much less worried about the policy that, since the late 1960s, has recognized almost precisely the same right, and still less about the existing variations in social programs (the administration of medicare, say, or the presence of a separate pension plan in Quebec). During the recent debates, many English-speaking Canadians objected to a formal clause recognizing Quebec's distinctiveness (or indeed to any clause expressly treating Quebec differently from other provinces), but they generally voiced no objection to Quebec being distinct in fact and very little to Quebec having greater autonomy in, for example, social programs.

The constitution is, for many Canadians, in a different league from other measures. It is a formal, highly symbolic, and permanent definition of the country. They are acutely sensitive to declarations that might, in their view, knock that definition off balance. Subconstitutional action does not carry the same freight. Indeed, this creates a significant limitation on reform by subconstitutional means: when the very appeal of a reform is symbolic – as was the case, for example, with the distinct society clause or some aspects of the aboriginal measures – subconstitutional reform may be utterly incapable of achieving the desired end.

Thus, rejecting a bundle of constitutional amendments is not the same as rejecting everything to do with the motives for those amendments. Constitutions are different from ordinary measures. Canadians may support a particular policy, yet still believe it should not be erected into a cardinal principle of the constitution. The rejection of the Charlottetown Accord in October 1992 did not involve the rejection of all moves towards aboriginal self-government, all efforts to accommodate Quebec's uniqueness, or every attempt to respond to the grievances of western or eastern Canadians.

Because this chapter is limited to those three proposals for reform, and because, even then, it focuses only on certain aspects of those proposals, it may seem to lack balance. It will tend to emphasize, at least in its structure, proposals premised on Canadians' differences or on the recognition of collectivities. What about individual rights? What about racism? What about First Nations' treaty rights? What about bilingualism? What about the health of Canada as a whole?

This chapter adopts its present structure because it is concerned chiefly with constitutional reform, and especially with reforms related to the principal themes of this study: language, culture, and Canada's various political communities. Many of the questions listed above are already dealt with in the constitution as it stands; indeed many were discussed in the previous two chapters. Others would take us to a level of detail beyond the scope of this book. I am not suggesting that Canadians should ignore those questions – the struggle against racism, for example, remains crucial, although I suspect that the most effective action now must occur through means other than constitutional amendment – only that this chapter's focus is on the accommodation of a separate set of issues. That said, my treatment of aboriginal self-government, Quebec's demands, and Senate reform remains strongly conditioned by consideration of the questions listed above, especially respect for individual rights and the need to maintain a vigorous pan-Canadian community. One of the objectives of the previous chapters was to demonstrate the possibility of reconciling our attachment to our local communities with our commitment to Canada as a whole. In so doing, those chapters addressed many of the most important issues regarding the relationship between the reforms discussed here and the integrity of Canadian citizenship or the protection of individual rights.

Finally, I should emphasize that the order of the issues in this chapter (indeed the failure to discuss some issues) does not in any way imply a hierarchy of worth. The order is determined by convenience of argument, aboriginal self-government raising issues similar to those affecting Quebec, the question of Quebec leading to a discussion of the provinces generally, and a brief return to the pan-Canadian community serving as an appropriate cap to the whole. Constitutions are interpreted as a single document, in no particular order, each section read alongside the others. Books, unfortunately, proceed page by page. I apologize for any offence caused by the fact that this is a book, not a constitution.

ABORIGINAL SELF-GOVERNMENT

At this point, the basic justification for aboriginal self-government needs no further elaboration. The whole direction of this argument has been favourable to some form of self-government, not simply because aboriginal peoples were here first, but because of the character of their communities and the significance of that character for their members. But what form? Many non-aboriginal Canadians continue to resist self-government because of doubts about how it will work in practice. This section examines, first, how we should understand the content of the right as it has been developed in recent negotiations, and second, the means of recognizing and implementing it.

Defining the Content of Self-Government

The starting-point of any discussion of self-government must be the diversity in the traditions and circumstances of aboriginal peoples. Although the underlying principle may be the same, the practical working out of that principle must vary from people to people – sometimes dramatically – and must therefore be accomplished through an extensive process of consultation and negotiation. This is all the more true since self-government cannot restore aboriginal governments to the state they were before the arrival of the colonists. Those institutions no longer exist in their pristine form, and even if they did, their societies have changed in ways that would require changes to the institutions. There are distinctive aboriginal structures – some descended from pre-colonial forms, some new – but their present character is the product of conditions very different from self-government. They will have to be adapted to serve new roles.

Thus, the precise content of self-government will be developed over a long period of time and is certain to include considerable variation. One can achieve some general sense of its contours, however, by looking at three things:

1 The status of the right, a status that will both define aboriginal governments' relationship to non-aboriginal institutions and influence the interpretation of those governments' powers
2 The likely extent of those governments' jurisdiction, especially the importance of territorial boundaries in the definition of that jurisdiction
3 The forces likely to shape the institutional structure of aboriginal governments.[3]

In recent constitutional negotiations, two phrases became very important regarding the status of aboriginal governments: first, the idea that aboriginal peoples possess an "inherent" right of self-government; and second, the recognition that aboriginal governments would constitute "one of three orders of government" in Canada. These phrases (or ones like them) are likely to remain central to discussions of the issue. They provide a useful framework through which to approach the status of aboriginal governments under a right of self-government.

The language of "inherent right," vigorously promoted by representatives of the First Nations during the aboriginal talks of the mid-1980s and eventually accepted in the Charlottetown Accord,[4] is often greeted with caution among non-aboriginal Canadians. Would it imply that aboriginal peoples possess utter sovereignty, that they are exempt from federal or provincial law, perhaps even the territorial sovereignty of the Canadian state? Would it mean that aboriginal governments can claim whatever jurisdiction they want? Some aboriginal leaders have indeed used the language of inherent right to make those assertions, and for a small number, all-encompassing authority is exactly what they want. For most, however, the right's inherent character speaks to its source – its justification, its status – rather than to its eventual scope, which they admit will be less than absolute. Recognition of the right as inherent makes clear that self-government is not merely a gift from a non-aboriginal sovereign. Instead, it is rooted in the very character of aboriginal peoples themselves and in their historic relationship with the Canadian state (and its predecessors, Britain and France). A constitutional amendment would recognize the right and indicate its general scope, but not create it.

Sometimes this argument is made simply in terms of the survival of a pre-existing right of aboriginal sovereignty through time: prior to colonization, aboriginal peoples possessed a right of sovereignty, and since that right was never extinguished, it still exists today.[5] This formulation often leads to confusion about the scope of aboriginal self-government. Do aboriginal peoples possess full sovereignty, or has it been partially extinguished? If so, how? More importantly, the approach is misleading because it suggests that aboriginal rights find their origin in specific doctrines of seventeenth- or eighteenth-century international, French, British, or aboriginal law, doctrines which conferred a right of sovereignty and which we are bound to apply because they were the legal rules of the time. This belies the true origin of aboriginal rights. Aboriginal rights are much more the product of the relationship *between* colonists and aboriginal peoples than of any pre-existing legal rules. They are the result of adaptation and mutual accommodation, a process often forced on the colonizing powers by the actual autonomy of aboriginal peoples, indeed by the colonizing powers' inability to impose control on aboriginal societies. That process was the source of the colonial law's recognition of substantial self-government for aboriginal societies. The development of aboriginal rights in today's law is, in large measure, an attempt to recapture the respect for autonomy that developed in those earlier arrangements.[6]

Thus, the fundamental impulse of the right is the practical autonomy of aboriginal societies, the fact that they have had and still have their own ways of addressing issues of social order, ways that have retained their independence despite the majority's periodic attempts to suppress them. Those ways should not now be swept aside by non-aboriginal forms, but should have space for expression.

That space need not be absolute. The great majority of aboriginal people seek to achieve autonomy within Canada (although on terms that recognize that their peoples have their own integrity, their own independently derived status, not on terms dictated by non-aboriginal governments). They acknowledge that their destiny is linked to Canada, given the modest population of particular peoples, the extent of their resources, and the interlocking nature of aboriginal and non-aboriginal habitation. The inherent right is, then, compatible with a kind of federalism, in which aboriginal communities would determine many issues internally but would nevertheless participate in the Canadian or provincial political communities on other matters. This was the structure suggested by the Charlotte-town Accord's provisions. The right of self-government would exist "within Canada," and the jurisdiction of aboriginal governments would be extensive but not absolute.[7]

Would this mean the end of the notion of aboriginal "sovereignty"? Sovereignty is a notoriously slippery concept, having many meanings. In the past, legal theorists often worked with a unitary conception: sovereignty involved the exercise of absolute power by a single government. More recently, however, theorists have come to adopt a more subtle approach, one that recognizes that sovereignty might be subject to broad constraints (for example, international human rights norms) or be shared among a number of different actors, each having authority over a set of subjects. The latter approach is especially appropriate to federal systems of government. Under Canada's constitution, for example, both the provinces and Ottawa are, within their appropriate spheres, sovereign, in the sense that each has primary authority over matters within its jurisdiction. Neither is subordinate to the other; neither derives its authority from the other. Each has its own independent sphere within which what it says goes. This is very different from the situation of Indian band councils (established under the Indian Act) or municipalities. Those entities are entirely dependent on the legislature that created them (Ottawa and the provinces respectively). Their powers can be revoked, at any time, by that legislature.

Under a regime of self-government like that proposed in the Charlottetown Accord, aboriginal governments would be recognized as having the kind of status possessed by the provinces and Ottawa. They would be sovereign, within their spheres, in the same way that Ottawa and the provinces are sovereign in their spheres. They would become, in the words of the accord, "one of three orders of government," having their own, original authority over matters falling within their jurisdiction.[8] They would have a form of "sovereignty," but one that would not be absolute. And of course, the justification for a constitutional status independent of the will of the non-aboriginal legislatures would be the inherent source of aboriginal peoples' entitlement to govern themselves.

Under this form of self-government, then, aboriginal people would participate in a number of political communities at once. Just as other Canadians are simultaneously members of at least two levels of political community – provincial and federal – aboriginal Canadians would be members (probably) of three: provincial, federal, and aboriginal. The precise jurisdiction of aboriginal governments would depend on the drawing of boundaries between aboriginal and non-aboriginal institutions. These would have to be determined by negotiations and would differ from people to people. Certain generalizations are possible, however.

In most situations, self-government would be tied to territory. Aboriginal peoples would exercise their most extensive authority over specific tracts of land, probably equivalent to their present reserves plus territory obtained in land-claims settlements. Even on these lands, there would be a continuing role for the federal and provincial governments. This role would exist with respect to institutions or standards deemed to be of substantial concern to the broader community, including, for example, national defence, Canadian citizenship, certain (perhaps all) criminal offences, and the overall regulation of banking and money. It might conceivably include minimum standards for social services or policing, so that while direct responsibility would be exercised by the community concerned, Ottawa or the province could intervene if something went drastically wrong. In addition, there would likely be certain responsibilities that aboriginal peoples would not, for their own reasons, wish to assume, some because they would be too expensive or time-consuming for the community to fulfil (it is unlikely, for example, that an aboriginal community would create its own system of unemployment insurance), others because they might be too difficult to resolve within relatively small communities (prosecutions for serious crimes may be better handled outside the community, although the community may wish to have a say in sentencing).

Apart from authority over a territory, aboriginal self-government might also take the form of jurisdiction over individual band members, wherever they live. This would only be appropriate for a very limited range of subjects, such as family or inheritance law. Aboriginal institutions might also have control of the provision of certain services to aboriginal people off reserve (for example, halfway houses for released prisoners, substance-abuse programs). Because of the inherent complexity of a jurisdiction based on persons rather than territory, however, the jurisdictional reach of self-government will be much more extensive for individuals living on aboriginal land than for those in the cities. Finally, self-government might mean participation in joint regulatory structures, combining aboriginal and non-aboriginal input. This could be the case for wildlife management or environmental regulation in areas used by aboriginal peoples.[9]

Note that in each of these cases, although culture would be an important factor in the structure of regulation, the governments would not be tied simply to ethnic origin. First, the very definition of an aboriginal people is likely to emphasize involvement and recognition within the community rather than mere bloodlines. Indeed, some peoples want political participation to be defined purely in terms of residence, without regard to ethnicity or culture.[10] Second, for territorially based powers, the application of aboriginally determined rules would depend chiefly on presence within the territory. Non-aboriginal users of aboriginal lands would be subject to the government's authority, and aboriginal people would be able to opt out by leaving the territory. Third, in the case of social service agencies off reserve, individuals would likely be able to choose between aboriginal agencies and those available to the general population. Some rights and obligations, such as those related to family or inheritance law, might follow individuals wherever they go, but that happens now in non-aboriginal legal systems with respect, for example, to the marital regimes of individuals changing countries or provinces.

What about the internal structures of aboriginal governments? What would they look like? Here again, the diversity of aboriginal traditions prevents easy answers. In many cases, the communities themselves are just beginning to address these questions. There are, however, some constraints that will shape that process, the most important relating to democratic controls. The traditional institutions of some aboriginal societies include hereditary elements. Those elements have led some critics to doubt whether aboriginal governments would be sufficiently democratic, a concern reinforced (in the minds of the critics) by Charlottetown's proposal that the Charter provisions regarding voting rights not apply to aboriginal governments, and by the claims of some aboriginal groups (such as the Longhouse faction in some Mohawk communities) that their nonelective structures, rather than the elected councils, are the legitimate power.

The concern is an important one and a matter of real dispute in a few communities.[11] Many of the arguments take insufficient account, however, of the extent to which democratic principles are rooted within aboriginal communities. To begin with, those principles fit well with aboriginal traditions of government, under which power was often widely dispersed. They have also been shaped by aboriginal peoples' experience with structures of band governance based on non-aboriginal models. Consequently, although under self-government some peoples would undoubtedly retain or reinstate hereditary elements (for example, a council of elders or of clan mothers), it is very likely that the principal power would be vested in democratically accountable institutions. Certainly, the choice of institutions would be founded on popular approval, expressed through a referendum or similar means. Indeed, there is, in contemporary aboriginal societies, no viable substitute for that support as the foundation for institutional legitimacy. Federal policy requires referenda or equivalent votes for major structural change, such as the ratification of the Yukon aboriginal self-government agreements, the division of the Northwest Territories, or the settlement of land claims. The dispute in the Mohawk community of Kanesatake over who was the legitimate spokesperson for the community – a conflict that placed in issue the very basis for aboriginal governments' legitimacy – was ultimately resolved by referendum.[12] The manner in which the principal aboriginal organizations participated in the Charlottetown debate similarly emphasized the importance of popular approval.

Of course, a simple commitment to democratic principles is not enough. Institutions can be subverted. There has to be very close attention to checks and balances, especially when structures are new, communities are small, and governments possess dramatically different powers from those of traditional societies. This is not the place for a detailed discussion of such checks, which would take us beyond the scope of this brief survey. Recognition of the concern does have implications for, among other things, the relationship between aboriginal and non-aboriginal governments, the manner in which the Charter should apply to aboriginal communities, and the creation of guarantees of, for example, aboriginal women's participation in community governance. Those implications will be worked out chiefly through the implementation process. It is to that that I now turn.

The Recognition and Implementation of Self-Government

Aboriginal self-government is one area in which reform need not be blocked by the failure of constitutional amendment on the Charlottetown model. Nevertheless, the different methods of implementation each have their own strengths and weaknesses. This section briefly reviews constitutional amendment, government-to-government negotiations, and (very briefly) judicial interpretation of the present constitution as means of securing self-government, suggesting the consequences associated with each of those methods. Our principal focus is on the central tension: how does one balance aboriginal peoples' demand for substantial progress now against the need for long and complex negotiations to determine the practical content of the right?

The constitutional conferences of the mid-1980s collapsed largely because of the failure to resolve this tension. A resolution acceptable to the governments and principal aboriginal organizations was achieved, however, in the Charlottetown process. The terms of that accord suggest how self-government might be achieved through formal amendment. Essentially, the strategy was to recognize the right in general terms, describing its broad dimensions, then establishing a framework for negotiations at the level of each community. In order to ensure that negotiations would be taken seriously, the right was made enforceable before the courts, following a five-year delay.

This structure demonstrates the principal strengths of the constitutional route. First, it permits all aboriginal peoples to obtain something immediately: the highly symbolic recognition that the right exists, for all aboriginal peoples, based on their inherent character. This formal, irrevocable declaration is something that all peoples can claim as an achievement, even if the practical implementation of self-government takes many years. Second, constitutional amendment confirms, without ambiguity, that aboriginal governments have the status of one of three orders of government. They would have their own independent anchor within the constitution. Third, a constitutional provision would bind the federal and provincial governments in law. They would have to act in a manner consistent with the right, or face judicial disapproval.

Thus, constitutional amendment is an effective way of achieving a right that would have symbolic punch and a status independent of the non-aboriginal governments. The problem is how to balance this instant, powerful entrenchment of the right against the need to work out its content over a set of negotiations. How do governments know what they are entrenching? Don't they run the risk of finding later, after the courts have interpreted the provision, that it has taken a quite different form than they expected?

Charlottetown dealt with this by encouraging the courts to focus, at least in the first instance, on policing the negotiations rather than directly defining the content of the right.[13] The courts were authorized to make orders designed to promote negotiations. Although the accord itself gave no examples of how this would happen, one can predict from labour law (where a duty to bargain also exists) that the orders could include such things as simply finding the government to be in bad faith, ordering it to meet with aboriginal representatives, ordering it to prepare a formal offer addressing certain issues, or even requiring that it renounce a position judged to be incompatible with the underlying principle of the right.[14] Thus, judicial surveillance of the right could be used to keep negotiations moving along but could not be used, at least initially, to create entire governments by judicial fiat. This would ensure that all affected governments had a say in the solution. It would also accord with the preferences of most judges: few would want to draft full-fledged constitutions of aboriginal self-government, given the vast range of possible structures and the multitude of interests affected.

This would have minimized the problems of constitutional amendment, but it would not have eliminated them. Despite the efforts of the courts, negotiations might still fail, and the courts would then have to deal with the content of the right. Indeed, the existence of a judicial recourse might prompt the parties to hold back on compromise, hoping for a better decision from the courts. It seems likely that even in that case, however, the courts would proceed cautiously, defining the right's content little by little and looking for opportunities to get the parties back to the table. Potentially more serious was the balance between matters to be constitutionalized and those to be left for later negotiations. Instituting the right to self-government by amendment meant that a number of decisions had to be made about the overall structure of aboriginal governments, with the results enshrined immediately in the constitution. Many such decisions, like those concerning the inherent character of the right and the general status of the governments, were not problematic. Others could have used more consideration. This was especially so for the provisions addressing the role of the Charter in aboriginal governments. The Charter raises a number of very thorny problems, especially since its phrasing sometimes assumes the existence of institutions that may not be present, or may be structured in very different ways, under self-government. Aboriginal communities may, for example, deal with some kinds of antisocial activity through mechanisms different from the conventional criminal trial. This may require a rethinking of such rights as the right to remain silent or to retain counsel without delay. The best result might not be a simple decision that the Charter should or should not apply, but a readjustment of the rights in question. This is extremely difficult to do in the pressure-cooker of a negotiation like Charlottetown. That process required a decision on many of these issues before they had been fully discussed. If the accord had been passed, those decisions would have been constitutionalized, making them virtually untouchable in the future. One clause in Charlottetown suffering from such haste was the provision regarding the use of the notwithstanding clause by aboriginal governments. It seemed to be more a product of concern with symbolic equality between aboriginal and non-aboriginal governments than of careful consideration of how the clause might be used in fact. It was extremely vague in its terms, necessarily so given the parties' ignorance of the particular institutions to which it might apply.[15]

Some of these problems are avoided if the right is achieved by negotiation between aboriginal and non-aboriginal governments in specific situations, without an immediately entrenched constitutional right. That kind of process allows the parties to address the issues much more concretely, in full knowledge of the institutional setting. Because the overall structure is not locked into the constitution, there is much more scope for debate, experimentation, and flexible transitional arrangements.

This approach is much better able to address the concerns of those persons, even within aboriginal communities, worried about the immediate entrenchment of self-government. In the Charlottetown process, it became obvious that a significant number of aboriginal people questioned the immediate entrenchment of self-government, especially on the conditions set out in Charlottetown. The Native Women's Association of Canada (NWAC) was particularly worried that the position of aboriginal women might be imperilled if aboriginal governments, generally male-dominated, had access to the notwithstanding clause. These differences were extremely difficult to resolve in the highly abstract debate surrounding Charlottetown. In the absence of knowledge of the precise structure and powers of aboriginal governments, each intervenor had little alternative but to express its confidence or its anxieties, the balance between these determining whether it ultimately supported or opposed the Charlottetown package. The result was a bitter, irreconcilable impasse.

Underlying this conflict was a very real question of trust in aboriginal governments. The lack of trust was not the result of a belief that aboriginal people were incapable of governing themselves or that the aims of self-government were misconceived. Many of the critics, especially those within the NWAC, were in favour of a move towards self-government. The root problem was the uncertainty about the institutions: at the very least the governments would be exercising powers they had not exercised before, and they might well have radically redesigned internal structures. Not only was there little or no experience with institutions exercising those powers, but often their fundamental structure had yet to be decided. The practical effectiveness of the governments, the efficacy of their internal controls, the extent to which aboriginal women would play a strong role in the process of government all were very much open to question. This uncertainty would be avoided if self-government were achieved through negotiations, prior to constitutionalization. This would permit the institutions to be designed and experienced without being locked-in in advance. It might even facilitate the phased introduction of aboriginal governments, so that the institutions – and trust – could be established gradually.[16]

The flexibility of this approach, however, also gives rise to its principal drawbacks. The federal and provincial governments might try to declare their commitment to aboriginal peoples. They might, for example, make a political declaration similar to that adopted by the Ontario and aboriginal governments in August 1991, formally recognizing that aboriginal peoples constitute "distinct nations" within Ontario, that they possess an inherent right of self-government, and that their relationship should be on a "government(s) to government" basis.[17] Such a declaration would be an important demonstration of good faith and, in those terms, of significant value. But it would not carry the legal force or symbolic weight of a constitutional provision. There would still be no additional constitutional constraint on non-aboriginal governments. The move to self-government would depend essentially on the goodwill and priorities of the federal and provincial governments. Their commitment could vanish overnight, leaving aboriginal peoples little to fall back on other than political protest. Moreover, the only immediate achievement of many aboriginal peoples would be the declaration of intent. They would not be able to point to a clear constitutional recognition, and any concrete progress on self-government would have to follow the slow pace of negotiations proceeding people by people. As for the status of the resulting governments, they would probably lack an independent constitutional foundation. They would not, in other words, be "one of three orders of government," but would remain subject to revision or abolition by non-aboriginal governments. Only if the non-aboriginal governments were willing to adopt a further constitutional amendment, or if self-government arrangements could be included within land-claims agreements entrenched by the existing constitution,[18] would aboriginal governments achieve that status.

Thus, the non-constitutional route does allow one to achieve a form of self-government while avoiding some of the pitfalls of constitutionalization, but with significant sacrifices. Aboriginal peoples would no longer be able to use the courts to push governments to the bargaining table, and both the right to self-government and the resulting governments would lack the status conferred by a constitutional guarantee.

There is one other way that a constitutional right to self-government might be obtained: through judicial interpretation of the Constitution Act, 1982's guarantee of "existing aboriginal and treaty rights." Aboriginal peoples have long claimed that self-government is included in those rights. If they succeed in making that case, the right would already have an independent basis within Canada's constitutional framework. This is not the place to discuss the full merits of that argument. I wish only to signal the possibility and note how it deals with the central tension identified above.[19]

First, courts would remain loath to undertake the complex task of defining entire structures of government. Thus, any attempt to establish the right through judicial interpretation would be a slow affair, proceeding incrementally, probably as an adjunct to claims to land, fishing, or analogous rights to resources. It would not, then, provide an immediate, general recognition of the right. Second, if the courts did undertake to recognize the right, they would have a much more difficult time achieving the combination of judicial oversight and reliance on negotiations present in Charlottetown. That accord clearly recognized the right and equally clearly contemplated negotiations as the preferred means of implementing it. Under the present provisions the courts could recognize the right, but once having entered into that process would have a hard time resisting demands to spell out its content. It would be difficult, in other words, for the courts (on the present provisions) to both recognize the right and escape the burden of defining its content. Finally, many of the general structural concerns addressed, albeit hastily, in Charlottetown would be almost impossible to handle effectively through the interpretation of the existing constitution. It would, for example, be very difficult to achieve any subtlety in the application of the Charter to aboriginal governments.

Recognition of a right of self-government through the interpretation of the present constitution may, in short, have some merit, but it would pose profound problems in the implementation process. A negotiated solution of either of the types described above would be preferable.

QUEBEC'S CONCERNS

Just as the discussion of aboriginal concerns focused on one key demand, this section will not address all the issues of interest to Quebec. Instead it will concentrate on three: the recognition of Quebec as a distinct society; the reform of the division of powers; and the amending formula. (The nomination of Supreme Court justices is discussed in the next section.) This choice is not intended to deny the importance of other issues. It simply permits me to show the implications of this argument within a reasonable compass. Most of this section will discuss constitutional amendment. In a concluding section I will address the possibilities for reform in the absence of amendment.

The Distinct Society Clause

Much of this book has been devoted to the argument that Quebec constitutes, within Canada, a distinct society. Chapter 6 explored the structure of Canada's political communities, suggesting why the vast majority of francophone Quebecers continue to see their province as fulfilling a cultural role, a role compatible with Quebecers' allegiance to Canada as a whole. Chapter 7 argued that this role can be consistent with respect for individual rights and with Canada's stability.

That unique role has been enormously important to the six and a half million Canadians whose first language is French; indeed, for many of them, it remains essential to their continued adherence to this country. It was one of the principal factors that shaped Canada's federal system of government. It is the kind of foundational, pervasive fact that should be taken into account in constitutional interpretation. The distinct society clause is an excellent way of ensuring that that occurs. It would, quite simply, direct the courts to consider Quebec's unique character when interpreting the constitution. Given the relevance of Quebec's distinctiveness to the entire constitution (the powers of the provinces under the Constitution Act, 1867; the constraints on provincial authority in the Charter), it makes sense that the clause should apply to the whole constitution, not just the Charter.

The distinct society clause is also appropriate in symbolic terms. One of the principal themes of this book has been that a superficial insistence on identical treatment is insufficient. We have to recognize that different kinds of difference may require different kinds of accommodation. The structures appropriate for addressing gender, the character of aboriginal peoples, or the heritage of the multicultural communities, for example, may well differ from one another. The distinct society clause is a good way of recognizing Quebec's particular kind of distinctiveness as compared to that of other provincial societies. Because Quebec is the only province in which Canada's francophone political community is dominant, it has a significance for francophone Quebecers unlike that of other provinces for their citizens. This is not to say that other provinces are unimportant or that their societies are blandly similar to one another. A substantial section of this book explored the compelling basis for attachment to all provincial societies. But linguistic differences have an impact on the shape of political communities unlike any others, strongly influencing the structure of debate and participation. Because of that dynamic, Quebec will inevitably hold a particular importance for French-speaking Canadians, as the only jurisdiction in which public life occurs predominantly in their language. This justifies its unique recognition in the distinct society clause.

It is important to emphasize that the clause does not resurrect an old and discredited version of the "two founding peoples." It does retain the element of truth in that slogan – the existence of two dominant languages of public debate in Canada, the importance of respecting the role of French in Canada's political life – but it avoids many of its unpleasant overtones.

First, the distinct society clause does not adopt a purely historical justification. The predominantly French character of Quebec is relevant, not because the French were here first, but because the French language remains a vital and defining feature of Quebec today. It is this fact, not the historical priority of a particular ethnic group, that counts.

Second, the clause is non-exclusive in its phrasing and its place within the constitution as a whole. "Distinct society" itself is open. It clearly evokes the predominant use of French and the distinctively French Canadian culture of Quebec, but it does so in a way that does not exclude the contribution of other linguistic or cultural groups.

In fact, the proposal in Charlottetown to define "distinct society" by listing three characteristics – a French-speaking majority, a "unique culture," and a civil law tradition – (a proposal promoted not by Quebec but by provinces wishing to limit Quebec's claim to distinctiveness) might suggest a more exclusive interpretation.[20] Moreover, the definition is inept and unnecessary. The French Canadian language and culture are clearly at the heart of Quebec's character, but their role is much more dynamic than a list of elements suggests. As this book has argued, the fact that public discussion occurs predominantly in French gives the entire discussion a substantial degree of autonomy, so that Quebec's character shapes the full range of social action (including the contribution of minority linguistic or cultural groups). This, of course, does not mean that legislative jurisdiction should be co-extensive with Quebec's distinctiveness. There remain very good reasons (not least the aspirations of Quebecers themselves) for Quebec's continued participation in the pan-Canadian community. But it does mean that Quebec's distinctiveness is richer and more far-reaching than the impoverished definition suggests, a richness worth taking into account in the interpretation of the constitution as a whole. That, after all, is what the distinct society clause, as an interpretive clause, asks us to do. It would not confer powers over everything distinctive. It would simply tell the courts to take Quebec's distinctiveness into account when interpreting the rest of the constitution.

Now, the openness of Quebec's "distinct society" may be as much potential as actual. There remains a tendency in Quebec, as in many societies, to blur the lines between cultural and political membership, speaking of *québécois* in two different but not always separated ways: as a cultural, perhaps even an ethnic group – the *québécois pure laine* – and as the members of the political entity called Quebec. The tendency to run these two together, to treat ethnic Quebecers as the only full citizens of Quebec, is much less pronounced than it once was. Recently even that bastion of conservative nationalism, the Société St-Jean Baptiste, has embraced a more open conception of *québécois*.[21] But whatever the present situation, the general form of the distinct society clause allows room for the evolution of Quebecers' self-identification (especially if the poor excuse of a definition is omitted). Moreover, the clause does not exclude the operation of the Charter's individual guarantees or those provisions recognizing other cultural groups: the various versions of the clause all recognize the need to protect official-language minorities; the Charter must still be interpreted "in a manner consistent with the preservation and enhancement of the multicultural heritage of Canadians"; and aboriginal peoples continue to enjoy their constitutional rights in Quebec.[22]

Third, the clause does not make the mistake of imposing a false parallelism on Quebec and the rest of Canada. The language of "two nations" tends to assume all too simply that if Quebec is a French-speaking nation, the rest of Canada is an English-speaking one – two distinct nations, facing each other across the Ottawa River. There may be some justification for thinking of Quebec as a nation (though this book argues that even that does violence to Quebecers' complex allegiances), but there is no justification for treating "English Canada" or any other subset of Canada as the "nation" of English-speaking Canadians. Their allegiance is clearly focused on the entirety of Canada, including Quebec, even if they have at times had difficulty understanding the role of French Canadians within that vision. The distinct society clause avoids these pitfalls by getting rid of the language of nation altogether and concentrating instead on the distinctive character of Quebec, a focus that does not presume any equivalent identity for an English Canada. We may eventually evolve towards a more cohesive idea of "English Canada" (rather than just "Canada") to match the cohesion of Quebec,[23] but I doubt it. We will probably continue to live with a more flexible patriotism, one that allows for the baroque asymmetry of our allegiances.

Division of Powers

That asymmetry is worth accommodating not only through the broad, interpretive means of the distinct society clause, but also through adjustments to the division of powers, especially to the federal spending power.

Chapter 6 suggested that Quebec's concerns with legislative jurisdiction are strongly linked to the growth of the spending power. Most of Quebec's demands for change to the division of powers – its most keenly felt grievances – relate to matters that were originally within provincial jurisdiction but are now subject to an extensive federal role because of Ottawa's superior financial resources. Those resources have allowed Ottawa to make policy in those areas simply by spending money with strings attached (though in two cases, unemployment insurance and old age pensions, this strategy has been supported by constitutional amendments conferring jurisdiction on Ottawa).[24] The provinces are forced to go along with these programs, or allow their taxpayers to suffer a severe fiscal penalty.

Outside Quebec, there has been broad support for this expanded federal role, as the weight of Canadians' allegiances has tended to shift from their provinces to Canada as a whole. Inside Quebec, there has been long-standing criticism, founded upon Quebecers' commitment to the autonomy of their province. The controversy over the use of the spending power is thus, in many ways, the concrete expression of the asymmetry of Canadians' allegiances. If we do intend to adjust our constitutional arrangements to fit those allegiances, the spending power is a good place to start.

The most appropriate response would be to adopt an amendment enabling Quebec to opt out of certain spending programs. This would have to be coupled with full financial compensation so that Quebec taxpayers would not be taxed twice for the same service. The ability to opt out should certainly apply to future programs in areas of exclusive provincial jurisdiction, as in the Meech Lake and Charlottetown accords. In order to maintain a rough parity of services across the country, the ability to opt out might be made conditional on the province's establishment of a comparable program, again as in the accords.[25] This would preserve the province's administrative control while ensuring that benefits would be portable between provinces and that the fiscal burdens of the program would be roughly comparable throughout the country. Quebec might also be permitted to withdraw from some existing programs, again with compensation. In this case, the programs to be affected would be determined by agreement, but could include such things as labour training, housing and urban affairs, welfare, and tourism.

When assessing the merits of this kind of proposal, one should assume, out of caution, that the full extent of the power would be used. Even on that basis, the kinds of powers envisaged here (certainly if limited to Quebec) would not undermine the viability of the federal government. But I doubt whether, in practice, granting Quebec an extensive right to opt out would result in the creation of many new programs, completely separate from their federal equivalents. Quebecers have an interest in maintaining the portability of services between provinces. Even if independent programs are established, they will probably be coordinated with federal schemes, as in the case of the existing Canada and Quebec pension plans. In some situations, Quebec may well decline to exercise the right to withdraw, because the benefits of a parallel scheme are not worth the added cost. In other cases, it may find ways to satisfy its concerns within the federal plan. Already, there is substantial variation between provinces in such important areas as income support and medicare (where even the payment of premiums differs from province to province). Since the early 1960s, Quebec has been permitted to opt out of a number of programs, with compensation. The reform suggested here would not, then, change the provision of services as much as one might think. It would, however, give Quebec a constitutional guarantee that it could opt out. Opting out would no longer depend on the goodwill of the federal government. Quebec could rest assured that it would be able to control the extent of federal intrusion into its legislative jurisdiction.

This kind of solution is especially appropriate for Quebec. The same considerations do not apply, at least not with the same force, to other provinces. Outside Quebec, there is much more support for the federal presence, much less concern about the expansion of the pan-Canadian political community.[26] Now, this alone might not justify confining opting out to Quebec. The ability to opt out merely gives a province a choice. Other provinces might still be given that ability; if they did not want to opt out, they could simply choose to remain within the federal schemes. But many citizens do not trust their provinces with this choice, fearing that institutional self-interest would play all too large a role in their decision. They believe that spending-power programs should, quite simply, be controlled at the level of Canada as a whole. For some, this is because they consider those programs to be a fundamental part of what it means to be Canadian. Others state their reasons in less exalted terms. They simply see many social issues as appropriately discussed at the level of Canada as a whole, or if they are from poorer provinces, they worry that granting rich provinces the ability to opt out will make it more difficult to establish future programs.

We therefore have a fundamental difference of opinion on the ability to opt out, Canadians outside Quebec tending to regard it with suspicion, Quebecers considering it crucial to the retention of the province's autonomy. This is one area in which we would do well to give up the rigid insistence that all provinces should be treated identically, and instead tailor our institutions to fit the structure of our political engagement. If we insist on identical treatment, we will have to extend the right to opt out to all provinces, as was the case in Meech Lake and Charlottetown. This will make it more difficult to create new programs and more complicated to administer old ones. We may also end up limiting the scope of the power more than is justified for Quebec, merely because we would have to worry about other provinces. Moreover, we would be extending the power to those provinces not because it made sense for them (their residents have little quarrel with the federal power) but simply because of a knee-jerk opposition to any variation in provincial powers. Isn't it better to confine opting out to Quebec, allowing all Canadians to achieve a solution much more in keeping with the actual structure of political communities in Canada and more favourable to the continued development of federal programs?

Of course, any right to opt out may result in constitutional asymmetry, in different powers being exercised in different forums. This brings us to one last objection to opting out, often voiced in recent discussions. Some argue that opting out, or any other form of asymmetry, would wreak havoc with the process of law making in Ottawa: MPs from a province that had withdrawn from a program would be able to vote on matters of no concern to them – either that, or Parliament would have to devise extremely complicated voting rules to exclude their participation.

This argument has always struck me as having an air of unreality about it, exhibiting little awareness of what actually happens in Parliament, argued without regard for the terms of opting out, and premised on a simplistic and untenable theory of representation. To begin with, our structure of representation has much more flexibility than the critics give it credit for. Right now, MPs have radically different degrees of interest in federal legislation, yet we haven't concluded that the system is rotten. MPs from Newfoundland vote on bills dealing with the international marketing of grain. MPs from Saskatchewan vote on the cod fishery. MPs from southern Canada vote on pollution control in the North. We certainly expect that those powers will be exercised in a manner responsive to the people directly affected, and we are justifiably angry when Parliament has been insufficiently sensitive, but no one suggests that the right to vote should be limited to MPs from grain-growing, cod-fishing, or northern oil-drilling constituencies. All measures have a differential impact in different parts of the country, and we expect our representatives to be able to act appropriately even when their constituents are not directly affected.

Moreover, this holds true even when the divergence of interest results from the conscious design of public institutions. There are many measures that are structured so that they only affect particular sections of the country, yet the whole legislature votes on them. A good example is the Royal Canadian Mounted Police. The RCMP's role varies dramatically from place to place. In many areas it is the sole police force. In others (cities with their own police force; Ontario and Quebec, which have provincial police forces), it has a very restricted role. Nevertheless, all MPs have an equal say in its governance. Another example, closely analogous to the constitutional asymmetry proposed here, occurs within provincial jurisdiction. Many powers are delegated to municipal governments. These governments do not exist throughout the province, and even where they do exist, their powers may vary considerably. This means that the province provides services in some areas (building roads, regulating land use, administering social welfare, and others) that are provided by municipalities elsewhere. Urban members of the legislature continue to vote on these matters, without dire consequences.

Even if one does want to require that every member of Parliament have an interest, at least theoretical, in every matter governed by Parliament, there may be little problem with opting out. We should be clear on the role we expect of our MPs. They do not decide every administrative detail. Their chief concern is with the broad outlines of policy. In the case of ongoing programs like financial assistance to hospitals or family allowances, their principal task is to vote on the money to be used in the program.[27] If, as a condition of opting out, Quebec has to establish a program compatible with national objectives (the Meech test), its MPs would continue to have an interest much like that of other provinces' MPs. All would be equally concerned with the broad outlines of the program and with the extent of federal resources devoted to it: Quebec's program would be bound by the objectives determined by Parliament; Quebec taxpayers would still have to provide, through their federal taxes, their share of the revenue for the program (even though those moneys would be remitted to Quebec for administration of the program). Surely this is enough to maintain the integrity of representation. Few MPs from any part of the country seek to exercise a more detailed control.

One can therefore imagine a sliding scale of interest, depending on the extent of integration between the federal and Quebec programs. If the level of integration is high (Quebec must establish an equivalent program, meeting the same objectives, with coordination in the administration of the programs), the interest of MPs would, for all practical purposes, be equivalent. Even if the only condition imposed on a province opting out was that compensation from Ottawa should be spent in the same general policy area, MPs would share a substantially common interest: all would be concerned with the relative share of resources going to this area as opposed to another. It is true that Parliament would not oversee the day-to-day administration of the program in Quebec, which may mean that

Quebec MPs should be less involved in committees and ministerial tasks in that area, but this is no different from the kind of specialization that already occurs in the oversight of, for example, fisheries or agriculture.

Thus, if the right to opt out is very extensive, with virtually no conditions attached, so that the interest of Quebec MPs departs systematically and substantially from that of other MPs, we may have to adjust voting rights. This is highly unlikely, given the flexibility already within the system, the limited scope of opting out proposed, and the fact that virtually any conditions on opting out would make MPs' interests roughly equivalent. In the end, the critics' understanding of parliamentary representation seems rigid, almost mechanistic. MPs are not ciphers for the material conditions of their electors. We presume that they can respond sensibly to interests beyond their immediate constituency. As long as the federal government remains sufficiently important to all Canadians to engage the attention and commitment of their representatives, the structure can absorb variations in interest.

These kinds of limitations on the federal spending power would go a long way towards satisfying Quebec's concerns with the division of powers. One additional step would be to formalize Quebec's role in immigration. Jurisdiction over immigration has been concurrent since the time of Confederation. Quebec has, by administrative practice, assumed a real presence in the field. It clearly has a special interest, because of its concern with attracting francophone immigrants and with encouraging non-francophones to learn French. Immigration policy generally ensures that immigrants will take reasonable steps to adapt to their new home. Given that the predominant public language in Quebec is French, the willingness to learn that language is a legitimate consideration in the selection of applicants.[28] The respective roles of Ottawa and the provinces are currently fixed by agreement. A number of proposals have suggested that these agreements be granted a measure of constitutional protection.[29] Given Quebec's special interest, this makes sense in its case. Once again, this is a field in which Quebec's situation differs markedly from that of other provinces. There may be good reason for the other provinces to retain a say in immigration; there is less need for constitutionalization.

Other measures to adjust powers of a strictly cultural character may be worth considering. These are discussed further below. It seems very likely, however, that only minor adjustments (if any) are necessary. Most Quebecers admit that their province already has the control it needs over linguistic and cultural matters, in the narrow definition of those terms. As I suggest below, a number of areas of jurisdiction described as "cultural" serve multiple purposes, many of which fully justify a continued federal role.

Finally, the time is ripe for the elimination of two long-standing anomalies within our federal structure, each of which undermines the principle of provincial autonomy. The power of disallowance (and its cousin, the power of reservation), which permits the governor general (in practice, the federal cabinet) to nullify validly enacted provincial laws, is obsolete and should be abolished. Second, the federal Parliament's "declaratory power," which permits Parliament to assume control of works within provincial jurisdiction, should be abolished or at least made subject to a form of provincial consent (though the effects of existing declarations should be preserved).[30]

There are other division-of-powers issues worth discussing – a perennial topic has been the unification of family law within provincial jurisdiction – but these do not have the same significance for provincial autonomy. If the spending-power and immigration issues were settled, these other matters could, I believe, be discussed in less contentious, functionalist terms.

Amending Formula

Another consequence of the arguments presented here concerns the amending formula. The fundamental message of this book is that Quebec has an interest in provincial autonomy unlike that of other provinces. It is the only jurisdiction in which Canada's francophone public debate shapes policy without risk of submersion by anglophone majorities. If we are serious in preserving the space for French Canadian political expression in Canada – if we want to guarantee that that space will not be eroded by the action of anglophone majorities – Quebec's consent must be required for constitutional change.

This need not mean a veto over all amendments. There are some matters that are of insufficient concern to Quebec to justify a veto. One example would be the adjustment of boundaries between provinces other than Quebec. Even where Quebec is directly affected, there may be other ways of protecting its interest. Thus, the amending formula proposed by the eight dissenting provinces in 1981, and repeated in the Meech Lake and Charlottetown accords, would have protected Quebec's autonomy against amendments transferring powers from the provinces to Ottawa by allowing Quebec to opt out of those amendments (receiving, in return, financial compensation).

I will not discuss the merits of each of these solutions. The essential principle is that Quebec's consent should be required for changes that pose a significant threat to its autonomy or to the role of French Canadians in federal institutions.[31]

This might be accomplished by providing identical protection to all provinces, so that all have a veto over, or all may opt out of, certain amendments. This would impose an unnecessary rigidity in constitutional reform. There is no doubt that all provinces do have a strong interest in constitutional change, an interest reflected in the present amending formula (which requires unanimity for a handful of changes, and the approval of at least seven provinces for most other amendments).[32] All provinces do not, however, have the same interest in a veto. All except Quebec can reasonably assume that amendments harmful to them will also be harmful to others. They can therefore expect to have allies. Quebec has no such assurance precisely because it is the only jurisdiction directly concerned with protecting a francophone political community. That is why virtually all francophone politicians, of whatever party, have supported a veto for Quebec.

It may, however, be necessary to extend the protections to all if that is the only way to get agreement. (Indeed, this is what happened in Meech Lake and Charlottetown.) This kind of solution has been criticized for its paralysing effect on future amendments. It would make some amendments hard to get, but that, although unfortunate, may be a price worth paying. Constitutional amendment is not our normal political process. If the most pressing issues are resolved, we may be wise to avoid the negotiating table for a while, especially on the very few matters requiring unanimity. A little rigidity may be beneficial, encouraging our leaders to pay more attention to the ordinary business of government.

Reform without Constitutional Amendment

Successive Quebec governments have long sought to achieve their ends through formal constitutional amendment. They have demanded that the constitution expressly recognize and accommodate Quebec's distinct society. Given that emphasis on formal change, can Quebec achieve its ends without full-scale amendment? Surprisingly, there is substantial scope within the existing framework. Whether this would be sufficient depends largely on whether Quebecers would be satisfied with substance without form – whether they would accept a constitutional status unique in fact though not perhaps in law.

Many of Quebec's concerns with respect to the division of powers can be addressed by agreement between Ottawa and Quebec. In those areas in which the federal presence is based purely on the spending power, the basic legislative jurisdiction is already provincial. Programs can be transfered by Ottawa simply withdrawing, giving the money it would have spent to the province. The province would fill the void, picking up where Ottawa left off. As mentioned above, Quebec's traditional grievances have focused overwhelmingly on the spending power. Moreover, Ottawa's activity under the power is far from negligible. It now accounts for approximately 35 per cent of total federal spending.[33] Many of the activities often described as cultural are founded on the spending power (I suggest below, however, that Ottawa should not abandon these matters entirely). Securing greater autonomy in those fields would thus satisfy many of Quebec's concerns.

Even where Ottawa's presence is not based solely on the spending power, there is room for flexibility. Ottawa cannot transfer any of its exclusive legislative powers to the provinces, but it can limit its involvement in areas in which *both* Ottawa and the provinces have jurisdiction. This includes areas of concurrent jurisdiction and those with a "double aspect," permitting both Ottawa and Quebec to act. Immigration would fall within the first category; indeed, in that field the governments' respective roles are already determined by agreement. Tourism probably falls into the second. Family law is another area in which there is substantial overlap. Finally, even in areas of exclusive federal jurisdiction, Ottawa can delegate administrative powers to provincial agencies, effectively allowing those agencies to make policy in the area (as has occurred, for example, in transport regulation, and might occur in communications).

There is thus considerable (though not unlimited) scope for practical adjustment within the present framework. In a great many fields, Ottawa's presence could be reduced and Quebec's increased without constitutional amendment. Under this kind of arrangement, Quebec would not receive the guaranteed protection it would get under a constitutional right to opt out. Each transfer would require the consent of both governments and even then would not be legally binding. Ottawa could in theory change its mind and move back in to the vacated field. For this reason, a constitutional arrangement would be preferable in order to assure Quebec's control over its jurisdiction. In practice, however, the difference between the two ways of proceeding would be less than at first appears. Once a spending-power program was transferred, it would be very hard for Ottawa to reoccupy the field without the province's consent. First, it would mean setting up a parallel program competing directly with the existing one; a government would rarely be able to justify this to its electorate (it is inconceivable, for example, that Ottawa would now forcibly displace the Quebec Pension Plan). Second, the underlying basis of the spending power would have been eroded. That power was initially founded on Ottawa's fiscal dominance: because Ottawa controlled most taxation revenues, it had money to spend in provincial jurisdiction. If revenues were transferred to the provinces so that they could run their own programs, this dominance would be reduced, especially if the resources were made available, not by periodic federal grants, but by federal withdrawal from areas of taxation. In short, the great expansion of the spending power took place at a time when Ottawa monopolized revenue, when many programs were just being created, and when many provinces welcomed Ottawa's leading role. It is very unlikely that the power could regain its full extent after Quebec had opted out of programs by intergovernmental agreement.

Many division-of-powers issues, then, might be dealt with by agreement, without constitutional change. But what about those quintessentially constitutional issues, the amending formula and the distinct society clause?

Quebec cannot obtain change to the amending formula without the agreement of Ottawa and all the provinces. Without that change, amendments can, in theory, always be imposed on Quebec without its consent (except in the very few areas in which unanimity is now required). This is therefore one demand that needs full-scale amendment. Once again, however, the difference is less extreme than at first appears, especially when one considers informal constraints on amendment.

There is already a substantial body of opinion within Canada that amendments affecting Quebec should not be adopted over its opposition. That sentiment alone presents a significant obstacle to amendments, influencing the position of, for example, Ontario, whose assent would be necessary to any amendment opposed by Quebec. It is, moreover, buttressed by a real political sanction. All amendments require ratification by the federal House of Commons. Support for the veto is very strong in Quebec, and Quebecers continue to elect a quarter of federal MPs. Any federal government would therefore be subject to great pressure if it tried to amend the constitution without Quebec's approval. Of course, in 1982 significant amendments were pushed through over Quebec's objections, but those were very special circumstances. The Parti Québécois was in power and had just lost the referendum. Ottawa could therefore easily challenge the PQ's claim to speak for Quebecers on constitutional matters. Even then, many federalist Quebecers had misgivings about the manner of patriation. Furthermore, if there is a prospect of very substantial harm from an amendment passed without its consent, Quebec can always, in the last analysis, move towards independence, although this could only be used in the most extreme cases. There are, then, very considerable political controls on amendments over Quebec's objections.

What about the distinct society clause? How can its chief characteristics – its great symbolic impact and its entrenchment as an interpretive principle – be obtained without formal amendment? Indeed, they cannot be so achieved, and for that reason this book has argued for amendment. That said, we should again be careful not to exaggerate the extent to which Quebec is harmed by the absence of the clause. Quebec's distinctiveness is patent and is already used by the courts in the interpretation of the constitution.[34] The distinct society clause would have reinforced that practice, giving added force to those interpretive principles, but it would not have effected a major revolution. Rather, its main impact would have been in the more popular, less technical role of the constitution, where it would have served as a forceful symbol of Canadians' acceptance of Quebec's distinctiveness. The clause would have recognized, in the heart of the constitutional order, that the government of Quebec has a crucial role in promoting that distinctiveness. It would have acknowledged that Quebec need not be a province like the others, and thus would have undone the harm caused by the denial of that claim during the patriation process.

I doubt that that kind of recognition can be achieved by any means other than constitutional change. It seems that English-speaking Canadians have moved haltingly in that direction, especially during the Charlottetown process, but even if they don't move far enough and the present tension between visions of the country continues, we should not become so preoccupied with the lack of formal recognition that we miss the practical dynamics of this country. At that level Quebec already has its distinct society. Quebec does fulfil a crucial role in the promotion of a French-speaking society in North America. It possesses very significant powers to do so, and it can reinforce that position by the kinds of non-constitutional arrangements canvassed above. Moreover, it remains a crucial partner in Confederation, and its character inevitably shapes Canadian politics and federal policy in very real ways. This is especially true of recent federal-provincial negotiations, which, for all their inadequacies, have been dominated by Quebec's disaffection with the terms of patriation. Quebec *is* distinct, and that distinctiveness does not depend on constitutional recognition. It is there, shaping Canadian politics, sometimes to the perpetual frustration of those who would force Quebec into some other mould.

Quebec already has, then, by virtue of its weight and distinctiveness, a unique role. It is destined, one might say, to be the perpetual lump in the Canadian constitutional bed, able to insist on its distinctiveness despite those who would like a more uniform surface. Recognizing that reality expressly through the distinct society clause would, I believe, allow us to work more constructively. We could better understand how cultural diversity relates to human rights and waste less time in interminable and ultimately futile attempts to impose a single, idealized Canadian allegiance – a rigid theory of citizenship at odds with the richness and diversity of this country. But in the end, Quebec's ability to flourish within Canada does not depend on constitutional recognition. It springs from within, from the robust and vigorous character of Quebec society.

THE CONCERNS OF THE OTHER PROVINCES

Thus far, we have explored the specific concerns of aboriginal peoples and Quebec. This section discusses the concerns of other provinces. It focuses on demands related to the autonomy of provincial societies or to the expression of their specific character. It will not discuss proposals, such as Ontario's social charter, that raise very different considerations.

In recent years, provinces other than Quebec have not pushed for changes to the division of powers. This is partly because their chief grievances concerned jurisdiction over natural resources and these were addressed in the patriation package of 1982. In the 1970s and 1980s, Newfoundland did argue for increased control over fisheries, but this demand has not been pressed by the Wells government. Under Meech Lake and Charlottetown, all provinces would have been affected by changes to the spending power and the constitutionalization of immigration agreements, but this is because of the insistence of some provinces (especially Alberta and Newfoundland) that all provinces be treated identically, not because of any strong commitment to the substance of the changes. Instead, the demands of the provinces have focused on "intrastate federalism" – that is, the reform of federal institutions, especially the Senate and the Supreme Court of Canada, to reflect regional interests.

This section will be almost entirely concerned with change through constitutional amendment, focusing solely on the Senate and Supreme Court of Canada. In the latter case, the measures recommended could be achieved without constitutional amendment, given that the Supreme Court is not yet constitutionalized. A constitutional amendment would, however, be preferable, both to guarantee the existing composition of the court (including three judges trained in Quebec's civil law) and to force greater openness in Supreme Court appointments. It is also possible to do some minor tinkering to the Senate through subconstitutional means. One major reform, the election of senators, could be quickly adopted. At present, a prime minister can appoint whomever he or she wishes as a senator; to introduce elections, he or she need only agree to appoint those elected. It would, however, be a mistake to adopt this expedient. The Senate is fundamentally flawed by features entrenched within the constitution, such as the tenure of senators until age seventy-five and the fact that the Senate has virtually equivalent power to the House of Commons. Until those features are changed, it would be very unwise to adopt any measures that might increase its legitimacy. It is better to have a radically imperfect institution that does not dare exercise its powers than one that remains almost as imperfect but is willing to challenge the Commons.

Senate Reform[35]

Canada's present Senate is made up of 104 senators (exceptionally more) – 24 from each of Ontario and Quebec, 10 from each of Nova Scotia and New Brunswick, 4 from Prince Edward Island, 6 from each of the remaining provinces, and one from each territory. Senators are appointed by the federal prime minister and hold office until age seventy-five. The Senate's formal powers are roughly comparable to those of the principal chamber of the federal Parliament, the House of Commons, but because the Senate's legitimacy is seriously undermined by the manner of its appointment, it generally does not exercise its powers to their full extent. It does study legislation in depth, propose amendments, and conduct inquiries on matters of public interest, but it rarely blocks legislation from the House of Commons.[36]

Over the years, there have been a number of proposals for reform, ranging from complete abolition to various methods of appointment and election, with many variations in powers and procedure. The underlying rationale for most of the proposals is that the Senate should serve as a stronger voice, in federal decision making, for citizens from the less-populated provinces. It should respond to the long-standing complaints of western and (to a lesser extent) Atlantic Canadians that they have insufficient influence in Ottawa, an insufficiency which, the advocates of Senate reform argue, translates into policies that frequently ignore western and Atlantic concerns. Central Canada does carry great weight in federal institutions. Seats in the House of Commons are distributed roughly on the basis of population. Because Ontario and Quebec have the most people, 174 of 295 MPs come from those two provinces alone (and even this underrepresents their share of the population). The present Senate does nothing to balance central Canada's influence in the Commons, since Ontario and Quebec have a sizeable block of seats there as well and, in any case, the fact that senators are appointed by the prime minister undermines any pretence of regional representation. Thus, supporters of reform argue, the Senate should be reformed to give easterners and westerners a real say in Ottawa.

Since the mid-1980s, Alberta has been the chief advocate of change, pressing for a "Triple-E Senate." Under this proposal, the Senate would be "equal," in the sense that each province would have precisely the same number of senators; it would be "effective," possessing – and exercising – real powers over legislation; and it would be "elected" by the people, in contrast to both the present Senate, in which senators are appointed by the prime minister, and other models, in which members would be nominated by provincial governments. This formula has the virtue of extreme simplicity, fitting in nicely with Alberta's traditional invocation of the "equality of the provinces." It would also dramatically change the balance of power in the Senate: the share of senators for each of Ontario and Quebec would drop from 23 to 10 per cent – in fact less, because in all proposals the territories and perhaps the aboriginal peoples would have senators as well. In the late 1980s, Manitoba and Saskatchewan also moved to support the Triple-E Senate (although with less passion than Alberta). British Columbia, too, has generally favoured Senate reform (indeed BC was its principal supporter in the late 1970s) but has tended to prefer a Senate with regional rather than provincial equality. In the late 1980s, Newfoundland's Wells government added its voice to Triple-E. The Charlottetown Accord contained a proposal for a Senate that approached Triple-E: it would have been equal, probably would have been effective, and, in most provinces, would have been elected.[37]

The precise design of an institution like the Senate involves questions extending well beyond the scope of this study. I will not attempt, then, to give a comprehensive model. But Senate reform is relevant to my general argument because it does raise particular problems about the relationship between the pan-Canadian political community and two kinds of local community discussed in this book: each province's political community and the predominantly francophone community of Quebec. These problems are difficult to resolve, especially given the potential for conflict between two types of minorities: the Atlantic and western provinces, which feel neglected in federal decision making, and Quebec, which feels that French Canadian interests must be protected against anglophone majorities. I think there is a way of achieving an acceptable reconciliation between these two kinds of interests. First, however, we have to be very clear on the purpose of representation in the Senate. This book has emphasized that Canadians are, simultaneously, members of a number of political communities. They are members both of the broader, pan-Canadian community and of their more local provincial or linguistic communities. Those latter communities are characterized by the autonomy of their public debates through time. This autonomy in fact – and its value to the communities' members – justifies the autonomy of their provincial institutions. That is the main way in which the unique character of provincial political communities is accommodated: by ensuring that those communities have room in which their particular character can shape public decision making.

Now, some aspects of Senate reform may be specifically concerned with the maintenance of that form of autonomy, and may therefore be of particular concern to the provinces. That is the case, for example, with the special role sometimes ascribed to the Senate in restraining the federal government's regulation of natural resources or limiting the use of the federal spending power.[38] But this is a small part of Senate reform. The primary purpose is to create a better decision-making process in the pan-Canadian community, not to protect provincial autonomy. It is about making sure that all voices have a chance of being heard in the central institutions, so that central institutions respond not merely to the loud voices of central Canada but also to those of other, less-populous parts of the country.

This is an important objective, one that does justify changing representation in the Senate to give proportionately more weight to geography, particularly given the existing dominance of population in the Commons. But once one sees that the focus is the dynamic of the pan-Canadian community, an absolutely identical representation of provinces in the Senate no longer seems appropriate. We are not concerned with representing *provinces* or protecting distinctively *provincial* interests. We want to protect interests associated with broader factors.

Those factors are difficult to define with precision. They involve a complex balancing of small Commons representation, distinctive economic interests, specific regional cultures, and distance from Ottawa – a distance that means that because few federal civil servants come from the West and East, few are directly familiar with Atlantic and western concerns; a distance that means that MPs and cabinet members have much more immediate contact with opinion and commentary in central Canada; a distance that makes lobbying and effective criticism much more difficult for Canadians from the West and East. In this section, I will refer to that mix of concerns as *regional* or *geographically related* interests (although in using "regional" I do not mean to imply that a system of regional equality is the most appropriate). Whatever the mix of concerns, it is clear that our interest is not in specifically provincial matters. Our justification is similar to what leads us, when designing electoral constituencies within a single political community, to have larger populations in urban than in rural ridings. Otherwise, rural ridings would be enormous in area, having very little weight within the legislature. We want to find some reasonable compromise between representation by population and the assurance that important differences associated with geography will also be represented.

During the recent round of constitutional discussions, it was noted that with eight senators per province there would be one senator for every 16,221 people in Prince Edward Island and one for every 1,260,611 people in Ontario. An Islander's Senate vote, in other words, would be seventy-eight times more powerful than that of an Ontarian. It was argued that this was too great a difference, and it does seem excessive. Indeed, the premier of Prince Edward Island was not one of the advocates of Triple-E. But almost more perplexing is the fact that an Islander's vote would be six times more powerful than that of a New Brunswicker, or four times more than that of a Newfoundlander.[39] On what conceivable basis are such huge discrepancies justified within a region? Why should an Islander have so much more say than someone across the strait in New Brunswick? We should not forget that when we adjust for geography, we move away from the identical treatment of individuals. That adjustment is justified to ensure that all have a fair ability to be heard. But there is a trade-off, and we should pay careful attention to see that that trade-off is justified.

In this light, there seems to be little reason for insisting on the rigidly "equal" representation of provinces. A system that gives greater weight to the Atlantic and western sections of the country, without requiring utter equality, would be most appropriate. This would do less violence to the principle of representation by population and would tailor representation more closely to the relevant geographical concerns, without producing results that seem, frankly, silly. The idea of provincial equality may be useful as a bargaining position. It is very simple, and it would give the maximum representation to its principal advocates. But would it really create an appropriate balance between geographical and individual representation? Would it create a balance at all?[40]

Greater clarity on the purpose of reform may also help us design other aspects of the Senate. Most participants in the negotiations agree that the principal objective is to increase the *voice* of the West and East (as one Triple-E supporter put it, to change perceptions in Ottawa so that the government of the day reflects the true dimensions of this country) but without radically changing the final power of decision making. Most concede that regional representation in the Senate should not displace the primacy of representation by population in the House of Commons. They agree, for example, that at the very least the Commons should remain the principal chamber, the house with ultimate control over the finances of government, to which governments are responsible.[41] A reformed Senate is intended to supplement the role of the Commons, achieving an effective federal government that is, in the main, responsible to the will of the majority of the population but that hears and responds to the needs of all Canadians.

A number of the proposed changes lose sight of this relationship, slipping from a concern with voice towards an excessive preoccupation with the final power of decision making. This upsets the balance between individual and regional representation and might, in the end, undermine the effectiveness of the federal government. Still other proposals seem to impair the effectiveness of regional voice itself. A more consistent focus on the goal of increasing the expression of all regions' concerns in Canadian deliberation, without equating voice with the ability to make the final decision, may produce a much better Senate.

This is especially true of the Senate's powers in the legislative process. Advocates of the Triple-E often insist that the Senate should have a veto over federal laws. No laws, with the exception of the government's budget, could be passed without some form of Senate approval. This, however, raises two problems. First, it tends to emphasize the equality of the two houses of Parliament, placing geographical on a par with individual representation. While there is broad agreement that people living in less-populous areas of the country should be full participants in federal decision making, it is not at all clear that most Canadians believe that those areas should have the last word over all federal legislation, including legislation supported by a large majority of Canadians. Second, conferring a veto on the Senate would greatly increase the prospect of a federal government being paralysed by a hostile Senate. Even though a newly elected government would be responsible (in formal terms) to the House of Commons, it may be unable to implement its agenda because of consistent opposition from senators of other parties, opposition that may have nothing to do with regional concerns but may result from party strategy or from ideological differences. Canadians may be willing to accept the prospect of deadlock in some limited areas (areas like natural resources, where the provinces predominate and the Senate might properly serve as a check upon encroachments by Ottawa), but there is much less justification for creating a veto across the full range of federal activities.

Some proposals, recognizing the problem of deadlock, try to avoid it by adjusting the majorities required for the defeat of a bill. The defeat of some kinds of legislation would, for example, require a vote of 70 rather than 50 per cent of senators. This is, however, an inferior solution. Aside from its complexity, it continues to distort the Senate's role. There seems to be no intrinsic justification for the figure of 70 per cent, yet the very nature of the proposal keeps attention focused on that percentage: less than that, and the action of the Senate has come up short; more, and the Senate blocks the law. Moreover, the formula emphasizes, by its very nature, the power to oppose, to veto, rather than the power to express a regional perspective on federal policy and thus to shape in a positive manner the content of federal laws.

It would be far better to adopt a solution that places less emphasis on the ability to frustrate federal legislation and more on the ability to shape legislation through argument and debate. One proposal would accomplish this admirably. It suggests that the Senate not be able to veto legislation outright (except, perhaps, certain precisely defined categories of laws), but instead have the power to suspend the passage of legislation for periods ranging (in different proposals) from three months to one year. This would preserve the balance between individual and regional representation. The Commons would be predominant in symbolic as well as in practical terms. The prospect of deadlock would be avoided: if worst came to worst, the Commons could simply outwait the Senate and readopt the law. The Senate, nevertheless, would have the power to make its voice heard. Delaying the passage of legislation would seriously inconvenience the government, especially if the delay was considerable. That alone would prompt a government to consult with senators prior to presenting legislation, to involve them at the committee stage, and could well generate negotiations over the terms of legislation rejected by the Senate. Moreover, the Senate would command attention even if it could only muster a bare majority against a law.

This solution would also be much better than that adopted in the Charlottetown Accord, under which deadlocks would have been broken by a vote taken in a combined sitting of both houses. First, the Charlottetown solution would have required that the Senate be small, so that there would be an appropriate balance in the joint sitting. Each province would have had only six senators, limiting considerably the range of interests that could be accommodated within each delegation. Second, voting patterns in the combined body would have been unpredictable, depending upon the combined effect of the apportionment of seats in two bodies elected on quite different principles. This would almost certainly have produced quirky results bearing little relationship to the underlying justification for Senate reform. But most important, the mechanism of joint sittings, especially when combined with the complexity of the voting rules and the diversity of ways in which senators could be chosen, would have produced an institution with a severe identity crisis. An institution's legitimacy is greatly influenced by the apparent integrity of its design, by the clarity of its role and the extent to which its functioning is comprehensible. The Charlottetown Senate would have had serious problems on this score.[42]

The creation of a suspensive veto should be combined with other measures designed to give senators a strong voice. One of these concerns the method of election. Most proposals for reform suggest that Senate seats be allocated on the basis of some form of proportional representation: the seats would, in other words, be divided among political parties roughly in proportion to their share of the popular vote. This is an excellent suggestion, one that would complement well the existing method of representation in the Commons. It would, for example, enable the Senate to represent more accurately the range of opinion in different parts of the country. Under the system now used to elect members of the House of Commons, minority positions are seriously underrepresented, especially if they are spread evenly over a broad area. At times, this has had a very unfortunate effect, exaggerating the extent to which party support is polarized in different regions. In the 1980 general election, for example, the Liberals had 23 per cent of the popular vote west of the Manitoba-Saskatchewan border, but none of the seats; the Conservatives had 13 per cent of the popular vote in Quebec, but only one seat.[43] Proportional representation in the Senate would prevent this kind of aberration, giving all parties a much better opportunity to elect candidates from all regions. It would reduce the public's perception of conflict between regions, more accurately reflecting the true range of opinion. In areas in which party support was thin, it could help provide an electoral basis on which to build. But most importantly, it would enable political parties to respond better to the broad range of regional perspectives. Parties could draw on their senators for expertise in areas poorly represented in their Commons delegations. Indeed, the need to secure constructive representation from all regions of the country is one very good reason for allowing senators to serve as cabinet ministers.[44] This would allow for balanced representation at the heart of the policy-making process.

To maximize these benefits, the Senate should adopt a form of proportional representation that uses party lists. Under this type of system, political parties publicize lists of candidates in advance of each election, ranking them in order of preference. Voters vote for the party, and the candidates elected are drawn from the top of each list. This system is sometimes criticized for the prominent role it assigns to parties. For that reason, some have recommended the system of "single transferable votes," in which voters indicate their preferences from among a list of candidates, and these preferences are then translated into votes by a complicated mathematical formula. A system of party lists has, however, three important advantages. First, it enables the major parties virtually to guarantee that those at the top of their lists will be elected. They can therefore attract into public life persons who might otherwise balk at the rough-and-tumble of a Commons election. One might not want all politicians elected this way; the rough-and-tumble has its advantages, especially in terms of immediate, democratic responsiveness. That benefit is already provided in the Commons, however. Basing the Senate on a different principle would enable us to draw upon persons of extensive experience and authority who may not have the skills required in a Commons campaign but who could contribute significantly to the quality of representation. Second, along with the need to prepare lists comes a high degree of party accountability of a sort much less evident in a system of single transferable votes. This is especially important for increasing the participation of minorities and women. Parties with a commitment to increasing women's presence might, for example, require that their party's list alternate between male and female candidates. Finally, from the citizen's perspective, the system of party lists is straightforward, especially when compared to the single transferable vote. The precise effect of their vote does not depend upon the vagaries of an incomprehensible formula.[45] In any event, again for reasons of institutional integrity, a reformed Senate should have a single electoral structure, not the kind of province-by-province option contemplated in Charlottetown.[46]

One last issue deserves discussion. Some participants in the Charlottetown campaign, notably the National Action Committee on the Status of Women, argued that half the seats in the Senate should be reserved for women. This would, I believe, be a mistake, not because affirmative action is unjustified (one of the reasons I argue for party lists is precisely that they would support that end), but because of the unfortunate consequences of building that form of representation into the constitutional structure. The reservation of seats for women, once constitutionalized, would be there forever: unanimity would be required to remove it. That kind of permanent structural change would be appropriate if we believed that the differences between men and women would be stable through time and would remain so fundamental that we should build the entire structure around them. The question of a stable, pervasive difference between men's and women's voices is, however, still a matter of great controversy, even within the feminist community. While many would insist on more access to political power for women, many hope that we will eventually reach the point where women and men participate interchangeably in each political community. Assigned seats in the Senate seems to cut against that, at least symbolically, and may undermine the demand for women's representation in other forums, such as the Commons. The alternative approach suggested above – structuring the electoral process so that parties can more easily be held accountable for gender balance – seems likely to accomplish the same end without prejudging the issue of distinctive voice. Moreover, the inherent flexibility of that approach allows it to be used for other ends, such as securing greater representation for visible minorities.

This has been a brief foray into the complex jungle of Senate reform. I hope, however, that it has suggested how Canada can achieve a strong Senate, one that gives effective voice to regional concerns without radically changing the balance between geographical and individual representation. Such a Senate would be appropriate in symbolic terms as well. Virtually everyone (with the possible exception of the Quebec government) now agrees that the Senate should not be a "House of the Provinces," representing distinctively provincial interests. Why, then, should we choose a form of representation emphasizing the provinces? The principal reason many

Quebecers object to the Triple-E Senate is that it appears to be another manifestation of the argument that all provinces should be treated the same, the argument used during the Meech Lake debate to oppose the distinct society clause. Why do we need to fight this battle again, especially if our real concern is with voices ignored within the pan-Canadian political debate, not with provincial interests as such? If we do sidestep this fight, we will find that agreement is much easier to achieve.

In fact, the two kinds of minority interest identified at the beginning of this section – Canadians living in the Atlantic and western provinces on the one hand, French-speaking Quebecers on the other – appear much less antagonistic when one concentrates on the precise objectives of each group. The principal aim of most Quebecers is to defend the autonomy of that province's political community. This has very little to do with Senate reform, which is concerned with decisions at the federal, not the provincial, level. Only if we insist on bringing provincial status back into the Senate debate – where it does not belong – does an irresolvable conflict arise. Citizens in the less-populous provinces, on the other hand, are chiefly concerned with increasing their influence within federal institutions. This does raise the possibility of conflict, for Quebecers also want to retain significant representation in Ottawa. After all, Ottawa would, under any scenario short of outright separation, continue to exercise very substantial powers with respect to them as well. There are three reasons, however, why the kind of Senate sketched above may be acceptable to Quebecers. First, the risk of direct harm to Quebecers' interests would be negligible. The Senate would be able to shape the content of laws, it might even be able to frustrate the adoption of measures favourable to Quebecers, but it would not be able to enact legislation on its own. All laws would still have to be passed by the House of Commons, and in that chamber Quebecers would retain their present weight. Second, the fact that under the above proposal the Senate would only possess a suspensive veto would ensure that representation by population remained dominant. Quebecers could accept a greater *voice* for western and Atlantic Canadians, but they would have a much harder time granting equal power to a chamber in which their population was drastically underrepresented. Third, providing better guarantees of Quebec's jurisdiction under the division of powers would take some of the pressure off the demand for "French power" in Ottawa. Quebecers might accept a loss of influence in the Senate in return for more direct protection of their province's autonomy.

The Supreme Court of Canada

Another set of proposed reforms concerns the Supreme Court of Canada. One of the most important of these is the suggestion that provinces participate in the appointment of Supreme Court judges. As it stands now, Supreme Court judges are appointed by the federal prime minister acting alone, without any requirement for consultation or approval. Under the Meech Lake and Charlottetown accords, the prime minister would still make the final selection, but would do so from names furnished by provincial governments.[47] Thus, any appointment would require the agreement of both the federal and provincial levels of government. The usual justification for this reform is that the Supreme Court polices the entire constitutional structure, including the division of powers. Given that role, it is inappropriate for one level of government to have the sole responsibility for appointing judges.

This argument has real force. The adjudicative process is not a matter of the mechanical application of law to facts. Especially in constitutional matters, it is conditioned by broader considerations of justice and constitutional structure, including judges' understanding of the underlying rationale for a given division of powers, or their general sense of the appropriate roles of federal and provincial legislatures. The substance of adjudication is therefore vulnerable to influence through the appointments process. The best way to ensure balance is by requiring the principal parties to agree on any appointment.

Some have argued that the preparation of lists of nominees by provincial governments would give those governments too much influence in the process. This is not a substantial concern in the case of provinces other than Quebec. Those provinces do not have designated seats on the court. If a prime minister did not like the names on a particular province's list, he or she could simply appoint a judge from another's list. The problem is more serious for Quebec because, under the proposals, three seats would be reserved for judges from that province. Some have argued that a government committed to Quebec's independence might use this provision to undermine the court, proposing judges hostile to the very idea of Canada. Under the Meech Lake provisions, this could have resulted in a stalemate, Quebec refusing to change its recommendation, Ottawa refusing to appoint. That is no longer a concern. The problem was solved in Charlottetown by permitting the chief justice to appoint interim judges to fill long-standing vacancies.[48]

The proposals for provincial participation are therefore workable and appropriate, given Canada's federal character. But they would also be valuable for reasons having nothing to do with federalism. In recent years, many have criticized the lack of openness and consultation in judicial appointments (not specifically to the Supreme Court of Canada but to courts generally). Sometimes, this criticism has focused on political patronage, sometimes on the existence, in the judiciary, of gender bias or other forms of insensitivity to the concerns of disadvantaged groups. These criticisms are often difficult to address effectively. The number of judges is so small, their skills so unique, that attempts to predetermine the characteristics judges should possess are likely to produce only general guidelines, imposing little constraint on the nomination process. If constraining guidelines are created, they are likely to be clumsy, doing violence to the subtlety of adjudication. The focus has therefore shifted to the design of the nomination process, so that weighing the criticisms can become an integral part of the complex task of choosing judges. In recent years, a number of very important reforms have been proposed (and, to a much lesser extent, implemented): public consultation on criteria for appointment; the creation of nominating committees to receive applications, interview candidates, and make recommendations; and participation by community representatives on these committees.[49] It would be useful to give support to these initiatives in the constitutional power of appointment. This is difficult to do in detail, given the need for flexibility in the structure of nominating committees and the need to respond to changing demands over time. One way to approach this outcome, however, is to require the concurrence of more than one government in appointments. At the very least, this would encourage more rigorous discussion and justification. Limiting politicians' ability to use appointments for partisan purposes would also open the way for a larger role for nominating committees. Quite apart from its federal role, then, a system of joint appointments may strengthen the quality of our judiciary.

THE DEMANDS OF THE CANADIAN COMMUNITY

This book has repeatedly emphasized that Canadians simultaneously belong to at least two political communities. Thus far, this chapter has concentrated on the accommodation of provincial or regional interests. This section addresses the other primary focus of

Canadians' allegiance, the pan-Canadian community. That community need not and should not displace Canada's constituent societies, but if we are to maintain what we value in Canada as a whole – if we are to maintain any significant political structure at that level – we must pay careful attention to the health of the pan-Canadian community.

I hope my own attention to that community has been evident throughout this chapter. My discussion of the Senate was strongly conditioned by the need to maintain and improve federal institutions, by enabling governments to achieve more balanced regional representation in caucus and cabinet, by emphasizing geographically related interests rather than provinces, and by greatly limiting the possibility of deadlock between the Senate and the House of Commons. Similarly, one of the reasons for recommending asymmetry in the division of powers is not merely to permit us to accommodate Quebec, but also to allow us more latitude in developing programs at the level of Canada as a whole, retaining that avenue for Canadian political debate (while nevertheless securing Quebec's ability to protect its autonomy).

Indeed, this book has attempted to give a framework, not merely for justifying autonomy, but also for designing the relationship generally between our concentric and overlapping communities. The need to consider the integrity of the pan-Canadian community cuts across all constitutional issues. This section cannot discuss all its implications, but it will address one that was important in the recent negotiations and integrally related to the main themes of this study: constitutional jurisdiction over culture.

There is a large ambiguity in our use of the term "culture" in constitutional discussions. We often speak as though the objective of cultural jurisdiction were to legislate culture – to determine the culture of a society. This has led some Quebec commentators to demand complete provincial control over the field so that their culture would not be determined by an English-speaking majority.[50] It is true that some cultural policy does seek to promote a specific culture. It tries to secure cultural survival, offer services in a particular language, or assist the expression of specific traditions. But culture is a much more complex category than is frequently assumed. When we grasp that complexity, we will see that there is a strong case for a jurisdiction shared between Ottawa and the provinces.

To begin with, cultural policy is not simply about the content of culture, about promoting or restricting a particular culture. Often, it is about creating and maintaining channels of communication within a society. It supports an infrastructure for discussion and debate,

without necessarily attempting to push a particular point of view
(or a particular language). That infrastructure, that opportunity for
exchange, is essential to any political community. In the first place,
it is the vehicle for political discussion itself. Beyond the exchange of
strictly political messages, it is the way we come to understand each
other's environment, each other's culture, each other's interests. It
is, in short, the way we learn about each other, the way we build a
rapport.

This is true not only of regional communities. It is also true of the
pan-Canadian community. If that community is to work well, there
must be channels of communication linking its constituent societies.
The federal government has an essential role to play in developing
the infrastructure of the pan-Canadian community.

Canada's cultural institutions form a very important part of that
infrastructure. The CBC greatly facilitates public debate across
provinces. This is most apparent within the two linguistic halves of
the CBC's operation (both radio and television). Each permits Canadians to have access to news and opinion from other provinces, access that would not exist (at least not to anything like the same
extent) if all broadcasting were privately owned or provincially controlled. There is much less interchange across the linguistic divide.
Only a modest proportion of the population listens to broadcasting
in the second language. Although this is probably inevitable, attempts to interpret the two linguistic communities to each other
have also been spotty and should certainly be improved. Even if the
full potential has not been realized, however, the CBC's importance
to Canadian political debate is undeniable.

The same is true of other cultural institutions, although perhaps
to a lesser degree. The National Film Board has served a crucial role
in producing and distributing films and training new filmmakers to
interpret Canada to Canadians. It has been important not only in
its treatment of expressly political themes (Denys Arcand's film on
textile workers, Studio D's work on women's issues, Donald Brittain's
historical documentaries), but also in its production of films reflecting Canada's regional cultures. Federal support for academic studies
and conferences has fulfilled a similar function, encouraging dialogue across regional and linguistic divisions. The same is true of
Ottawa's assistance to artists, writers, journals, museums, and the
performing arts. It is also true of policies that do not fall under the
cultural rubric at all, but that nevertheless are important agents of
communication and exchange, sometimes as much in symbolic as in
practical terms: the post office, mail subsidies for newspapers and
magazines, the passenger rail system.

The need to foster communication across the cultures is also one of the justifications for Ottawa's role in the promotion of bilingualism. Here we set foot on more controversial terrain. Certain forms of bilingualism can increase the danger of language loss, especially if there is already significant pressure for assimilation. This was the insight underlying Acadian arguments to the B&B Commission that schools in New Brunswick should not become fully bilingual: the pressure to use English was already so great that a secure haven was needed within which francophone children could develop their own language. The same kind of perception led the B&B Commission to suggest three forms of linguistic accommodation, two of which recognized the need for a degree of independence between the cultures. This did not exclude the construction of bridges across cultures. The B&B Commission recommended that the strategies should be combined so that there would be areas in which one language would be predominant but second-language education and other forms of interchange would be promoted.[51] Those bridges need to be constructed wisely, however, taking into account the actual dynamics of language use in order to avoid eroding the position of the more threatened of the communities.

Indeed, this brings us to one of the principal dilemmas of cultural policy. Even though the primary objective may be to encourage communication, channels of communication are never completely separable from cultural content, especially if the relevant "content" is the language of communication itself. After all, one of the primary justifications for assimilating minority-language groups has been the claim that in so doing communication can be fostered across the entire society. Canadians have rejected that approach and have accepted that Canada should retain two principal languages of public debate. We have to be careful, however, that in fostering communication by other means, we do not indirectly promote the same end.

There is certainly a balance to achieve here, but it is a balance, not a zero-sum game where one loses what the other gains. There are some measures that are supportive of cultural pursuits or cultural exchange without posing a risk to any of the participants. This is another way in which the simplistic conception of "legislating culture" is misleading. The CBC, for example, helps maintain a Canadian conversation – certainly within linguistic groups, but also across the linguistic divide – without materially threatening either linguistic group.

This is not simply an argument for the status quo. There may be room for clarification and adjustment in powers over culture, motivated by the need to foster interaction and debate within Canada's constituent societies and the desire for protection against federal policies adversely affecting language use. I doubt, however, whether any major transfer is required. Provincial powers over these matters are extensive already.[52] Adjustments might include the following:

• ensuring that certain programs (for example, federal support for minority-language education) are administered by the provinces;
• guaranteeing that provincial public television stations (the Knowledge Network; TVOntario; Radio-Québec) have access to the television distribution system (which falls under federal jurisdiction);
• allowing provinces the right to opt out of certain cultural programs; and
• establishing a formula for dividing revenues used to support cultural activities so that each level of government controls a set proportion.

Any such changes should, however, be premised on the multifaceted character of cultural programs and the consequent legitimacy of a significant federal role. Many of the adjustments may be best achieved by intergovernmental cooperation, without express constitutional change.

There are, therefore, strong arguments for the recognition of concurrent federal and provincial jurisdictions in what has been called the cultural field. There has been a tendency in recent constitutional discussions to denounce concurrency as inefficient and duplicative. While inefficiency may be a possibility, especially in economic regulation, this book's argument suggests why Canadians have tolerated – and may wish to continue to tolerate – a significant degree of concurrency. It is difficult, in an undivided world, to define with any precision where one power begins and another ends, and it may be that some subjects genuinely have, in the popular debate, a double aspect – one more closely tied to the provincial political community, the other to the pan-Canadian community.

Conclusion

9 The Canadian Conversation

This book has examined how conceptions of language, culture, and national identity came together in our constitutional debates of the last thirty years. We saw that at first, during the 1960s, the demand for constitutional change came from Quebec, as that province sought to work through the constitutional implications of the Quiet Revolution, especially the shift from church to state as the focus of French-speaking Quebecers' cultural aspirations. We saw how the Trudeau government firmly resisted those demands, equating them with a dangerous and potentially destabilizing nationalism, and tried instead to redirect Quebecers' loyalties from the province to Ottawa, notably through the introduction of bilingualism. The tug of war between Ottawa and Quebec came to a climax during the time that the Parti Québécois ruled the province. During that period, a host of other interests also made their presence felt on the constitutional scene. In the federal-provincial relationship, the western provinces and Newfoundland challenged Ottawa's powers over natural resources and urged reform of central institutions. Aboriginal peoples decried the failure to address land claims and self-government. Many groups rallied around the prospect of a new charter of rights, hoping by that means to achieve a greater measure of equality within Canadian society.

That ferment did result in patriation in 1982. Patriation made the constitution amendable within Canada, and added a charter of rights protecting a host of freedoms, including special provisions guaranteeing schools for official-language minorities. The patriation package also extended provincial control over natural resources. It contained a guarantee of aboriginal and treaty rights, promising a set of constitutional conferences on aboriginal rights to follow patriation (conferences that ultimately ended in failure). Quebec's concerns, however, were not addressed. Indeed, Quebec was not a party to the patriation agreement. And so the stage was set for the negotiations that led first to Meech Lake and then, with the failure of that accord, to Charlottetown.

There were many reasons for the breakdown epitomized by the failure of Meech Lake. One was the Meech process: the Conservative government had not recognized the value of a vigorous public debate, of solid justification of public policy in the popular arena. Another was Canada's regrettable neglect of aboriginal issues. The very structure of constitutional talks also made lasting agreement difficult: they come along so rarely, their symbolic force is so great, that it is extremely difficult to focus on a confined set of issues, on a "Quebec Round." But more important than all these, the Meech discussions forced us to address the relationship between culture, language, nation, and individual in a way we had never done before. And when we tried to do that, we found we had great difficulty coming to agreement. Although we addressed some of the defects of Meech in Charlottetown, our inability to agree on this underlying relationship remained and was largely responsible for the rejection of Charlottetown as well.

The two accords addressed constitutional issues in the way Canadians had traditionally dealt with them: ad hoc, without much philosophy or political theory, addressing the parts without giving much thought to how the whole fit together. In fact, this kind of ad hoc improvisation was the very purpose of the reforms designed to address Quebec's concerns. Those reforms were meant to blur the philosophical purity of the 1982 package, but without setting the content of that package aside. The patriation package had been rigorous in its opposition to any recognition of a unique role for Quebec within the Canadian federation. It had protected individual rights – an objective that the great majority of Canadians, including Quebecers, supported – but it had also striven to emphasize the unity of Canadian citizenship, the symmetry of the Canadian state, and the protection of the rights of English- and French-speaking Canadians at the level of Canada as a whole, not at the level of the province. The content of the patriation package, the way it was achieved, and the arguments used by its advocates all carried the strong message that Quebecers' loyalties should be focused on the federal government and that Quebec could not be trusted with a cultural role.

Meech Lake tried to change that, subtly, by recognizing through the distinct society clause that Quebec was not a province like the others and that its uniqueness should be considered in the interpretation of the constitution.

This, however, set the cat among the pigeons. Canada had changed since our earlier attempts to compromise the questions of our languages and our allegiances. Now there was a written constitution protecting fundamental rights. We had to work with the highly visible and symbolically charged Charter. No longer could we fudge and accommodate and adjust, without clearly understanding why. Now we had to write everything down, we had to explain how it all fit together, and we had to try to state in constitutional terms forms of interaction we had lived with for years but that defied easy expression. We tried to do that in Meech, then we tried again in Charlottetown, but the terms of our debate failed us.

In our attempts to discuss our constitutional structure (as opposed to our attempts to live with it), we had never really come to grips with how our country made sense – with how we could combine strong allegiance to our more local societies with strong allegiance to Canada as a whole, how culture might appropriately shape the structure of Canadian government. We had fallen into easy simplifications that, when pursued to their ultimate conclusion, failed to do justice to the complex pattern of our political lives.

This was never more true than during the Trudeau-Lévesque years. During that time, especially to many English-speaking Canadians, everything seemed to fall into neat dichotomies. The conflict of allegiance was clear: either you were for Quebec or for Canada. So was the issue of language rights. Either you had a liberal approach, one in which everyone could choose whichever language he or she wished to use, in which "every Canadian would feel at home in every part of the country," or you had a collectivist, nationalistic approach, in which government told you which language to speak. All subtleties were lost. One side argued that the national community was the same as the cultural community and that therefore Quebec must inevitably become its own country. The other argued that culture was a matter for individuals to decide and that government should be neutral when it came to cultural matters, claiming no cultural role, treating all cultures alike.

There was real doubt whether either of the parties to this debate truly lived by these simplicities. Certainly, the Trudeau government was much more willing to assert a cultural role with respect to Canadian culture, making one wonder whether its arguments were as much about culture as they were about nation. But the arguments were potent in the public debate, the identification of culture with nation attracting many in Quebec, the argument for the cultural neutrality of government (and the focus on Ottawa rather than the provinces) attracting many in the rest of Canada. And in the end, that simple opposition stunted our understanding of how the country could make sense, for of course neither perspective could explain very well the impulsion behind Canadian federalism; neither could explain why federalism had been necessary in the first place, why we might wish to preserve it. For one, federalism was an accident of history, throwing together two fundamentally separate nations; for the other, it was simply one way of achieving functional decentralization (although the theory had a hard time explaining why we should bother putting decentralization into the constitution, when we might as well let a central government organize its affairs as it saw fit).

We were left with a gaping hole, and we had to ask ourselves whether all our history of adjustment and accommodation was simply a matter of political bargaining among elites – whether Canada's politics had been just one long, unprincipled compromise – or whether there was something more substantial to it. We had to think more seriously about the role of culture in government and especially about the relationship between culture and individual rights. We were ill-equipped to do that during the debates, still caught as we were in a discussion that tended to contrast individual to collective rights, treating everything cultural as falling into the second category.

What we needed was a way of making sense of our practice, which, after all, had been relatively successful and relatively tolerant. We needed a way of seeing how cultural concerns related to individual concerns, one that did not leap to the conclusion that they were automatically opposed. We had to come to a solid understanding of how culture might legitimately affect the structure of government. We needed, in short, a convincing theory of pluralist federalism.

This book has attempted to lay out the beginnings of that theory. It is founded upon the interests of individuals, not groups. Its premise is the fundamental importance of political participation to individuals, not necessarily participation in the sense of active campaigning and running for office, but rather in the more gentle sense of engagement in the debates of one's society – the desire to see one's concerns reflected in public decision making, the sense that public debates are one's own. It is this sense of engagement in deliberation that, I suggest, is the substance of political allegiance in a democracy. It is also what makes the particular character of a society's public life valuable to individuals, a value worth accommodating in governmental structures.

In some societies, that accommodation can be adequately achieved through institutions at the level of the country as a whole. The country is sufficiently homogeneous, its debates sufficiently common, that all feel a part of one political community. In Canada, however, the pattern of political interaction is more complex.

At one level, we certainly have a common life as Canadians. The quality of that life could be improved, especially by fostering the participation of those now underrepresented: the poor, racial minorities, women, Canadians of ethnic origins other than British or French. Senate reform would also ensure that western and Atlantic Canadians had a stronger voice in federal decision making. But despite the room for improvement, there is nevertheless a very real Canadian community, with its own dynamic and history, retaining the allegiance of the great majority of Canadians. The Canadian community is not, however, the only community that means something to Canadians. We also cherish more local societies, each with its own distinctive character, its own dynamic, each having substantial autonomy from that of Canada as a whole. We don't want to see those communities washed out in a single, Canada-wide political debate. We want the particular quality of those discussions to have their expression in public decision making as well. Federalism is valuable precisely because it enables us to achieve both. The pan-Canadian community is predominant for some issues, our local communities for others.

This desire to retain the specific character of our local debates is not a matter of retreating into a close-minded, parochial shell, shut off from the world (it is no more close-minded than wanting to maintain the distinctive character of Canada vis-à-vis the United States). It is simply the value we attach to the form of interaction that has marked our own political engagement. In fact, confidence in our own discussions, far from closing us off, probably assists us in participating in public affairs generally. We never engage in discussion in a wide-open, unmarked field. We always make our interventions against the background of what has gone before, we formulate our comments so that they speak to the concerns of others, and we draw upon our wealth of experience to support our positions. We always and inevitably converse from a position within a particular history. That doesn't stop us from moving beyond our immediate circle, although even then, we undoubtedly work from a base shaped by our own formation.[1] On the contrary, it often seems that we feel most able to go out and engage the world when we feel sufficiently secure in our own identities.

A number of factors have contributed to the pattern of our various allegiances. One is the simple fact of living in different provinces, with different citizens, having their own institutions. As I suggested above, those institutional differences can grow into very real provincial cultures, well worth preserving. Another is the fact that public debate occurs in different languages. The use of different media almost inevitably separates political discourse, creating substantial autonomy. That autonomy is never absolute. There may well be substantial reasons, accepted by members of all linguistic communities, for continuing a dialogue across linguistic boundaries. Nevertheless, linguistic differences are likely to generate a relative autonomy, producing the kind of distinctive dynamic that supports demands for institutional autonomy. We saw in the case of the aboriginal peoples that the same kind of process could occur as a result of pronounced cultural differences.

This book has argued that it is perfectly appropriate to take those cultural differences into account in the structure of government institutions. That does not mean that collective rights are winning over individual rights, that a uniform culture is being imposed on all, or that a society is being frozen in time, stifling prospects for challenge and renewal. All public institutions, even those of the pan-Canadian community, are marked by the distinctive character of their debates; all have, in that broad sense, a cultural character. Taking linguistic and cultural difference into account in the design of political institutions simply means that minority as well as majority cultures have a space in which their terms of debate, their traditions, can serve as the dominant framework for political discussion.

The structure of our various communities is not symmetrical. This book has argued that our institutions can reflect that asymmetry. Federalism is a much more flexible device than is often supposed. From the perspective of the liberty and equality of individual citizens, there is little difference between an asymmetrical and a symmetrical structure. In either case, different laws apply to citizens in different parts of the country. Asymmetry simply means that the forum in which the decisions are taken also varies from one province to another. Moreover, the integrity of representation in central institutions is robust. It is able to tolerate substantial variations in the impact of policies without the representative process being undermined. In fact, much of the resistance to asymmetry seems to be prompted, not by a concern with material inequality or constraints on the liberty of individuals as such, but by a much more visceral opposition to differences in treatment – a feeling that any difference, among provinces or individuals, is inherently unequal, and is perhaps the product of special privilege. There is a continuing belief that in a nation all citizens are treated the same, the same rules apply to all, perhaps even that citizens themselves should be, in some important respects, the same. This belief is fundamentally incompatible with the spirit of accommodation underlying federalism, a spirit that has long recognized that when people are different in relevant ways, treating them equally may require treating them differently.

This book has explored the complex interrelationship between language, culture, and political community in the specific context of Canada's constitutional debates. It has spoken in a distinctively Canadian voice. The issues it raises are, however, of much broader interest. It has long been the hope of some strains of liberalism that government could treat everyone neutrally, abstracting from many of the characteristics that set us apart from each other, especially questions of culture. But culture is pervasive, affecting the whole gamut of human action. Wherever there is a distinctive minority community with subtantial autonomy in its conception of public action, there are demands for complementary forms of institutional autonomy. Given the different sizes of minority populations, the range of their concerns, and the lack of symmetry between their desire for decentralization and that of the majority population, the demands frequently tend towards asymmetrical solutions. This is the case, for example, with Catalans in Spain, Scots in the United Kingdom, Corsicans in France, or Puerto Ricans in their unique relationship to the United States. Many countries face issues of cultural accommodation broadly similar to those of Canada. Such issues require careful consideration of the true demands of political stability and individual equality, consideration that goes beyond the simplicities of a nationalism that insists on single allegiances and uniform treatment.

These issues have never been easy to resolve. They are still more difficult in the strongly democratic polities of today. It is no accident that the rise of nationalism coincided with the rise of mass politics in nineteenth-century Europe. Democracy demands a high degree of responsiveness between citizens and governments. Citizens must have the feeling that their concerns are taken seriously, that their complaints are being heard, that their aspirations are being considered. In deeply divided societies – societies in which there are two or more largely autonomous political communities – this pattern of demand and response becomes much more complicated, especially for a central government attempting to maintain a viable community while recognizing the differences between each of the component societies. Such a government has to respond to a popular debate that may well be divided along linguistic or cultural lines. If it attempts to overcome divisions by brokering at the level of each communities' leaders, without sufficient concern for speaking to the population as a whole (as Ottawa did during the Meech Lake debate), it becomes very difficult to maintain responsiveness, direct engagement, and concern with the members of each of the component communities. The central government tends to lose its popular base, opening the way for populist appeals confined to one of the component groups, appeals that, in their simplistic intolerance, may undermine the possibility of the societies continuing within a single state.

This is not, of course, to say that we should go back to a time before democracy. The very foundation of this book has been profoundly democratic, based on the value of political engagement and the need for public institutions to respond to the distinctive character of communities' debates. But there is a tension in pluralist democracies that needs to be addressed in any attempt to accommodate cultural differences. There is a danger that political decision making can become disconnected from public discussion, accommodation occurring at the elite level but leaving the rest of the population behind. Either that or action at the level of the country as a whole can begin to reflect the interests of only one segment of society, neglecting the perspective of others. The best way to counter both these evils is to retain a firm commitment to tolerance and accommodation, but also to promote a vigorous discussion of the terms of that accommodation within political discussion generally. Political activity in pluralist societies has to be conscious of the existence of different, largely autonomous perspectives on issues, and when issues concern the society as a whole, political actors should deliberately work to encourage discussion across cultures – to encourage, in other words, a pattern of public discussion that can support the overarching political institutions.

Governments often take the demand for public consultation as implying a largely passive role for themselves: they simply need to listen to, absorb, and act on what the people say. That is not so. The government is always in a different position from the citizens in public debate. It possesses more information on the specific policy options under study. It will inevitably have to sort through the presentations and take the final decision. If it keeps that information and its evolving idea of potential solutions secret from the public, it will have difficulty securing public support for its initiatives (or even public understanding of the issues involved), and the effectiveness of the popular contribution will be greatly reduced. Moreover, the citizenry will know that it has been given the form rather than the substance of consultation. The government has to listen, it is true, but it also has to engage in a dialogue with the public, letting the public know what it is considering, where it is heading. And in a society as diverse as Canada's, the central government has a special obligation to do that in a way that fosters understanding across the boundaries of its constituent communities.

Facing the difficulties of maintaining that conversation, we may be tempted to conclude that it is simply not worth it. We may wonder whether we should stop struggling against the natural separation of our political life and instead divide our country so that our political communities match the divided pattern of our debates. Then we can fall back on a simpler, more understandable conception of democratic responsiveness, one that does not require the institutional creativity suggested here.

That, of course, is a false hope. We cannot entirely separate from each other. We can make it easier or more difficult to work together, we can change the intensity of our interaction, but we cannot opt out of the problems discussed here. If Quebec separates from Canada, we will still be sharing the northern half of North America, still struggling to maintain the distinctive characteristics of our societies in the face of pressure from the south, still possessing extensive family and business links in other parts of the new states, still having interlocking communication, transportation, environmental, and economic interests. If we are going to deal with any of these issues satisfactorily – if we are not going to suffer very severe costs of separation – we are going to have to work together, and that means finding solutions to precisely the kinds of issues raised here. Those solutions will not be achieved easily after the cost and bitterness of separation.

Moreover, if we do divide the country, we will find, within our newly independent states, very similar problems of cultural autonomy and therefore similar demands for accommodation. There will be, following separation, substantial aboriginal populations in each of the new states. There will be large linguistic minorities. We may try to adopt the solution of the 1969 white paper on aboriginal rights[2] and treat members of these minorities in the same way we treat all citizens. Even if we intend to treat them more generously, we may find that we drift inevitably towards that solution (not just in Quebec, but also in other parts of what was once Canada), given the pressures to build new states, the costs and insecurity of transition, and the emphasis on cultural unity at the origin of at least one of the new states. But even then we will not escape tensions similar to those we now face. Resistance from the minorities concerned will elicit considerable attention in the international community. We may find that we face choices very similar to those we face now, but without the same resources or goodwill to resolve them.

But of course the most serious cost of separation would be the loss of our country itself, the loss of a significant component of all our identities. I believe we underestimate the extent to which we have affected each other. I do not mean that someone from British Columbia knows someone in Quebec or has a fine-grained understanding of the work of Quebec writers or is well aware of the currents within Quebec politics. The mutual interaction has been subtle, much less self-conscious. Almost without knowing it, our societies have grown up together, contributing to our political life at the level of the country as a whole, but also intersecting at the popular level more than we realize. Indeed, we may not realize it until it is too late, until we find ourselves complaining about some political issue only to find that the issue is gone – the whole debate is gone – and we are faced with figuring out who we are as citizens of some new country. We would have emigrated to a country we didn't know, and in the process we would have lost a considerable portion of the richness, the diversity, the dynamism of our lives as Canadians.

The problem of finding a sense of country (as opposed to the material costs of separation) would be most severe for English-speaking Quebecers and Canadians outside Quebec. Francophone Quebecers would lose more than many yet realize (the *indépendantiste* Pierre Bourgault rightly speaks of achieving independence as being, for Quebecers, like emigrating),[3] but at least one object of "national" allegiance would remain largely intact. The same would not be true of Canadians outside Quebec (and of course English-speaking Quebecers). Their principal identification would have been with a political entity – Canada – which would no longer exist. They would have to create another object of allegiance, perhaps some entity reconstituted out of the remaining Canadian provinces, perhaps some subset of that remainder. But they could not continue as before. Nor would reconstituting the country be easy. Ontario would have almost precisely the same population as all the remaining provinces and territories put together, giving it half the total representation in federal institutions.[4] The two sections of the new entity would be geographically separated, no longer making much sense, intuitively, as a country. The existing capital would be awkwardly situated, straddling the border with a foreign state. Most importantly, the continuity of history and commitment would be broken, making it more difficult to understand why we should sacrifice to overcome the very substantial difficulties of maintaining a single country.

Canada is more than the sum of its parts. There have been many attempts over the last 125 years to capture its distinctive character. Some have focused on the great beauty of all Canada's varied landscapes. Others have emphasized the definition of our character against that of the United States; in recent years, this has focused on the more communitarian nature of Canada evident (among other things) in our greater willingness to create extensive social programs. All these are extremely important, but they seem, on their own, incomplete, lacking one crucial element. When I think what Canada means to me, it is not just the land or our communitarian traditions, despite their importance. It is also the people of this country, their rich diversity, and the way in which they have cooperated, disagreed, and in the end shaped each other. What matters most – what makes up the soul of our identity as Canadians – is the conversation we have had in this rich and magnificent land.

Notes

1 "Meech Lake accord fatally defective, Asper tells panel," *Winnipeg Free Press*, 19 August 1987, 13.

2 Canada, *Federal By-elections: Report of the Chief Electoral Officer: 1990* (Ottawa: Supply and Services Canada, 1991), at 23–6.

3 L. Bozinoff and P. MacIntosh, "Federal Conservatives Tie Record Low Level of Support," *The Gallup Report*, 23 January 1992, 1–2. The support for the Bloc Québécois and the Reform Party had remained substantially the same since the previous spring.

4 *Un Québec libre de ses choix: Rapport du Comité constitutionnel du Parti libéral du Québec* (28 January 1991) (chair: J. Allaire); *Rapport de la Commission sur l'avenir politique et constitutionnel du Québec* (March 1991) (co-chairs: M. Bélanger and J. Campeau).

5 E. Thompson, "Carr fights off challenge for CLC leadership; Labor group keeps peace by withdrawing opposition to Meech accord," *Gazette* (Montreal), 18 May 1990, A3.

6 Canada, Senate and House of Commons, *Minutes of Proceedings and Evidence of the Special Joint Committee of the Senate and of the House of Commons on the 1987 Constitutional Accord*, 26 August 1987, at 13:24–13:27 (testimony of Louise Dulude).

7 One remarkable example was the 1991 conference of the Quebec section of the Association Henri-Capitant (a prestigious association committed to the study of private law within the civil law tradition). Its topic was "Droit civil et droits autochtones: confrontation ou

complémentarité," and involved sessions on the relationship between aboriginal and civilian conceptions of property, aboriginal family law, the juridical status of the reserve, and aboriginal administration of justice, all with significant aboriginal participation. There have, of course, been additional sources of tension, especially the long controversy over Hydro-Québec's Great Whale project.

8 This version is taken from Charles Taylor, "Quebec Focus" (1990) 70 (1) *McGill News* 8.

9 For those persuaded by polls, a number of public opinion surveys have shown this kind of dual commitment, often indicating the simultaneous attachment of Quebecers to the symbols of Quebec and Canada. See, for example, the CROP poll reported in 17 (11) *L'actualité* (July 1992); and Richard Johnston and André Blais, "Meech Lake and Mass Politics: The 'Distinct Society' Clause" (1988) 14 (Supplement) *Canadian Public Policy* S25 at S33–S38. See also Gérard Bergeron, *Notre miroir à deux faces* (Montreal: Québec/Amérique, 1985); and Christian Dufour, *Le défi québécois* (Montreal: L'Hexagone, 1989).

10 In fact, the ability to substitute a referendum on a new constitutional package for the proposed referendum on sovereignty was not spelled out in the report of the Bélanger-Campeau Commission (although it was in the Allaire report). Nevertheless, everyone understood that this was the government's intention if it received an acceptable package, and indeed the Bélanger-Campeau recommendations proposed the establishment of a special parliamentary commission to study any new constitutional offers.

11 This is the way committed sovereignists understood the Allaire report. They remained very suspicious of the Bourassa government's intentions, believing that the government was not strongly committed to the report's constitutional prescription.

12 A full description of what I mean by "political community" will have to wait until chapter 6. Briefly, however, I use the term to refer to a forum of debate and decision making on public issues. As will become clear, my notion of political community includes people of very different interests. It is the autonomous pattern of political interaction that is important, not any strong sharing of interest.

Public debate is, of course, diffused throughout a country like Canada. Political communities are not, then, hermetically sealed. But even though their boundaries are indistinct and flexible, it does make sense to talk about certain forums as being the focus of attention for their members for particular issues. Those are the contexts within which the web of political interaction is most intense for those issues. One thus ends up with a set of overlapping or concentric communities, a set that addresses different issues or the same issues in different

323 Notes to pages 27–38

ways but nevertheless has its own distinctive structure. I explore the structure of Canada's chief political communities in chapter 6.

"Multicultural communities" and the women's movement are not "political communities" in this sense, since they generally do not aspire to a large degree of autonomy in public decision making but rather to more effective inclusion within a broader political forum. I draw this distinction not to undermine their legitimacy, but to point out that the difference in aspiration justifies a different response (as should become clear from chapter 6). A group like the women's movement is certainly a very important and oft-neglected segment within that broader community – one that may deserve its own specific forms of accommodation (and indeed I explored that accommodation in the judicial setting in "The Adjudication of Contested Social Values: Implications of Attitudinal Bias for the Appointment of Judges," in Ontario Law Reform Commission, *Appointing Judges: Philosophy, Politics and Practice* [Toronto: OLRC, 1991], 3) – but that accommodation is unlikely to take the form of governmental autonomy.

13 On aboriginal adoptions see Review Committee on Indian and Metis Adoptions and Placements (Manitoba), *No Quiet Place: Final Report to the Honourable Muriel Smith, Minister of Community Services* (1985) (chair: Assoc. Chief Judge Edwin C. Kimelman); Emily F. Carasco, "Canadian Native Children: Have Child Welfare Laws Broken the Circle?" (1986) 5 *Canadian Journal of Family Law* 111; and Patricia A. Monture, "A Vicious Circle: Child Welfare and the First Nations" (1989) 3 *Canadian Journal of Women and the Law* 1. On the use of French in Ontario schools, see Royal Commission on Bilingualism and Biculturalism, *Report* (1968), vol. 2, at 47–51.

14 Discussed below, at page 47.

INTRODUCTION TO PART ONE

1 For an important overview of Canada's constitutional discussions, which adopts a longer time frame than the one used here and develops more fully the issues of process, see Peter H. Russell, *Constitutional Odyssey: Can Canadians Become a Sovereign People?* (Toronto: University of Toronto Press, 1992).

2 This mood was captured, for example, in Harold Cardinal, *The Unjust Society: The Tragedy of Canada's Indians* (Edmonton: Hurtig, 1969); George Ryga, *The Ecstasy of Rita Joe* (Vancouver: Talonplays, 1970); and George Manuel and Michael Posluns, *The Fourth World: An Indian Reality* (Don Mills: Collier-Macmillan, 1974).

3 See, for example, the landmark Royal Commission on the Status of Women in Canada *Report* (Ottawa: Information Canada, 1970).

1 On the varieties of Quebec nationalism during this period, see Ramsay
   Cook, *Canada and the French Canadian Question* (Toronto: Macmillan,
   1966).

2 On Duplessis, see Robert Rumilly, *Maurice Duplessis et son temps* (Montreal: Fides, 1973); Conrad Black, *Duplessis* (Toronto: McClelland
   and Stewart, 1977); and Herbert F. Quinn, *The Union Nationale: Quebec
   Nationalism from Duplessis to Lévesque*, 2d ed. (Toronto: University
   of Toronto Press, 1979).

3 See, for example, William Kaplan, *State and Salvation: The Jehovah's Witnesses and Their Fight for Civil Rights* (Toronto: University of Toronto
   Press, 1989); and Robert Comeau and Bernard Dionne, eds., *Le droit
   de se taire: histoire des communistes au Québec, de la Première Guerre mondiale à la Révolution tranquille* (Outremont: VLB Éditeur, 1989). As
   Kaplan makes clear, discrimination against Jehovah's Witnesses was
   certainly not confined to Quebec. Nor was discrimination against Communists or Jews. F.R. Scott's caution, included in an article discussing *Roncarelli* v. *Duplessis*, [1959] S.C.R. 121, the famous Canadian civil
   liberties case brought by a Jehovah's Witnesses sympathizer against
   Duplessis, bears repeating (Scott was one of Roncarelli's lawyers): "It
   may be worth warning too zealous defenders of civil liberties against
   using this incident as an excuse for another attack upon Quebec. The
   most serious breach of civil liberties in this country is British Columbia's – and the federal government's – treatment of Canadian citizens of Japanese origin. Beside it the case of Jehovah's Witnesses
   in Quebec is less reprehensible. For the Japanese-Canadians do not
   insult their fellow citizens by calling them evil names in widely distributed pamphlets" (F.R. Scott, "Duplessis *versus* Jehovah," in Scott,
   Essays on the Constitution: Aspects of Canadian Law and Politics
   [Toronto: University of Toronto Press, 1977], 196).

4 As with any major historical transformation, the Quiet Revolution had
   its antecedents. See Michael D. Behiels, *Prelude to Quebec's Quiet Revolution: Liberalism versus Neo-nationalism, 1945–1960* (Kingston: McGill-
   Queen's University Press, 1985). For discussions of the Quiet
   Revolution itself, see Dale C. Thomson, *Jean Lesage and the Quiet
   Revolution* (Toronto: Macmillan, 1984); Kenneth McRoberts, *Quebec:
   Social Change and Political Crisis*, 3d ed. (Toronto: McClelland and Stewart, 1988), 128–72; and Robert Comeau, ed., *Jean Lesage et l'éveil
   d'une nation: les débuts de la révolution tranquille* (Sillery: Presses de
   l'Université du Québec, 1989). For discussions more immediately
   immersed in the events but still retaining their interest, see Royal Com-

mission on Bilingualism and Biculturalism (hereafter: B&B Commission) *Preliminary Report* (Ottawa: Queen's Printer, 1965); Cook, *Canada and the French-Canadian Question*; and Peter C. Newman, *The Distemper of Our Times: Canadian Politics in Transition: 1963–1968* (Toronto: McClelland and Stewart, 1968).

5 James Iain Gow, *Histoire de l'administration publique québécoise 1867–1970* (Montreal: Les Presses de l'Université de Montréal, 1986); P.-A. Linteau et al. *Histoire du Québec contemporain: le Québec depuis 1930* (Montreal: Boréal, 1989), 653; *Le Québec statistique: Édition 1985–1986* (Quebec: les publications du Québec, 1985), at 307.

6 See, for example, the review of the language of work in B&B Commission, *Report* (1969), vol. 3B, 447–69.

7 B&B Commission, *Report* (1969), vol. 3A, 21. The figures for "anglophones" and "francophones" in the text are, respectively, those for English-speaking persons of British ethnic origin and those for French-speaking persons of French ethnic origin. These probably correspond most closely to the use of "anglophone" and "francophone" today, especially given the increasing use of "allophone" to refer to those whose mother tongue is neither English nor French. (I have ignored the figures for the very small proportion of the population whose ethnic origin was British or French, but who were unilingual in the other ethnic group's language.)

8 For a full account of the controversy, see Kenneth Bryden, *Old Age Pensions and Policy-Making in Canada* (Montreal: McGill-Queen's University Press, 1974), at 137–75.

9 Quoted in R. Bothwell, I. Drummond, and J. English, *Canada Since 1945: Power, Politics, and Provincialism*, rev. ed. (Toronto: University of Toronto Press, 1989), at 266.

10 Richard Johnston and André Blais, "Meech Lake and Mass Politics: The 'Distinct Society' Clause" (1988) 14 (Supplement) *Canadian Public Policy* S25 at S29–S33 and S38–S39. See also the report of the CROP/ *L'actualité* poll in *L'actualité*, January 1992, 20ff.

11 S.Q. 1975, c. 6.

12 Canada, House of Commons, *Debates*, 17 December 1962, 2722–6.

13 Statistics from B&B Commission, *Report* (1967), vol. 1, 27, and (1969), vol. 3A, 101. See the summary of findings on language use in the federal civil service in B&B Commission, *Report* (1969), vol. 3A, at 113–80.

14 B&B Commission, *Report* (1969), vol. 3A, 261–92.

15 B&B Commission, *Preliminary Report* (1965), 111–13; (1967), vol. 1, xxviii–xxix, xxxiii–xxxiv, xliii–xlvii, 12. The recognition that Quebec was not "a province like the others" (vol. 1, xlvii) also shaped the commission's later recommendations regarding the language of

326 Notes to pages 54–60

work in Quebec's private sector, which proposed that French become "the principal language of work at all levels." One commissioner dissented (B&B Commission, *Report*, [1969], vol. 3B).

16 B&B Commission, *Report* (1967), vol. 1, 93–117, 121–31; (1968), vol. 2, 141–96.

17 B&B Commission, *Report* (1967), vol. 1, 91–3, 138–41; (1968), vol. 2, 199–266; (1969) vol. 3A, 89–347.

18 On Trudeau generally, see George Radwanski, *Trudeau* (Toronto: Macmillan, 1977); Stephen Clarkson and Christina McCall, *Trudeau and Our Times*, vol. 1: *The Magnificent Obsession* (Toronto: McClelland and Stewart, 1990).

19 Official Languages Act, S.C. 1968–69, c. 54.

20 Pierre Elliott Trudeau, "Federalism, Nationalism, and Reason," in Trudeau, *Federalism and the French Canadians* (Toronto: Macmillan, 1968), at 188.

21 Quotation from ibid., 193 (emphasis in original). Even within this essay, Trudeau acknowledged that emotion could not be banished from politics and that nationalism would probably continue to play a role in political life (195). He also devoted considerable time to attacking the previous form of Canadian nationalism (which, he claimed, had disregarded the French presence in Canada) and to arguing that any successful nationalism would have to appeal to all major groups within society. One is left wondering whether he doubted, even then, that an appeal to functionalism alone would work. Perhaps he had already reconciled himself to the need to rely on emotion in politics.

One wonders too whether his ambiguous treatment of nationalism flowed from imprecision in the use of the term. Frequently, he used "nationalism" to refer to the emotional identification of ethnicity with self-determination – the tendency to require, in other words, that each ethnic group have its own state. His express definitions adopted this meaning. He clearly rejected this form of nationalism. But in his argument, he often slipped away from that strict definition to include within "nationalism" all emotional identification with the state. The discussion of the creation of nationalism at the federal level (quoted in the text) used the term in this sense. Indeed, he must have used "nationalism" in this way whenever he referred to it crossing ethnic boundaries in ethnically divided states. When it came to this form of nationalism, his opposition was much more equivocal.

22 For a sense of Pearson's openness, see Lester B. Pearson, *Mike: The Memoirs of the Right Honourable Lester B. Pearson*, vol. 3 (Toronto: University of Toronto Press, 1975), at 236ff.

23 Pierre Elliott Trudeau, *Federal-Provincial Grants and the Spending Power of Parliament* (Ottawa: Queen's Printer, 1969).

24 Again, his essay "Federalism, Nationalism, and Reason," in *Federalism and the French Canadians*, may provide the explanation. He notes the centrifugal tendencies of federations and adds: "If the heavy paste of nationalism is relied upon to keep a unitary nation-state together, much more nationalism would appear to be required in the case of a federal nation-state" (192). Once Trudeau accepted, perhaps reluctantly, the need for a Canadian nationalism to counter the Quebec version, the very logic of nationalism drove him to focus exclusively on Canada.

25 B&B Commission, *Report* (1969), vol. 4, 19. The "other" category also includes those who did not state their ethnic origin.

26 B&B Commission, *Report* (1967), vol. 1, 173 (terms of reference); *Preliminary Report* (1965), 28, 50–2, and vol. 1, xxii–xxiv (defending against ethnic hierarchy); vol. 1, 155–69 (Rudnyckyj's report); and (1969), vol. 4.

27 For a description of some of these activities, together with the text of the 1971 policy statement, see Canada, Minister of State Multiculturalism, *Multiculturalism and the Government of Canada* (Ottawa: Supply and Services Canada, 1978).

28 Canada, Department of Indian Affairs and Northern Development, *Statement of the Government of Canada on Indian Policy, 1969*. For a full discussion of the white paper, see Sally M. Weaver, *Making Canadian Indian Policy: The Hidden Agenda 1968–70* (Toronto: University of Toronto Press, 1981).

29 Ibid.; "Prime Minister Trudeau: Remarks on Aboriginal and Treaty Rights. Excerpts from a Speech Given August 8th, 1969, in Vancouver, British Columbia," in Peter A. Cumming and Neil A. Mickenberg, eds., *Native Rights in Canada*, 2d ed. (Toronto: Indian-Eskimo Association of Canada and General Publishing, 1972), Appendix IV, 331–2. Interestingly, there is a discrepancy between the French and English versions of the 1969 document, the French saying that treaty rights should be brought up to date, the English that they should be ended! See page 11 of the English version, page 12 of the French.

30 *A.G. Can.* v. *Lavell* (1973), [1974] S.C.R. 1349; *Canadian Bill of Rights*, S.C. 1960, c. 44, s. 1(b); *Lovelace* v. *Canada* (1981), 1 Can. Human Rights Y.B. 305; *International Covenant on Civil and Political Rights*, Article 27. The importance of the distinctive nature of aboriginal communities to aboriginal women was emphasized when, following *Lovelace*, the Native Women's Association of Canada joined with the Assembly of First Nations in arguing for a degree of band control over the definition of band membership, instead of a single standard Canada-wide – this against the opinion of the federal Department of Justice that local control (at least for the reinstatement of those ex-

cluded by the discriminatory provision) would violate the Charter of
Rights and Freedoms (Douglas Sanders, "Indian Status: A Women's
Issue or an Indian Issue?" [1984] 3 *Canadian Native Law Reporter* 30.
31 *Calder* v. *A.G. B.C.* [1973] S.C.R. 313.
32 *Chief Max "One-Onti" Gros-Louis* c. *Société de développement de la Baie James*,
    [1974] R.P. 38 (Sup. Ct.); *Société de développement de la Baie James*
    c. *Kanatewat* [1975] C.A. 166.
33 *The James Bay and Northern Québec Agreement* (Quebec: Éditeur officiel,
    1976).
34 Mr Justice Thomas R. Berger, *Northern Frontier, Northern Homeland: The*
    Report of the Mackenzie Valley Pipeline Inquiry, vol. 1 (Toronto:
    Lorimer, 1977).
35 An agreement in principle was concluded, but it ultimately foundered
    on the issue of the extinguishment of aboriginal rights. Separate
    negotiations have continued with some of the peoples who make up
    the Dene Nation.

CHAPTER THREE: CONSTITUTIONAL THEMES

1 The constitution of Canada is made up of a diverse set of documents,
   of which the principal are the Constitution Act, 1867 and the Constitution Act, 1982. The Constitution Act, 1867 is essentially the same
   as the British North America Act, 1867, as amended from time to
   time. The latter act (along with a host of other constitutional documents)
   acquired its new name in 1982, at the time of patriation. It still gov-
   erns the basic institutional structure of Canadian government and the
   division of powers. The Constitution Act, 1982 contains the Canadian Charter of Rights and Freedoms, the amending formula, and a
   number of other provisions, the most important of which is the
   guarantee of aboriginal rights.
2 For one of the best examples of this argument, see Pierre Elliott
   Trudeau, "The Practice and Theory of Federalism," in Trudeau,
   Federalism and the French Canadians (Toronto: Macmillan, 1968), 124.
3 Constitution Act, 1867, section 90.
4 For useful introductions to Canadian fiscal relations, see Donald
   V. Smiley, *Canada in Question: Federalism in the Eighties*, 3d ed. (Toronto: McGraw-Hill Ryerson, 1980), 158–213; and Peter W. Hogg, *Con-*
   stitutional Law of Canada, 3d ed. (Scarborough: Carswell, 1992),
   135–59.
5 Constitution Act, 1982, section 36.
6 An Act to amend the statute law relating to income tax, S.C.
   1974–75–76, c. 26, section 7; Petroleum Administration Act, S.C.
   1974–75–76, c. 47; *Can. Industrial Gas and Oil* v. *Saskatchewan*, [1978]

2 S.C.R. 545; Constitution Act, 1867, section 92A, added by the Constitution Act, 1982.
7 Constitution Act, 1867, sections 91(3) and 92(2). The distinction between direct and indirect taxation is complex. In principle, direct taxes (e.g., property or income taxes) are paid by the person on whom the taxes are levied; indirect taxes (e.g., excise taxes) are passed on to someone else (usually the consumer).
8 *Report of the Royal Commission on Dominion-Provincial Relations* (Ottawa: King's Printer, 1940).
9 This was of more than theoretical interest. Ever since the late 1970s, successive federal governments have tried to limit their contributions. The provinces have strongly resisted these efforts, arguing that it would be a breach of faith, perhaps even a breach of contract, for the federal government to reduce its funding unilaterally. In their view, federal governments have been trying to have it both ways, retaining control over the programs in the name of national identity, but attempting to shift more of the cost onto provincial treasuries. In recent years, the Mulroney government's unilateral attempt to limit contributions to the wealthiest provinces under the Canada Assistance Plan (which subsidizes welfare payments by the provinces) was challenged in the courts, without success. See *Reference re: Canada Assistance Plan* (1991), 83 D.L.R. (4th) 297 (S.C.C.). This led some provinces to push, in the post-Meech round of constitutional negotiations, for an amendment making federal-provincial agreements binding under certain conditions. See, for example, Senate and House of Commons, *Report of the Special Joint Committee on a Renewed Canada* (Ottawa: Queen's Printer, 1992) (co-chairs: G. Beaudoin and D. Dobbie) (hereafter: Beaudoin-Dobbie Commission), at 68–9 and 116; and also proposed section 126A of the Constitution Act, 1867, in the Charlottetown Accord's *Draft Legal Text*, section 17.
10 For an excellent discussion, see Brian Slattery, "The Independence of Canada" (1983), 5 *Supreme Court Law Review* 369.
11 Canada's evolution towards independence can be seen as part of a still longer process that includes the struggle for "responsible government" – for government responsible to assemblies elected by Canadian residents, not to governors appointed from London. For a discussion of the critical transition, see J.M.S. Careless, *The Union of the Canadas: The Growth of Canadian Institutions 1841–1857* (Toronto: McClelland and Stewart, 1967).
12 Statute of Westminster, 1931 (U.K.), R.S.C. 1985, Appendix II, No. 27; An Act to amend the Supreme Court Act, S.C. 1949 (2d sess.), c. 37.
13 Sections 42–50 of the Constitutional Amendment Bill (Bill C-60), 20 June 1978, in Anne F. Bayefsky, ed., *Canada's Constitution Act*

1982 and Amendments: A Documentary History, vol. 1 (Toronto: McGraw-Hill Ryerson, 1989), at 358–61.

14 For human rights protection in Canada prior to the Charter, see Walter Surma Tarnopolsky, *The Canadian Bill of Rights*, 2d ed. (Toronto: McClelland and Stewart, 1975). The literature on the Charter itself is now very extensive.

15 See Ken Adachi, *The Enemy That Never Was: A History of the Japanese Canadians* (Toronto: McClelland and Stewart, 1976); Douglas Cole, *An Iron Hand upon the People: The Law against the Potlatch on the Northwest Coast* (Vancouver: Douglas & McIntyre, 1990); Alan R. Marcus, *Out in the Cold: The Legacy of Canada's Inuit Relocation Experiment in the High Arctic* (Copenhagen: International Work Group for Indigenous Affairs, 1992); Irving Abella and Harold Troper, *None Is Too Many: Canada and the Jews of Europe 1933–1948* (Toronto: Lester and Orpen Dennys, 1982); William Kaplan, *State and Salvation: The Jehovah's Witnesses and Their Fight for Civil Rights* (Toronto: University of Toronto Press, 1989); Robert Comeau and Bernard Dionne, eds., *Le droit de se taire: histoire des communistes au Québec, de la Première Guerre mondiale à la Révolution tranquille* (Outremont: VLB Éditeur, 1989); Lita-Rose Betcherman, *The Little Band: The Clashes between the Communists and the Political and Legal Establishment in Canada, 1928–1932* (Ottawa: Deneau, n.d.); and Merrily Weisbord, *The Strangest Dream: Canadian Communists, the Spy Trials, and the Cold War* (Toronto: Lester and Orpen Dennys, 1983).

16 For a review of the cases, see Hogg, *Constitutional Law*, at 774–7.

17 The Saskatchewan Bill of Rights Act, S.S. 1947, c. 35; Canadian Bill of Rights, S.C. 1960, c. 44; The Alberta Bill of Rights, S.A. 1972, c. 1; and Charter of Human Rights and Freedoms, S.Q. 1975, c. 6. These statutes purport to control the actions of government. In addition, the provinces and Ottawa have enacted extensive statutes (often referred to as "human rights codes") banning discrimination in certain private relationships, such as employment, the lease of a residence, and a host of other circumstances.

18 The reform of central institutions to reflect regional differences has been termed "intrastate federalism." For an excellent discussion of these issues, not only regarding the Senate but also the federal executive, the House of Commons, and the Supreme Court, see Donald V. Smiley and Ronald L. Watts, *Intrastate Federalism in Canada* (Toronto: University of Toronto Press, 1985).

19 Population figures from the 1991 census: Statistics Canada, *A National Overview: Population and Dwelling Counts* (Ottawa: Supply and Services Canada, 1992), at 7.

20 Constitution Act, 1867, sections 24 and 29.

21 It is unclear whether, following the constitutional amendments of 1982, the Supreme Court is subject to the constitutional amending formula or is still subject to the unencumbered will of Parliament. The answer depends on a particularly thorny problem of interpretation of the Constitution Act, 1982. For contrasting opinions, see R. Cheffins, "The Constitution Act, 1982 and the Amending Formula: Political and Legal Implications," (1982) 4 *Supreme Court Law Review* 43, at 53–4; Stephen A. Scott, "The Canadian Constitutional Amendment Process" (1982) 45 *Law and Contemporary Problems* 249 at 258–62; and Hogg, *Constitutional Law*, at 72.

22 Quebec's tradition of private law proceeds from different sources and uses a different style of reasoning than the private law of other provinces. Judges from those provinces are usually unfamiliar with the civil law tradition. If the Supreme Court is to continue as the final court of appeal for Quebec, it has to have enough judges trained in the civil law so that it can credibly decide those cases. The Supreme Court of Canada consists of nine judges. Each case is decided by a panel consisting of at least five judges. As it stands now, cases arising under Quebec's civil law are almost always heard by the minimum number of judges (five), including the three Quebec judges. In this way, the court ensures that a majority of the panel is trained in the civil law. If there were less than three civil law judges, civil law cases would be decided by panels having a majority of judges untrained in the civil law. The practice of having three Quebec judges is enshrined in section 6 of the Supreme Court Act, R.S.C. 1985, c. S-26.

23 The Royal Proclamation, 7 October 1763, R.S.C. 1985, Appendix II, no. 1. For an overview of the British and Canadian treaty processes, see Olive Patricia Dickason, *Canada's First Nations: A History of Founding Peoples from Earliest Times* (Toronto: McClelland and Stewart, 1992), chaps. 12 and 19.

24 The Quebec Act, 1774 (U.K.), R.S.C. 1985, Appendix II, no. 2; The Constitutional Act, 1791 (U.K.), R.S.C. 1985, Appendix II, no. 3. See Hilda Neatby, *Quebec: The Revolutionary Age 1760–1791* (Toronto: McClelland and Stewart, 1966); and Mason Wade, *The French Canadians 1760–1967*, rev. ed. (Toronto: Macmillan, 1968), at 47–92.

25 For the structure of government, see Wade, *The French Canadians*, 47ff.; and Neatby, *Quebec*. For the application of English law, see A.L. Burt, *The Old Province of Quebec* (Toronto: Ryerson, 1933), at 433–45; Hilda Neatby, *The Administration of Justice under the Quebec Act* (Minneapolis: University of Minneapolis Press, 1937), at 224ff.; and John E.C. Brierley, "The Co-existence of Legal Systems in Quebec: Free and Common Socage in Canada's 'pays de droit civil'" (1979) 20 *Cahiers de Droit* 277.

26 *The Report of the Earl of Durham, Her Majesty's High Commissioner and Governor General of British North America* (London: Methuen & Co., 1922 [1839]), 8.

27 For the political arrangements of the Union period, see Careless, *The Union of the Canadas*, especially at 208–13.

28 These provisions are still part of the Constitution Act, 1867, although the section 80 limitations have been validly abrogated by the Quebec legislature: An Act respecting the electoral districts, S.Q. 1970, c. 7.

29 A good example of these symbolic arguments is the long debate between the "compact" and the "statute" theories of Confederation. The first sees Confederation as a pact between self-governing, autonomous provinces, in which the provinces (or, in other versions, the linguistic groups) come first and the central government is little more than their creature. The second sees Confederation as a wholly new entity, not dependent on the will of constituent groups or provinces. Here, the idea of the whole predominates, and the provinces are its administrative subdivisions. The two theories purport to describe the historical origin of Confederation, but the historical argument is little more than an excuse for emphasizing autonomy on the one hand or unity on the other. Note too how the language of the debate forces polarization on its participants: it leaves no room for a solution including both commitment to the whole and commitment to the parts. Rather, it presumes that either the whole or the parts must be prior, and automatically relegates the other to a lower status. For a discussion of the compact theory through time that argues that the coexistence of both theories and the preservation of the tension between them has been essential to Canadian constitutional life, see Roderick A. Macdonald, "... Meech Lake to the Contrary Notwithstanding" (1991) 29 *Osgoode Hall Law Journal* 253 and 483; and, in much the same vein, Richard Simeon, "Meech Lake and Visions of Canada," in Katherine E. Swinton and Carol J. Rogerson, eds., *Competing Constitutional Visions: The Meech Lake Accord* (Toronto: Carswell, 1988), 295.

CHAPTER FOUR: TOWARDS PATRIATION

1 For accounts of the negotiations of this period, see Dale C. Thomson, *Jean Lesage and the Quiet Revolution* (Toronto: Macmillan, 1984); Donald V. Smiley, *Canada in Question: Federalism in the Eighties*, 3d ed. (Toronto: McGraw-Hill Ryerson, 1980), 66–90; and Edward McWhinney, *Quebec and the Constitution 1960–1978* (Toronto: University of Toronto Press, 1979). For one view from Quebec, see Jean-Louis Roy, *Le choix d'un pays: le débat constitutionnel Québec-Canada 1960–1976* (Ottawa: Leméac, 1978).

2 The Fulton-Favreau formula is reproduced in Anne F. Bayefsky, ed., *Canada's Constitution Act 1982 and Amendments: A Documentary History* (Toronto: McGraw-Hill Ryerson, 1989), at 16–21.

3 This is a common problem for those committed to specific forms of constitutional change. Alberta later ran into a similar situation during the Meech negotiations. It wanted Senate reform, but it also wanted to control the nature of that reform. It therefore agreed to the requirement of unanimity for changes to the Senate in Meech Lake, even though that might make reform more difficult to secure. It opted, in other words, for control instead of ease of modification.

4 See, for example, Pierre Elliott Trudeau, "Federal Grants to Universities," in Trudeau, *Federalism and the French Canadians* (Toronto: Macmillan, 1968), 79.

5 See especially Alan C. Cairns, "Recent Federalist Constitutional Proposals," in Cairns, *Disruptions: Constitutional Struggles, from the Charter to Meech Lake*, ed. D.E. Williams (Toronto: McClelland and Stewart, 1991), 35 at 43–5; Peter H. Russell, "The Political Purposes of the Canadian Charter of Rights and Freedoms" (1983) 61 *Canadian Bar Review* 30; and Rainer Knopff and F.L. Morton, "Nation-Building and the Canadian Charter of Rights and Freedoms," in Alan Cairns and Cynthia Williams, *Constitutionalism, Citizenship and Society in Canada* (Toronto: University of Toronto Press, 1985), 133. For examples of this approach in federal statements of the time, see P.E. Trudeau, *A Time for Action: Toward the Renewal of the Canadian Federation* (Ottawa: Supply and Services, 1978); and House of Commons, *Debates*, 15 April 1980, 32–6, quoted in Roy Romanow, John Whyte, and Howard Leeson, *Canada ... Notwithstanding: The Making of the Constitution 1976–1982* (Toronto: Carswell/Methuen, 1984), xv.

6 See Pierre Elliott Trudeau, "A Constitutional Declaration of Rights," in Trudeau, *Federalism and the French Canadians*, 52; and P.E. Trudeau, *Federalism for the Future: A Statement of Policy by the Government of Canada* (Ottawa: Queen's Printer, 1968).

On a number of occasions, Trudeau claimed that he was not strongly committed to constitutional reform and only advocated reform in response to provincial demands. (See, most recently, Trudeau, "Convocation Speech at the Opening of the Bora Laskin Law Library" (1991) 41 *University of Toronto Law Journal* 295 at 305.) This is disingenuous, given that he had long advocated an entrenched charter of rights (see, for example, "A Constitutional Declaration of Rights," at 53, and "Quebec and the Constitutional Problem," in *Federalism and the French Canadians*, 3 at 44–6), began promoting a charter shortly after assuming the justice portfolio, and throughout the 1970s advocated constitutional reform even when (as in 1974 or 1976) the provinces were

334 Notes to pages 97–107

lukewarm. His professed reticence is best explained on tactical grounds. Trudeau knew he was struggling with the provinces for control of the reform process. When the initiative seemed to lie with the provinces or after a federal initiative had resulted in failure, it was better to affect disinterest than confess to defeat in an important branch of government policy.

7 For a statement of his views, see Daniel Johnson, *Égalité ou indépendance* (Montreal: Éditions de l'homme, 1965).

8 For a good summary of these discussions, see Smiley, *Canada in Question*, 69–79.

9 The Victoria Charter is reproduced in Bayefsky, *Canada's Constitution Act 1982*, at 214–23.

10 For accounts of the constitutional negotiations of this period, see Robert Sheppard and Michael Valpy, *The National Deal: The Fight for a Canadian Constitution* (Toronto: Fleet Books, 1982); Edward McWhinney, *Canada and the Constitution 1979–1982* (Toronto: University of Toronto Press, 1982); David Milne, *The New Canadian Constitution* (Toronto: Lorimer, 1982); Romanow et al., *Canada ... Notwithstanding*; and Stephen Clarkson and Christina McCall, *Trudeau and Our Times*, Vol. 1: *The Magnificent Obsession* (Toronto: McClelland and Stewart, 1990). Romanow et al. is particularly good on the challenge from the Prairies, British Columbia, and Newfoundland.

11 Official Language Act, S.Q. 1974, c. 6 (Bill 22).

12 *A.G. Quebec v. Blaikie (No.1)* [1979] 2 S.C.R. 1016.

13 Charter of the French Language, S.Q. 1977, c. 5.

14 For useful expressions of the PQ's constitutional position, see René Lévesque, *Option Québec* (Montreal: Éditions de l'homme, 1968); and Claude Morin, *Quebec versus Ottawa: The Struggle for Self-government 1960–72* (Toronto: University of Toronto Press, 1976).

15 The discussions of 1978–79 did, however, produce greater agreement on some issues, agreement that later found its way into the patriation package. This was the case, for example, with constitutional jurisdiction over natural resources. See Romanow et al., *Canada ... Notwithstanding*, at 24–9.

16 Bill C-60 is reproduced in Bayefsky, *Canada's Constitution Act 1982*, 340–413. See also Trudeau, *A Time for Action*.

17 *Reference re: Authority of the Parliament in Relation to the Upper House*, [1980] 1 S.C.R. 54.

18 Constitutional Committee of the Quebec Liberal Party, *A New Canadian Federation* (1980).

19 Canada, Office of the Prime Minister, "Transcript of a Speech Given by the Right Honourable Pierre Elliott Trudeau at the Paul Sauvé Arena in Montreal on May 14, 1980," news release, 16 May 1980, at 4–5.

20 See above, note 10.

21 The federal proposal is reproduced in Bayefsky, *Canada's Constitution Act 1982*, 743–61.

22 Constitution Act, 1867, section 92A.

23 In its final version, that clause reads: "Notwithstanding anything in this Charter, the rights and freedoms referred to in it are guaranteed equally to male and female persons" (Constitution Act, 1982, section 28).

24 The dissenting provinces' proposal is reproduced in Bayefsky, *Canada's Constitution Act 1982*, at 804–13.

25 The National Indian Brotherhood adopted the new name at its annual conference in June 1982, although it is still incorporated under its former name. The third organization mentioned in the text is the Inuit Tapirisat. In 1983 a fourth national organization, the Métis National Council, was formed after a dispute among members of the NCC. The MNC draws its support from Métis in the western provinces and Ontario.

26 (1981), 117 D.L.R. (3d) 1 (Man. C.A.); (1981), 118 D.L.R. (3d) 1 (Nfld. C.A.); [1981] C.A. 80 (Que. C.A.).

27 *Reference re: Resolution to Amend the Constitution*, [1981] 1 S.C.R. 753.

28 Constitution Act, 1982, section 35. It is unclear what effect the addition of "existing" had. Probably none. It certainly limited the recognition to rights still in existence at the time of patriation, therefore excluding rights already extinguished. But it is very unlikely that the courts would have interpreted the provision as resurrecting already-extinguished rights even if "existing" had not been included. It is also true that aboriginal rights remained a vague category, their content yet to be determined. But this process would not be conceived as the creation of rights, but rather the definition of rights presumed to exist already. Unless they had been extinguished, all aboriginal rights were "existing" at the time the Charter entered into force. They merely had to be described.

29 For an account of the struggle, see Penney Kome, *The Taking of Twenty-Eight: Women Challenge the Constitution* (Toronto: Women's Educational Press, 1983).

30 See, for example, René Lévesque, *Attendez que je me rappelle ...* (Montreal: Québec/Amérique, 1986), at 389.

31 Québec, Assemblée nationale, *Journal des Débats*, 1 December 1981, 605 (quotations are my translation).

32 *Reference re: Objection to a Resolution to Amend the Constitution*, [1982] 2 S.C.R. 793.

33 Act respecting the Constitution Act, 1982, S.Q. 1982, c. 21.

34 For useful discussions of "Charter patriotism," see Charles Taylor, "Can Canada Survive the *Charter*?" (1992) 30 *Alberta Law Review* 427; and

Alan C. Cairns, *Charter versus Federalism: The Dilemmas of Constitutional Reform* (Montreal and Kingston: McGill-Queen's University Press, 1992), especially at 118–23.

35 For an account of this litigation strategy, see Sherene Razack, *Canadian Feminism and the Law: The Women's Legal Education and Action Fund and the Pursuit of Equality* (Toronto: Second Story Press, 1991).

36 See, for example, Lévesque's own account in *Attendez que je me rappelle,* at 444–8.

37 See Richard Simeon, "Meech Lake and Visions of Canada," in Katherine E. Swinton and Carol J. Rogerson, eds., *Competing Constitutional Visions: The Meech Lake Accord* (Toronto: Carswell, 1988), 295.

38 The personalization has also marred a number of otherwise thoughtful treatments of the issues. This is true, for example, of Clarkson and McCall, *Trudeau and Our Times*, and Donald Brittain's National Film Board documentary, "The Champions" (parts 1 and 2, 1978; Part 3, 1986). For a thought-provoking examination of the personalized politics of the times from a Quebec perspective, see Gérard Bergeron, *Notre miroir à deux faces* (Montreal: Québec/Amérique, 1985).

CHAPTER FIVE: AFTER PATRIATION

1 Canada, Senate and House of Commons, *Report of the Special Joint Committee of the Senate and House of Commons on Senate Reform* (Ottawa: Queen's Printer, 1984) (co-chairs: G. Molgat and P. Cosgrove).

2 For accounts of the aboriginal rights conferences following patriation and texts of relevant documents, see Norman K. Zlotkin, "The 1983 and 1984 Constitutional Conferences: Only the Beginning" [1984] 3 *Canadian Native Law Reporter* 3; David C. Hawkes, *Negotiating Aboriginal Self-Government: Developments Surrounding the 1985 First Ministers' Conference* (Kingston: Institute of Intergovernmental Relations, 1985); Bryan Schwartz, *First Principles, Second Thoughts: Aboriginal Peoples, Constitutional Reform and Canadian Statecraft* (Montreal: Institute for Research on Public Policy, 1986); Norman K. Zlotkin, ed., "Documents from the 1987 First Ministers' Conference on Aboriginal Matters" [1987] 3 *Canadian Native Law Reporter* 1; and David C. Hawkes, *Aboriginal Peoples and Constitutional Reform: What Have We Learned?* (Kingston: Institute of Intergovernmental Relations, 1989).

3 The combination of this provision with the unusual wording of section 35 of the Constitution Act, 1982 (aboriginal rights were not "guaranteed" but merely "recognized and affirmed") added to the uncertainty over the clause's effect. Some argued that the clause had recognized the general principle of aboriginal rights, and that the content of those rights would have to be determined in later negotiations. On this

reading, section 35 was largely symbolic or at least did nothing more than preserve aboriginal rights from any suggestion that patriation might obliterate them. It did not entrench aboriginal rights in the constitution. This reading was rejected by the Supreme Court of Canada in *R.* v. *Sparrow* (1990), 70 D.L.R. (4th) 385, where the court held that section 35 did entrench aboriginal rights.

4 Constitution Act, 1982, sections 35(3) and (4), 35.1, and 37.1.

5 *Report of the Special Committee on Indian Self-Government* (the Penner report), in Canada, House of Commons, *Minutes of Proceedings of the Special Committee on Indian Self-Government*, no. 40.

6 For detailed accounts of the Meech Lake saga, see A. Cohen, *A Deal Undone: The Making and Breaking of the Meech Lake Accord* (Vancouver: Douglas & McIntyre, 1990); and Patrick J. Monahan, *Meech Lake: The Inside Story* (Toronto: University of Toronto Press, 1991). For a penetrating discussion of the content and significance of the accord against the backdrop of the history of linguistic relations in Canada, see Roderick A. Macdonald, "... Meech Lake to the Contrary Notwithstanding" (1991) 29 *Osgoode Hall Law Journal* 253 and 483.

7 "Texte du discours prononcé par M. Gil Rémillard," Annexe A in P.M. Leslie, *Rebuilding the Relationship: Quebec and Its Confederation Partners: Report of a Conference, Mont Gabriel, Quebec, 9–11 May 1986* (Kingston: Institute of Intergovernmental Relations, 1987), 47 at 50. Although it was not one of the five conditions, Rémillard also emphasized the need to improve the situation of francophones outside Quebec. In particular, he suggested that the right of official-language minorities to manage their schools be expressly guaranteed, and that the condition qualifying minority-language education rights ("where numbers warrant") be reviewed. Neither of these things occurred in the Meech process, although in *Mahé* v. *Alberta* (1990), 68 D.L.R. (4th) 69, the Supreme Court of Canada held that, where practicable, the minority-language community should have a role in administering its own schools.

8 For the text of this agreement, see "Meech Lake Communiqué of April 30, 1987," Appendix 1, in Peter W. Hogg, *Meech Lake Constitutional Accord Annotated* (Toronto: Carswell, 1988), 56.

9 Strictly speaking, the only amendments in the Meech Lake Accord requiring unanimous approval were those dealing with the amending formula and the Supreme Court of Canada (although even for the latter, it was doubtful whether unanimity was required for every provision). All the other amendments – including the distinct society clause and the ability to opt out of future spending-power programs – only required the consent of Parliament plus seven provinces having 50 per cent of the population. Nevertheless, from the beginning

the first ministers acted on the assumption that none of the amendments should become law unless all did. This meant that, effectively, unanimity was required for the whole package.

10 This section discusses the draft constitutional amendments themselves, rather than the initial accord reached on 30 April (reproduced in Hogg, *Meech Lake Annotated*, Appendix 1). These draft amendments were the focus of the Meech Lake debate and were what most people referred to as the "Meech Lake Accord." For their text, with commentary, see Hogg, *Meech Lake Annotated*.

11 Proposed section 2 of the Constitution Act, 1867 in Constitutional Amendment 1987 (the Meech Lake Accord).

12 Charter of the French language, R.S.Q. 1977, c. C-11, sections 135–56.

13 The Supreme Court of Canada's decision in *Ford* v. *Quebec (A.G.)*, [1988] 2 S.C.R. 712, provides another example of how the court might have used the distinct society clause. In that case, the provision in Bill 101 banning the use of English on commercial signs was challenged. The court struck the legislation down, holding that the law was contrary to freedom of expression in Quebec's own Charter of Human Rights and Freedoms, R.S.Q. 1977, c. C-12 (although the same reasoning would have applied under the Canadian Charter). The protection of Quebec's *visage français* would, it held, have justified making French predominant, but not exclusive. Here, then, the court gave effect to the Charter right but took into account the unique character of Quebec in the discussion of limits on that right.

14 For a similar evaluation, see Macdonald, "... Meech Lake," 511 ff.; Charles Taylor, "Shared and Divergent Values," in Ronald L. Watts and Douglas M. Brown, eds., *Options for a New Canada* (Toronto: University of Toronto Press, 1991), 64–5; and Taylor, "Can Canada Survive the *Charter*?" (1992) 30 *Alberta Law Review* 427 at 436.

15 The B&B Commission, *Preliminary Report* (1965), at 92, caught the essence of the claim in its discussion of support for special status in Quebec: "The goal to be achieved was expressed more exactly than the means by which it might be obtained: it was a question of having Quebec officially recognized as 'a province not like the others,' one which is the fatherland of the French Canadian 'nation,' and as such, a province which should be given special powers."

16 Constitution Act, 1867, section 95.

17 Proposed sections 95A to 95E of the Constitution Act, 1867, in the Meech Lake Accord.

18 See Andrew Petter, "Federalism and the Myth of the Federal Spending Power" (1989) 68 *Canadian Bar Review* 448.

19 Proposed section 106A of the Constitution Act, 1867, in the Meech Lake Accord.

20 Indeed, there was a significant argument that Meech Lake would buttress the constitutionally questionable spending power. See Peter Hogg, "Analysis of the New Spending Provision (Section 106A)," in Katherine E. Swinton and Carol J. Rogerson, eds., *Competing Constitutional Visions: The Meech Lake Accord* (Toronto: Carswell, 1988), 155.

21 Constitution Act, 1982, section 41.

22 Proposed section 41 of the Constitution Act, 1982, in the Meech Lake Accord.

23 Proposed section 40 of the Constitution Act, 1982, in the Meech Lake Accord.

24 Proposed section 101C of the Constitution Act, 1867, in the Meech Lake Accord. The present provisions governing the Supreme Court of Canada are found in the Supreme Court Act, R.S.C. 1985, c. S-26.

25 Proposed section 101B(2) of the Constitution Act, 1867, in the Meech Lake Accord.

26 Proposed sections 25 and 148 of the Constitution Act, 1867, and section 50 of the Constitution Act, 1982, in the Meech Lake Accord.

27 Polling data from *The Gallup Report*, 28 April 1988, 1, and 18 May 1990, 2. In the May 1990 poll, in Canada as a whole 42 per cent opposed the accord and 33 expressed no opinion. The percentage opposed to the distinct society clause outside Quebec ranged from 60 to 70 per cent.

28 For blow-by-blow descriptions, see above, note 6.

29 Alan C. Cairns, "Citizens (Outsiders) and Governments (Insiders) in Constitution-Making: The Case of Meech Lake," in Cairns, *Disruptions: Constitutional Struggles, from the Charter to Meech Lake*, ed. D.E. Williams (Toronto: McClelland and Stewart, 1991), 108; Alan C. Cairns, "Constitutional Minoritarianism in Canada," in R.L. Watts and D.M. Brown, eds., *Canada: The State of the Federation 1990* (Kingston: Institute of Intergovernmental Relations, 1990), 71.

30 Constitution Act, 1982, section 27. For the link between section 28 and cultural concerns, see Sherene Razack, *Canadian Feminism and the Law: The Women's Legal Education and Action Fund and the Pursuit of Equality* (Toronto: Second Story Press, 1991), at 34.

31 See, for example, *A.G. Que.* v. *Que. Protestant School Bds.* [1984] 2 S.C.R. 66; and *Ford* v. *Que.* [1988] 2 S.C.R. 712.

32 An Act to amend the Charter of the French language, S.Q. 1988, c. 54 (Bill 178).

33 Charter of the French Language, S.Q. 1977, c. 5 (Bill 101).

34 In a CROP–La Presse poll taken in January 1985, for example, 62 per cent of francophone respondents said that bilingual commercial signs should be permitted, another 18 per cent that the language of signs should be left entirely up to the business concerned. Only

20 per cent answered that the language of signs should remain French only. The report noted that this was consistent with other recent polls. See A. Noël, "La grande majorité des Québécois acceptent l'affichage bilingue," *La Presse* (Montréal), 20 January 1985, 4.

35 *Ford* v. *Quebec (A.G.)*, [1988] 2 S.C.R. 712. The related provision required that only the French version of company names be used. The result in the case turned on the complicated interrelationship of the Quebec and Canadian charters (both of which could be set aside by notwithstanding clauses) and two separate invocations of the Canadian Charter's notwithstanding clause. The Quebec National Assembly had not invoked the Quebec Charter's notwithstanding clause, so that charter applied to both the sign-law and company-name provisions, invalidating them. The blanket invocation of the Canadian Charter's notwithstanding clause (enacted under the PQ) had lapsed, and so it no longer insulated the provisions from the Canadian Charter's application. The sign-law provision had been amended more recently, however (again under the PQ), and the *amending* law had contained another invocation of the notwithstanding clause. *That* clause had not lapsed, and so the sign-law provision itself was not subject to the Canadian Charter.

36 For a remarkable example of this, see Philip Resnick, *Letters to a Québécois Friend* (with a reply by Daniel Latouche) (Montreal: McGill-Queen's University Press, 1990), at 20–5. Resnick supported the more stringent provisions of Bill 101, yet was outraged by the enactment of Bill 178!

37 I discuss this idea of normative compromise in "The Adjudication of Contested Social Values: Implications of Attitudinal Bias for the Appointment of Judges," in Ontario Law Reform Commission, ed., *Appointing Judges: Philosophy, Politics and Practice* (Toronto: OLRC, 1991), 3.

38 Discussed briefly above at page 100.

39 For example, a Telepoll Research poll taken at the time of the adoption of Bill 178 found that 44 per cent of Quebec respondents believed the province should have the right to pass legislation notwithstanding the Charter, 40 per cent believed it should not; 58 per cent approved the solution in Bill 178, 37 per cent disapproved (I. Block, "Quebecers strongest backers of override clause use, poll says," *Gazette* [Montreal], 23 December 1988, A4. A Gallup poll taken in the two weeks after the passage of Bill 178 found that 61 per cent of French-speaking respondents were in favour of permitting bilingual signs in Quebec. At the same time, when asked what was more important, English-speaking Quebecers' freedom of speech or French-speaking Quebecers' right to preserve their culture, 78 per cent of fran-

cophone respondents answered the latter. See L. Bozinoff and P. Mac-
Intosh, "Tory Honeymoon Continues; Country Divided on
Language Rights," in Gallup Canada, Inc., release, 12 January 1989.
40 In the post-Meech period, we began to see the point made explicitly.
See, for example, the exchange between Ovide Mercredi, grand
chief of the Assembly of First Nations, and Trudeau reported in Benoît
Aubin, "A rights discussion," *Gazette* (Montreal), 14 December 1991,
B3; Lise Bissonnette, "Éditorial: Question aux premiers peuples," *Le
Devoir* (Montreal) 16 March 1992, 12; or Gordon Gibson, "Let's not
use racism to tackle native needs," *Globe and Mail* (Toronto), 1 June
1992, A15.
41 Note that this "transfer" would not, however, have changed the legislative power formally attributed to the federal Parliament under
the Constitution Act, 1867. It would merely have allowed for opting
out of federal spending programs *in areas of provincial jurisdiction*,
constitutionally questionable in any case.
42 B&B Commission, *Preliminary Report* (1965), 128.
43 Proposed section 25 of the Constitution Act, 1867, in the Meech Lake
Accord.
44 B&B Commission, *Preliminary Report* (1965), 111.
45 Hogg, "Analysis of the New Spending Provision."
46 Paul Gérin-Lajoie, *Constitutional Amendment in Canada* (Toronto: University of Toronto Press, 1950); The Honourable Guy Favreau,
Minister of Justice, "The Amendment of the Constitution of Canada,"
in Anne F. Bayefsky, ed., *Canada's Constitution Act 1982 and Amendments: A Documentary History* (Toronto: McGraw-Hill Ryerson, 1989),
22.
47 See, for example, Quebec, *Report of the Royal Commission of Inquiry on
Constitutional Problems*, vol. 2 (Quebec, 1956), 78; and the speech
by Lesage quoted in Ramsay Cook, *Canada and the French-Canadian Question* (Toronto: Macmillan, 1966), at 164.
48 Newfoundland, House of Assembly, *Verbatim Report (Hansard)*, 2 April
1990, at R67.
49 The claim that anglo-Quebecers might be better off than other minorities seemed ludicrous to many, especially many anglo-Quebecers.
Wasn't Quebec the only province that had legislated against a minority
language? The substance of the claim can be seen if one distin-
guishes between three different kinds of prejudice that linguistic minorities can suffer. First, they can suffer tremendous pressure to
change their language because of the non-governmental environment:
they may form an isolated pocket within a large population speaking the other language; media of communication may use the other
language; they may have to speak the other language in order to

do business or to find work. Second, the absence of governmental services in their language – schools, universities, hospitals, social services – can hamper language acquisition, force assimilation in order
to progress, or simply increase the advantage of using the other language. Third, governmental policy can directly restrict language use.
With respect to each of the first two categories (probably the most
important for the ability to retain one's language), anglophone Quebecers were in a much better position than francophones outside
Quebec. Only with respect to the third were they in a worse position,
and even then the prejudice was more symbolic than material.

50 There was some controversy over the deadline. Just how binding was
it? The amending formula established by the Constitution Act, 1982
stipulated that, for amendments requiring the support of seven provinces having 50 per cent of the population (most of the Meech
amendments), the legislatures had to adopt resolutions ratifying the
amendments within three years of the first ratifying resolution. The
rationale for this requirement was to prevent a ratification period from
dragging on indefinitely. On 23 June 1987 Quebec became the first
to ratify Meech, therefore establishing the deadline of 23 June 1990.
After the latter date, it would certainly have been possible for all
the provinces to readopt the package, beginning the process all over
again. It may also have been possible for Quebec alone to readopt
the package. All the other parties might then have treated the second
ratifying resolution, that of Saskatchewan on 23 September 1987,
as the initiating resolution, effectively extending the deadline three
months. Either of these expedients would probably have been effective; the courts would have been loath to rule an amendment invalid
if all legislatures had ratified it within a three-year period. However,
each would have undermined the purpose of the deadline: the ratification period – and therefore the period during which the to-
and-fro of constitutional debate continued – might have stretched on
indefinitely. Ottawa and the provinces may have been willing to
adopt this expedient if all were committed to ratification, but not if any
of them wanted to renegotiate the accord.

51 See above, note 27.

52 The drafting of the Charlottetown Accord proceeded in two steps. The
agreement actually concluded at Charlottetown, entitled *Consensus
Report on the Constitution, Charlottetown, August 28, 1992: Final Text*, described the proposal in ordinary language without draft amendments (except for the "Canada clause," described below, for which a
draft was provided). The parties to the original agreement then
worked on the text of the amendments, eventually producing the *Draft
Legal Text: October 9, 1992*. The discussion that follows is based on

the latter document. If the referendum had passed, it is likely that there would have been further minor changes to the wording of the provisions.

53 For these provisions, see *Draft Legal Text*, sections 12 (immigration), 16 (spending power), 15 (Supreme Court of Canada), 32 and 33 (amending formula), and 21, 4, and 32 (new provinces).

54 Government of Newfoundland and Labrador, *Constitutional Proposal: "An Alternative to the Meech Lake Accord"* (submitted to the First Ministers Conference, 9 and 10 November 1989).

55 The latter phrase is from the *Consensus Report*, 1.

56 Proposed section 2(1) and (2) of the Constitution Act, 1867, in *Draft Legal Text*, section 1.

57 Proposed section 2(1)(c) of the Constitution Act, 1867, in *Draft Legal Text*, section 1.

58 This, for example, had been the tendency in the 1991 federal proposals, although these would have provided for both an interpretive clause in the Charter and a reference to distinct society in a Canada clause at the beginning of the Constitution Act, 1867; see Government of Canada, *Shaping Canada's Future Together: Proposals* (Ottawa: Supply and Services, 1991), at 51–53. A similar approach was adopted by the Beaudoin-Dobbie Committee in February 1992 in its report, *A Renewed Canada: The Report of the Special Joint Committee of the Senate and the House of Commons* (Ottawa: Supply and Services, 1992), at 21–27.

59 *Draft Legal Text*, sections 7 (disallowance), 9 (declaratory power), 12 (immigration), and 16 (spending power).

60 Proposed section 93A of the Constitution Act, 1867, in *Draft Legal Text*, section 11.

61 Proposed sections 92B and 92C of the Constitution Act, 1867, in *Draft Legal Text*, section 10 (culture); proposed sections 92(12A), 93B and 93C of the Constitution Act, 1867, in *Draft Legal Text*, sections 9(2) and 11 (labour market development and training).

62 Proposed section 92D of the Constitution Act, 1867, in *Draft Legal Text*, section 10 (telecommunications); proposed section 93D of the Constitution Act, 1867, in *Draft Legal Text*, section 11 (regional development).

63 Proposed section 37 of the Constitution Act, 1982, in *Draft Legal Text*, section 31.

64 This point was forcefully made by the political scientist, Ronald Watts, during the Meech Lake debate: Canada, House of Commons, *Minutes of Proceedings and Evidence of the Special Committee to Study the Proposed Companion Resolution to the Meech Lake Accord* (the Charest committee), 10 April 1990, at 3:73–3:74.

65 The provisions dealing with the new Senate were proposed sections 21–36C of the Constitution Act, 1867, in *Draft Legal Text*, section 4.

66 Proposed section 51A(2)(b) of Constitution Act, 1867, in *Draft Legal Text*, section 5.

67 *Draft Legal Text*, sections 8 and 12 (jurisdiction over Métis), 23 (Métis land), 29 (treaty interpretation), and 33 and 29 (amendment).

68 Proposed sections 35.1 (1) and (2) of the Constitution Act, 1982, and proposed section 2(1)(b) of the Constitution Act, 1867, in *Draft Legal Text*, sections 29 and 1 respectively.

69 Proposed sections 35.2, 35.3, and 35.1(4) of the Constitution Act, 1982, in *Draft Legal Text*, section 29.

70 Proposed section 35.1(5) of the Constitution Act, 1982, in *Draft Legal Text*, section 29.

71 Proposed section 35.4(2) of the Constitution Act, 1982, in *Draft Legal Text*, section 29.

72 Proposed sections 32(1)(c) (application of the Charter), 33.1 (notwithstanding clause), 3 (voting rights), 35.5 and 25(c) (affirmative action, etc.) of the Constitution Act, 1982, in *Draft Legal Text*, sections 26, 27, 24, 29, and 25 respectively. Charlottetown contemplated that governments established under the provisions might extend voting rights to all residents of a given area. This was the structure favoured by aboriginal peoples in the Northwest Territories. See proposed section 35.2(4) of the Constitution Act, 1982, in *Draft Legal Text*, section 29; and Michael Asch, *Home and Native Land: Aboriginal Rights and the Canadian Constitution* (Scarborough: Nelson Canada, 1988), at 93–104.

73 Proposed sections 36.1 and 36.2 of the Constitution Act, 1982, in *Draft Legal Text*, section 31.

74 Proposed section 16.1 of the Constitution Act, 1982, in *Draft Legal Text*, "Bilateral amendment – New Brunswick and Canada."

75 For an excellent discussion of the defeat, see Alain Noël, "Deliberating a Constitution: The Meaning of the Canadian Referendum of 1992" (revised version of a paper presented at the Colorado College Colloquium, 13 November 1992).

CONCLUSION TO PART ONE

1 The phrase is Trudeau's, used in a convocation speech at the University of Toronto: M. Trickey, "Trudeau disputes view that '82 deal left Quebec in cold: 'Sorcerer's apprentice' blamed," *Gazette* (Montreal), 22 March 1991, B1. That remark is not in the published version of the speech: Trudeau, "Convocation Speech at the Opening of the Bora Laskin Law Library" (1991) 41 *University of Toronto Law Journal* 295. Instead, he criticizes the 1981 decision of the Supreme Court of Canada, which held that a unilateral federal request for patriation would be contrary to constitutional convention (discussed above, at

page 113), blaming it for patriation's lack of legitimacy in Quebec. That must be wrong, and it is more an expression of spleen and desire to shift the blame than reasoned analysis. Quite apart from the fact that it is unseemly to criticize a judicial decision on the grounds that it was inconvenient for one's government, the criticism drastically exaggerates the legitimizing effect of Supreme Court judgments in Quebec. Indeed, if they really did have such an effect, patriation without Quebec's assent would have been accepted, for the Supreme Court explicitly denied that Quebec's assent was required (*Reference re: Objection to a Resolution to Amend the Constitution*, [1982] 2 S.C.R. 793). The 1981 decision did cast a cloak of illegitimacy over unilateral action, but this effect was most telling outside of Quebec. Quebecers' discomfort had much deeper roots.

CHAPTER SIX: LANGUAGE, CULTURE, AND POLITICAL COMMUNITY

1 Pierre E. Trudeau, *The Constitution and the People of Canada* (Ottawa: Queen's Printer, 1969), 4–6. See also Peter H. Russell, "The Political Purposes of the Canadian Charter of Rights and Freedoms" (1983) 61 *Canadian Bar Review* 30; and Rainer Knopff and F.L. Morton, "Nation-Building and the Canadian Charter of Rights and Freedoms," in Alan Cairns and Cynthia Williams, research coordinators, *Constitutionalism, Citizenship and Society in Canada* (Toronto: University of Toronto Press, 1985), 133.
2 Indeed, it found its way into the Charlottetown Accord: *Consensus Report on the Constitution, Charlottetown, August 28, 1992: Final Text*, at 1.
3 The recognition that national identity lies as much in a country's disagreements as in its agreements has much in common with Louis Hartz's analysis of the ideological dynamic of new societies. He argues that colonial societies are marked by only a portion of the ideological spectrum of the colonial power. They are fragments of the old country's society, thrown off at a particular historical juncture. Their ideological balance therefore differs from that of the old country, lacking the depth and breadth of that society. This fragment then forms the basis for the evolution of political debate in the colony, an evolution shaped by the balance of ideological forces present at the origin. See Louis Hartz, *The Founding of New Societies: Studies in the History of the United States, Latin America, South Africa, Canada, and Australia* (New York: Harcourt, Brace & World, 1964).
   Hartz's analysis may exaggerate both the extent to which the initial fragment fixes the course of subsequent debate and the autonomy of that debate from more concrete relations within society, but the rec-

ognition that national character is best conceived in terms of a course of discussion through time – possessing its own dynamic, its own language of justification, unfolding in its own way in response to largely internal pressures – is very close to that presented here.

4 This, for example, is the truth lying behind Pierre Bourgault's comment, quoted above, at page 19, that true separatists no longer care what the rest of Canada thinks.

5 For a recent attempt to measure Quebecers' continued attachment to Canadian symbols, showing that considerable attachment does exist, see the poll reported in 17 (11) *L'actualité* (July 1992). The same phenomenon is especially pronounced among aboriginal peoples. There, the long experience of loss of resources, loss of governmental autonomy, poor living conditions, disease, and very strong pressure to abandon aboriginal cultures understandably makes aboriginal people reluctant to make effusive statements of commitment to Canada. Yet at the same time, there is great willingness among most aboriginal people to remain within Canada, on the basis of a just accommodation.

6 Quotation from Rainer Maria Rilke to Franz Xaver Kappus, 14 May 1904, in Rilke, *Briefe*, vol. 1 (Wiesbaden: Insel-Verlag, 1950), 74–80 at 80. Translation from unnumbered introductory pages of Hugh MacLennan, *Two Solitudes* (Toronto: Collins, 1945). See also Elspeth Cameron, *Hugh MacLennan: A Writer's Life* (Toronto: University of Toronto Press, 1981), at 176–7. The reference to Lord Durham refers to his famous report on the constitution of the Canadas: *The Report of the Earl of Durham, Her Majesty's High Commissioner and Governor General of British North America* (London: Methuen & Co., 1922 [1839]), at 8.

7 F.R. Scott, "Dancing," in Scott, *The Dance Is One* (Toronto: McClelland and Stewart, 1973), 20. I do not know whether Scott would have extended the metaphor to our national lives, and if he had, he almost certainly would have rejected the conclusions for the constitution advanced here. His position was much more centralist than mine, unsympathetic to provincial claims to autonomy. When it comes to the constitution, I tend to agree with Scott when he acted (to borrow Shelley's expression) as unacknowledged rather than acknowledged legislator of his society!

8 This form of commonality may, in other words, be less a matter of express consensus than of largely unintentional accommodation, where parties to the same conversation come to define their positions primarily in relation to each other. The existence of continued disagreement may hide the fact that the terms of discussion have converged and now represent a significant level of commonality, at least with regard to what questions are important and how they should be

approached. For examples of this kind of convergence or mutual self-definition in ideologies, see Pierre Ansart, *Idéologies, conflits et pouvoir* (Paris: PUF, 1977), at 77ff; Jeremy Webber, "The Mediation of Ideology: How Conciliation Boards, through the Mediation of Particular Disputes, Fashioned a Vision of Labour's Place within Canadian Society" (1989) 7 (2) *Law in Context* (Melbourne) 1.

9 By saying that we work within the debate, I don't mean simply that we decline to emigrate (although I do mean that as well), but that at a deeper level, the starting-point of all our political opinions lies in the debate we have inherited. In fact, the form of political community described here, the evaluation of its significance for its members, and the conclusions for institutional design in this book are all founded on the perception that in public life – indeed, in any discussion with another individual, any attempt to read a text – we must always begin with a set of presumptions, a set of cultural understandings. Those presumptions are crucial to any constructive engagement in the debate or with the text. If we don't share some understanding of the terms of the debate with the other participants in the discussion or with the text, we have to begin by developing that rapport. Our presumptions may well be modified or rejected in the course of conversation, but they are the inescapable starting-point. It therefore means a great deal to us if we can begin the discussion within our own debate, where we understand its framework and its presumptions and can expect that others do as well.

This conception tries to capture the fact that we all develop within specific communities (or traditions or cultures), are inevitably marked by those communities, and yet find that we can develop some critical distance from particular opinions or institutions within them. A citizen's engagement with his community is dialectical, it shaping him, but he in turn reflecting upon it, engaging in its debates and perhaps changing it. For the conceptual foundations of this discussion, see Hans-Georg Gadamer, *Truth and Method* (New York: Crossroad, 1988); Charles Taylor, "Atomism," in Taylor, *Philosophy and the Human Sciences: Philosophical Papers*, vol. 2 (Cambridge: Cambridge University Press, 1985), at 187–210, *Sources of the Self: The Making of the Modern Identity* (Cambridge, Mass: Harvard University Press, 1989), and *Multiculturalism and "The Politics of Recognition"* (Princeton: Princeton University Press, 1992); Alisdair MacIntyre, *Whose Justice? Which Rationality* (Notre Dame: University of Notre Dame Press, 1988), especially chap. 18; and Gerald Postema, "On the Moral Presence of Our Past" (1991) 36 *McGill Law Journal* 1153. MacIntyre's work tends to close in upon a specific tradition that MacIntyre considers superior. This seems unnecessary. I tend towards the approach to MacIntyre's work suggested in Brian Slattery, "Rights, Communities and Tradition" (1991) 41 *University of Toronto Law Journal* 447.

10 Indeed, it rejects the traditional opponent of the compact theory, that is, the "statute theory." Arguments that rely on nothing more than historic right provide a poor foundation for political arrangements today. History is important not because it reveals implicit contracts (or other juridical acts) that determine what we must do today, but because it has had a profound impact on the *present* character of our political communities. Our present communities have their roots in the past. If we want to understand them, we have to come to terms with their past. If we want to understand their value to their members, we have to understand how they came to assume their present form.

11 For one account leaning in this direction, see Robert Bothwell, Ian Drummond, and John English, *Canada Since 1945: Power, Politics, Provincialism*, rev. ed. (Toronto: University of Toronto Press, 1989), especially at 255–86, 359–99.

12 In fact, this is an oversimplification. Prior to Confederation there was a second level (afterwards a third), which served as a very important object of allegiance for many Canadians and a source of real governmental authority for all: the imperial government. See, for example, Carl Berger, *The Sense of Power: Studies in the Ideas of Canadian Imperialism 1867–1914* (Toronto: University of Toronto Press, 1970). For simplicity's sake, I will confine myself to the levels discussed in the text.

13 Constitution Act, 1867, section 92(13).

14 Constitution Act, 1867, section 91(26).

15 Constitution Act, 1867, section 92(8).

16 Constitution Act, 1867, section 92(7) and (9).

17 Constitution Act, 1867, section 92(16).

18 Constitution Act, 1867, section 91(2). There is a vigorous controversy over the proper extent of the trade and commerce power, some saying that it was intended to cover more than merely interprovincial and international trade but that it was unduly restricted by judicial interpretation. I do not intend to join that controversy here. At any rate, it is clear that the power was intended to cover transactions extending beyond a province.

19 Constitution Act, 1867, 91(5), (9), (10), (13)–(20), 92(10), and 95.

20 For an exceptionally rigorous example of a functionalist approach, see Albert Breton and Anthony Scott, *The Design of Federations* (Montreal: Institute for Research on Public Policy, 1980).

21 See, for example, Frank R. Scott, "The Privy Council and Mr. Bennett's 'New Deal' Legislation," in Scott, *Essays on the Constitution: Aspects of Canadian Law and Politics* (Toronto: University of Toronto Press,

1977), 90; *Report of the Royal Commission on Dominion-Provincial Relations* (Ottawa: King's Printer, 1940), at 247–52 and 257–9; Bora Laskin, "'Peace, Order and Good Government' Re-Examined" (1947) 25 *Canadian Bar Review* 1054; and for an influential overview, Alan C. Cairns, "The Judicial Committee and Its Critics," in D.E. Williams, ed., *Constitution, Government, and Society in Canada: Selected Essays by Alan C. Cairns* (Toronto: McClelland and Stewart, 1988), 43.

22 Government of Canada, *Canadian Federalism and Economic Union: Partnership for Prosperity* (Ottawa: Supply and Services, 1991). See also the Trudeau government's version of the same argument: *Powers over the Economy: Securing the Canadian Economic Union in the Constitution* (Ottawa: Government of Canada, 1980).

23 See, for example, *Un Québec libre de ses choix: Rapport du Comité constitutionnel du Parti libéral du Québec* (28 January 1991) (chair: J. Allaire), 14–20.

24 In the 1950s, Quebec's Tremblay Commission suggested that the 1867 division of powers was largely based on the scope of legislation in the Province of Canada during the Union Period: *Report of the Royal Commission of Inquiry on Constitutional Problems*, vol. 1 (Quebec, 1956), at 35–44. During that period, some laws applied to one of the province's component parts (what later became Quebec or what later became Ontario), while others applied to the entire province. After Confederation the first category of laws became provincial, the second federal. That suggestion rings true and would help explain some apparently anomalous aspects of the division of powers. It is also consistent with the statement in the text that the division resulted from a complex balancing of factors. Finally, it supports the idea that the division of powers was less a matter of highly rationalized construction on the functionalist plan than one of evolution over a long period of time. The division of powers was more likely to reflect, then, an existing sense of community rooted in concrete patterns of political interaction.

25 *Report of the Earl of Durham*, at 16 and 218. (For the historical and intellectual background to the report, see Gerald M. Craig, "Introduction," in Craig, ed., *Lord Durham's Report* (Toronto: McClelland and Stewart, 1963), i; and Janet Ajzenstat, *The Political Thought of Lord Durham* (Montreal: McGill-Queen's University Press, 1988). For liberal nationalism's treatment of linguistic differences, see E.J. Hobsbawm, *Nations and Nationalism Since 1780: Programme, Myth, Reality* (Cambridge: Cambridge University Press, 1990), chaps. 1 and 2. Hobsbawm's analysis, however, tends to be insufficiently attuned to the varieties of "nationalism" and it attempts such an immense sweep

that at times it is, in its detail, simply wrong. (See, for example, his rep-
etition of the myth of the "strongly anglicized French *joual* of the
Montreal lower-class neighbourhoods," 161.)

26 Ibid., at 8–9.

27 Ibid., at 23–9.

28 Ibid., at 24–5, 29ff.

29 Ibid., at 221–2.

30 See J.M.S. Careless, *The Union of the Canadas: The Growth of Canadian
Institutions 1841–1857* (Toronto: McClelland and Stewart, 1967).

31 According to the 1986 census, 48 per cent of people living in the Montreal metropolitan area are bilingual (Statistics Canada, *Montréal:
Part 2: Profiles* [Ottawa: Supply and Services Canada, 1988], Table 1–1).
Yet of the weekly volume of English-speaking television viewing,
only 8 per cent is by francophone viewers, and of French-speaking television, only 5 per cent by anglophone viewers (S. Baillargeon, "Mo-
nologues des sourds," *L'actualité*, January 1992, 47, quoting BBM 90–91).
The same phenomenon is evident from the figures compiled by
NADbank®'91 regarding newspapers and radio. NADbank divides Montreal's population into two groups, English/Ethnic (31 per cent of
the population) and French (69 per cent). The readership of the weekday *La Presse* is 92 per cent French, the weekday *Journal de Montréal*
89 per cent French, and the weekday *Gazette* 82 per cent English/Ethnic.
Regarding radio, 92 per cent of those who reported listening to
CJAD-AM 800 (an English talk-show station) were English/Ethnic, and
90 per cent of those listening to CKAC-AM 730 (a French talk-show
station) were French. (My thanks to David Klimek of the Gazette for
these figures.)

32 At pages 46–8.

33 See, for example, the frank discussion in *Royal Commission on Constitutional Problems*, vol. 2, at 81–83.

34 See, for example, the remarks of John A. Macdonald on 6 February
1865 in P.B. Waite, ed., *The Confederation Debates in the Province of
Canada/1865* (Toronto: McClelland and Stewart, 1963), at 40–1.

35 There was a good example of this phenomenon during the Meech Lake
debate, when many English-speaking intervenors urged politicians
to listen to ordinary Canadians, clearly assuming that the latter were
united on the issue. There were, of course, profound divisions between the anglophone Canadian and francophone Quebec grass roots.
The problem, then, did not simply concern responsiveness to popular opinion (though this was certainly a large part of the problem),
but also concerned how such profound division should be dealt
with.

36 Not all English-speaking Canadians have been ready to make those compromises, and indeed on occasion the majority has opposed com-

promise. But note the dynamic: if English-speaking Canadians refuse to compromise, they need not give up their identification with the pan-Canadian community; they simply use their majority status to force their position on the entire community. Francophone Quebecers lack that option. That is why they cannot afford such substantial identification with a pan-Canadian perspective.

37 Constitution Act, 1867, section 133 (use of both languages in Parliament, legislation, and the courts); and Constitution Act, 1982, sections 16–22 (declaring both languages official, restating section 133's guarantees, and giving a right to federal government services in the citizen's language in certain circumstances).

38 Parliament's Beaudoin-Dobbie Committee got the message. Its recommendations regarding the division of powers were focused on the spending power; they restrained its future exercise, suggested provincial participation in the redesign of existing shared-cost programs, and provided for federal-provincial agreements to reduce the federal role in areas where the spending power had been used. There was no immediate effect on existing programs, however; restrictions would have occurred through intergovernmental agreements to be negotiated later. This lack of concrete results produced significant criticism in Quebec, but the committee was right to identify the spending power as the main irritant in division-of-powers issues. See *A Renewed Canada: The Report of the Special Joint Committee of the Senate and the House of Commons* (the Beaudoin-Dobbie report) (Ottawa: Queen's Printer, 1992), at 63–5 and 70–83.

39 This is the figure adopted in the Beaudoin-Dobbie report, 63.

40 Although Quebecers' commitment to the 1867 division of powers is therefore independent, to some degree, of the functional justification for allocating powers to the provinces, I do not want to suggest that the initial division was arbitrary, without functional or cultural justification. The original division tended to reflect the scope of legislation adopted during the Union period: legislation applying to both halves of the colony was generally allocated to Ottawa; legislation applying to one, allocated to the provinces. This suggests that the division of powers did have, at least originally, an organic foundation in the political life of the colony. Since that time, of course, the division of powers has taken on a life of its own, generating its own expectations. This is especially true in the case of social programs, many of which were beyond contemplation at the time of Confederation. Nevertheless, the overall structure of governmental authority, especially the fact that charitable institutions, hospitals, and education fell within provincial jurisdiction, suggested that the novel services (such as greatly expanded health care, or welfare payments) should be provincial.

41 I should not overstate the unity of the Canadian criminal law. Although
the substantive offences are the same (and it is this that results in
the symbolic unity discussed in the text), ancillary matters, such as the
treatment of young offenders, the criteria applied by prosecutors
in the exercise of their functions, or even the right to a jury trial, can
vary from province to province. (See *R. v. Turpin*, [1989] 1 S.C.R.
1296 and *R. v. S.*, [1990] 2 S.C.R. 254, where the Supreme Court of
Canada found this variation to be acceptable under the Charter.)
Indeed, the interpretation of the substantive offences in Quebec may
be different from that in the rest of Canada. See Nicholas Kasirer,
"The Annotated Criminal Code en version québécoise: Signs of Territoriality in Canadian Criminal Law" (1990) 13 *Dalhousie Law
Journal* 520.

42 Figures for Montreal from 1986 census: (Statistics Canada, *Montréal:
Part 2: Profiles*).

43 The figures for French-speaking Quebecers are drawn from the 1986
census, and include all who declared they could speak French. The
number of Quebecers for whom French is their mother tongue is a little
over five and a half million (Statistics Canada, *Quebec: Part 2: Profiles*
[Ottawa: Supply and Services Canada, 1988], 1; Statistics Canada,
Quebec: Part 1: Profiles [Ottawa: Supply and Services Canada, 1987],
at 1). The populations of the other provinces were also drawn from
the 1986 census (Statistics Canada, *Census Divisions and Subdivisions:
Population* [Ottawa: Supply and Services Canada, 1987], 1–1 to 1–5).

44 Figures for New Brunswick are from Statistics Canada, *New Brunswick:
Part 1: Profiles* (Ottawa: Supply and Services Canada, 1987), 1.
Figures for Ontario are from Statistics Canada, *Ontario: Part 1: Profiles*
(Ottawa: Supply and Services Canada, 1987), at 1.

45 My thanks to my colleague Armand deMestral for having insistently
pressed this idea of two Canadian multiculturalisms, one with
French, one with English as its general language.

46 They have not been displaced to anything like the extent often assumed
by non-aboriginal Canadians. See, for example, the comments in
Royal Commission on the Donald Marshall, Jr., Prosecution, *Findings
and Recommendations*, vol. 1 (chair: T.A. Hickman) (Halifax: Province
of Nova Scotia, 1989), at 171–3.

47 See the discussions of adoption that occur throughout the ethnograph-
ical literature. Many examples can be found, for example, in Bruce
G. Trigger, *The Children of Aataentsic: A History of the Huron People to
1660* (Montreal: McGill-Queen's University Press, 1987); and Richard White, *The Middle Ground: Indians, Empires, and Republics in the Great
Lakes Region, 1650–1815* (Cambridge: Cambridge University Press,
1991). Similar flexibility is often built into twentieth-century compre-

hensive agreements on aboriginal claims. See, for example, the
treatment of membership in "Umbrella Final Agreement between the
Government of Canada, the Council for Yukon Indians and the
Government of the Yukon," 30 May 1992, sections 3.2.2.3 and 3.2.2.4.
48 See, for example, William Kornhauser, *Politics of Mass Society* (Glencoe:
Free Press, 1959), especially 74ff.

CHAPTER SEVEN: AN ASYMMETRICAL CONSTITUTION

1 Constitution Act, 1867, section 91(24).
2 See *Guerin* v. *The Queen*, [1984] 2 S.C.R. 335.
3 See David Milne, "Equality or Asymmetry: Why Choose?" in Ronald
L. Watts and Douglas M. Brown, eds., *Options for a New Canada*
(Toronto: University of Toronto Press, 1991), 287–91.
4 This was the case, for example, with the Meech Lake Accord's distinct
society clause, which would certainly have had an impact upon constitutional interpretation, but in a way that is difficult to analyse in terms
of more and less. See above, at pages 127–9.
5 There is, of course, one constituency that is concerned with governmental powers as such and for whom the notion of equality of provincial governments has real substance: the governments themselves.
Institutional self-interest provides important incentives to blur the
distinction between equality of governments and equality of citizens in
order to harness the potent language of equality to narrowly institutional ends.
   One centralist strain in Canadian scholarship has tended to seize upon
this, painting demands for decentralization as the product of this
interest (see the examples in note 37, below). Institutional concerns are
indeed reflected in all governmental action, and thus one should
not merely accept governmental pronouncements at face value. There
is nevertheless a more substantial foundation to our provincial commitments. This book attempts to chart the contours of that foundation.
6 Among the predominantly anglophone provinces, there are of course
significant variations. The poorer provinces and Ontario tend to
be strongly supportive of the federal role. Alberta tends to be among
the most committed to provincial autonomy.
7 For a brief introduction to this principle, on which there is now a considerable literature, see Dale Gibson, *The Law of the Charter: Equality
Rights* (Toronto: Carswell, 1990), at 133–7.
8 Certain features of Canadian constitutionalism already recognize that
provinces may have to be treated differently in the interest of a
more fundamental equality. One example is the principle of equalization, now enshrined in the Constitution Act, 1982, section 36. If

provinces were treated identically, equalization would not exist. Each
province would pay for its own services out of its own resources.
There would be no transfer from taxpayers in richer provinces to governments in poorer provinces. But although the elimination of
equalization would preserve a superficial equality between provinces,
it would undermine another expression of equality: the ability of
citizens in any province to have access to comparable levels of service.
As Canadians we accept equalization – at considerable cost to
wealthy provinces – because we believe that Canadians in every part
of the country should be able to derive roughly equivalent benefits
from their citizenship. If we accept different treatment in the interest
of a decent level of governmental services, surely we can consider
measures designed to accommodate the different challenges faced by
cultural groups.

9 For an interesting exploration of the potential tension between federalism and a constitutional norm of equality, see José Woehrling, "Le
principe d'égalité, le système fédéral canadien et le caractère distinct
du Québec," in Pierre Patenaude, ed., *Québec – Communauté fran-
çaise de Belgique: autonomie et spécificité dans le cadre d'un système fédéral*
(Montreal: Wilson and Lafleur, 1991), 119.

10 Some jurists argued that regional differences in the application of the
criminal law violated the equality guarantee in the Charter. Fortunately, the Supreme Court of Canada rejected this position. See the
decisions cited in chapter 6, note 41. In any case, one wonders
whether objections to the differential application of federal law are
more potent in the abstract than in concrete situations. The enforcement of the criminal law has long varied from province to province because of the overlapping of federal and provincial jurisdiction in
the area. See Peter W. Hogg, *Constitutional Law of Canada*, 3d ed.
(Toronto: Carswell, 1992), 467ff.

11 This scepticism is much less apparent when it comes to measures designed to promote Canadian culture. In part, this reflects the difference between the two kinds of opposition to cultural measures
described in the text. One suspects, however, that it also reflects the
fact that arguments of rights are often tied up with conceptions of
nation.

12 For an intriguing attempt to justify the accommodation of cultural difference within an expressly liberal framework, see Will Kymlicka,
Liberalism, Community and Culture (Oxford: Clarendon Press, 1989).

13 For a stimulating discussion of this aspect of the relationship of culture
to law, see Clifford Geertz, "Local Knowledge: Fact and Law in
Comparative Perspective," in Geertz, *Local Knowledge* (New York: Basic
Books, 1983), 167; and, with respect to aboriginal rights in Canada,

Mary Ellen Turpel, "Aboriginal Peoples and the Canadian *Charter*: Interpretive Monopolies, Cultural Differences" (1989–90) 6 *Canadian Human Rights Yearbook* 3.

14 This will strike many lawyers as a dramatic oversimplification of dubious accuracy. Concepts such as "ownership" seem incompatible with the theoretical structure of land rights in the common law, which, it is often argued, differ from the civil law precisely because they lack a concept of ownership. The common law has retained a doctrine of estates of feudal origin, quite different from the civilian concept of ownership. Those differences remain important for the creation of limited rights in land, and in the common law may potentially serve as the basis for a reinvigoration of the notion that all rights in land are limited (under the impulsion of an increased concern with environmental protection). That said, however, the largest and most common estate in the common law, the fee simple, has in contemporary society assumed a content and a role that make it not much different from ownership, for the purposes of the discussion in the text – and indeed, the similarity has found its way into common usage, in which the holder of a fee simple is generally called an owner, if there are no lesser estates in the land. For a very brief discussion of the difference between ownership in the common and civilian legal traditions, see F.H. Lawson, *Introduction to the Law of Real Property* (Oxford: Clarendon Press, 1958), especially at 79ff. See, further, John E.C. Brierley and R.A. Macdonald, eds., *Quebec Civil Law* (Toronto: Emond-Montgomery, 1993).

15 The comparison between Montagnais and Quebec conceptions of landholding is drawn in Alain Bissonnette, "Droits autochtones et droit civil: opposition ou complémentarité? Le cas de la propriété foncière," in *Droit civil et droits autochtones: Confrontation ou complémentarité?* (Montreal: Association Henri-Capitant [Section québécoise], 1992). For a detailed discussion of Montagnais conceptions, see José Mailhot and Sylvie Vincent, "Le droit foncier montagnais" (1982) 15 (2–3) *Interculture* 65.

16 For situations in which courts expressed regret at their inability to vest custody of children in an aboriginal community, see *Tom* v. *Winnipeg Children's Aid Society*, [1982] 2 W.W.R. 212 (Man. C.A.); *Re C. and V.C.* (1982), 40 B.C.L.R. 234 (Prov. Ct.). My thanks to Gerald Donegan for bringing these to my attention.

17 On occasion, the courts have remarked that the preferential treatment of English and French is an exception to equality. See, for example, *Mahé* v. *Alberta* (1990), 68 D.L.R. (4th) 69 at 87–8. That is true insofar as it suggests that the law is not neutral in its treatment of language. Lack of neutrality should not, however, be automatically assimilated

to inequality, at least not without more careful analysis. The differential roles languages serve in society (discussed above, at pages 215–18) may mean that languages have very different significance to individuals, justifying different treatment without violating equality.

18 See above, at pages 45–6.

19 Pierre E. Trudeau, "Quebec and the Constitutional Problem," in Trudeau, *Federalism and the French Canadians* (Toronto: Macmillan, 1968) 3 at 24.

20 Charter of the French language, R.S.Q. 1977, c. C-11, sections 4, 45–6, 135–56.

21 Durham's report also emphasized this tendency for the common language to predominate. Indeed, it was precisely this which, Durham believed, had led to the rapid assimilation of the French-speaking population of Louisiana and would lead to the assimilation of French Canadians under a legislative union of the Canadas. See *The Report of the Earl of Durham, Her Majesty's High Commissioner and Governor General of British North America* (London: Methuen & Co., 1922 [1839]), at 219–25.

22 Canada, Commissioner of Official Languages, *Annual Report 1991* (Ottawa: Supply and Services Canada, 1992), at 27–8. Indeed, see the recommendations of the B&B Commission and the means of implementing bilingualism in the civil service, discussed above, at pages 52–4. Both were sensitive to the kind of dynamic sketched here.

23 B&B Commission, *Preliminary Report* (1965), at 66–7 and 85; and André Laurendeau, *Journal tenu pendant la Commission royale d'enquête sur le bilinguisme et le biculturalisme* (Outremont: VLB Éditeur, 1990), at 193–5.

24 Often, judges must adjudicate questions (such as the constitutionality of abortion, the extent of aboriginal title, or the effect of the Charter on Quebec's language legislation) on which there is no unambiguous answer in constitutional or legislative texts, and deep disagreement within society on the considerations that should govern the decision. I address the issue of how judges themselves should approach those questions in "The Adjudication of Contested Social Values: Implications of Attitudinal Bias for the Appointment of Judges," in Ontario Law Reform Commission, ed., *Appointing Judges: Philosophy, Politics and Practice* (Toronto: OLRC, 1991), 3. This section of the book is concerned with a somewhat different issue. It argues that in the interpretation of constitutional norms, differences of culture are often relevant to an adequate understanding of the context of constitutional decision making – an understanding necessary when judging whether constitutional norms are contravened by the challenged conduct. It is therefore acceptable for judges to consider these differences when

making their decisions, and indeed for the text of the constitution to direct them to do so.

25 See, for example, *Irwin Toy* v. *Quebec (Attorney General)* (1989), 58 D.L.R. (4th) 577 (S.C.C.).

26 See, for example, *R.* v. *Butler* (1990), 60 C.C.C. (3d) 219 at 230 (Man. C.A.), overturned on appeal by the Supreme Court of Canada, (1992) 134 N.R. 81.

27 See *Reference re ss. 193 and 195.1(1)(c) of the Criminal Code (Man.)* [1990] 1 S.C.R. 1123.

28 See *R.* v. *Keegstra* (1990), 1 C.R. (4th) 129 (S.C.C.).

29 See notes 25–28 above, especially the summary of the scope of freedom of expression in *Irwin Toy*, note 25. In every case, the Supreme Court held that the communication fell within the freedom, although in every case the court also decided that the limits were justified under section 1 of the Charter.

30 Constitution Act, 1982, section 1.

31 *Mahé* v. *Alberta* (1990), 68 D.L.R. (4th) 69 at 106–7.

32 *Ford* v. *Quebec (Attorney-General)* (1988), 54 D.L.R. (4th) 577 (S.C.C.).

33 Above, at pages 127–9 and 237–47.

34 See above, at pages 241–3.

35 See above, at page 247.

36 One of the most consistent advocates of this argument is Trudeau. See, most recently, "Trudeau Speaks Out: The Former Leader Attacks Quebec Nationalists and English Canadians who Support Them," *Maclean's*, 28 September 1992, 22–6. For a non-polemical version of this argument, see Alan C. Cairns, "Constitutional Change and the Three Equalities," in Watts and Brown, *Options*, 90–3.

37 The lack of even-handedness is especially evident in the popular debate, but it also colours some of the specialist discussions. See, for example, Alan Cairns, "The Governments and Societies of Canadian Federalism," in D.E. Williams, ed., *Constitution, Government, and Society in Canada: Selected Essays by Alan C. Cairns* (Toronto: McClelland and Stewart, 1988), 141; Robert Bothwell, Ian Drummond, and John English, *Canada Since 1945: Power, Politics, Provincialism*, rev. ed. (Toronto: University of Toronto Press, 1989), at 255–86, 359–99. In contrast, Albert Breton's influential 1964 article, one of the sources of this argument in the Canadian context, was even-handed: "The Economics of Nationalism" (1964) 72 *Journal of Political Economy* 376.

38 See, for example, Cairns, "Constitutional Change," 90–3.

39 Axworthy continued, "My vision of Canada is based on individual rights and liberties, and within that individual recognition we can all be different or distinct" (exchange between Barbara Frum and Tom Ax-

worthy, on the CBC television program, "Is Canada Drifting Apart," 23 May 1990 [my thanks to Hubert Gendron and Sandy Bourque for their help in locating this reference]).

40 Pierre E. Trudeau, "Federalism, Nationalism, and Reason," in Trudeau, *Federalism and the French Canadians*, 182 at 198.

41 Ibid.

42 17 (11) *L'actualité* (July 1992).

43 It is instructive, for example, that in the first of the 1992 conferences on constitutional issues leading up to Charlottetown – a conference that brought together participants from many walks of life and from across Canada to discuss the issues in depth – the participants came out in favour of an asymmetrical distribution of powers. See S. Delacourt, "Forum urges separate deal for Quebec," *Globe and Mail* (Toronto), 20 January 1992, A1.

44 See, for example, Roderick A. Macdonald, "… Meech Lake to the Contrary Notwithstanding" (1991) 29 *Osgoode Hall Law Journal* 253 and 483; and the evocative article by James Tully, "Diversity's Gambit Declined," in Curtis Cook, ed., *Canada's Constitutional Crisis and the Referendum of October 26, 1992* (Montreal: McGill-Queen's University Press, 1993).

CHAPTER EIGHT: PRACTICAL IMPLICATIONS

1 See, for example, David Milne's suggestions for reconciling provincial equality and asymmetry: Milne, "Equality or Asymmetry: Why Choose?" in Ronald L. Watts and Douglas M. Brown, eds., *Options for a New Canada* (Toronto: University of Toronto Press, 1991), 285.

2 For excellent discussions of this symbolic role of the Charter, see Rainer Knopff and F.L. Morton, *Charter Politics* (Scarborough: Nelson, 1992), especially 81–90; and Alan C. Cairns, *Charter versus Federalism: The Dilemmas of Constitutional Reform* (Montreal: McGill-Queen's University Press, 1992).

3 For useful discussions of aboriginal self-government, see Michael Asch, *Home and Native Land: Aboriginal Rights and the Canadian Constitution* (Scarborough: Nelson Canada, 1988); Frank Cassidy and Robert L. Bish, *Indian Government: Its Meaning in Practice* (Lantzville and Halifax: Oolichan Books and Institute for Research on Public Policy, 1989); and Royal Commission on Aboriginal Peoples, *The Right of Aboriginal Self-Government and the Constitution: A Commentary* (Ottawa, 13 February 1992).

4 Proposed section 35.1 of the Constitution Act, 1982, in *Draft Legal Text: October 9, 1992*, section 29.

5 See, for example, Bruce Clark, *Native Liberty, Crown Sovereignty: The Existing Aboriginal Right of Self-Government in Canada* (Montreal: McGill-Queen's University Press, 1990).

6 I make this argument in more detail in "Rapports de force, rapports de justice: la genèse d'une communauté normative entre colonisateurs et colonisés," paper prepared for the *Réseau québécois* of the Law and Society Progamme of the Canadian Institute of Advanced Research. See also Brian Slattery, "Aboriginal Sovereignty and Imperial Claims" (1991) 29 *Osgoode Hall Law Journal* 681; and idem, "Understanding Aboriginal Rights" (1987) 66 *Canadian Bar Review* 727.

7 See *Draft Legal Text*, section 29.

8 Proposed sections 2(1)(b) of the Constitution Act, 1867 and 35.1(2) of the Constitution Act, 1982, in *Draft Legal Text*, sections 1 and 29.

9 Structures like these already exist or are proposed under various comprehensive land-claims agreements. See, for example, *The James Bay and Northern Québec Agreement* (Quebec: Éditeur officiel, 1976).

10 See, for example, the position of aboriginal peoples in the Northwest Territories: Asch, *Home and Native Land*, at 93–9. See the provision contemplating this in the Charlottetown Accord: proposed section 35.2(4) of the Constitution Act, 1982, in *Draft Legal Text*, section 29.

11 See, for example, Gerald R. Alfred, "From Bad to Worse: Internal Politics in the 1990 Crisis at Kahnawake" (1991) 8(1) *Northeast Indian Quarterly* 23; and Dan Gaspé, "The Mohawk Struggle," in William Dodge, ed., *Boundaries of Identity: A Quebec Reader* (Toronto: Lester Publishing, 1992), 16.

12 A. Norris and P. Kuitenbrouwer, "Kanesatake votes solidly for elected band council," *Gazette* (Montreal), 1 June 1991, A5.

13 See proposed section 35.1(4) of the Constitution Act, 1982, in *Draft Legal Text*, section 29. This suggested how courts should deal with the matter once an action had been brought; the ability to bring an action was itself suspended for five years to permit negotiations.

14 For a good introduction to the duty to bargain in Canadian labour law, see Labour Law Casebook Group, *Labour Law: Cases, Materials and Commentary*, 5th ed. (Kingston: Industrial Relations Centre, Queen's University, 1991), 430–93.

15 Proposed section 33.1 of the Constitution Act, 1982, in *Draft Legal Text*, section 27.

16 For an example of such a phased introduction, see "Draft Yukon First Nation Model Self-Government Agreement," 29 November 1991, sections 18.1–18.2.

17 Agreement entitled "Statement of Political Relationship," between Ontario premier Bob Rae and the minister responsible for Native

affairs, on the one hand, and fourteen chiefs of the Ontario First Nations, on the other, 6 August 1991.

18 Constitution Act, 1982, section 35(3) provides constitutional protection to "land claims agreements." In the chief example to date the agreement stipulated that the self-government arrangements would not be constitutionalized, although it left open the possibility that this might be done in the future. See "Umbrella Final Agreement between the Government of Canada, the Council for Yukon Indians and the Government of the Yukon," 30 May 1992, sections 24.12.1–24.12.2.

19 The section in question is Constitution Act, 1982, section 35(1).

20 Proposed section 2(1)(c) of the Constitution Act, 1867, in *Draft Legal Text*, section 1. This exclusive interpretation was a possibility but was not required. The wording of the clause, especially the fact that it said that the distinct society merely "includes" those characteristics, is still compatible with the approach presented here. It is nevertheless regrettable that the possibility was left open.

21 See R. Dutrisac, "Jean Dorion a eu raison des traditionnalistes qui voulaient sa tête," *Le Devoir* (Montréal), 16 March 1992, 3.

22 Proposed sections 2(1)(a) and 2(2) of the Constitution Act, 1867, in the Meech Lake Accord; proposed section 2(1)(d) of the Constitution Act, 1867, in *Draft Legal Text*, section 1; and Constitution Act, 1982, sections 27 and 35.

23 There have been suggestions of such a trend recently among some anglophone, left-leaning Canadian nationalists who, after free trade and Meech Lake, seem to have given up on Quebec. See, for example, Philip Resnick, *Toward a Canada-Quebec Union* (Montreal: McGill-Queen's University Press, 1991), especially 19–32. One wonders, however, whether they ever had much feeling for the ways in which our allegiances are intertwined. Frequently, they are the same persons who, during the 1970s, all too easily confused support for Quebec's aspirations with support for Quebec's independence.

24 Constitution Act, 1867, sections 91(2A) and 94A.

25 Proposed section 106A of the Constitution Act, 1867, in the Meech Lake Accord; and proposed section 106A of the Constitution Act, 1867, in *Draft Legal Text*, section 16.

26 There are good reasons for restraint in the exercise of the spending power outside Quebec. Many of our most innovative social programs were developed at the provincial level. Provincially administered programs are often better adapted to local conditions. For these reasons, an influential section of the Saskatchewan NDP has long defended provincial authority over social programs. (For opinions from this tradition, see Andrew Petter, "Federalism and the Myth of the Federal Spending Power" (1989) 68 *Canadian Bar Review* 448; and John

Richards, "Suggestions on Getting the Constitutional Division of Powers Right," in Jean-Michel Cousineau, et al., *Delivering the Goods: The Federal-Provincial Division of Spending Powers* (Toronto: C.D. Howe Institute, 1992), 1.) It seems to me that the best response is not to give all provinces a right to opt out, however. These arguments are best considered within the federal debate, when deciding whether to create new programs.

27 This is not just the result of the decay of our political institutions. In large measure, the MPs' limited role results from the complexity of government. MPs cannot, for example, routinely verify the merits of each level of exposure stated in an environmental regulation or evaluate the precise budgetary guidelines applicable to hospitals. There has to be some distinction between general oversight by the legislature and more detailed control by the executive. See, for example, J.S. Mill's argument in chapter 5 of *Considerations on Representative Government*.

28 This, of course, should not be the sole criterion, and indeed, Quebec still accepts prospective immigrants who are unilingually anglophone. Applicants are evaluated on many criteria, converted into a system of points. Under Quebec's point system, the ability to speak French is important. It can, however, be outweighed by other factors.

29 Proposed sections 95A–95E of the Constitution Act, 1867, in the Meech Lake Accord; and proposed sections 95A–95D of the Constitution Act, 1867, in *Draft Legal Text*, section 12.

30 See, for example, proposed sections 90 and 92(10)(c) of the Constitution Act, 1867, in *Draft Legal Text*, sections 7 and 9.

31 The Gang of Eight's amending formula can be found in Anne F. Bayefsky, ed., *Canada's Constitution Act 1982 and Amendments: A Documentary History* (Toronto: McGraw-Hill Ryerson, 1989), 806–11. Proposed section 40 of the Constitution Act, 1982, in the Meech Lake Accord; proposed section 40 of the Constitution Act, 1982, in *Draft Legal Text*, section 32.

I do not intend to discuss in detail the subjects that should require Quebec's consent. I will, however, mention one that was contentious during the Meech Lake debate: the creation of new provinces. The potential prejudice to Quebec of the creation of a new province is really quite focused: principally its effect on Quebec's relative weight in the amending formula and in a reformed Senate. Those concerns can be addressed by splitting the act of creating a new province from the effects of that action on matters like the amending formula and Senate representation. Quebec's veto could be limited to the latter. This indeed was the approach adopted in the Charlottetown Accord: proposed sections 21(2) of the Constitution Act, 1867, 2 and 3 of the

Constitution Act, 1871, and 41(c) and 42.1 of the Constitution Act, 1982, in *Draft Legal Text*, sections 4, 21, and 32.

32 Constitution Act, 1982, sections 38–49.

33 *A Renewed Canada: The Report of the Special Joint Committee of the Senate and the House of Commons* (the Beaudoin-Dobbie report) (Ottawa: Queen's Printer, 1992), at 63.

34 One of the clearest examples is *Ford* v. *Quebec (A.G.)*, [1988] 2 S.C.R. 712. In that case, the Supreme Court struck down the sign law provisions of Quebec's Bill 101. It acknowledged, however, that Quebec's *visage français* would have justified requiring that signs use French and perhaps even that the French lettering be predominant.

35 For a good introduction to the voluminous literature dealing with Senate reform, see Donald V. Smiley and Ronald L. Watts, *Intrastate Federalism in Canada* (Toronto: University of Toronto Press, 1985).

36 Constitution Act, 1867, sections 21–36. See Robert A. Mackay, *The Unreformed Senate of Canada*, rev. ed. (Toronto: McClelland and Stewart, 1963).

37 *Draft Legal Text*, section 4.

38 Charlottetown, for example, would have permitted the Senate to block natural resources tax policy bills (proposed section 34[3] of the Constitution Act, 1867, in *Draft Legal Text*, section 4).

39 Calculations based on 1991 census figures: Statistics Canada, *A National Overview: Population and Dwelling Counts* (Ottawa: Supply and Services Canada, 1992), at 7.

40 Another way of putting the issue is that in political discussion, the provinces serve two different roles. They are, of course, political entities with their own powers and their own institutional interests to defend, but they are also the most obvious of Canada's constituent units – units which, moreover, are valued precisely because they allow for regional variation and express distinctively regional concerns. We easily slip into the habit, then, of using them as the appropriate forums for the expression of regional concerns generally. They certainly are useful regional voices in federal-provincial relations, but they lose that significance when we talk about Senate reform. Then, we are talking about building regional representation right into the federal institutions themselves. At that point, we no longer need to rely on "provinces" as shorthand for "regional voices." We can seek to represent the geographically related interests directly, and the balance of representation can be adjusted so that it achieves the best balance, which may have little to do with the fact that one or two or three provinces exist in a certain area. The provinces are no longer particularly relevant for determining representation, although for simplicity's sake we may well construct the constituencies so that they respect provincial boundaries.

41 See, for example, the document that was largely responsible for Alberta's advocacy of the Triple-E Senate: P. McCormick et al., *Regional Representation: The Canadian Partnership* (Calgary: Canada West Foundation, 1981), at 117–18.

42 The provisions mentioned are all found in *Draft Legal Text*, section 4. For similar reasons, the rules requiring a double majority (a majority, in other words, of all senators and of all French-speaking senators) for measures affecting the French language or culture were ill-advised (proposed sections 36 to 36B of the Constitution Act, 1867, in *Draft Legal Text*, section 4).

43 Canada, *32nd General Election 1980: Report of the Chief Electoral Officer* (Ottawa: Supply and Services Canada, 1980), xxiv–xxv. For a trenchant analysis of this effect of the electoral system, see Alan C. Cairns, "The Electoral System and the Party System in Canada, 1921–1965" and "The Constitutional, Legal, and Historical Background to the Elections of 1979 and 1980," both in Douglas E. Williams, ed., *Constitution, Government, and Society in Canada: Selected Essays by Alan C. Cairns* (Toronto: McClelland and Stewart, 1988), at 111 and 88 respectively.

44 I therefore disagree with the ban on senators as cabinet ministers in Charlottetown. See proposed section 24 of the Constitution Act, 1867, in *Draft Legal Text*, section 4.

45 Indeed, even the supposed benefits of the single transferable system (freedom from party domination, openness to the participation of independent candidates) are open to question. The predominant role of parties results much more from the cost of campaigning than from the structure of the electoral system. This would be all the more true in Senate elections, which would have very large constituencies. It is very doubtful whether, even under a system of single transferable ballots, there would be any significant role for independents. Moreover, one can achieve a great deal of openness under a party-list system by making it relatively easy to create a party.

46 Proposed section 23 of the Constitution Act, 1867, in *Draft Legal Text*, section 4.

47 Proposed section 101C of the Constitution Act, 1867, in the Meech Lake Accord; and proposed section 101C of the Constitution Act, 1867, in *Draft Legal Text*, section 15.

48 Proposed section 101D of the Constitution Act, 1867, in *Draft Legal Text*, section 15.

49 For useful discussions of reform to the nominating process, see *Report of the Canadian Bar Association Committee on the Appointment of Judges in Canada* (Ottawa: Canadian Bar Foundation, 1985); Canadian Association of Law Teachers Special Committee on the Appointment of Judges, *Judicial Selection in Canada: Discussion Papers and Reports*

(1987); and Ontario Law Reform Commission, ed., *Appointing Judges: Philosophy, Politics and Practice* (Toronto: OLRC, 1991).

50 See, for example, *Un Québec libre de ses choix: Rapport du Comité constitutionnel du Parti libéral du Québec* (28 January 1991) (chair: J. Allaire), at 32.

51 See above, at pages 53–4.

52 Moreover, the maintenance of channels of communication on the pan-Canadian level almost inevitably promotes interaction within local or regional communities as well (at least if access to those channels is relatively open). This is the case for a federally-regulated field like broadcasting; in both radio and television, most of the programming is determined locally, for a local audience. Federal jurisdiction tends to maintain, in other words, an infrastructure suitable for *both* levels of political community – a situation which would be less certain if jurisdiction were provincial.

CHAPTER NINE: THE CANADIAN CONVERSATION

1 See, for example, the wonderful evocation of how a concern with human rights can be rooted in the circumstances of a very specific experience in Brian Slattery, "Rights, Communities and Tradition" (1991) 41 *University of Toronto Law Journal* 447.

2 Discussed above, at pages 68–9.

3 "Faire l'indépendance, c'est comme immigrer," interview with Pierre Bourgault in 17(11) *L'actualité* (July 1992) 29.

4 Figures based on the 1991 census. The precise numbers are 10,084,885 for Ontario and 20,400,896 total for all the provinces and territories except Quebec (Statistics Canada, *A National Overview: Population and Dwelling Counts* [Ottawa: Supply and Services Canada, 1992], at 7).

Index

Aboriginal land claims, 66, 69–73, 113, 122, 171, 172, 259, 267, 269, 274, 309

Aboriginal peoples: aboriginal rights conferences, 5–6, 117, 122–5, 170, 179, 270, 310; adoption, 239, 249; alienation, 5–6, 17, 176; constitutional jurisdiction, 75, 151, 231; Crown's fiduciary obligation, 231; cultural definition, 222, 268; diversity, 66–7, 220; failure of Meech Lake, 4–6, 11, 16; 1969 white paper, 67–9, 72, 317; 1991 Ontario declaration, 273; patriation, 93, 109, 111–13, 114–15, 117, 122; relationship to land, 238–9, 250; relations with Quebec, 16–17, 160–1; self-assertion, 38, 67–9; social conditions, 67; suppression of aborig-

inal customs, 67, 83; women's Indian status, 69, 122, 135–6. *See also* Cree; Inuit; Mohawk; Montagnais; National Indian Brotherhood; Native Council of Canada

Aboriginal rights. *See* Aboriginal land claims; Aboriginal self-government; Constitution Act, 1982

Aboriginal self-government, 17, 28, 66, 72–3, 112, 113, 117, 220–2, 226, 227, 231, 233, 239, 247, 249, 309; and aboriginal rights conferences, 122–5, 179; and Charlottetown, 17, 163, 170–2, 175, 228, 265–7, 269, 270–5; and Charter, 151–2, 171, 269–70, 272–3, 275; democracy, 268–70; "inherent" character, 124–5, 170, 264–7, 273; justiciability, 124, 170–1, 270–2,

274–5; and Meech Lake, 132, 147, 155; recommendations, 263–75; sovereignty, 265–7; subconstitutional reform, 261–2, 272–4; and women, 172, 249, 270, 272–3

Aboriginal treaty rights, 68, 73, 87, 109, 170

Abortion, 136

Acadians, 8, 49, 137, 196, 243, 304. *See also* Francophones outside Quebec

Ad Hoc Committee of Canadian Women on the Constitution, 15

A.G. Quebec v. *Blaikie* [1979] 2 S.C.R. 1016, 100

Allaire report, 13, 19–20

Allegiance: asymmetry, 206–12, 214, 227, 233, 254–5, 278, 280–1, 314; multiple, 24–6, 126, 129, 143–4, 205–6, 223, 225, 227, 254–6, 258–9, 263, 312–14,

248–51; expression, 244–6; focus for nationalism, 116–17, 143–4, 151–2, 157, 178, 179, 251; and Meech Lake, 6–7, 14–15, 127–9, 134–42; minority language rights, 114–19 *passim*, 128–9, 137, 139–40, 159–60, 245–6, 250, 278; multiculturalism, 109, 136, 150–1, 159, 217, 278; in negotiations before patriation, 96–7, 98, 104–5, 106, 108–10, 183–4; notwithstanding clause, 113–14, 116, 138–41, 171, 213, 272; reaction in Quebec, 117, 140, 151–2, 157, 213; section 1, 245; section 28 (gender equality), 14, 109, 115, 117, 135–6, 154. *See also Ford* v. *Quebec*; Constitution Act (1982)

Canadian identity: constitutional definition, 183–4, 192; evolution, 208–11; nature, 29–33, 205, 318–9; reconception, 185–93, 197, 223–8. *See also* Nationalism

Canadian Labour Congress, 14

Canadian Radio-television and Telecommunications Commission (CRTC), 244

Catholic Church in Quebec: before Quiet Revolution, 41–2; in Quiet Revolution, 44–6

Centre de recherches sur l'opinion publique, 258

CF-18 contract, 4, 9, 142, 149, 155, 158

Charlottetown Accord: aboriginal self-government, 17, 163, 170–2, 175, 228, 265–7, 269, 270–5; aftermath, 21–2, 180, 261, 262; amending formula, 163, 170, 284–5; Canada clause, 164–6; distinct society clause, 163, 164–6, 174, 262, 277, 288; division of powers, 163, 164, 166–7, 172; economic union, 163, 172–3; failure, 173–5, 180, 310–1; House of Commons reform, 169, 175; and individual rights, 165, 166, 269; New Brunswick language rights, 173; process, 10, 20–1, 162–3, 173–4; relationship to Meech Lake, 163–6, 180; Senate reform, 20–1, 163, 168–70, 174–5, 291, 296, 298; social charter, 163, 172–3; spending power, 164, 166–7, 172–3, 214, 279, 280; Supreme Court of Canada, 164, 300. *See also* Referendum

Charter. *See* Canadian Charter of Rights and Freedoms; Quebec Charter of Human Rights and Freedoms

Charter of the French Language. *See* Bill 101; Bill 178

Chrétien, Jean, 10–11, 118

Churchill Falls hydro contract, 4, 158

Civil rights movement (US), 67, 96

Clark, Joe, 10, 107; in government, 105–6

Collective rights, 28, 165, 166, 238, 312

Communications, 9, 48, 77, 93, 104, 129, 158, 167, 213, 244, 256, 286; recommendations, 302–5

Communists, 83

Compact theory, 195

Confederation, 71, 195, 197–9, 208, 231

Confederation for Tomorrow Conference (1967), 97

Conservative Party. *See* Clark; Diefenbaker; Mulroney

Constitution Act (1867), 75, 116. *See also* British North America Act (1867)

Constitution Act (1982), 116; aboriginal rights guarantee, 108–9, 111, 113, 114–15, 122, 124, 151, 154, 159, 170, 231, 249, 274–5, 278, 310. *See also* Canadian Charter of Rights and Freedoms; Patriation

Constitutional interpretation, 727–9, 244–7, 248–9, 300

Constitutional process, 259, 315–17. *See also* Charlottetown Accord; Meech Lake Accord

Cree people, 71–2

Criminal law, 239; and aboriginal self-government, 267–8, 272; differential application, 235; jurisdiction, 75, 76, 199, 214–15

Cross, James, 98

Culture: and democracy, 315–17; definition, 237–8; and human rights, 224–5, 235–51; jurisdiction, 167, 213, 215, 302–3; and law, 237–9, 244–7; and public institutions, 26–8, 68–9, 87–91,

Victoria Charter, 98–9

Wells, Clyde, 142, 155,
158, 289, 291
Women's organizations,
38; constitutional
focus, 92, 117; and
Meech Lake, 6–7,
14–15, 135–6; and
patriation, 109, 115,
117, 135–6; suffrage,
96. *See also* Ad Hoc
Committee of Canadian
Women on the Consti-
tution; Fédération des
femmes du Québec;
National Action
Committee on the
Status of Women;
Native Women's Asso-
ciation of Canada

JL 27.5 .W433 1994 c.1
Webber, Jeremy H. A., 1958-
Reimagining Canada

DATE DUE

OCT 3 0 2001	

GAYLORD   PRINTED IN U.S.A.